Thompson Westcott

Chronicles of the Great Rebellion against the United States of America

Thompson Westcott

Chronicles of the Great Rebellion against the United States of America

ISBN/EAN: 9783337210151

Printed in Europe, USA, Canada, Australia, Japan

Cover: Foto ©ninafisch / pixelio.de

More available books at **www.hansebooks.com**

CHRONICLES

OF THE

GREAT REBELLION

AGAINST THE

UNITED STATES OF AMERICA.

BEING A CONCISE RECORD AND DIGEST OF THE EVENTS CONNECTED WITH THE STRUGGLE—CIVIL, POLITICAL, MILITARY AND NAVAL—WITH THE DATES, VICTORIES, LOSSES AND RESULTS, EMBRACING THE PERIOD BETWEEN APRIL 23, 1861, AND OCTOBER 31, 1865.

PHILADELPHIA:
A. WINCH, 505 Chestnut Street.

Entered according to Act of Congress, in the year 1867, by
A. WINCH,
In the Clerk's Office of the District Court in and for the Eastern District of Pennsylvania.

INTRODUCTION.

THE Rebellion, by certain States, against the United States, was the result of a discontent long existing, produced by causes imaginary rather than actual, and which were exaggerated in regard to their true bearings and importance, by the cunning of unscrupulous politicians. The insurrection had its political and civil features a terior to the breaking out of the war. The design of the Southern States to secede from the Union, was foreshadowed by the secession of several delegations from the Democratic National Convention, held at Charleston, S. C., April 23, 1860. It assumed activity and determination upon the election of Abraham Lincoln and Hannibal Hamlin as President and Vice-President of the United States, Nov. 6, 1860. This signification of the people's will was followed by the withdrawal of South Carolina Senators from the United States Senate, Nov 9 and 11, 1860, and by other withdrawals from Congress and the Cabinet. As early as Nov. 18th, but twelve days after the Presidential election, the Legislature of Georgia appropriated $1,000,000 to arm the State. South Carolina formally seceded Dec. 20th. The evacuation of Fort Moultrie by Major Robert Anderson, took place six days after; and immediately followed the seizure of revenue cutters, forts, and public property, by the secessionists. The steamer *Star of the West* was fired into by the secessionists of Charleston, S. C., on the 9th of January, 1861, that being the first act of actual war. On the 11th of April the surrender of Fort Sumter was demanded. On the 12th a cannonade was opened on that work by the rebels, and on the 15t' the fort was surrendered.

This event aroused the whole country; and from that period the war was warmly carried on, until the surrender of General Robert E. Lee, the rebel commander-in-chief, to Lieutenant-General J. S. Grant, at Appamattox Court House, Virginia, April 9, 1865, caused the subsequent surrender of the rebel General Joseph E. Johnston to Major-General W. T. Sherman, at Raleigh, N. C., April 26; of the rebel General Kirby Smith to Major-General Canby, at Galveston, Texas, June 2d; and the rebel Red River fleet to the United States navy, June 3d. From that date, hostilities in the United States were at an end—the only remnant of the rebellion being the depredations of the pirate Shenandoah, which were continued for some months after the war was closed.

During the bloody and disastrous war which resulted from the pride and ambition of bad men, there were actually in service in the armies of the United States, during the war, 2,656,553 men. The Government had made calls at various times for troops, in aggregate, 2,759,049—there being a deficiency at the close of the war of 102,496, which, if necessary, would have been made up by recruiting. Beside the men who came upon the Government calls, there were enlisted for certain emergencies, upwards of 120,000 men, not contained in the regular forces. The calls made by the President upon the people for troops were as follows:

April 15, 1861, for 75,000 men—three and six months.
May 3, July 22, July 25, 1861, for 500,000 men—one, two and three years.
July 2, 1862, for 500,000 men—three years.
August 4, 1862, for 300,000 men—nine months.
June 15, 1863, for ———— militia—six months.
Oct. 15, 1863, Feb. 1, 1864, for 500,000 men—three years.
March 14, 1864, for 200,000 men—three years.
1864, ———— militia mustered into service—one hundred days.
July 18, 1864, for 500,000 men—three and four years.
Dec. 19, 1864, for 300,000 men—three and four years.

The number of troops furnished by the various States, to the Union army, were as follows:

Maine,	71,745
New Hampshire,	34,605
Vermont,	35,256
Massachusetts,	151,785
Rhode Island,	23,711
Connecticut,	57,270
New York,	455,568
New Jersey,	79,511
Pennsylvania,	366,326
Delaware,	13,651
Maryland,	49,730
West Virginia,	30,003
District of Columbia,	16,872
Ohio,	317,133
Indiana,	195,147
Illinois,	258,217
Michigan,	90,119
Wisconsin,	96,118
Minnesota,	25,034
Iowa,	75,860
Missouri,	108,773
Kentucky,	78,540
Kansas,	20,097
Total,	2,653,062

During the war there enlisted in the service of the Government, 178,795 colored soldiers.

What the losses of the army were, during the whole war, will never be known with accuracy. It was carried on over such a wide extent of country, and there was so much private hostility—if we may use these words to designate the treachery which cut off single soldiers—that the record can never be made complete.

The United States navy, by the necessities of the contest, was increased from 7500 men, the full complement before the war, until it employed 51,500 men in service, and 16,880 laborers and assistants at the navy yards. Since the 4th of March, 1861, the navy was increased by the addition of 418 purchased vessels, and 208 built by the Government. After the close of hostilities, the greater portion of these vessels, not originally constructed for war purposes, were sold.

In regard to the rebel army, it is impossible to obtain any statistics, as to its strength and efficiency, during the four weary years of war, or as to its losses. We know that it was kept up until all the fighting force of the South was exhausted; that it lost severely in the battles of the war; and that only when it could no longer continue the contest, did it surrender. Its losses must have been very heavy; and the cause for which it fought was unsuccessful, because it was wrong.

CHRONICLES OF THE REBELLION.

1860. *April* 23.—The Democratic National Convention met in Charleston, South Carolina. April 30, the Cincinnati Platform of 1856 substantially adopted; whereupon delegations from several slave States *seceded* from the Convention, and organized an opposition convention. Both conventions finally adjourned without making nominations.

May 9.—A convention of delegates claiming to represent the friends of the Union and Constitution met at Baltimore, and nominated for President, John Bell of Tennessee; for Vice-President, Ed. Everett, of Mass.

May 16.—The Republican National Convention met at Chicago. May 18, Abraham Lincoln, of Illinois, nominated for President of the United States; and Hannibal Hamlin, of Maine, for Vice President.

June 11.—The Convention of Democratic Seceders met at Richmond, and adjourned until the 21st.

June 18.—The regular Democratic Convention met at Baltimore. Efforts were made to obtain the readmission of the seceding delegates at Charleston, which were defeated; in consequence of which, other Southern delegations seceded. The convention nominated for President, Stephen A. Douglas of Illinois; for Vice-President, Herschel V. Johnson, of Georgia.

June 28.—The Seceders' Convention met in Baltimore, and nominated J. C. Breckinridge, of Ky., for President, and Joseph Lane, of Oregon, Vice-President.

November 6.—Abraham Lincoln and Hannibal Hamlin elected President and Vice-President of the United States by the electoral vote of seventeen States,—189 in number. John. C. Breckinridge and Joseph Lane received the votes of eleven States,—72 in number; John Bell and Edward Everett received the votes of 3 States,—39 in number; Stephen A. Douglas received the vote of one State and three-seventh of the vote of New Jersey,—in number 12. Total electoral vote, 303. Popular vote for Lincoln and Hamlin, 1,857,610; Douglas and Johnson, 1,365,976; Breckinridge and Lane, 847,953; Bell and Everett, 590,631.

November 9 *and* 11.—South Carolina Senators in the United States Congress resigned.

November 18.—Major Anderson ordered to Fort Moultrie, to relieve Col. Gardner, ordered to Texas.

——Georgia Legislature appropriated $1,000,000 to arm the State.

November 22.—Washington and Philadelphia banks suspended specie payments. The banks of Baltimore and Richmond did so two days before.

December 10.—Howell Cobb, Secretary of the Treasury, resigned his seat in the Cabinet.

December 13.—Meeting of the Cabinet in relation to reinforcement of Fort Moultrie: President Buchanan opposed to its reinforcement; Secretary Cass and Secretary Toucey urged the measure; Mr. Buchanan had not the nerve to order the reinforcement.

December 14.—Lewis Cass, Secretary of State, resigned his seat in the Cabinet because the President would not reinforce Fort Moultrie.

Dec. 19.—Governor Hicks, of Maryland, refused to convene the Legislature of the State upon demand of A. H. Handy. Secession commissioner from Mississippi.

Dec. 20.—S. Carolina ordinance of secession passed.

Dec. 23.—Defalcation discovered in Indian Trust Fund, Washington amounting to $830,000. Godard Bailey, clerk in the Department, arrested as the culprit.

December 26.—Maj. Robert Anderson, U. S. A., in command of Fort Moultrie, in Charleston Harbor, evacuated the fort, and, with his garrison, took possession of Fort Sumter, in the same harbor.

Dec. 27.—U. S. revenue cutter Aiken given up by its commander, Capt. N. L. Coste, to State of S. Carolina.

Dec. 28.—The Palmetto Flag raised on the customhouse and post-office at Charleston, Castle Pinckney and Fort Moultrie taken possession of by State troops.

Dec. 29.—John B. Floyd resigned his situation as Secretary of War because President Buchanan refused to withdraw the troops from Fort Sumter.

1861.—*Jan.* 2.—Act of secession passed by Miss.

——Captain Charles Stone appointed to organise the militia of the District of Columbia.

Jan. 3.—Fort Macon, North Carolina, Fort Wilmington, and the United States Arsenal at Fayetteville, seized by order of Governor Ellis of North Carolina.

——The Legislature of Delaware unanimously refused to receive H. Dickinson, Secession commissioner from Mississippi.

——U. S. forts and property seized in Miss.

——Forts Pulaski and Jackson, near Savannah, seized by order of Governor Brown, of Georgia.

January 4.—Commissioners sent from South Carolina to treat with President Buchanan for a peaceable cession of the U. S. property in South Carolina; left Washington,—the President, after some correspondence, declining further intercourse with them.

——United States Arsenal at Mobile, with arms and munitions of war, seized by Secessionists.

——Fort Morgan, Mobile, seized by order of the Governor of Alabama.

Jan. 8.—Forts Caswell and Johnson, N. C., taken possession of by persons residing in the vicinity.

——Secretary Jacob Thompson resigned from the Cabinet upon hearing that the Star of the West had been sent to Charleston with troops.

January 9.—Steamer Star of the West, with 250 United States troops, for Fort Sumter, fired into by rebel batteries near Charleston.

January 11.—Act of secession passed by Alabama.

——U. S. Marine Hospital, near New Orleans, taken possession of by State troops, and 216 sick and feeble patients of the institution ordered to be immediately removed. Forts Jackson and St. Philip, at the mouth of the Mississippi, Fort Pickens, Lake Ponchartrain, and U. S. Arsenal, Baton Rogue, also seized.

January 12.—Act of secession passed by Florida.

——Pensacola Navy Yard and Fort Barrancas surrendered by Commodore Armstrong, U. S. Navy.

——Lieut. A. J. Slemmer, in command at Fort McRae, withdrew his troops to Fort Pickens.

January 15.—United States Coast Survey Schooner Dana, seized by the State of Florida.

January 19.—Act of secession passed by Georgia.

January 24.—United States Arsenal at Augusta, Georgia, seized by the State authorities.

January 27.—John B. Floyd, late Secretary of War, presented by the Grand Jury at Washington, D. C., for maladministration of office, for complicity in the abstraction of Indian bonds to the amount of $830,000 and for conspiracy against the Government.

January 28.—Act of secession passed by Louisiana.

Jan. 29.—U. S. revenue cutter McClellan surrendered at N. Orleans, by Capt. Breshwood, a Virginian.

January 31.—United States branch mint at New Orleans seized, and United States funds to the amount of $511,000 taken by the State of Louisiana.

February 1.—Act of secession passed by Texas.

February 2.—United States revenue cutter Cass surrendered at Mobile by Captain Morrison, a Georgian.

Feb. 4.—Peace Conference assembled at Washington.

February 5.—United States Arsenal at Little Rock, Arkansas, taken possession of by the State.

February 6.—Congress of seceding States met at Montgomery, Alabama.

February 9.—Jefferson Davis, of Mississippi, elected President, and Alexander H. Stephens, of Georgia, Vice-President, of "the Confederate States of America."
—— Vote upon secession taken in Tennessee.
February 13.—Abraham Lincoln and Hannibal Hamlin officially declared to be elected President and Vice-President of the United States, upon counting the votes.
February 18.—Jefferson Davis inaugurated President of the Southern Confederacy.
February 23.—Abraham Lincoln, President-elect, arrived unexpectedly in Washington, having made that part of the journey from Philadelphia to Washington secretly and at night, in consequence of a supposed plot to assassinate him in his passage through Baltimore.
February 26.—Gen. D. E. Twiggs, U. S. Army, by treacherous collusion, surrendered to the State of Texas all the troops under his command, and Federal property worth a million and a half of dollars.
February 27.—The Peace Conference, in convention, submitted to the United States Senate a plan of adjustment and seven amendments to the Constitution of the United States.
March 2.—Revenue cutter Dodge seized in Galveston Bay by the State of Texas.
March 4.—Abraham Lincoln inaugurated as President of the United States.
March 5.—Peter G. Toutant Beauregard, late major of United States Engineers, ordered by Jefferson Davis to take command of the Confederate forces at Charleston, South Carolina.
March 6.—Fort Brown, Texas, surrendered by Captain Hill, U. S. Army.
March 9.—Act for the establishment of an army of the Confederate States passed by the rebel Congress.
March 27.—Rumors from Charleston, South Carolina, that Fort Sumter was to be evacuated.
April 4.—The Virginia Convention, adopting several resolutions reported by the Committee on Federal Relations, rejected an ordinance of secession (moved as an amendment) by a vote of 89 to 45.
April 7.—Steamship Atlantic, with Barry's battery, troops, and provisions, left New York.
April 8.—The authorities of South Carolina were notified that the United States would send an unarmed vessel with provisions and supplies for Fort Sumter; reply was made that the vessel would be fired into if it attempted to enter the port; notice was then given that the United States would supply the fort peaceably, if possible,—if not, by force.
April 9.—The State Department declined to receive the commissioners from the rebel Confederacy.
April 11.—Demand made of Major Anderson, at Fort Sumter, that he should evacuate the fort; the request was declined by Major Anderson.
April 12, 2 A.M.—General Beauregard sent a message to Major Anderson, stating that, if he would evacuate the fort and agree not to fire in the mean time upon the State batteries unless they fired upon him, no fire would be opened upon Fort Sumter. Major Anderson replied that he would evacuate at noon on the 15th, if not previously ordered or not supplied with provisions.
—— 3.30 A.M.—General Beauregard notified Major Anderson that fire would be opened from the batteries on Fort Sumter in one hour.
—— 4.30 A.M.—A fire was opened on Fort Sumter from Fort Moultrie and from batteries at Mount Pleasant, Cumming's Point, and the floating battery, Morris Island, and other points,—there being seventeen batteries in all. The fire was returned from Fort Sumter at 7 A.M., and continued throughout the day. The enemy's cannonade was very hot. Fire broke out in the barracks at Sumter three times during that day, and was extinguished.
—— Rejoicings throughout the South upon account of the attack upon Fort Sumter. L. Percy Walker, Secretary of War of the Confederate States, made a speech at Montgomery, in which he declared that the Confederate army would be in possession of Washington by the 1st of May.

April 12.—Fort Pickens reinforced by troops landed from the United States fleet.
April 13.—The cannonade resumed at Charleston, the rebels having fired at intervals during the night. The officers' quarters took fire about eight o'clock from a shell. Hand-grenades and shells ready for use caught fire and exploded within the fort. The whole roof of the barracks was in flames at twelve o'clock. The magazine was in great danger. Ninety barrels of gunpowder were taken out of the magazine, which, as the fire increased, had to be thrown into the sea. The heat, smoke, and galling fire gradually exhausted the garrison, and nearly suffocated them. At this time, Ex-Senator Wigfall presented himself in a boat near one of the batteries, and demanded a surrender, falsely stating that he had been sent by General Beauregard for that purpose. At 12.55 the flag of Fort Sumter was hauled down. The fort surrendered upon honorable terms,— the garrison to carry away the flag and all company arms and property, and all private property, with every facility to remove the troops to any part of the United States. Of the garrison of the fort none were killed; on the side of the rebels it was reported that "nobody was hurt." After the bombardment had commenced, a fleet of transports with provisions appeared off the bar.
April 15.—Major Anderson and his command evacuated Fort Sumter, saluting his flag with fifty guns,— the band playing "Yankee Doodle" and "Hail to the Chief!" During the salute, a gun exploded, killing two men and wounding four others. Major Anderson and his men were taken to New York on the steamer Baltic.
—— Proclamation issued by the President of the United States, calling on the States for 75,000 militia, to suppress "insurrectionary combinations," and warning the persons engaged in such combinations to disperse in twenty days; also calling a special session of Congress on the 4th of July.
April 16.—Governor Magoffin, of Kentucky, responded to President Lincoln's proclamation, "Kentucky will furnish no troops for the wicked purpose of subduing her sister Southern States."
—— The Ringgold Flying Artillery of Reading, Pennsylvania, Captain James McKnight, 180 men, with four field-pieces, set out for Washington *viâ* Harrisburg,—being the first troops to respond to the call of the President.
April 17.—Governor Letcher, of Virginia, refused to call out the militia of that State in response to the President's proclamation.
—— Steamship Star of the West taken near Indianola, Texas, by the Galveston volunteers.
—— Governor Letcher, of Virginia, issued a proclamation recognizing the independence of the Southern Confederacy, and ordering the State militia to hold itself in readiness for service.
—— The Virginia State Convention passed an ordinance "to repeal the ratification of the Constitution of the United States of America by the State of Virginia, and to resume all the rights and powers granted under the said authority."
—— Jefferson Davis issued a proclamation declaring that letters of marque and reprisal would be issued by the Confederacy, "in resisting the wanton and wicked aggressions" of the United States.
April 18.—Governor Harris, of Tennessee, refused to furnish troops for "coercion."
—— Governor Jackson, of Missouri, replied to the United States Secretary of War that "his requisition was illegal, unconstitutional, revolutionary, diabolical, and cannot be complied with."
—— John Bell (candidate of the Constitutional Union party for President) issued an address calling upon the people of Tennessee to maintain a position of independence against all assailants whether from the North or South.
—— Lieutenant Jones, U. S. Army, commanding at Harper's Ferry, with 43 men, burned the arsenal and workshops there, and retreated to Pennsylvania; a large quantity of munitions of war and 15,000 stand of arms destroyed.

April 19.—The President of the United States issued a proclamation announcing the blockade of the Southern ports.

——— The 6th Massachusetts regiment, Colonel Jones, and a portion of Colonel William F. Small's Philadelphia regiment, (which was unarmed,) were attacked in Baltimore, on their way to Washington. The Massachusetts men, after suffering injury and insult for some time, fired into the mob, killing 9, and wounding many, who were carried off. Loss of the 6th regiment, 3 killed, and 7 wounded. The Pennsylvania regiment was dispersed and shamefully treated: a portion of them succeeded in getting off. The mob then took possession of the town, plundered the gun-shops, and prepared for forcible measures.

April 20.—The draws of the bridges over the Gunpowder and Bush Rivers, on the Philadelphia & Baltimore Railroad, and the whole of the Canton Bridge, at Baltimore, burned by mobs.

——— United States Arsenal at Liberty, Missouri, seized by the Missourians.

——— Gosport Navy-Yard, opposite Norfolk, burned by United States officers. The United States ships-of-the-line Pennsylvania, 74, Delaware, 74, Columbus, 74, steam-frigate Merrimac, 44, frigates Raritan, 45, Columbia, 44, United States (in ordinary) sloops-of-war Germantown, 22, and Plymouth, 22, brig Dolphin, and a powder-boat, scuttled and burned. A portion of the immense stores of cannon in the yard were spiked; but a large number of guns fell into the hands of the rebels, which afterward furnished them with armament for their field-fortifications in all parts of the South.

April 21.—United States branch mint at Charlotte, North Carolina, seized by the State authorities.

——— Intense excitement at Baltimore in consequence of rumors that Pennsylvania troops had reached Cockeysville, Maryland, to invade the city, and that the garrison at Fort McHenry was prepared to shell the city.

April 22.—Robert E. Lee, late of the United States Army, nominated by the Governor of Virginia commander of the land and naval forces of the State.

——— United States Arsenal at Fayetteville, North Carolina, surrendered to the State of North Carolina.

——— United States military supplies seized at Napoleon, Arkansas, by order of the Governor of the State.

——— A meeting held at Clarksburg, in Western Virginia. Resolutions passed censuring the course of Governor Letcher in relation to Secession. Delegates appointed to meet other Union delegates at Wheeling, May 13, to consider what course of action should be pursued.

——— In consequence of the burning of the railroad-bridges over the rivers near Baltimore, and of the bad state of feeling in that city, a new military route was opened. The 8th Massachusetts regiment was sent from Philadelphia to Perryville, Maryland, opposite Havre de Grace, and from thence (*via* Susquehanna River and Chesapeake Bay) to Annapolis, in steam-transports, where, on the 22d, they were joined by the New York 7th regiment, which had left Philadelphia by steamship Boston. The two regiments took possession of Annapolis, released the United States frigate Constitution, which was in danger of capture, repaired the railroad from Annapolis to Annapolis Junction, and opened the railroad to Washington City.

April 25.—Colonel Van Dorn, of Texas, captured 450 United States troops at Saluria.

——— Fort Smith, Arkansas, taken possession of by State troops under Colonel Solon Borland.

——— General Harney arrested at Harper's Ferry, in Virginia, but afterward released.

——— Illinois volunteers visited the United States Arsenal at St. Louis, and carried off a large amount of munitions of war, to secure them from the Secessionists.

——— The New York 7th regiment reached Washington.

April 25.—Governor Letcher, of Virginia, issued a proclamation announcing that the State had been transferred to the Southern Confederacy although the people had not yet voted upon the ordinance of secession.

April 30.—The House of Delegates of Maryland defeated an ordinance of secession by a vote of 13 for secession, and 53 against it.

May 3.—The President of the United States issued a proclamation calling for 42,034 volunteers to serve for three years, unless sooner discharged, and ordering the regular army to be increased by the addition of ten regiments,—making altogether a maximum aggregate increase of 22,714 officers and enlisted men,—and directing the enlistment of 18,000 seamen for not less than one nor more than three years.

May 5.—The Relay House, on the Baltimore & Washington Railroad, taken possession of and fortified by Federal troops under command of General B. F. Butler.

May 6.—The Convention of Arkansas passed an ordinance of secession.

——— Captain Nathaniel Lyon, U. S. Army, in possession of the arsenal at St. Louis, required by the police commissioners of that city to remove United States troops from all places outside of the arsenal grounds. The demand was refused.

May 7.—Governor Harris, of Tennessee, before the said State had become a member of the Confederacy, made a treaty putting the whole military force of the State under the control of the Confederacy.

May 9.—420 United States regulars, a company of United States artillery, with Sherman's battery, and the 1st Philadelphia Artillery regiment, Colonel F. E. Patterson, (17th of the line,) marched through Baltimore, —the first troops since the attack on the Massachusetts regiment, April 19.

May 10.—The Winans steam-gun captured near the Relay House.

——— Camp Jackson, commanded by General Frost, near St. Louis, surrounded by United States troops under Captain Lyon, and 639 men taken prisoners, with their arms and munitions. After the surrender, a mob, which followed the United States troops with riotous demonstrations, was fired into by one company; 22 persons were killed, and many wounded.

May 11.—The Home Guards of St. Louis, marching from the arsenal, were annoyed by riotous demonstrations. A pistol was fired at them; after which the Guards turned and fired on the mob: 7 persons were killed, and many wounded.

——— Charleston blockaded by United States frigate Niagara.

May 13.—Federal troops under Gen. Butler marched into Baltimore from the Relay House, and took possession of Federal Hill.

May 14.—Ross Winans arrested at the Relay House, and sent to Fort McHenry, to be imprisoned there.

May 15.—A proclamation of neutrality between the belligerents issued by the Queen of Great Britain, forbidding her subjects to enter the service of either party, "or to break a blockade lawfully and effectually established."

May 20.—At three o'clock P.M. the officers of the United States Government made a descent upon all the telegraphic offices in the free States, and seized MSS. of the despatches sent during the previous twelve months, —the object being to discover what persons had corresponded with the rebels by that medium.

——— An ordinance of secession passed by the North Carolina Convention.

——— Governor Magoffin, of Kentucky, issued a proclamation declaring that the State would be neutral, and that the movement of the troops of either party on the soil of the State was forbidden.

May 21.—Act of the Confederate Congress forbidding Southern debtors from paying their creditors at the North, and compelling payment instead into the rebel treasury, approved by Jefferson Davis.

May 24.—Troops advanced from Fortress Monroe by General Butler encamp on "the sacred soil of Virginia," at Hampton.

May 24.—A general movement into Virginia made from Washington, at the Chain Bridge and Long Bridge. A railroad-train captured, with 300 prisoners. The New York Fire Zouaves, under Colonel E. E. Ellsworth, also took possession of Alexandria, Virginia. Ellsworth, after entering the town, was killed at the Marshall House—a hotel—by John S. Jackson, the proprietor. Jackson was shot and bayoneted on the spot by Private Brownell, of the Fire Zouaves. The number of men engaged in the advance into Virginia, in the neighborhood of Washington, was about 13,000.

May 26.—The privateer Calhoun arrived at New Orleans with one brig and two schooners,—all whalers, —taken near the passes of the Mississippi.

—— The rebel Congress passed an act prohibiting the exportation of cotton except through the Southern seaports.

May 27.—A writ of habeas corpus issued by Chief-Justice Taney for the body of John Merryman, confined, upon a charge of treason, in Fort McHenry. General Cadwalader, in command at Baltimore, refused to obey the writ, by order of the President. Attachment was issued on General Cadwalader for contempt of court; but the officer having the writ could not obtain admission to the fort. Judge Taney filed an opinion in the nature of a protest.

May 30.—Grafton, Virginia, occupied by Virginia and Ohio troops, under Colonel Kelly. The Secessionists fled without firing a gun.

May 31.—An action at Acquia Creek, on the Potomac, between the United States gun-boats Freeborn (Captain Ward) and Anacosta, and rebel batteries on shore, with no perceptible effect.

June 1.—The bombardment of the batteries at Acquia Creek resumed by the Freeborn and United States gun-boat Pawnee, and continued for five hours. The vessels received several shots, but no person was hurt. It is supposed that several of the rebels in the batteries were killed by the shells thrown from the boats.

—— Lieutenant Tompkins, of the United States Cavalry, on scouting-service, fired upon at Fairfax Court-House. The dragoons charged through the town upon riflemen, wheeled and returned, and met two detachments with a field-piece; they then turned again and cut their way through a third detachment in the rear, running a gauntlet of musketry, taking 5 prisoners, and killing, as they believed, 27 men. Loss of the cavalry, 2 killed, 2 wounded, and 1 missing.

June 3.—1500 rebel troops at Philippi, Virginia, surprised by Ohio and Indiana regiments, under Colonel Kelly. The rebels fled after a straggling fire, in which Colonel Kelly was severely wounded. Two of the Federal soldiers were killed, and 25 wounded. Loss of the Secessionists, 16 killed, several wounded, and 10 prisoners.

—— The pirate privateer Savannah, Captain Baker, captured by the United States brig Perry, off the coast of South Carolina.

—— Senator Stephen A. Douglas, of Illinois, died at Chicago.

June 7.—General Patterson's army corps commenced its march toward Virginia from Chambersburg,—Brigadier-General Thomas leading the advance.

June 8.—The bridges over the Potomac at Point of Rocks and Berlin were burned by order of the rebel General Lee. Also, burned, the same day, four bridges on the Alexandria, Loudon & Hampshire Railroad.

June 10.—A night attack concerted upon rebel batteries supposed to exist at Great Bethel, in Virginia, about 12½ miles from Fortress Monroe, by United States troops under command of Gen. Pierce. In the darkness, before coming upon the enemy, a portion of the New York 7th, under Colonel Bendix, fired upon the New York 3d, Colonel Townsend: 1 man was killed, and 10 were wounded. The firing warned the enemy of the proximity of the force, and they were thus prepared for the emergency. Upon advancing to the neighborhood of Back River, near Great Bethel, a heavy fire was opened upon the Federal troops from two masked batteries mounting rifle cannon and thrown up on the other side of the stream. The enemy's fire was returned, and an attempt made by the Federal troops to carry the place by assault. The first battery was taken by a portion of the United States troops. But another mistake was made: one officer supposed a force upon the left was the enemy, and fell back. This caused a general retreat, and all the advantages gained were given up. Federal loss, 13 killed, 30 wounded, and several missing. Among the killed were Lieutenant Greble, U. S. Army, in command of the artillery, and Major Theodore Winthrop. The loss of the enemy is *reported* by the Southern papers to have been 17 killed. The force of the rebels was about 2200, under the command of General Magruder.

June 11.—Colonel Wallace, with the Indiana regiment, surprised a body of rebels at Romney, in Western Virginia, who fled in confusion. Killed, 2 rebels, and several wounded; 1 of Wallace's men was wounded.

June 12.—Governor Jackson, of Missouri, issued a proclamation calling out 50,000 militia to resist the Federal Government.

June 13.—Election for members of Congress in Maryland. Union candidates elected in all but one instance.

June 14.—Harper's Ferry evacuated by the Confederates. The railroad-bridge over the Potomac burned, with the Government armory buildings; also the railroad-bridge at Martinsburg, and the bridge over the Potomac at Sheppardstown; and a large number of locomotives, cars, and machinery at Martinsburg, belonging to the Baltimore & Ohio Railroad.

June 16.—The declaration of the independence of Western Virginia of the rebel State Government unanimously made by the Convention at Wheeling, and signed by 56 members.

June 17.—A skirmish at Edward's Ferry, on the Potomac, between 300 of the 1st Pennsylvania regiment and a force of Secessionists who attempted to take possession of the ferry. Federal loss, 1 killed, and 4 wounded; rebel loss, from 15 to 20 killed and wounded.

—— Colonel Kallman's regiment, at St. Louis, being pressed by a mob, turned and fired near the Recorder's office, killing 6 persons, and wounding 1.

—— A train on the Loudon & Hampshire Railroad, carrying the 1st Ohio regiment, Colonel McCook, under immediate command of General Schenck, was fired upon near Vienna, by a battery of field-pieces worked by a Virginia artillery company. The troops left the train, formed and returned the fire, and succeeded in retreating in good order. Federal loss, 8 killed, and 7 wounded; rebel loss, 6 killed.

—— A Union Convention of Eastern Tennessee met at Greenville. Thomas A. R. Nelson chosen President.

June 18.—Battle near Booneville, Missouri, between Federal troops under General Lyon, and State troops belonging to General Price's command. The account of this battle is vague. The number of killed was reported at 300, and a large number of prisoners were taken.

—— 800 Union Home Guards, under command of Captain Cook, attacked at Cole Camp, Missouri, by a large number of Secessionists under Governor Jackson: 23 Federal soldiers were killed, 20 wounded, and 30 taken prisoners. The rebels were repulsed, and retreated, suffering a loss of 25 killed and wounded.

June 21.—East Tennessee Convention adopted a declaration of grievances and resolutions protesting against the election held on the 8th as unfair. The vote on the 8th in Eastern Tennessee was, "For separation," 14,780; against it, 32,923. Whole vote of the State, "for separation," 104,913.

June 24.—Proclamation of the Governor of Tennessee that the people of the State had dissolved all political connection with the late United States Government.

June 25.—The steamboat St. Nicholas, of Baltimore, seized by persons who came aboard pretending to be passengers, led by one Captain Richard Thomas, who was disguised "as a French lady."

June 26.—13 mounted volunteers, belonging to Colonel Wallace's Indiana regiment, attacked 41 rebels, in Western Virginia; killed 8 of them, and chased the rest two miles. On their return, they captured 17 horses, and were attacked by 75 of the enemy. They held them at bay until dark, when they got off with a loss of 1 killed and 1 wounded; 2 lieutenants and several Secessionists were wounded in the last skirmish.

June 27.—George P. Kane, marshal of police at Baltimore, arrested for treason.

———— Attack upon rebel batteries at Matthias Point; on the Potomac, by United States gun-boats Freeborn, Pawnee, and Resolute. Captain Ward, of the Freeborn, killed.

July 1.—Members of the police board, Baltimore, arrested for treason.

———— Election in Kentucky for members of Congress. Nine Union men and one "State rights" man elected. Aggregate Union majority, nearly 60,000.

July 2.—General Patterson's army corps crossed the Potomac and advanced into Virginia. A force under the rebel Colonel Jackson fled, and their camp at Falling Waters, or Hoke's Run, was captured. Loss of the Federal troops, 3 killed, and 10 wounded; loss of the rebels, as far as known, 3 killed, and 27 wounded.

July 3.—Colonel Smith, commanding Illinois troops, about 600 in number, was attacked near Monroe, Missouri, by the rebel General Harris, with 1600 men. The rebels were repulsed, with a loss of 4 killed, and several wounded. The rebels retreated to Monroe, where they made a stand, and were again beaten back. Smith posted himself in the academy buildings, in the town, and was surrounded by 1600 rebel cavalry and other troops. He held out until reinforcements came up from Quincy, which fell upon the rear of the rebel force, completely routing them, with a loss of 20 or 30 killed, 75 prisoners, and several horses taken.

July 4.—Congress met in accordance with the special proclamation of the President. Present, 43 Senators, and in the House 159 members. Galusha A. Grow was elected Speaker of the House, and Emerson Etheridge Clerk.

July 5.—Battle near Carthage, Missouri, between 10,000 rebels under Governor Jackson and General Rains, and about 1500 United States troops commanded by Colonel Sigel. Sigel made a masterly retreat.

July 7.—Hampton, Virginia, burned by order of the rebel General Magruder. Property destroyed supposed to be worth $1,000,000.

———— Captain Thomas, who, "disguised as a French lady," led the pirates who seized the steamboat St. Nicholas, of Baltimore, was arrested on board the steamboat St. Mary, being hid in a *bureau-drawer* in the ladies' cabin.

July 11.—Battle at Rich Mountain, in Western Virginia, between a body of rebels under Colonel Pegram and United States troops under General Rosecrans. Pegram surrendered 600 prisoners.

July 12.—600 rebels in the neighborhood of Barboursville, in Western Virginia, attacked by three companies of Colonel Woodruff's 2d Kentucky regiment, and routed, with a loss of 10 killed, and several wounded.

———— General Garnett, commanding the main body of the Confederates, retreated from Laurel Hill.

July 13.—The retreating rebels were overtaken near Carricksford by United States troops under General Morris. The rebels were defeated, and General Garnett killed. Rebel loss in both battles, more than 250 killed, 1000 prisoners, 5 guns, 12 colors, and 1500 stand of arms; Federal loss, 20 killed, and 60 wounded.

July 15.—General Patterson's army corps left Martinsburg, Virginia, and advanced to Bunker Hill.

July 16.—The Federal army of the Potomac, under General McDowell, commenced the advance from Arlington, in four columns: the extreme right under General Hunter; the right centre under General Tyler; the left centre under Colonel Dixon I. Miles; and the extreme left under Colonel Heintzelman. As the United States troops advanced, the rebels retired from Falls Church, Fairfax Court-House, and other points within their lines.

July 17.—General Patterson's army corps marched from Bunker Hill to Charlestown, which was reached the same night.

———— Skirmish at Fulton, Missouri, between 1000 rebels under Harris, and Colonel McNeill, with 600 Federals. The rebels dispersed. Eleven Union soldiers killed and wounded.

July 18.—170 Union Home Guards, under Major Van Horn, attacked near Harrisonville, Missouri, by 500 rebels under Captain Duncan. The rebels were repulsed, with a loss of 14 killed.

———— General Tyler, leading the column of the right centre, Federal army, after passing Centreville and marching by the Manassas road, was informed that there were masked batteries ahead, near Bull Run. He sent forward Colonel Richardson, with one brigade, to reconnoitre, the rest of the division remaining at Centreville. The advancing body (about 2000 in number) was fired upon, near Blackburn's Ford, by two batteries of eight pieces, which commanded the road. The regiments fell back, covered by a gun of Sherman's battery. Two rifled cannon were brought in front by Captain Brackett, and there was a steady fire for some time. The woods were again reconnoitred and the Union troops fired upon, which was replied to by Ayre's battery. At halfpast four o'clock, General Tyler recalled the troops. Number of killed, wounded, and missing on the Federal side, 158; rebel loss, large.

July 21.—General McDowell desiring to turn the position of the enemy, force him from the road, and, if possible, destroy the railroad leading from Manassas to the Valley of Virginia, the troops were detailed to execute this duty in four columns,—the fifth remaining, as a reserve, seven miles in the rear of Centreville. Burnside's brigade of Hunter's division was the first to receive the fire of the rebels from artillery and infantry. Being reinforced, they drove the enemy's right, commanded by Beauregard, for some distance. Heintzelman's division was opposed to the enemy's centre, under command of J. E. Johnston. This part of the rebels being desperately galled by Griffith's battery, made three efforts to take it, but were driven back, having previously been driven a mile and a half by the Federal troops. At three o'clock in the afternoon, the Union forces—which had been fighting since half-past ten in the morning, and had been marching and under arms from two o'clock in the morning—was in possession of the Warrenton road, from the stone bridge westward. The rebels were disheartened and flying; but the Federal troops were exhausted and worn, the heat being intense, and the soldiers suffering for water and food. At this time, reinforcements, which had come up from Winchester by railroad and had been under Johnston there, threw themselves, under command of General Kirby Smith, into the woods at the right of the Federalists, and opened fire upon them, which caused the latter to break and retire. This movement soon resulted in disorder. Efforts to rally them were in vain. The retreat soon became a rout, and this soon degenerated further into a panic. Richardson's brigade, which had been ordered to attack the batteries at Blackburn's Ford, in order to keep the enemy in check, and had executed that service with gallantry, were now also retiring by order; but the command being assumed by Major-General McDowell, they covered the retreat, permitting the fugitives to pass without being very actively pursued. The flying soldiers were now perfectly frantic. They abandoned their artillery, threw down their guns, and seemed to vie with each other in disgraceful speed. The enemy scarcely attempted to follow, being badly cut up, and seemingly ignorant of the unaccountable panic which had seized upon the Federal troops. The number of Federalists actually in this battle was about 18,000.

The Federal loss was 19 officers, and 462 non-commissioned officers and privates; wounded, 64 officers, and 947 non-commissioned officers and privates; the prisoners and missing, about 900.

The principal Federal officers killed were Colonel James Cameron, 79th New York; Colonel Slocum

2d Rhode Island; Lieutenant-Colonel Haggerty, 69th New York.

Wounded.—Colonel David Hunter, U. S. Army; Colonel S. P. Heintzelman, U.S. Army; Colonel O. B. Wilcox. Michigan volunteers, (taken prisoner;) Colonel Corcoran, New York 69th, (taken prisoner;) Colonel H. W. Slocum, 27th New York; Colonel H. M. Wood, 14th New York; Colonel Marston, 2d New Hampshire.

Two batteries (in all, 10 guns) were actually taken upon the field; 7 which were abandoned in the flight were subsequently picked up by the rebels,—making 17 guns in all that they took possession of. The whole force of artillery, of all calibres, in service on the Federal side, were 49 pieces, of which 28 were rifled.

Upon the Secession side there was killed, General Bernard E. Bee, of South Carolina; General Francis S. Bartow, Georgia; Colonel Nelson, Virginia; Colonel Fisher, North Carolina; Colonel Mason; Lieutenant-Colonel B. F. Johnson.

Wounded.—General Kirby Smith; Colonel Wade Hampton; Colonel S. J. Gartrell, Virginia; Colonel Jones, Alabama; Colonel Thomas, Colonel H. C. Stevens, Major Robert Wheat, Louisiana; Major Scott, Alabama.

A correspondent of the Richmond "Dispatch," writing from Manassas, July 22, places the rebel loss at 600 killed, and 2500 wounded. A correspondent of the New Orleans "Picayune" declared that there were between 500 and 600 killed, and between 2000 and 3000 wounded. The number of rebels at Manassas was stated by Jefferson Davis, in a speech made at Richmond, after the battle, to be but 18,000; but, as he said in the same speech that "60 pieces of splendid cannon" were taken from the United States army, and "provisions enough to feed an army of 50,000 men for twelve months,"— which would have required 12,000 wagons to transport to the battle-ground,—his *facts* are not reliable. A Richmond paper estimated the troops at Manassas to be 40,000; a correspondent of the "Picayune," 30,000. W. H. Russell, of the London "Times," estimated it to be 60,000. Whatever the force may have been, their loss was heavy, and they were too much cut up to pursue the fugitives.

July 24.—Nine sloops and schooners belonging to the rebels were burned in Back River, Virginia, by a naval expedition under command of Lieutenant Crosby.

July 27.—Hampton, Virginia, previously occupied by Federal troops under Gen. Butler, abandoned by them.

July 29.—General Cox, in command of United States troops, reached Gauley Bridge, in Western Virginia. Governor Wise, in command of the rebels, burned the bridge and retreated.

July 30.—The State Convention of Missouri, assembled at Jefferson City, by a vote of 56 to 25, declared that the offices of Governor, Lieutenant-Governor, Secretary of State, and members of Assembly, were *vacant*. Hamilton R. Gamble was appointed provisional Governor until the regular election in November.

August 1.—The rebel privateer Petrel was sunk off the coast of South Carolina by the frigate St. Lawrence. The Petrel, mistaking the St. Lawrence for a merchantman, fired into her. The St. Lawrence answered with a broadside which cut the privateer in two: 5 pirates were drowned, and 36 picked up and taken prisoners.

——— General Lyon attacked a large force of Confederates, under General McCulloch, at Dug Spring, Missouri. A gallant charge was made upon the rebels by United States cavalry. General Lyon retired to Springfield. Loss of the rebels reported to be heavy.

August 5.—A camp of 350 Union soldiers, at Athens, Missouri, attacked by 1200 rebels, under Martin Green, who was repulsed by Captain Moore, in command. Being reinforced with 150 men, Moore followed the enemy, killing 20, wounding 25, and taking 18 prisoners. Loss of the Union men, 3 killed, and 18 wounded.

August 8.—Senator John C. Breckinridge, of Kentucky, and Mr. Vallandigham, of Ohio, complimented by a public dinner, at Baltimore, by Secession sympathizers. Breckinridge afterward attempted to speak, upon being serenaded, but was prevented by the outcry and noise of a large number of Union men who were on the ground. They cheered for "The Union," for "General Scott," and for "Henry Winter Davis." When attempts were made to silence the disturbers, they responded, "Remember the 19th of April!" "Remember the week of terror!" "You had us then,—we have got you now!"

August 10.—Battle at Wilson's Creek, near Springfield, Missouri, between 5200 Federal troops under General Lyon, and about 22,200 rebels under Generals Ben McCulloch and Price. General Lyon was killed. The command devolved on General Sigel, who, finding the enemy too strong, retreated, without being pursued, to Springfield, and then to Rolla, to wait for reinforcements. Federal loss, by official report, 223 killed, and 721 wounded; rebel loss, under Price, by official report, 156 killed, and 517 wounded; McCulloch's loss, by his own report, 265 killed, and 800 wounded. Entire rebel loss, admitted by themselves, 421 killed, and 1317 wounded. The Federal troops took 70 prisoners and 400 horses, and compelled the rebels to burn a large quantity of baggage, to prevent it from falling into our hands.

August 12.—Charles J. Faulkner, minister to France under President Buchanan, arrested at Washington, and sent to Fort Lafayette, New York Harbor, as a prisoner of State.

August 13.—Skirmish at Grafton, Western Virginia, between 50 men of the 4th Virginia regiment, under Captain Dayton, and 200 rebels commanded by Zuchariah Cochran: 21 rebels killed, and the rest put to flight. No loss on the Federal side.

August 14.—Martial law proclaimed in St. Louis by Major-General Fremont.

August 15.—The rebel Governor Jackson issued a proclamation at New Madrid, declaring that the union between Missouri and the other States was dissolved, and that Missouri was an independent State.

——— The banks of Philadelphia, New York, and Boston agreed to take $50,000,000 of the national loan, with the privilege of taking $50,000,000 more in 60 days and $50,000,000 more in 120 days.

August 16.—The President issued a proclamation declaring the seceding States to be in a state of insurrection, prohibiting all intercourse between them and the other States of the Union.

August 18.—The "Jeff Davis" rebel privateer wrecked on the bar at St. Augustine, Florida.

August 20.—Skirmish at Hawk's Nest, Western Virginia: 400 rebels attacked the 11th Ohio regiment, and were driven back, with a loss of 50 killed, and a large number wounded: 2 Federal soldiers were wounded.

——— The Western Virginia Convention, at Wheeling, resolved that thirty-nine counties in that part of the State should be formed into a new State, called "Kanawha," if the people should so decide at an election to be held October 24.

——— The office of the "Jeffersonian" newspaper, at West Chester, Pennsylvania, entered, and the type and material destroyed,—the paper being opposed to the war.

August 21.—A rebel force of 600, under General Rains, seized 90 mules near Fort Scott, Kansas. Rains was pursued by Colonel Montgomery for several miles. Rains had cannon, and Montgomery but a single howitzer. A running fight was kept up until nightfall, when Montgomery retired.

——— 4000 Cherokee Indians, assembled in mass meeting at Tahlequa, declared their adhesion to the Confederate States. The head chief (John Ross) gave orders for raising a regiment of mounted men, under Colonel John Drew.

August 22.—Rebel steamer N. B. Terry taken at Paducah, Kentucky, by United States gun-boat Lexington, with 1 field-piece, 30 minie rifles, and other contraband goods, on board.

——— The office of the Stark County "Democrat"— a secession paper published at Canton, Ohio—destroyed by Union volunteers.

August 23.—The "Jeffersonian" newspaper, at West Chester, Pennsylvania, seized by the United States Marshal as a treasonable publication.

August 26.—A military and naval expedition, under General Butler and Commodore Stringham, sailed from Fort Monroe, Virginia.

———— A portion of the 7th Ohio regiment, Colonel Tyler, taken in flank at Cross Lanes, near Summerville, Virginia, by a large force of rebels, with 10 guns. The Union troops succeeded in cutting their way through the enemy, with the loss of 15 killed, and about 40 wounded.

August 28.—The bombardment of the forts at Hatteras commenced: 300 soldiers landed, under command of Colonel Max Weber.

August 29.—Fort Hatteras and Fort Clark, at Cape Hatteras Inlet, North Carolina, captured by a joint naval and land expedition under Commodore Stringham and Major-General Butler: 31 cannon, 1900 stand of arms, 75 kegs of powder, and 715 prisoners taken, including Captain Samuel Barron, Secretary of the Navy of North Carolina. The surrender was unconditional. None of the United States forces were injured. On the part of the rebels, 5 were known to be killed, and several wounded were sent away before the surrender. The naval force consisted of the frigates Minnesota and Wabash, the gun-boats Pawnee, Monticello, and Harriet Lane, with transports conveying about 1000 troops.

August 30.—Major-General Fremont, commanding the department of the West, issued a proclamation declaring the State of Missouri under martial law, and declaring the property of all persons who had taken up arms against the United States, or who should thereafter do so, confiscated to the public use, and that their slaves—if they have any—shall be declared *freemen*.

September 1.—From 400 to 600 rebels, at Boone Court-House, Western Virginia, routed by Union troops (Kentucky and Virginia) under command of Captain Wheeler. The rebels were charged upon and ran away: 35 of them were killed, several wounded, and 5 taken prisoners. The Federalists lost none; but 6 men were wounded, 22 horses were taken, and a considerable quantity of arms. After this, the town was fired and every house in it burned.

September 2.—The Charlestown Home Guards cavalry surrounded at Bellers' Mill, near Harper's Ferry, Virginia, by a portion of the 13th Massachusetts regiment: 3 rebels were killed, 5 wounded, and 22 taken prisoners.

September 3.—A bridge over the Little Platte River, Missouri, on the line of the Hannibal & St. Joseph Railroad, was so weakened by the rebels that it was expected to break down with the first train that crossed it. The passenger-express, bound West, was precipitated into the river, and a large number of innocent persons —men and women—killed and wounded. This was one of the most fiendish acts perpetrated in Missouri.

September 4.—600 Union troops, at Shelbina, Missouri, attacked by about 3500 rebels under Martin E. Green, with two pieces of artillery. After waiting two hours for reinforcements from General Hurlbut, the Federalists retreated, with a loss of horses, wagons, &c. No other loss.

———— Kentucky invaded by rebel troops, who took position at Hickman, Chalk Cliffs, and Columbus, and commenced to throw up fortifications.

September 6.—Paducah, Kentucky, occupied by General Grant, in command of Union forces numbering about 2100. He was assisted by two gun-boats upon the Ohio River.

———— General Pope, U. S. Army, marched against Martin E. Green, at Hunneville, Missouri, who fled with 3000 men, leaving behind them baggage, provisions, and forage.

September 7.—The House of Representatives of Kentucky directed the flag of the United States to be hoisted over the State-House, by a vote of 77 against 20.

September 11.—The President of the United States ordered that the proclamation of Major-General Fromont, that the slave-property of rebels should be confiscated, be modified in accordance with the act of Congress, which specifies that whenever slaves are employed in or upon any fort, navy-yard, dock, armory, ship, or entrenchment, or in any military or naval capacity, against the Government of the United States, the person owning said slaves shall lose all right to their future services.

———— The House of Representatives of Kentucky adopted a resolution directing the Confederate troops to leave the State.

———— A reconnoitring party, under Colonel Stevens, of the New York 79th, had a skirmish near Lewinsville, Virginia, with four rebel regiments, including Stewart's cavalry. Several rounds were fired on each side. The object of the reconnoissance being accomplished, the Federalists retired in good order, and the rebels retreated beyond Lewinsville. General Smith, commanding the division, was early on the ground. On the part of the Federalists, 6 killed, and 7 wounded.

September 12.—General Rosecrans, commanding the United States troops in Western Virginia, made a strong reconnoissance in front of the rebel entrenchments at Carnifex Ferry, where were posted about 5000 men under General Floyd, late of Buchanan's Cabinet. Detachments of the rebels, in advance of the lines, were driven in by the command of General Benham. The enemy had about 16 pieces mounted, and played upon the Federal lines with shell and musketry, and were answered with spirit. After four or five hours' engagement, night coming on, General Rosecrans withdrew his troops out of range, and posted them for the night, with the expectation of 'renewing the battle at dawn. In the night, however, Floyd abandoned his position, and, crossing the Gauley River with his troops, destroyed the county bridge, sunk the bridge of boats communicating with his camp, and fled to the mountains. His camp-equipage, tents, and arms were captured by Rosecrans, who, in consequence of the destruction of the bridges, could not pursue the fugitives. The Federal loss was about 16 killed, (among them, Colonel Lowe, 12th Ohio,) and 97 wounded; rebel loss not known.

———— 9000 rebels under General R. E. Lee, with about 10 pieces of artillery, advanced upon the positions held by General Reynolds, commanding Union troops at Elkwater, Western Virginia. Various strategetic movements were made in that vicinity and at Cheat Summit, for some days in succession, which were resisted by the United States forces. Skirmishing took place at several points. On the 17th, the rebels retired, —having lost about 100 killed, (including Colonel John A. Washington, the Mount Vernon speculator,) and 20 prisoners. Federal loss, none killed, 2 missing, and 60 prisoners.

———— The rebel General Price, and Claiborne F. Jackson, at the head of 15,000 or 20,000 men, attacked the Federal soldiers under command of Colonel James A. Mulligan, of Illinois, who were strongly entrenched at Lexington, Missouri.

September 13.—Mayor Brown, of Baltimore, Ross Winans, and other members of the Legislature, Henry May, M.C., and others, were arrested by the United States authorities in Baltimore and Maryland, the Government being in possession of information that they were engaged in a plot to pass an ordinance of secession at the adjourned session of the Legislature of Maryland, which was to assemble during the next week. By this bold measure, the Legislature was left without a quorum, the session contemplated was not held, and the plot of the Secessionists to vote Maryland out of the Union—which was believed to have been entered into by a conspiracy with the rebel Government—was totally frustrated.

———— Fight near Booneville, Missouri, between 150 Union Home Guards, under Captain Eppstein, and 600 rebels, under Colonel Brown. The Home Guards were entrenched, and drove back the enemy. On the rebel side, Colonel Brown and Captain Brown were killed, with 10 others, and 30 wounded.

September 14.—A boat-expedition, under Lieutenant John Russell, of the United States ship Colorado, cut out the privateer Judith, under the guns of the rebels, at Pensacola Navy-Yard, and destroyed the vessel by fire. Loss on the Federal side, 3 killed, and 15 wounded.

September 15.—An attack made by about 500 rebels upon a portion of the 28th Pennsylvania regiment, Colonel Geary, opposite Prichards' Mill, on the Potomac. The rebels were repulsed, with a loss of 18 killed, and some wounded; Federal loss, 1 killed.

September 16.—Chandeleur Island, near the mouth of the Mississippi River, taken possession of by the crews of the United States steamer Massachusetts and the sloops-of-war Preble and Marion, who threw up batteries, and rekindled the light at the light-house, which had been long extinguished.

September 17.—A railroad-train on the Ohio & Mississippi Railroad, containing a portion of Col. Torchin's 19th Illinois regiment, fell through a bridge near Huron, Indiana, killing and wounding nearly 100.

—— 570 of the 3d Iowa regiment, under Lieutenant-Colonel Scott, with 1 piece of artillery, gallantly sustained an attack from 4500 rebels, at Blue Mills, Missouri. After a fight of an hour, Scott retreated slowly and in good order, and took up a better position. Whilst there, Colonel Smith, with 1400 Federal troops, came up by another route. The two forces then united, and pursued the rebels, who crossed the river before daylight, and retreated: 16 Unionists killed, 94 wounded, and 6 missing; rebel loss not known.

—— Fight at Marratstown, Missouri, between 600 United States troops, under Colonels Montgomery and Johnson, and 400 rebels. The latter were routed, with a loss of 7 killed. 100 horses were taken, and all the tents and provisions of the enemy. Colonel Johnson was killed, and 2 Federal soldiers; 6 were wounded.

September 20.—Colonel James A. Mulligan, after a gallant defence at Lexington, Missouri, during which several brilliant sorties were made by his troops and the charges of the enemy were repulsed, was compelled to surrender in consequence of a want of water,—the men having fought fifty-nine hours without it, having only three barrels of vinegar with which to quench their thirst; 3500 men were surrendered to the rebels by this mishap, with 3000 muskets and rifles, a number of wagons, some provisions, 5 pieces of artillery, 2 mortars, 750 horses, and army stores worth $100,000. From 900 to 1200 rebels were reported to be killed and wounded. General Price, in his report, named the amount as 25 killed, and 72 wounded. After thus succeeding in this siege, the rebel general abandoned Lexington a few days afterward, fearing an attack from the Federal troops under Fremont advancing against him. The Federal loss at Lexington was Colonel White, killed, with about 40 others, and 75 wounded: $900,000 in money, belonging to Missouri banks, was taken by Price, who reported that he had restored the same to the rightful owners.

September 23.—700 rebels were driven out of Mechanicsville Gap, Western Virginia, by 875 Union soldiers, under Colonels Cantwell and Huske. The latter then advanced on Romney, and stormed the rebel lines, which were defended by 1400 infantry and cavalry. The rebels retreated to the mountains, with a loss of 35 killed, and a large number wounded; Federal loss, 3 killed, and 10 wounded.

September 24.—Skirmish at Point of Rocks, Maryland, between 400 rebels and Colonel Geary's 28th Pennsylvania regiment. The rebels were upon the Virginia side of the Potomac, but were driven off by shells and musket-balls. Two or three houses on the Virginia side were burned by the Federalists,—a few men crossing the river Potomac for the purpose.

September 25.—A reconnoissance made near Lewinsville, Virginia, by 5000 United States infantry, three companies of cavalry, and three batteries, under command of General William F. Smith. A large quantity of forage, cattle, sheep, &c. was taken. At Lewinsville an attack was made on this force by five regiments of infantry and a regiment of cavalry, having 6 pieces of artillery. Shots were exchanged on both sides. The rebel batteries were silenced. No loss on the Union side. The troops marched back to the Chain Bridge in good order. Colonel Stewart, of the rebel cavalry, was taken prisoner.

September 29.—The United States forces opposite Washington advanced, under General W. F. Smith, upon Munson's and Upton's Hills, which had been held by the rebels, but were now deserted. In the advance, by some unfortunate mistake, some regiments of Baker's brigade—viz. the California regiment, 24th Pennsylvania, (Colonel Owens,) Baxter's Philadelphia Fire Zouaves, and Friedman's dragoons—fired upon each other in the darkness of the night, killing 9, and wounding 18.

October 1.—The propeller Fanny, chartered by the United States Government, captured by three rebel steam-tugs while on the passage from Hatteras Inlet to Chicomacomico, on the coast of North Carolina: 25 soldiers belonging to the 20th Indiana regiment, who were on board, were taken prisoners, and 2 rifled cannon were captured.

—— 1000 Ohio and Virginia Union troops, under Lieutenant-Colonel Engart, surrounded and attacked a number of rebels at Chapmanville, Virginia, and routed them, killing 60, and taking 70 prisoners. In their flight, the rebels were intercepted by Colonel Hyatt, who killed 40, and took a large number of prisoners.

October 3.—Reconnoissance in front of the rebel lines at Green Brier River, Western Virginia, by 5000 men of General Reynolds's division. A lively skirmish ensued. Federal loss, 10 killed, and 11 wounded; 13 rebel prisoners were taken, and some baggage and horses. The rebels were stationed at Buffalo Hill, and were driven from their lower entrenchments; but, being reinforced and strongly posted, the Union troops did not attempt any thing further.

—— 2500 rebels, transported from the mainland in six small steamers and flat-boats, attacked the 20th Indiana regiment, Colonel Hawkins, at Chicomacomico, North Carolina: 50 of the United States troops were taken prisoners, with all their tents and baggage. Colonel Hawkins succeeded in reaching Fort Hatteras with the remainder.

October 4.—A party of New Mexican Union volunteers, under Captain Mink, was surprised at Alimosa, thirty-five miles below Fort Craig, by 110 Texan rebels, and their horses stampeded. Captain Mink proposed to surrender his company; but his men dissented, secured their horses, and retreated to Fort Craig. Subsequently about 100 United States troops, from Fort Craig, pursued the rebels, overtook them, killed their captain and 10 men, wounded about 30, and killed 30 horses. The balance of the Texans escaped to Messella.

October 5.—The United States gun-boat Monticello made an attack, with shot and shell, upon the rebels at Chicomacomico, North Carolina, who had routed the Indiana Union volunteers two days before: 218 shot and shell were fired from the Monticello in three hours and a half. The slaughter is supposed to have been heavy, and the rebels were compelled to take to their boats and make their escape. They represented afterward that "nobody was hurt."

October 9.—1500 rebels, under command of General Anderson, landed in the night on Santa Rosa Island, near Pensacola, Florida, and made an attack upon the camp of Colonel William Wilson's Zouaves, (6th New York regiment.) There were but 215 of them there, the others being detached upon special duty. This small party, being suddenly aroused about two o'clock in the morning, met the invaders with determination, and the fight was spiritedly contested. The noise of the conflict brought portions of two companies of regulars from Fort Pickens,—making the whole Union force 365. On their way to the relief of Wilson, 80 of these met about 700 of the enemy, and cut their way through them. After some time, the rebel General Anderson gave orders to retreat; in doing which his force was badly cut up.

The boats in which they embarked were fired into, and several were killed and wounded. Loss of the Zouaves, 10 killed, and 16 wounded; regulars, 6 killed, 20 wounded, and 10 prisoners,—among them, Major Vogdes. The Union forces took 35 prisoners. 21 of the rebel soldiers were killed and left on the island. By their own statements in Southern newspapers, the rebels lost 350 killed, wounded, and missing. During the fight, the tents of the Zouaves were burned by the rebels, who had brought over combustibles for that purpose.

October 9.—General Smith's division of the United States army, in front of Washington, made an advance to Lewinsville, Virginia, which was occupied in force.

October 10.—300 rebels, under the command of Captain Holliday, were attacked near Hillsboro', Kentucky, by 50 Home Guards, under Lieutenants Sadler and Sergeant, who dispersed them, capturing 127 Enfield rifles, and a quantity of sabres, pistols, &c. Union loss, 3 killed, and 2 wounded.

October 11.—A rebel schooner, lying in Quantico, in Dumfries Creek, Virginia, was cut out by armed boats from the United States gun-boats Rescue and Resolute, under the command of Midshipman W. F. Stewart, Master Edward L. Haynes, and Master Amos Foster. They succeeded in firing the vessel, which was totally destroyed. The enemy fired at the boats on their return; but the crews were not injured.

October 12.—The rebel Commodore Hollins, with a steam-ram, iron-clad, called the Manassas, and a fleet of fire-ships, attacked the United States blockading squadron at the Southwest Pass of the Mississippi. The ram ran against the United States steamer Richmond in the dark, starting two planks on her quarter, near the stern, but doing no other damage. To avoid the fire-ships, the squadron—consisting of the steamers Richmond, Huntsville, Waterwitch, sloops-of-war Preble and Vincennes, and steamship Nightingale—got under weigh and drifted down the river. The Richmond, Preble, Vincennes, and Nightingale got on the bar, and, whilst there, were attacked by the rebels, who did but little damage. They were beaten off by the Richmond, with 2 guns. The Richmond, Preble, and Vincennes were towed off the next day. No one was hurt in the Federal fleet. Captain Hollins, on the strength of this achievement, sent a despatch to New Orleans, declaring that he had sunk the sloop-of-war Preble, and, after the other vessels "were fast in the sand, I peppered them well." New Orleans was illuminated in consequence of this "brilliant victory."

—— 80 United States cavalry, under Major James, attacked 30 rebels in a corn-field near Lebanon, Missouri: 8 rebels killed, and 5 taken prisoners; 2 of the Union troops were killed.

October 13.—Two companies of cavalry belonging to Wright's battalion, under Captains Montgomery and Switzler, made a dash at about 300 rebels, near Wet Glaze, eighteen miles below Lebanon, Missouri, killing 62, wounding 12, and taking 36 prisoners; Federal loss, 1 man killed, and 1 wounded.

—— A skirmish at Beckwith, Missouri, between 25 of Captain Nolens' Federal cavalry and 100 rebel cavalry. The Federalists were repulsed, with a loss of 5 killed, and 5 wounded. The rebel captain was killed.

October 14.—57 United States soldiers, who were prisoners at Richmond, Virginia, were released by the rebel authorities. The United States Government ordered an equal number of rebel prisoners to be released upon their taking the oath of allegiance, or an oath not to engage in arms against the United States.

—— The Hon. William H. Seward, Secretary of State, addressed a circular letter to the Governors of the Northern States, recommending that measures should be taken by the respective States to put their harbors and ports on the seas and lakes in a condition of complete defence against foreign intervention or aggression.

October 15.—About 600 rebels, under Jeff Thompson, surrounded 50 Union soldiers near Big River Bridge, Missouri. The latter fought as long as they could, but were forced to surrender, with a loss of 1 killed, and 7 wounded. The rebel loss was 5 killed, and 4 wounded. Jeff Thompson then proceeded to burn the Big River Bridge,—which work being accomplished, he retreated with his men.

October 15.—The Missouri State Convention passed an ordinance postponing the election of Governor until November, 1862.

October 16.—The rebel army in front of Washington retired from Vienna, and fell back, with their whole column, to Fairfax Court-House. The Union troops advanced and took possession of Vienna.

—— A company of Wisconsin volunteers, stationed near Bolivar, Virginia, was attacked by a superior force of rebels under Colonel Turner Ashby, (about 2000 in number,) with 7 pieces of artillery. The Unionists charged upon the enemy, and captured 1 gun, (a 32-pounder,) and took 10 prisoners; but, the enemy coming upon them strongly, they were compelled to retreat,—leaving the gun behind them. Reinforcements were then sent over from Harper's Ferry, under command of Colonel John W. Geary, with 1 gun. With this piece the rebels were driven back, and finally put to flight, and the 32-pounder which had been taken and lost was again captured. This fight continued for about eight hours. The rebel loss was supposed to be 50 killed, and 100 wounded.

—— 150 Missouri scouts, under Major White, surprised the rebel garrison left at Lexington, Missouri, by General Price, and recaptured the place, taking 300 prisoners.

—— Major Gavitt, of the 1st Indiana cavalry, made an attack on rebels near Pilot Knob, Missouri, but, finding them strongly posted, fell back, and was reinforced by Colonel Alexander, with 600 Illinois infantry. The enemy followed, fighting all the way. Gavitt then got his gun into position, and the enemy were drawn into an ambuscade, in which they suffered a heavy loss.

October 17.—Lieutenant Kirby, with 15 men of Major Wright's battalion, fought 45 rebels at Linn Creek, Missouri, killing 5, and wounding 12.

October 19.—A fight at Big Hurricane Creek, Carroll county, Missouri, between Colonel Morgan, 18th Missouri, with 220 men and 2 guns, and 400 rebels, who were put to flight, with a loss of 14 killed, and 8 prisoners.

—— The schooner Fairfax — a transport loaded with hay—captured by the rebels on the Lower Potomac. Several new batteries were unmasked, and the river was considered unsafe for navigation,—being commanded by rebel batteries on the banks for several miles.

October 21.—Battle at Ball's Bluff, Virginia, and defeat of the Union forces under command of Colonel E. D. Baker, in which were engaged on the Union side about 1700 men, belonging to the Pennsylvania 71st ("California") regiment, Massachusetts 15th and 20th, and the Tammany New York regiment. The movement was made from Harrison's Island,—the design being to draw the attention of the enemy from the crossing into Virginia of the main bodies of the Union army, under General Stone and General Banks, at Conrad's Ferry and Edwards' Ferry, above and below Harrison's Island. To execute this movement, a small number of men of the 15th Massachusetts regiment crossed the Potomac into Virginia on the night of the 20th. The soldiers were attacked in the morning by rebels in rifle-pits, who were driven therefrom by a charge. The enemy kept in the protection of woods, and were held in check by three pieces of artillery. Colonel E. D. Baker, with a battalion of the 71st Pennsylvania "California" regiment, crossed to their assistance in the morning. At two o'clock, being strongly reinforced, the rebels enclosed this little force on three sides,—the trees being filled with their sharpshooters. The battle then raged sharply until night. Colonel E. D. Baker was killed at the head of his regiment about four o'clock, and his regiment fell into some disorder. Colonel Coggswell, of the Tammany regiment, succeeded in command, and, finding the hope of success weak, in consequence of the disparity of numbers, ordered a retreat about dark. The Union troops were driven toward the river. The means of transportation were miserable, being but two small scows that would not hold fifty men each. The current was swift and deep. Many soldiers threw away their guns and accoutrements, and plunged in the Potomac. Some succeeded in swimming across, some were drowned, and others shot in the water. The surviving fugitives took refuge on Harrison's Island, and were not pursued. The Unionists lost Colonel E. D. Baker, 71st Pennsylvania, killed; Colonel Cogswell, New York Tammany regiment, a prisoner; many officers were wounded and taken prisoners. The entire Union loss, killed, wounded, and missing, was about 800. The rebels admitted a loss of 300 killed and wounded; but it is believed to have been much greater.

———— 5000 rebels, under Jeff Thompson and Lowe, were defeated at Fredericktown, Missouri, by Illinois, Wisconsin, and Indiana troops, about 2000 in number, under Colonel Curlin, Colonel Ross, Colonel Baker, Major Plummer, and Major Scofield. The engagement lasted two hours, when the rebels fled from the field in disorder, and took to the woods. Major Gavitt and Captain Higham were killed in making a charge. Colonel Lowe, the rebel leader, was killed, and 4 heavy guns were captured. The rebels were pursued for twenty-two miles, when the chase was given over. 200 dead rebels were left in the field. Union loss, 6 killed, and 40 wounded.

———— Colonel Garrard, having 2000 men, was attacked by a rebel force, under General Zollicoffer, at Camp Wildcat, Kentucky. Zollicoffer had 5000 men. The rebels made three charges, but were repulsed each time. Their loss was estimated at 200 killed and wounded. Union loss, 30 killed and wounded. Zollicoffer retreated.

———— A large naval expedition sailed from Annapolis, Maryland, destined for some point on the Southern coast, under command of Samuel F. Dupont, senior flag-officer. It comprised 8 steam and sailing frigates, 16 steam gun-boats, and 34 armed steam and sailing transports,—mounting, in all, 400 guns. Commanders of the troops, General E. L. Viele, General Isaac J. Stevens, and General H. G. Wright,—the whole under direction of General Thomas W. Sherman. This expedition stopped at Fort Monroe, where some more soldiers were taken on board. The soldiers numbered about 15,000; the seamen several thousand.

———— The Union troops, stationed on the Virginia side, at Edwards' Ferry and Harrison's Island, were withdrawn to Maryland, upon reports that large numbers of the rebels were advancing.

October 24.—The election in Western Virginia, to determine whether that part of the State should be formed into a new State, called "Kanawha," was held, and resulted in favor of the proposition by a very large majority.

———— Major Charles Zagoni, commanding General Fremont's body-guard, (150 in number,) made a charge upon 2000 rebels, under Colonel Pierce, at Springfield, Missouri. The enemy did not stand, but were routed in a very short time. Union loss, 18 killed, 20 wounded, and 20 missing; rebel loss, 80 killed, 60 wounded, and 27 prisoners.

October 25.—William Smith, one of the crew of the rebel privateer Jeff Davis, was convicted of piracy at Philadelphia.

October 26.—General B. F. Kelly, with troops, marched from New Creek, in Western Virginia, to Romney, and routed the rebels there, taking all their wagons and camp-equipage, 3 pieces of cannon, 200 horses, and 450 prisoners. The fight lasted for two hours. The rebels were commanded by Colonel Armstrong. Union loss, 1 killed, and 5 wounded.

———— Three companies of 9th Illinois regiment had a skirmish at Saratoga, Kentucky, with a company of rebel cavalry, 100 strong. The rebels were routed, with a loss of 13 killed, 24 prisoners, 52 horses, and their camp-equipage. United States loss, 2 wounded.

October 26.—400 rebels laid down their arms at Fulton, Missouri, and surrendered to 1500 Union troops, under General Henderson, and were permitted to return to their homes.

October 30.—The great naval expedition sailed from Fortress Monroe, bound to some part of the Southern coast.

October 31.—Lieutenant-General Winfield Scott, commander of the United States army, was retired from active service, at his own request,—and Major-General George B. McClellan appointed commander of the armies of the Union.

November 1.—Rebel batteries commanded by General Floyd, situated on the Gauley River, Western Virginia, near the junction of the Gauley and New Rivers, opened fire upon the camp of General Rosecrans' division, on the opposite side of the river. Firing continued all day and for a day or two after, without any great loss to the Unionists. The latter responded from their own guns, and silenced some of the rebel batteries.

November 2.—Prestonburg, Kentucky, occupied by General Nelson and Union troops. The rebels retired without resistance.

———— Major-General John C. Fremont, commander of the Western Department of the army, having received orders, when at Springfield, Missouri, to resign his command to Major-General Hunter, (the second in command,) did so, and took a formal leave of his troops on the 3d.

November 4.—An expedition under Colonel Gresnel took possession of Houston, Texas county, Missouri, and captured a large amount of rebel property, and several prominent Secessionists, including some officers of the rebel army; also 500 cattle, and 90 horses and mules.

November 6.—120 Union troops, under Capt. Schields, were captured by the enemy near Little Santa Fé, Missouri. The Union troops were on their way to join General Fremont's column. The reported force of the enemy was 500 men.

November 7.—The United States gun-boat Resolute went up the Rappahannock River, as far as Urbanna Creek, where a large schooner was captured; all her stores and movable property were then taken out, and the vessel was burned.

———— An expedition of 3500 Union troops, which left Cairo, Illinois, the night before, under command of Generals Grant and McClernand, landed below Belmont, Missouri, opposite Columbus, Kentucky, and made an attack upon the force of rebels there, under command of General Cheatham. The latter were about 7000 strong, and they were posted behind entrenchments. They were driven from thence across the river, their camp taken and burned, and baggage, cannon, horses, and mules captured. The rebel loss was estimated at 300 killed and wounded, and 130 prisoners taken. After this victory, strong rebel reinforcements crossed the river, and the Unionists, after hard fighting, retired to the steamers from which they landed. The Union loss was about 125 killed and mortally wounded, and about 125 wounded.

———— Forts Walker and Beauregard, commanding the channels of entrance to Beaufort, South Carolina, captured by the United States fleet. The rebels evacuated the forts and fled, leaving ammunition, stores, and provisions. Union loss, 8 killed, and 20 wounded. Beaufort was deserted by its inhabitants, and taken possession of by United States troops.

November 8.—Messrs. James M. Mason and John Slidell, appointed by the rebel Government ministers to England and France, were taken off the English mail-packet steamer Trent, in the Bahama Channel, by a force from the United States frigate San Jacinto, Capt. Charles Wilkes, commander. They had succeeded in running the blockade, and had left Havana in the Trent.

November 10.—250 Union troops at Guyandotte, Western Virginia, massacred by rebel troops brought in by the treachery of the inhabitants.

November 11.—Guyandotte burned by Union troops under Colonel Zeigler, in revenge for the part taken by its residents in the massacre of the day before.

ion force under General
t Piketon, Kentucky, was
t twelve miles from the
sh, the rebels, who were
John S. Williams, fled.
20 wounded; rebel loss,
missing.
on attacked the rebels at
ir sustaining a loss of 400
soners were taken.
nnessee burned by Union
oyed between Knoxville
ennessee Railroad.
rawn among the United
Virginia, by order of the
ared that the officers upon
d as hostages for the rebel
iladelphia and New York.
swell, Wilcox, Woodruff,
iels Bowman and Neff,
Vogdes, Captains Rock-
were thus designated as

Floyd fell back from
'irginia, before the troops
. After a slight skirmish
d to Raleigh.
the War Department, the
nted to the command of
New Mexico, Colonel E.
r-General Hunter; Mis-
; Ohio, Brigadier-General
dier-General Rosecrans.
rivateer Beauregard, Cap-
h Carolina, was captured
States vessel W. G. Ander-
commanding.
in Virginia, opposite the
ortion of the 28th Penn-
onel Geary, and a force of
ed, with a loss of 3 killed,

oner Mabel, attempting to
ton, South Carolina, was
op-of-war Dale.
nt of Union troops, under
t routed Hawkins's rebel
, near Rumsey, McLean
veral, and taking 25 pri-
kets, &c. Union loss, 10

seized by rebels the pre-
dissouri, recaptured.
ner Adelaide, of Nassau,
lockade, was captured by
nnecticut, near Cape Cana-
est. She was loaded with
goods contraband of war.
almyra, Missouri: a num-
o join Price's army, were
i cavalry, and dispersed,
d 16 prisoners.
II. Foote, U.S. Navy, ap-
t in the Western Military
rank equal to that of a

legates, representing forty-
f North Carolina, met at
passed repudiating the act
the loyalty of the State to
'aylor was named as Pro-
e by this convention.
Falls Church, Virginia, be-
tion of the 14th New York
ed to fall back; but, being
e rebels, who retired, with
ounded.

November 18.—150 rebels captured by a company of Union cavalry, near Warrenburgh, Missouri.

—— The steamer Platte City boarded at Price's Landing, Missouri, by the rebel Jeff Thompson and 200 men: two men were taken off and hung as spies.

November 19.—The rebel steamer Nashville, Captain Pegram, captured in the British Channel the American ship Harvey Birch, bound from Havre to New York. The captain and crew were taken off and the ship burned. The Nashville then ran into Southampton, England, where the prisoners were landed. The captain and officers of the Nashville were fêted and congratulated by the people of the town.

—— An engagement upon the Tennessee River, beyond Paducah, Kentucky, between the United States gunboat Conestoga and shore-batteries. The rebels were driven off with loss. The Conestoga received but slight damage.

November 20.—Review of seven divisions of troops, numbering 70,000 men, by Major-General McClellan, near Washington, D.C.

—— A fight near Kansas City between Colonel Burchard and 24 men of Jennen's brigade and 150 rebels under Colonel Hays. The latter were defeated and driven away, and Hays's house was burned, with that of Captain Gregg, another rebel officer. Rebel loss, 5 killed, and 8 wounded.

—— 3000 rebels assembled in Accomac and Northampton county, Virginia, on the Eastern Shore, dispersed upon the advance of troops under General Lockwood, by order of General Dix and proclamation of the policy of the Government. General Lockwood took 10 pieces of cannon and 1000 stand of arms.

—— Marble Nash Taylor, Provisional Governor of North Carolina, issued a proclamation calling upon the people of the State to return to their allegiance to the United States Government.

—— The rebel General Floyd broke up his camp near the Gauley River, Western Virginia, and retreated, destroying his tents, equipage, and a large quantity of arms and ammunition.

November 22.—The camp of the 2d Louisiana regiment, on the James River, Virginia, five and a half miles above Newport News, was shelled by two Union gunboats, and destroyed, with loss to the rebels.

—— Fire opened from Fort Pickens, Florida, upon the rebel steamer Time, near the navy-yard at Warrington. The cannonading was returned by the rebel forts McRae and Barrancas: it continued all day.

November 23.—The bombardment of Pensacola and Warrington continued,—ships of the United States fleet taking part. Fort McRae was silenced, the town of Warrington destroyed, and the navy-yard at Warrington much damaged. Union loss, 1 killed, and 6 wounded.

November 24.—A skirmish at Lancaster, Missouri, between 450 Union troops under Colonel Moore, and 420 rebels under Lieutenant-Colonel Blanton. The rebels were routed, with a loss of 13 killed, and several wounded; Union loss, 2 killed, and 1 wounded.

—— The stock of grain, wheat, and corn upon the farm of the traitor Simon Bolivar Buckner, of Kentucky, near Munfordsville, was seized and confiscated by Union cavalry under Captain Moreau.

—— Tybee Island, at the mouth of the Savannah River, taken possession of by crews from the United States gunboats Flag, Augusta, Pocahontas, and Seneca.

November 26.—A reconnoissance was made from Langleys to Drainesville, northwest of Washington, in Virginia, by a portion of the 1st Pennsylvania cavalry, under Colonel Bayard. A few rebel pickets were captured; but, on the return, the cavalry was attacked by a rebel force in ambush. Several were killed on both sides, and some of the cavalry taken prisoners.

—— The rebel Commodore Tatnall, with three small steamers and a gunboat, attacked the Federal fleet in Cockspur Roads, Georgia. His purpose was to draw the Federal ships within range of the guns of Fort Pulaski,—in which design he failed.

November 26.—A reconnoissance by a squadron of the 3d Pennsylvania cavalry, Captain Bell, in the neighborhood of Vienna, Virginia. The party was caught in ambush by a superior rebel force of cavalry and infantry. The Unionists succeeded in cutting their way through, with a loss of 29 killed, wounded, and missing.

November 27.—News of the forcible taking of Messrs. Mason and Slidell, rebel commissioners, from the English steamer Trent, was received at Liverpool, causing intense excitement throughout Great Britain.

—— A reconnoissance made by Union cavalry to the neighborhood of Fairfax Court-House, Virginia, where there was a skirmish with rebel cavalry, with small loss on each side.

—— The United States Government assumed entire command of the commerce and navigation of the Mississippi River below St. Louis, and established regulations for the government of navigation and intercourse with points below.

November 28.—Two schooners belonging to Baltimore, Maryland, captured by the rebel steamer George Page, near rebel batteries on the Potomac.

November 29.—The shipment of saltpetre from Great Britain forbidden by order of the Government.

—— A fight at Black Walnut Creek, Missouri, between Union Missouri cavalry, under Major R. M. Hough, and a rebel force: 17 rebels killed and wounded, and 5 taken prisoners; Major Hough and 4 Federals slightly wounded.

—— The rebels at Harper's Ferry opened fire upon the 28th Pennsylvania regiment, on the Maryland side, with shot and shell, without doing any damage.

November 30.—General Price issued a proclamation to the people of Missouri, dated at Neosho, calling for 50,000 volunteers to aid him in keeping the State as a part of the Confederacy.

December 1.—The British schooner Albion, of Nassau, N. P., loaded with contraband of war, and captured while attempting to run the blockade at Charleston, South Carolina, was sent into New York by the United States gunboat Penguin.

December 2.—A skirmish near Hunter's Chapel, Virginia, between Union and rebel cavalry: 4 rebels killed and wounded, and 2 taken prisoners.

December 3.—300 rebels, under Colonels Freeman and Turner, attacked the Union cavalry under Major Bowen, at Salem, Kent county, Missouri. They charged upon a house in which Federal soldiers were sleeping, killing and wounding 15 of the latter, by shooting through the windows. The Federals rallied, and a street-fight took place. The rebels were driven from the town, many being killed and wounded.

—— The Western Virginia Convention changed the name of the new State from "Kanawha" to "Western Virginia."

—— A scouting party of horsemen, under the command of Captain Bell, 3d Pennsylvania cavalry, numbering 120 men, encountered a large force of rebel cavalry and infantry in a narrow defile beyond Vienna, Virginia. The Federals succeeded in cutting their way through, with a loss of 45 killed, wounded, and missing.

December 4.—A party of rebel horsemen fell into an ambush near Annandale, Virginia, which was placed there in order to catch the rebels who had been in the habit of coming out to capture the Federal pickets. The rebels' horses were thrown down by a strong telegraph-wire stretched across the road. When the Federals fired into them, 6 or 7 of the horsemen were killed, and 3 captured, including a lieutenant. Union loss, 1 man killed.

—— A formal proclamation issued by Queen Victoria, of Great Britain, forbidding the export from British ports of nitrate of soda, brimstone, lead, and firearms.

—— An expedition, under General Phelps, which left Fortress Monroe November 29, on board the steamer Constitution, landed a force of men on Ship Island, Mississippi Sound, in the Gulf of Mexico, near the coast. General Phelps issued a proclamation in terms which gave much offence at the South and to many persons at the North.

December 4.—Federal cavalry made a dash for the Memphis Branch Railroad, Kentucky, and burned Whippoorwill Bridge.

—— Major-General Halleck issued an order to his officers in Missouri, directing the imprisonment of persons who give aid to the rebels; that persons in the disguise of citizens who give information to the rebels shall be treated as spies and shot; and that the Union families in St. Louis (refugees), driven out of their homes in other parts of Missouri by the rebels, shall be maintained at the expense of the secessionists of the city of St. Louis.

December 5.—A skirmish near Brownsville, Kentucky, between Union Home Guards and part of the rebel General Hindman's forces. Slight losses on both sides.

December 6.—One brigade of the Pennsylvania Reserves, under General Meade, went from Camp Pierpont, Fairfax county, Virginia, toward Dranesville, on a foraging expedition, and returned with large spoils, not having seen any of the enemy.

December 7.—An engagement in Mississippi Sound, Gulf of Mexico, between the United States gunboat New London and steamer De Soto, and the Pamlico and California, two rebel armed vessels which were attempting to run the blockade.

—— General John Pope was assigned to the command of the National forces between the Missouri and Osage Rivers.

—— Captain Sweeney and his band of guerrillas (35 in number) taken near Glasgow, Missouri, by Merril's Union cavalry.

—— A rebel force of 400 infantry, 200 cavalry, with 6 pieces of artillery, appeared near Dam No. 5, on the Virginia side of the Potomac, near Williamsport, Maryland, and commenced throwing shot and shell across the river at a position which was held by one company of Massachusetts volunteers on picket-duty and an unarmed Illinois regiment. During the succeeding night a company of sharp-shooters was stationed near the Maryland shore, which the next morning did such execution that the rebels fled, leaving their battery,—which our troops could not take for want of the support of a battery on the Maryland side.

December 9.—Freestone Point, Virginia, on the Lower Potomac, shelled by the United States flotilla, consisting of the Harriet Lane, Anacostia, Jacob Bell, Reliance, Stepping-Stones, and Herbert. The rebel batteries at Shipping Point kept up a brisk fire, which was responded to by the Union battery at Budd's Ferry. A party from the fleet landed and burned the rebel buildings and stores at the point.

December 11.—A skirmish near Bertrand, Missouri, between Union forces of infantry and cavalry under command of Lieutenant-Colonel Rhodes, and Major Mudd and a number of rebels. The latter lost 16 prisoners, with horses and firearms.

—— A party of rebels fired from the Virginia shore of the Potomac River upon the Union pickets at Dam No. 4, near Sharpstown, Maryland. The latter, by superiority of fire, compelled the enemy to retreat. A party of Federals who crossed the river to reconnoitre were in turn compelled to retreat by rebel infantry. Before they reached the river, they were cut off by a portion of rebel cavalry, and the whole of them captured.

December 12.—A terrible conflagration at Charleston, South Carolina, consuming and totally destroying the business portion of the city.

December 13.—A skirmish on the banks of Green River, Kentucky, between a company of the 15th Ohio regiment and 150 rebel cavalry. Several were wounded on both sides.

—— The villages of Papinsville and Butler, Missouri, burned by troops under command of Major Williams, of the 3d Kansas regiment. These towns had for a long time been head-quarters of the guerrillas.

December 13.—A battle at Alleghany Camp, Pocahontas county, Western Virginia, between 750 men of Indiana, Ohio, and Virginia regiments, under General Milroy, and 2000 rebels under General Johnson, of Georgia. Union loss, 30; rebel loss, 200 killed and wounded, including General Johnson, shot in the mouth, a major, and other officers.

——— W. H. Johnson, of the Lincoln cavalry, shot as a deserter, in camp, near Washington, D.C.

——— The British ship Admiral, attempting to evade the blockade by pretending to be one of the Union stone fleet, was captured near Savannah by the Augusta. The Admiral was loaded with coal, and had sailed from Liverpool.

December 15.—Pickets belonging to the 28th Pennsylvania regiment taken in ambush opposite Berlin, Maryland. Federal loss, 1 wounded, and 2 taken prisoners; rebel loss, 2 killed, and 5 wounded.

——— A portion of Platte City, Missouri, including the court-house and post-office, set on fire by rebel guerrillas and burned.

December 17.—A reconnoissance made up the Orange & Alexandria Railroad to Bone Mills, by a squadron of the 1st New Jersey cavalry, under command of Captain Shelmire. A portion of this force was surrounded and a lieutenant shot in six places. The orderly escaped and brought up his comrades, when the rebels retreated.

——— Four companies of Colonel Willich's German Indiana regiment were attacked opposite Munfordsville, Kentucky, by Texan Rangers and two regiments of rebel infantry, with 6 pieces of artillery, under Colonel Terry. Colonel Willich was reinforced, and drove the rebels back, with a loss of 33 killed (including Colonel Terry), and 50 wounded; Union loss, 1 lieutenant and 8 privates killed, and 16 wounded.

——— A rebel camp near Shawnee Mound, Missouri, with 2200 men, attacked by Union forces under General Pope, and broken up: 150 prisoners were taken, with wagons, tents, baggage, horses, &c.

December 18.—A rebel camp near Milford, Missouri, attacked by a command under Colonel Jefferson C. Davis and Major Marshall: 1300 prisoners were surrendered (including 3 colonels and 17 captains), 1000 stand of arms, 1000 horses, 65 wagons, tents, baggage, and supplies; Federal loss, 2 killed, and 8 wounded.

December 19.—Colonel Geary's 28th Pennsylvania regiment, near Point of Rocks, Maryland, shelled from the Virginia shore by a rebel battery of 3 guns, supported by infantry. The Unionists replied with 2 pieces, and disabled one rebel gun at the first shot; the others were driven back, together with a fourth gun, brought up as a reinforcement: 14 rebels were killed, and several wounded. After the retreat of the enemy, Geary's forces shelled out 150 rebels secreted in some houses on the Virginia shore, near the Potomac, killing and wounding several.

——— British ship Cheshire, of Liverpool, with contraband of war, captured near Tybee Island, Georgia, arrived at New York, sent in by United States gunboat Augusta.

——— Ripley, Jackson county, Virginia, taken possession of by the "Moccasin Rangers" (a rebel band).

December 20.—Battle at Drainesville, Virginia, between a brigade of the Pennsylvania Reserves, the Bucktail Rifles, and a battery of artillery, under General E. O. C. Ord, and a rebel brigade of infantry, with a battery of 6 guns, under General Stuart. The rebels were routed and driven half a mile. The object of the expedition (the procurement of forage) was accomplished, and the Federal troops returned to their camps with large quantities of forage. Federal loss, 7 killed, and 61 wounded; rebel loss, 90 killed, left on the field (including Colonel Tom Taylor, of the 1st Kentucky regiment), a number wounded and carried off, and 7 prisoners.

——— One hundred miles of the Missouri Railroad destroyed by a rebel force belonging to General Price's command,—burning bridges and depôts, destroying water-tanks, tearing up rails, prostrating telegraph poles and wires, &c. between Hudson and Warrenton.

December 20.—Major McKee and 101 men encountered and repulsed 400 rebels, four miles south of Hudson, Missouri, who had attacked a stock-train, captured the stock, and held the railroad-men as prisoners: 10 rebels were killed, 17 taken prisoners, with 30 horses.

——— Sixteen old whale-ships, denominated the "stone fleet," were sunk in the main channel of Charleston Harbor, South Carolina, under the direction of Captain C. H. Davis, in order to seal up the channel.

December 22.—Rebel ordnance and commissary stores at Nashville, Tennessee, destroyed by fire. Loss estimated at $1,000,000.

——— General Halleck, at St. Louis, issued an order declaring that persons who burn bridges and destroy telegraph-lines and railroads shall be shot if captured and found guilty by the sentence of a court-martial; also that United States officers shall have power to impress all secessionists in the neighborhoods where such damage is committed, and to compel them to make the necessary repairs, and that whatever other cost may be necessary to pay for such repairs shall be assessed on the towns and counties where the destruction is committed.

December 23.—47 Union men, at Jos. Coerson's house, Perry co., Kentucky, attacked 118 rebels and dispersed them, with 16 wounded. No loss on the Union side.

December 24.—General Pope's cavalry captured 2: rebel captains at Lexington, Missouri, and other prisoners, and destroyed a foundry and ferry-boats.

December 25.—Two spans of a bridge across the Hannibal & St. Joseph Railroad, Missouri, at Charlestown, burned by the rebels.

December 26.—150 to 200 Government horses were burned by a fire which broke out at the Observatory, Washington, D.C.

December 28.—Fight at Mount Zion, Boone county, Missouri, between 450 Federal troops, under General Prentiss, and 900 rebels, under Colonel Dorsey. The latter lost 150 killed and wounded, 35 prisoners, 95 horses, and 105 muskets; Union loss, 3 killed, and 11 wounded.

——— Two squadrons of cavalry, under Major Murray, which left Calhoun, Kentucky, on a scouting expedition, were separated. One squadron fell in with 700 rebels, under Colonel Forrest, who attacked them. A desperate hand-to-hand conflict ensued, the Union men only retreating when their ammunition gave out. Captain Albert G. Bacon, of the Federals, was killed, and 7 or 8 wounded. The rebels lost Captain Merriwether, and several wounded.

——— The diplomatic correspondence between the United States and British Governments upon the capture of Messrs. Mason and Slidell and their secretaries was published. The United States Government decided to surrender them, upon the ground that the proceedings were irregular, no method existing for the trial of the fact whether the prisoners were contraband of war, and because also the United States had hitherto invariably contended that the flag protected all who sailed under it.

December 31.—The town of Biloxi, Mississippi, surrendered, without firing a gun, to three United States gunboats under command of Commander Melancthon Smith. The fort there was dismantled, and the gunboats returned to the fleet.

1862. *January* 1.—Messrs. Mason and Slidell, rebel commissioners, and their secretaries, captured on board the Trent by Captain Wilkes, were put on board the steamboat Starlight and taken to Provincetown, Cape Cod, where they were transferred to the British gunboat Rinaldo, to be conveyed to England.

——— Firing at Pensacola, Florida, between Fort Pickens and the rebel forts and batteries, caused by Fort Pickens opening on the steamer Time, landing stores at the navy-yard at Warrington.

——— A rebel fort at Port Royal Ferry, South Carolina, shelled by United States gunboats under command of Commander C. R. P. Rodgers, with a column of infantry under General Stevens. The fort was taken and garrisoned with the Pennsylvania Roundhead regiment.

The rebels now appeared in line of battle, and the gunboats opened on them again, which caused severe losses in the rebel ranks.

January 2.—The steamship Ella Warley (formerly the Isabel) ran the blockade at Charleston, South Carolina.

January 3.—A rebel camp, with 280 men, broken up at Hunnewell, Missouri, by 300 National troops, under Colonel Glover. The rebels fled.

January 4.—A rebel depôt of supplies, at Huntersville, Western Virginia, captured and destroyed by National troops, 740 in number. The place had been occupied by about the same number of rebel soldiers.

——— 500 Federal troops, at Bath, Virginia, attacked by a large rebel force under General Jackson, which was twice repulsed; but, the Unionists being taken in flank, they fell back to Hancock.

January 7.—Colonel Dunning, with a portion of General Kelly's forces, attacked 2000 rebels at Blue's Gap, Virginia, east of Romney. The rebels were routed, with a loss of 15 killed, 2 pieces of cannon, wagons, tents, and 20 prisoners.

January 8.—A skirmish near Paintsville, Kentucky, between Virginia cavalry, under Colonel Bowles, and Humphrey Marshall's troops. Rebel loss, 6 killed, 14 wounded, and 7 prisoners; Union loss, 2 killed and 1 wounded.

——— Colonel Garfield occupied Paintsville with his brigade. The rebels fled on his approach, and were pursued, with some loss. Marshall's army broke up and fled in confusion, abandoning and burning a portion of his stores.

——— A gallant fight near the Dry Fork of Cheat River, Virginia, between Captain Latham, with 17 men of the 2d Virginia Union regiment, and 30 guerrillas, in which, after an hour's fighting, the rebels were forced to fly, with a loss of 6 killed, and several wounded; Federal loss, 6 men wounded.

——— A fight at Roan's tan-yard, Randolph county, Missouri, between 1000 rebels, under Colonel Poindexter, and 480 men under Majors Torrence and Hubbard. The rebels were routed in half an hour, losing every thing. The rebel camp, of 105 tents, 25 wagons, a large number of saddles, blankets, &c., with provisions, was burned.

January 10.—Colonel Garfield, having left Paintsville in pursuit of Humphrey Marshall's force, came on them at the forks of Middle Creek, Kentucky, 2500 strong, with 3 pieces of cannon, and routed them completely, killing 60, taking 25 prisoners, with horses, stores, &c.

January 11.—Waldo P. Johnson and Trusten Polk, Senators from Missouri, adhering to the rebels, were expelled from the United States Senate.

——— Colonel Garfield occupied Prestonburg, Ky.

January 13.—Simon Cameron resigned his position as Secretary of War. Edwin M. Stanton, of Pennsylvania, was appointed in his place.

January 17.—Steamer Emma captured, in an attempt to run the blockade off the coast of Florida, by the United States steamship Connecticut.

January 18.—John Tyler died at Richmond, Virginia, in his seventy-second year.

January 19.—Battle of Mill Spring, Kentucky,—Federal forces commanded by General George H. Thomas; rebel forces (12,000 strong) commanded by General F. K. Zollicoffer and General George B. Crittenden. The rebels made the attack, expecting to cut off the junction of Thomas with Schoepf. The fight commenced at half-past five o'clock in the morning, and lasted until late in the afternoon. The rebel General Zollicoffer was killed by a shot fired by Colonel S. S. Fry, 4th Kentucky regiment. The rebels retreated to their intrenchments, which they evacuated in the night, and crossed the Cumberland River. Loss of the rebels, in killed, wounded, and prisoners, 349, as far as known to the Union forces, many dead and wounded having been taken off the field; they also lost 12 guns, a large number of small arms, 1200 horses and mules, wagons, commissary stores, ammunition, &c. Federal loss, 39 killed, and 207 wounded.

January 23.—Rebel steamer Calhoun captured near the Southwest Pass, Mississippi River.

——— Second stone fleet sunk in Maffit's Channel, harbor of Charleston, South Carolina.

January 28.—It having been discovered that the Savannah River could be entered at some distance above its mouth, and beyond Fort Pulaski, which might thus be cut off from communication with the city of Savannah, two expeditions of United States gunboats were organized, under command of Captain C. H. Davis and Captain C. R. P. Rogers. These vessels, by following the course of Wilmington Narrows, on the south side of the river, and Wall's Cut and Wright River, on the north, penetrated respectively to within short distances of the Savannah River, where they were stopped by piles and obstructions and shallowness of water. Whilst thus impeded, Commodore Tatnall, of the rebel navy, with five gunboats, came down the Savannah River with a fleet of lighters with provisions for Fort Pulaski. The United States gunboats opened on him; but three of the rebel gunboats, with their lighters, succeeded in reaching the fort and returning to Savannah. No damage appears to have been done on either side.

January 29.—A fight at Porter's house, near Occoquan Bridge, Virginia, between a party of the 37th New York volunteers and a party of Texans in the house, who, when surprised about midnight, were enjoying themselves in a dance. They refused to surrender on summons, and fired at the United States troops through windows and port-holes which they made through the weather-boards of the house. The whole party of Texans—a major, and 9 privates and a civilian—were killed by a platoon which fired through the weather-boards of the house. Federal loss, 1 killed, and 4 wounded.

January 31.—Act of Congress was passed, giving to the President of the United States authority to take possession of all the railroads and lines of telegraph in the United States, whenever in his judgment the public safety required it.

February 1.—Skirmish near Bowling Green, Kentucky, between a party of rebels and a company of cavalry (41st Indiana volunteers), commanded by Captain J. B. Presdee. Rebel loss, 3 killed, and 2 wounded; Union loss, none.

February 3.—The rebel steamer Nashville allowed to leave Southampton, England. The Union gunboat Tuscarora, at anchor near Cowes, was prevented from following the Nashville by the British frigate Shannon, 51 guns, and detained twenty-four hours, until the Nashville escaped.

February 4.—A skirmish at Occoquan, Virginia, between National and rebel parties: 4 rebels killed and wounded; 1 Federal wounded.

February 6.—Fort Henry, on the Tennessee River, taken by the squadron of Union gunboats commanded by Flag-Officer A. H. Foote,—consisting of the iron-clads Cincinnati, Commander Stembel; Essex, Commander Porter; Carondelet, Commander Walke; St. Louis, Lieutenant Paulding; also the wooden gunboats Conestoga, Lieutenant Phelps; Tyler, Lieutenant Gwyn; and Lexington, Lieutenant Shirk. It was arranged that there should also be a land-attack, under command of General Grant, by General McClernand and other officers; but, before the troops were in position, the gunboats moved into attack. After they had shelled the fort for an hour and a half, the rebels struck their colors and surrendered to the naval officers. General Grant arrived at the fort an hour after it had surrendered. In the action the gunboat Essex received a shot in her boiler, which caused the scalding of Commander Porter and 28 of his officers and men. The Cincinnati received 31 shots, the Essex 15, St. Louis, 7, Carondelet, 6. Loss, 1 killed on the Cincinnati, 9 wounded; Essex, 1 killed, 9 wounded, 29 scalded. No loss was sustained by the rest of the fleet. There surrendered the Confederate General Lloyd Tilghman and 70 men. A few were wounded; but the majority of the rebels encamped outside of the fort escaped before the surrender: they were estimated at from 3000 to 10,000. There were captured in the fort 20 heavy guns, barracks and tents to accommodate 15,000 men, arms, ammunition, stores, &c.

February 7.—General Lander occupied Romney, Virginia, without a fight, the rebels having retreated toward Winchester.

—— Skirmish, Friedman's Pennsylvania cavalry, with rebels, near Germantown, Virginia: 1 rebel killed, 12 prisoners, and 8 horses taken.

—— Harper's Ferry, Virginia, shelled by Colonel Geary, of the 28th Pennsylvania regiment, in retaliation for an act of treachery by rebel troops under color of a flag of truce. The Wager Hotel and other houses were burned.

—— Two rebel transport steamers chased by Union gunboats, under Lieutenant Phelps, in the Tennessee River, above Fort Henry, were abandoned and burned, with military stores. Same day, the rebel gunboat Eastport (partly iron-plated) was captured, with large quantities of lumber.

February 8.—Two steamboats taken at Chickasaw, Mississippi, by Lieutenant Phelps, United States Naval Expedition. Three steamboats were burned, and a large quantity of supplies taken and destroyed.

—— A skirmish on Linn Creek, Kentucky, between Captain Smith, 5th Virginia regiment, with 21 men, and 32 of Jenkins's rebel cavalry: 8 rebels were killed, 7 wounded, and all the rest taken prisoners, with 32 horses; Federal loss, 1 killed, and 1 wounded.

—— Roanoke Island, North Carolina, captured by land and naval forces of the United States, under General Burnside and Commodore Goldsborough. The action commenced February 7, between a portion of the United States fleet and rebel gunboats stationed near Forts Bartow and Blanchard. After some firing, the rebel gunboats retired, with the design of drawing the Union gunboats to a part of the channel where piles and obstructions were placed and where the guns of the forts had range. In this they failed; and the United States gunboats opened on the forts and set fire to the barracks of Fort Blanchard. In the afternoon a portion of the troops were landed on the island, being covered by the United States gunboats, which drove off a force of rebels stationed to dispute the landing. During the afternoon the rebel gunboats renewed the action with the Federal fleet, which resulted in the loss of the Curlew (the largest rebel steamer), and the Forest (one of his propellers) was disabled. On the morning of the 8th the Union gunboats renewed the action with Fort Blanchard; but the firing shortly afterward ceased, in consequence of the operations of the troops upon the island. The United States forces moved upon Fort Blanchard, under General Parke on the right, General Foster in the centre, and General Reno with the left flanking column. The centre engaged the Wise Legion (rebel), under Lieutenant-Colonel Frank Anderson, which was repulsed, with the loss of Captain Robert Coles, killed, and Captain O. Jennings Wise, mortally wounded. On the right the 9th New York (Hawkins Zouaves) carried the enemy's works by storm; and Reno's storming-party at the same time appeared in full charge on the left. The enemy, without waiting for a further contest, fled precipitately, abandoning the fort. Three regiments pursued. Some of the enemy escaped in boats; but a force of North Carolinians, to the north of the batteries, surrendered unconditionally, after a slight skirmish. Fort Forrest, on the main, was shortly after surrendered, and the victory was complete. The enemy lost 3000 prisoners (among them Colonel Shaw, Colonel J. Wharton Greene, Lieutenant-Colonel Poore, Colonel J. V. Jordan, and Major G. H. Hill), 40 killed and wounded, 6 forts and batteries, mounting 40 pieces, 3000 small arms, munitions, and an immense amount of stores. The remnant of the rebel flotilla, under Commander William F. Lynch, escaped. The Federals lost Colonel Russell, 10th Connecticut regiment. Lieutenant-Colonel Victor de Monticuil (D'Epineuil Zouaves), 33 killed, and 200 wounded.

February 9.—Brigadier-General Charles P. Stone, U.S. Army, arrested on a charge of treason, and sent to Fort Lafayette, New York.

February 10.—Commander Rowan, U.S. Navy, with 14 vessels, attacked the remnant of the rebel squadron off Cobb's Point, North Carolina, which were protected by two shore-batteries. One schooner belonging to the rebels struck her colors and was burned by her crew. Shortly afterward, the crews of the Powhatan, Fanny, Seabird, and Forrest (rebel vessels) ran them ashore and set fire to them. The Raleigh and Beaufort ran into the canal and escaped. The Ellis was captured and brought away by the Union fleet. The battery on Cobb's Point was abandoned by the enemy and taken possession of by United States sailors. Same day, Elizabeth City surrendered.

February 12.—General Price (rebel) retreated from Lexington, Missouri. General Curtis took possession, with a great quantity of military stores.

—— Colonel Reggin's expedition to Paris, Tennessee, returned to Fort Henry, having captured contraband goods worth $75,000, and the tents and camp-equipage of the rebel troops that fled from Fort Henry.

—— Edenton, North Carolina, occupied by men of a naval expedition commanded by Lieutenant A. Maury, U.S. Navy.

February 14.—Blooming Gap, Virginia, taken by General Lander: 13 rebels killed, and 75 taken prisoners; Union loss, 2 killed.

—— Acting Volunteer Lieutenant Edward Conroy, U.S. Navy, with an expedition, cut out three rebel schooners and sloops loaded with rice, in Bull's Bay, South Carolina.

February 15.—Four rebel gunboats attacked United States batteries, which, by prodigious efforts, had been erected on Venus Point, Savannah River. They were driven off after an engagement of an hour.

—— Bowling Green, Kentucky, evacuated by rebels, and occupied by General D. C. Buell.

February 16.—The Tennessee Iron-Works, above Dover, Tennessee River, destroyed by United States gunboat St. Louis, Flag-Officer Foote. It had been used in making iron plates for the rebel Government.

—— Fort Donelson, on the Cumberland River, Tennessee, captured by the Union forces of General Grant, divisions under Generals McClernand, Smith, and Wallace, assisted by the gunboats St. Louis, Pittsburg, Louisville, Conestoga, and Carondelet. A portion of the army was in position on the 12th, but nothing was done until the 13th, when the gunboat Carondelet engaged the batteries for two hours, after which she was withdrawn. On the 14th, the St. Louis, Louisville, Pittsburg, and Carondelet, with the Conestoga and Tyler in reserve, made an attack, and silenced the rebel water-battery and drove off the gunners. They suffered from the plunging shot of the upper batteries, which did considerable damage. After this the fleet retired. On the morning of the 15th, the enemy in force attacked the right of the Federal line of troops, capturing two field-batteries. Reinforcements were brought up, and, by desperate fighting, three of the guns were retaken; but, after a great struggle, the Union troops fell back. More reinforcements were brought up,—during which movement, by some unfortunate blunder, the 25th Kentucky (Union) regiment poured a volley into the 31st Illinois regiment, causing a terrible loss, and a confusion which incited the enemy to fresh exertions. Colonel Wallace's brigade, which was also brought up, was unable to stem the rebel torrent, and also fell back, with heavy loss. In this emergency, General Charles F. Smith was ordered to assault the left portion of the rebel lines, and carry their position at all hazards. Renewed preparations were made to regain the ground lost on the right. General Smith performed his part of the work gallantly. Moving forward without firing a gun, he charged into the lower battery of the rebels, and drove the defenders out of it at the point of the bayonet. This success encouraged the rest of the troops, and, with fresh men, General Grant beat back the rebels, carried by storm the hill which they occupied, and recovered the ground lost in the morning. At night the parties lay on their arms. The next day there was no serious renewal of hostilities. During the following night, Generals Floyd and Pillow, with about 5000 of the garrison, escaped. On the morning of the 16th, white flags were flying from the fort, and a surrender was made. The attacking force numbered 15,000; the force in the fort, about 20,000. Of the latter, after Floyd and Pillow escaped, Generals Simon B. Buckner and Bushrod Johnson were taken prisoners, with about 15,000 officers and men, 40 pieces of artillery, small arms, ammunition, stores, &c. Union loss estimated at 1200 killed, wounded, and missing. Among the killed were Lieutenant-Colonel William Erwin, 20th Illinois, and Lieutenant-Colonel Thomas H. Smith, 48th Illinois. The enemy were reported by Floyd, in his report to the rebel President Davis, to have lost 1500 killed and wounded.

February 17.—Skirmish at Sugar Creek, Arkansas. The 1st Missouri cavalry were fired upon from an ambush: 13 were killed, and 5 wounded. An artillery engagement followed, with but little loss on either side.

—— Two regiments of rebel Tennesseeans marched into Fort Donelson, with colors flying and drums beating, to reinforce Floyd and Pillow. They were unaware of its capture. They were all taken prisoners.

February 18.—Skirmish at Independence, Missouri, between Ohio cavalry and Quantrill's and Parkor's rebel band. The latter were routed, with a loss of 3 killed, several wounded and taken prisoners, with some arms; Federal loss, 1 killed, and 3 wounded.

February 19.—Clarksville, Cumberland River, Tennessee, surrendered to Flag-Officer Foote, of the Navy.

February 20.—Winton, North Carolina, burned by National troops, a heavy fire having been opened upon them by rebels from that place.

February 21.—Battle at Valverde, New Mexico, between rebel forces under Colonel Steele, and Union troops commanded by Colonel Canby. It lasted all day. The Union forces were about 1500; the rebels about 2000. The rebels made a desperate charge upon Captain McRae's battery of 6 pieces, which was defended by the latter without shrinking until he was shot down at his gun. The loss of these pieces turned the fortunes of the day,—which, in consequence of the cowardice of the New Mexican volunteers, could not be retrieved. Colonel Canby retreated to Fort Craig.

February 22.—Jeff Davis inaugurated at Richmond, Virginia, as permanent President of the rebel States.

February 23.—Fayetteville, Arkansas, taken by General Curtis. The rebels who had occupied it fled. They left a quantity of poisoned meat behind them, by which 42 officers and men of the Missouri cavalry, who ate it, were poisoned.

February 24.—Harper's Ferry, Virginia, occupied by General Banks, U.S. Army, without opposition.

February 25.—Nashville, Tennessee, occupied by Federal forces under General Nelson.

February 26.—Skirmish at Keittsville, Barry county, Missouri, between one company of Union troops, under Captain Montgomery, and 800 rebels: 2 Federals were killed, and 1 wounded; 1 rebel was killed. The others took off with them 70 horses.

February 27.—Evacuation of Columbus, Kentucky, commenced by the rebels.

February 28.—The rebel steamer Nashville, Captain R. P. Pegram, ran the blockade at Beaufort, North Carolina, and reached the town in safety.

—— Skirmish west of Charlestown, Missouri, between 64 men of the 7th Illinois cavalry, Captain Nolen, and 90 rebel cavalry under Jeff Thompson. The latter had 4 guns, which were taken by the Federals in a gallant charge. The rebels fled, carrying off their wounded.

March 2.—An engagement between the Federal gunboats Tyler and Lexington, and a rebel battery, at Pittsburg, Tennessee. The rebels were routed: their loss not known. Federal loss, 5 killed and missing, and 5 wounded.

—— General Frederick W. Lander died in camp, at Pawpaw, Virginia, from the effect of wounds received near Edwards Ferry, Virginia.

March 3.—Columbus, Kentucky, taken possession of by United States troops.

—— An engagement, two miles north of New Madrid, Missouri, between Federal troops under General Pope, and rebels, assisted by their gunboats. The National forces retired after suffering some losses.

—— Fernandina, Florida, surrendered to Commodore Dupont and General Wright, the rebels having abandoned their fortifications and fled.

March 6.—President Lincoln, by special message to Congress, recommended the adoption of a resolution in favor of co-operation by the Federal Government with any State that will agree to abolish slavery, giving to such State whatever pecuniary aid may be necessary to compensate for the inconvenience, public and private, produced by such a change of system.

March 7.—Cannonading on the Lower Potomac between the United States gunboat Freeborn, with other vessels, and rebel batteries, between Liverpool Point and Acquia Creek.

March 8.—Morgan's rebel cavalry made an attack upon a foraging-party of the 4th Ohio cavalry, five miles south of Nashville, Tennessee, and captured 18 wagons, burned 1, and took mules and teamsters prisoners. They were pursued by the 4th cavalry, and all the wagons retaken, with the prisoners: 4 rebels were killed, and 4 wounded.

—— Fort Johnston, at Leesburg, Virginia, occupied by Colonel Geary, 28th Pennsylvania regiment. The rebels fell back on Middleburg.

—— Occoquan, Va., evacuated by rebel troops.

—— The battle of Pea Ridge, Arkansas (called by the rebels the "battle of Elkhorn") was concluded, after three days' hard fighting. The Union army (20,000 strong) was commanded by General Samuel R. Curtis, and the rebels by Generals Ben McCulloch, Price, and Van Dorn (estimated to number 30,000). The rebels made the attack, March 6, on the right wing of Curtis's army, and assailed the rear-guard, which was commanded by General Franz Sigel. The latter succeeded in reaching and forming a junction with the main body of Federals, at Sugar-Creek Hollow. Hostilities ceased for that day about four o'clock in the afternoon. During the night, General Curtis changed his front, to meet a movement which he suspected that the enemy intended to make. This stretched his lines from Pea Ridge to Sugar-Creek Hollow and Big Sugar Creek. His right of the day before was now his left. An attack was ordered on the enemy's centre. Whilst this was in progress, the rebels, in immense force, threw themselves upon the right of the Federal lines. The contest was kept up all day. The enemy gained a position held by Colonel Carr, commanding a brigade, but were afterward repulsed, with great loss,—during which Ben McCulloch, their commander, fell mortally wounded. The attack upon the enemy's centre was then vigorously pushed, with many advantages,—during which another change of front was rendered necessary and was partially executed. At sunrise on the 8th this manœuvre was in progress, when the rebels again moved into attack with spirit. They were handsomely met; and, by some fine tactical movements executed by Sigel, Asboth, and Colonel Jeff C. Davis (commanding a brigade), the rebel lines were forced back on the right and left, until they formed the arc of a circle. A charge of infantry was then made by the Union troops, in solid mass, throughout the whole line, when the rebels broke and fled in confusion. The Federals lost 212 killed, 926 wounded, and 174 missing,—in all, 1312. Among the killed was Colonel Hendricks, 22d Indiana regiment. The rebels lost Generals McCulloch and McIntosh; and their loss in killed and wounded has been estimated at 1600. In this battle, Albert Pike headed a force of Cherokee Indians, who fought in the rebel ranks, and afterward scalped the bodies of friends and foes with a horrible impartiality. After the fight, Van Dorn retreated to the Boston Mountains.

—— By order of the President of the United States, the army of the Potomac was divided into army corps, as follows:—First corps, of four divisions, to be com

mner; second, three divi-
ll; third, three divisions,
n; fourth, three divisions,
th, Banks's and Shields's
al N. P. Banks.
d war-steamer Merrimac
irginia"), commanded by
came out from Norfolk,
he United States frigates
hich were anchored near
The Merrimac was accom-
'atrick Henry and Thomas
iron-plated), and by three
rland opened fire on the
ed off without effect. The
and fired a broadside into
umberland, near the bow,
e time. Backing off, this
sinking ship was then left
an attack was made upon
e Jefferson and Patrick
ge to the Congress. After
s seen, an effort was made
—which was accomplished
Zouave. This movement
acting as a ram in sink-
el monster, aided by the
tacked the Congress with
this fire for more than an
help from the other vessels
d Lieutenant Smith, who
killed, and the ship being
flag of the Congress was
removed in boats to the
burn, and was consumed.
fleet, which was lying be-
tifully to come to the rescue
cked. The steam-frigate
aground. The St. Law-
at long range, but could
of service. The frigate
gunboat Oregon was dis-
boiler; and the gunboat
having engaged the Min-
little effect, the Merrimac
to Norfolk in triumph.
was about 120 men. On
eph B. Smith, command-
loore, and about 100 men,
oners. On the Merrimac,
usly wounded, 2 men were
e Patrick Henry had 4
hipman Hutter was killed
ls, and 2 officers wounded.
of the 8th, the Ericson
under the command of
arrived at Fort Monroe.
ared to go into immediate
he Minnesota, which was
her lee. It was supposed
lerrimac would make an
he advent of this new foe
lock on the 9th the Merri-
the Henry and Jefferson,
as supposed were intended
the Merrimac stood out
itor put out for her. The
ut was soon astonished by
te Monitor, which caused
away rapidly. The fight
ben commenced, and was
it distances varying from
The Merrimac attempted
ut failed in the attempt.
were quick and exciting,
antage in lightness, speed,
Merrimac, in the encoun-
gan to leak badly; in con-
ed away to Norfolk, fol-
Monitor received no serious
damage. The only person on board who was hurt was
Lieutenant Worden, whose eyes were injured by the
scales and dust struck off from the interior of the iron-
plated pilot-house, which was struck by a round ball
whilst he was looking through a narrow slit left open
as a peep-hole.

March 9.—Point Pleasant, Missouri, ten miles below
New Madrid, was occupied by United States troops,
thus cutting off the rebel communications.

—— Cockpit Point, Virginia, occupied by Federal
troops, the rebels evacuating it, and burning their tents
and stores, the steamer George Page and other craft.

—— A skirmish at Burk's Station, near Fairfax
Court-House, Virginia, between 14 Union cavalry under
Lieutenant Hidden, and 150 rebel infantry. The latter
were routed. 3 rebels were killed, 5 wounded, and 11
taken prisoners. Lieutenant Hidden was killed.

March 10.—A band of rebels, in a log house and barn
in Lafayette county, Missouri, were attacked by Lieutenant J. D. Jenk, 1st Iowa cavalry, with 30 men, and
defeated, after a short engagement. Union loss, 1 killed,
and 4 wounded; rebel loss, 9 killed, and 3 wounded.

—— The United States gunboat Whitehall, in
Hampton Roads, Virginia, took fire and was totally
destroyed.

—— A fight at Big Creek Gap, Tennessee, between
Colonel James Carter's regiment of loyal Tennesseeans,
and rebel cavalry. The latter were routed, 2 being
killed, 4 wounded, and 1 lieutenant-colonel and 14 men
prisoners; 27 of the rebels' horses were killed, and 58
captured, with 300 tents, provisions, and arms; National
loss, 2 wounded.

—— Centreville, Virginia, occupied by Union
troops, the rebels evacuating it and destroying property
on their retreat.

March 11.—Manassas, Virginia, occupied by Federal
troops, without opposition. The rebels had evacuated
it, and committed great destruction of their stores.
They left behind, however, 80 army-wagons, 6 caissons,
clothing, medical stores, and other articles.

—— An army order, dated January 22, was now
published for the first time. It directs a general movement against the rebels, by land and sea, on the 22d of
February. General McClellan, having personally taken
command of the army of the Potomac, is relieved from
the general command of the army. General Halleck is
placed in command of the department of the Mississippi,
composed of his own, General Hunter's, and a part of
General Buell's command. The Mountain Department
(Western Virginia, and East Tennessee north of Knoxville) is placed under command of General Fremont.

March 12.—Winchester, Virginia, occupied by Union
forces.

—— A skirmish at Paris, Tennessee, between Union
troops under Colonel W. W. Lowe, and 600 rebels, who
were defeated. Rebel reinforcements coming up, Colonel
Lowe retreated, bringing off a considerable number of
prisoners.

—— Berryville, Va., occupied by Union troops.

—— Jacksonville, Fla., occupied by National forces.

March 13.—A bridge on the Mobile & Ohio Railroad,
twenty miles from Jackson, Tennessee, destroyed by
Ohio cavalry in command of Major Charles S. Hayes.

—— A skirmish between six companies of New
York 7th volunteers, and 350 rebel cavalry pickets, at
the junction of the Great Bethel and Williamsport road,
Virginia. The latter, after a few shots, set fire to the
houses which they had lately occupied, and fled.

—— United States House of Representatives passed
a resolution of thanks to General Curtis, his officers and
men, for the victory at Pea Ridge, Arkansas.

March 14.—Reconnoissance by General Stoneman,
with cavalry, 1500 strong, and 800 infantry, from Manassas, up the Orange & Alexandria Railroad, to Cedar
Run. At the latter place, a large number of rebel pickets
were driven in upon the main body; but the latter made
no attempt to follow. The bridges at Cedar Run and
Bristow were found to be burned. The road travelled
over was strewed with hats, caps, muskets, knapsacks, &c.
and many loaded wagons which had been abandoned.

March 14.—New Madrid, Missouri, was discovered, early in the morning, to have been evacuated by the rebels. They left all their artillery, field-batteries, wagons, mules, and other properties, their baggage, knapsacks, suppers on their tables, and candles burning in their tents; their dead were also found unburied, showing that the evacuation was made in great haste. This flight was produced by the operations of the Federal forces during the previous day. In the night of the 12th, a heavy battery was established within eight hundred yards of New Madrid, from which a furious fire by 60 pieces of artillery was kept up on the 13th. Fearing an assault on the 14th, the rebels fled. Some prisoners were taken, and the colors of several Arkansas regiments secured. National loss during the siege, 51 killed and wounded. There were taken 33 pieces of artillery, ammunition, several thousand small arms, tents for 10,000 men, horses, mules, wagons, &c. The killed of the enemy during the siege was considerably over 100.

—— General McClellan issued an address to his army, spirited and cheerful, informing them that the "period for inaction" had passed, and that he was about "to bring them face to face with the rebels."

—— Battle of Newbern, North Carolina, fought between a combined land and naval force, under General Burnside and Commodore Goldsborough, U.S. Navy, and a rebel force under General L. O. B. Branch. In the morning of the 13th, the United States troops were landed, under cover of the gunboats, at Slocum's Creek. They then marched twelve miles and bivouacked for the night on the railroad; while the gunboats proceeded farther up and shelled a rebel battery. In the morning the march was resumed. After a short time, the rebel batteries were discovered extending over a distance of two miles, mounting 46 guns in position, with field-artillery. The Union troops took these batteries in detail, the enemy retreating from one to another. The last and strongest was captured by a bayonet-charge by the 21st Massachusetts and 51st Pennsylvania. The rebels then fled across the river Trent, destroyed the bridges behind them, and escaped by railroad, the cars being ready, to Goldsboro', North Carolina. They attempted to burn the town of Newbern in the retreat, but failed. They sent down fire-ships against the United States vessels, which drifted against the railroad-bridge and burned it, but did no damage to the United States fleet. The Union troops captured 46 siege-guns, 3 field-batteries, 3000 small arms, and 300 prisoners (among whom were 1 colonel, 3 captains, and 4 lieutenants). The rebel killed and wounded were about 500. The National troops were gallantly led by Generals Foster, Parke, and Reno. Our losses were 91 killed, and 466 wounded. Lieutenant-Colonel Henry Merritt, 23d Massachusetts, Lieutenant Lawton, 27th Massachusetts, Captain Charles Tillinghast, 4th Rhode Island, were killed, and many officers wounded. Among the rebel killed were Colonel Avery and Major Hoke, 33d North Carolina.

March 15.—Engagements on the Potomac, at Acquia Creek, Virginia, between the National steamers Island Belle, Yankee, and Anacostia, and shore-batteries.

—— Railroad-bridge at Purdy, Tennessee, burned by Federal troops under General Lew Wallace, thus stopping railroad communication between Humboldt and Corinth, Mississippi.

March 16.—Pound Gap, Tennessee, taken by General Garfield, with 600 men of Ohio and Kentucky regiments. The enemy were taken by surprise, and routed. The entire camp, with arms, munitions, &c., were taken and burned. The expedition returned without loss or damage to a single man.

—— Skirmish at Pittsburg Landing, Tennessee, between a battalion of 4th Illinois regiment and rebel cavalry. The latter were defeated. The Union troops had 4 men wounded.

March 18.—Jeff Davis sent a message to the rebel Congress, recommending that all of their paroled soldiers should be released from their obligations and be compelled to bear arms against the United States.

—— A scouting-party of 250 men, under Lieutenant-Colonel Wood, encountered, at Salem, Missouri, 1000 rebel cavalry, under Colonels Coleman, Woodside, and McFarland. After a severe fight, the rebels were defeated. Colonel Woodside was killed, 100 killed and wounded, and several taken prisoners; Federal loss, 25 killed and wounded.

March 18.—British ship Emily St. Pierre, attempting to run the blockade at Charleston, South Carolina, was captured.

—— Acquia Creek, Va., evacuated by the rebels.

—— A rebel gunboat sunk near New Madrid, Missouri, by one of General Pope's batteries: 15 on board were killed. Five other rebel gunboats were suffered to pass, and thus became trapped between Pope's upper and lower batteries.

March 20.—Meeting of loyal citizens at Jacksonville, Florida: resolutions were adopted against secession, the convention of Florida having assumed a right to take the State out of the Union without submitting the question to the people.

March 21.—Captain Stevens, with 65 men, on a scouting-party, near Indian Creek, Missouri, surrounded the house of one Boone, a secessionist, and took prisoners 3 rebel captains and 17 men, with 1000 pounds of bacon stored at Boone's house for the use of the rebel army.

—— St. Augustine, Florida, taken possession of by the United States ship Wabash, Commodore Rodgers.

—— Major-General B. F. Butler, U.S. Volunteers, appointed to the command of the Department of the Gulf. General David Hunter appointed to the command of the Department of the South.

—— A fight at Mosquito Inlet, Florida, in which Lieutenant Thomas A. Budd, Acting-Master Mather, and three sailors who had ventured on shore, were killed.

—— Washington, North Carolina, occupied by National forces under General Burnside.

March 22.—Reconnoissance by Federal troops in the neighborhood of Cumberland Gap, Virginia. There was a skirmish with pickets, and some firing by artillery and from rifle-pits; but the distance between the parties was too great to cause damage to either side.

—— Quantrill's guerrillas routed in a skirmish near Independence, Missouri, by a portion of the 6th Kansas regiment. The enemy lost 7 killed, 11 missing, and 20 horses; 2 Unionists were killed.

—— Battle of Winchester, between 7000 Federal troops, under General Shields, with 24 pieces of artillery, and 11,000 rebels, with 27 pieces of artillery. The action commenced on the 22d, with a skirmish between Ashby's rebel cavalry and Michigan and Maryland cavalry. At sunrise on the 23d, General Thomas J. ("Stonewall") Jackson—who had been reinforced—advanced to the attack. After several hours' fighting, the Federals made a charge and drove the enemy half a mile; but, they taking a strong position with artillery, the Unionists were compelled to retreat. The victory was won by flanking the rebels on the left, which was executed with considerable loss, the rebels being protected by stone walls, behind which they were formed. The 84th Pennsylvania and 13th Indiana regiments charged boldly; the enemy gave way, and soon became panic-stricken and fled from the field. They were driven until dark, and lost 3 guns, muskets, equipments, &c. The Federals lost 115 killed (among them Colonel W. G. Murray, of the 84th Pennsylvania), and 450 wounded. The rebels confessed a loss of 869 killed, wounded, and missing. Their killed is known to have been about 500 left and buried on the field, and their wounded was estimated by General Shields at 1000.

—— The rebel Senate confirmed the following persons as members of Jeff Davis's Cabinet:—Secretary of State, J. P. Benjamin, Louisiana; Secretary of War, George W. Randolph, Virginia; Secretary of Navy, S. R. Mallory, Florida; Secretary of Treasury, C. G. Memminger, South Carolina; Attorney-General, Thomas H. Watts; Postmaster-General, —— Reagan, Texas.

—— Morehead City, North Carolina, taken possession of by General Parke's brigade of Burnside's divi-

)n, two miles off, was sum-
s held by 500 men under
)d to surrender; in conse-
ment was forthwith com-

meeting at Jacksonville,
he State Secession Conven-
:d.

ty batteries, Wilmington
y a force from the United
Wyandotte, and Norwich,
10 guns were taken and

rrillas, 200 strong, attacked
and of Major Emery Fos-
iri. The latter were pro-
s, and made such a gallant
driven off. Major Foster
nded, and 9 others; 1 man
9 killed, 17 wounded, and

d four companies of State
ssouri, and were defeated,
id several wounded. The
d, but none were killed.
iy, with 4 guns, shelled a
;, Virginia, killing 1, and
n driven off by the Federal

;inia, occupied by Union
; it upon the appearance of

lumfries, Virginia, between
Colonel Wyndham, and a
o were routed, with a loss
wounded. Several wagon-
en.
he Louisville & Nashville
in's rebel cavalry, who de-
e locomotive into a ditch.
ntucky, and other officers,

Cañon, New Mexico, be-
;uns, under Major Cheving-
;un. The rebels lost about
d 93 prisoners, 64 wagons,
)0 mules, small arms, &c.
ints Chambers, Baker, and
several officers and men

:en Shelbyville and Talla-
Colonel Kennett's Union
:tery, and 300 of Wood's
after making the attack,
dead and several wounded.
)and were attacked by Cap-
cavalry, west of Warrens-
re killed, and 25 taken pri-
e Colonel Parker and Cap-
tilled, and several wounded.
rginia, occupied by Federal

: Middleburg, Virginia, be-
ce, and rebel cavalry, under
intry. The 28th Pennsyl-
ugh the town. The rebels
loss.
in A. Dix assigned to the
partment: head-quarters at

is made upon Union City,
ree under Colonel Buford,
nty-four hours. The place
ry and infantry under Clay
ing several killed, 100 pri-
l a large quantity of forage.
Florida, taken by the United
)mmander Stellwagen.
nan's Landing, Arkansas,
vith the Federal advance

under General Steele, and a rebel force which disputed
the crossing of the river: 1 rebel lieutenant was killed,
and several rebels wounded, 5 prisoners were taken,
with horses, mules, forage, and small arms.

April 1.—The advance of General Banks's division,
in pursuit of Stonewall Jackson, had several slight
skirmishes with Ashby's cavalry. Woodstock and
Edenburg, in the Shenandoah Valley, were occupied
by National troops. Jackson burned the bridges after
he had passed over them, including a very large railroad-bridge at Edenburg.

—— A reconnoissance was made from Newport
News, Virginia, to Watt's Creek. A skirmish with
artillery took place, the secessionists being estimated
to be 3000 in number. The rebels were dispersed.

—— A reconnoissance was made to Big Bethel,
Virginia, by National troops. The rebels were found
to have returned and reoccupied the earth-works from
which they had previously retired. No attempt was
made to dislodge them.

—— An armed expedition, under command of
Colonel Roberts, of the 43d Illinois regiment, in five
boats with 100 men, surprised the lower rebel battery
at Island No. 10, Mississippi River. The sentinels and
soldiers occupying it fired upon them and fled. The
party landed and spiked 6 guns of a battery which had
previously been very annoying to the Federal fleet.
This daring feat was executed at great hazard, but
without any injury to those who participated in it.

April 2.—The War Department ordered that officers
of the United States army engaged in the recruiting-
service should return to their respective regiments, and
that no enlistments or new levies would be received
until further orders, "the force now in the field being
deemed amply sufficient for the suppression of the rebellion and the speedy termination of the war."

April 3.—Major-General Banks was assigned by the
War Department to the command of the department of
the Shenandoah. Major-General McDowell was appointed to the command of the department of the
Rappahannock.

—— The bombardment of Island No. 10 continued.
The rebel steamboat Winchester was set on fire by a
shell from the Union mortar-boats and burned to the
water's edge. During the day, the rebel floating battery was struck by a shell and disabled: 3 men on
board were killed.

—— A naval action near Pass Christian, Mississippi River, between the United States gunboats New
London, Jackson, and Lewis, and the rebel steamers
Oregon, Pamlico, and Carondelet. The Lewis was
crowded with troops, and was soon withdrawn, upon
that account, from the action. After an engagement of
one hour and forty-five minutes, the enemy withdrew.

April 4.—An attack was made by rebels, near Edenburg, Virginia, upon a portion of General Banks's army
engaged in rebuilding the bridge burned a few days before. They were replied to with spirit, and their object
failed.

—— Captain Waugh, in the gunboat Carondelet,
ran past the rebel batteries at Island No. 10, under a
heavy fire, and thus supplied General Pope with a great
assistance.

—— A reconnoissance in strong force was made by
General Sumner, U.S. Army, beyond Warrenton Junction, Virginia. After some skirmishing, with slight
losses on each side, the rebels withdrew beyond the
Rappahannock, and blew up the railroad-bridge.

April 5.—General McClellan telegraphed from Yorktown that, upon reaching that place, the enemy was
found to be strongly fortified. There was cannonading
on both sides,—during which, 3 United States soldiers
were killed, and 6 wounded. The enemy's fortifications
seemed to be two miles in length, with heavy guns and
impassable ground in front. The number of rebel troops
then in Yorktown were estimated at 30,000.

—— Major-General Wool telegraphed the War
Department from Fort Monroe that firing was heard
toward Yorktown (the movement of General McClellan's
army having commenced),—adding, "All goes on

smoothly. *I do not believe that the army of the Potomac will find many troops to contend with.*"

April 6.—The gunboat Pittsburg ran the gauntlet at Island No. 10, under a tremendous fire from the rebel batteries. This boat, and the Carondelet, together with four steam-transports and five barges, which were taken through a canal twelve miles long, cut through the swamps from Phillips Landing, above Island No. 10, to New Madrid, below it, afforded General Pope means of transportation. The canal—a great work—was devised by Colonel Bissell, of the Engineers, and executed under his direction. General Pope was now prepared to carry troops across the Mississippi, to commence land-operations against Island No. 10, which had previously been attacked only by the fleet and mortar-boats, but with little effect.

―――― Battle of Pittsburg Landing, or Shiloh. Early in the morning, the rebels, under Generals Albert Sidney Johnston, Beauregard, and Polk (estimated to be 60,000), made an attack upon the Union troops at Pittsburg Landing. 400 men of Prentiss's division, being the most advanced, fell back, the enemy following with irresistible force. By six o'clock in the morning the battle had become general along the whole line. The Union troops were about 38,000; and the attack was made with an expectation of crushing them before they could be reinforced by General Buell, who was known to be advancing by rapid marches. Their progress was resisted for a long time by the troops of General Prentiss, who were more exposed than the rest; but, after suffering severe losses, his division were surrounded, and the general, with 2000 of his men, were taken prisoners. On other parts of the field, the divisions of Generals Sherman, Hurlbut, and McClernand resisted gallantly, but were forced back gradually, with heavy losses, losing all their camps, which were occupied by the enemy, until the Union troops were almost driven into the river Tennessee. General Lew Wallace, who had set out in the morning to reinforce the Federal troops, took the wrong road, and did not arrive until late in the day, but then contributed to turn the tide of defeat,—in which he was aided by the gunboats Lexington and Tyler,—which, when the enemy neared the river, opened upon them with immense slaughter, causing them to fall back in confusion, out of range, but holding for the night nearly all the tents and encampments occupied by the Federals before the commencement of the battle. The loss on both sides was very severe. The Union army lost, besides killed and wounded, with their camp-equipage, 36 field-pieces. The gunboats in position kept up a fire in the direction of the rebels all night, which compelled them to change their position.

April 7.—During the heavy battle at Pittsburg Landing the previous day, the advance of General Buell's army reached the Tennessee River and commenced to cross. Transports were engaged in this work all night; and, when morning dawned, these troops were in the front, to the number of 30,000, all fresh and ready for the contest. They were under the command of Generals Grant, Buell, Nelson, McCook, and Crittenden,—the whole force engaged on the Federal side being estimated at 70,000. At daybreak they attacked the rebels vigorously; and, after a spirited resistance, the latter began to fall back. They were beaten out of the Union camps which they had occupied the previous night, leaving large numbers of their dead and wounded upon the field. The decisive blow was given by General Grant, who made a gallant charge at the head of six regiments,—upon which the rebels broke and fled. The slaughter on both sides was terrible. The Federals lost among their killed Brigadier-General W. H. L. Wallace; Colonel Pegram, Acting Brigadier; Colonel Ellis, 10th Illinois; Colonel Hall, 16th Illinois; Major Godard, 15th Illinois; Lieutenant-Colonel Kyle, 41st Indiana; Colonel Davis, 46th Illinois; Major Page, 37th Illinois; Major Hunter, 32d Illinois; Captains Carson, Newlin, Dillon, Moore, Carter; and other officers. Among the wounded were Colonel Sweeney, Acting Brigadier; Colonel David Stuart, 55th Illinois; General Sherman, Colonel Craft, Colonel Hayne, Colonel John A. Logan, Colonel Davis, and Colonel Peabody, 25th Wisconsin. The official report of the Federal losses was 1735 killed, 7882 wounded, and 3956 missing,—total, 13,763. The rebels lost General Albert Sidney Johnston, killed in the first day's fight; George W. Johnson, Provisional (rebel) Governor of Kentucky; Colonel Blythe, of Mississippi; Colonel Kitt Williams; Lieutenant-Colonel Tyler, 4th Louisiana; Major Doken, Tennessee. Of their killed, 2700 were found on the field, and many had been carried off. Among the wounded were General Clark, General Gladden, General Hindman, Colonel Brown, Colonel Richards, Colonel Rich, Colonel Bates, Colonel Bowen, and Lieutenant-Colonel Stewart. Their killed, wounded, and missing has been estimated at from 15,000 to 18,000. On the day after the battle, General Beauregard sent a flag of truce to General Grant, asking permission to bury the rebel dead upon the field,—which was refused, because they had already been buried by United States soldiers.

April 7.—General Banks, having completed the bridge over Stony Creek, Virginia, crossed it with his troops. They were fired upon by Ashby's cavalry, who were driven from their positions, which were occupied by the Union forces.

―――― General Pope sent a force across the river at New Madrid, Missouri, and took possession of four rebel batteries and spiked the guns.

―――― Island No. 10 was abandoned by the rebels in the night, leaving all their artillery, baggage, and supplies, with their sick and wounded. There were thus taken 11 earth-works and batteries, mounting 70 heavy guns, large magazines filled with shot and shell, and quantities of small arms, besides 17 officers and 568 men. The iron-plated rebel battery was turned adrift and upset: it mounted 16 guns. There were taken in the works 123 pieces of heavy artillery, and large quantities of stores and ammunition.

―――― General Pope, having sent a force of two divisions of troops, under Generals Paine, Stanley, and Hamilton, across the Mississippi, below Island No. 10, the rebel troops retreating from the island were intercepted and captured. There were taken Major-General W. D. Makall, Brigadiers Gaul, Walker, and Schaum, 273 field and company officers, 6700 privates, 30 field-guns, and 7000 stand of small arms.

―――― A rebel battery on Bull's Island, South Carolina, captured by the United States gunboat Onward, Lieutenant Nickels, and destroyed.

April 11.—The House of Representatives of the United States passed a bill, previously passed by the Senate, providing for the abolition of slavery in the District of Columbia, with compensation to the owners of the slaves that were freed.

―――― The rebel steamer Merrimac came out from Norfolk, accompanied by the Jefferson and Henry and several tugs. Three small Union transport vessels were captured, and there was some firing between the Merrimac, Monitor, and Naugatuck, but no general engagement.

―――― Fort Pulaski, Georgia, having been fully invested by the Federal troops, and having sustained a terrific bombardment for thirty hours, during which seven large breaches were made in the walls, surrendered unconditionally. It was occupied by Colonel Olmstead and 385 men. Although the firing was tremendous, but little hurt was done to the troops on either side. Union loss, 1 killed, and 5 wounded; rebel loss, 3 wounded. The Federal forces were commanded by General Gilmore. 47 heavy guns were taken, 7000 shot and shell, with other ammunition and stores.

―――― Huntsville, Alabama, taken by surprise by National troops under General O. M. Mitchell, after a forced march. 200 prisoners were taken, also 15 locomotives and a large number of cars. The line of rebel communication by the Memphis & Charleston Railroad was thus cut.

April 12.—An expedition from Huntsville, in cars captured by General Mitchell, went to Stevens Station, under command of Colonel Till, 33d Ohio regiment, where they captured 2000 men, and seized 5 locomotives and a number of cars.

April 12.—Another expedition from General Mitchell's corps went to Decatur, Alabama, under Colonel Turchin, and saved from destruction the railroad-bridge at that place, which had been set on fire by the rebels.

———— 4000 United States troops, in transports, accompanied by the gunboats Tyler and Lexington, went up the Tennessee River to the neighborhood of Eastport, Mississippi. They set fire to and destroyed two bridges of the Mobile & Ohio Railroad over and near Bear Creek, cutting off all access by the rebel army at Corinth with Alabama and the Eastern States of the Confederacy.

———— 150 rebels made a sortie from Fort Macon, North Carolina, and attacked four companies of the 8th Connecticut regiment, and drove in the pickets. After a short engagement, they were driven back. 2 Unionists and 4 rebels were wounded.

April 13.—1000 rebels, with two cavalry companies and 2 pieces of artillery, attacked the pickets of General Milroy, at Monterey, Western Virginia. They were repulsed after a brisk skirmish, with loss. The Union troops had 3 men wounded.

———— The President of the United States signed the bill passed by Congress, declaring that the United States will co-operate with any State which may adopt measures for the abolition of slavery.

April 14.—The United States flotilla proceeded up the Rappahannock River, Virginia. At the town of Urbana they were fired upon from rifle-pits. Shot and shell were opened upon the occupants, and they scattered in all directions. Proceeding up the river, rebel batteries at Lowrie's Point were shelled out; some of the crews landed, and burned 150 plank and log houses used by the rebels for quartering troops. At Tappahannock, farther on, white flags were raised, and the American flag was run up on one of the houses. The object of the reconnoissance being effected, the vessels returned, capturing three secession craft, laden with provisions, &c. for the rebel army.

April 15.—A large boat, containing a number of officers and men of the 75th Pennsylvania regiment, Colonel Bohlen, was upset at Castleman's Ferry, on the Potomac, and several officers and 40 or 50 men drowned.

April 16.—A skirmish upon Wilmington Island, Georgia, between a Federal surveying-party, with roops (about 200 in number), and 600 rebels, who crossed over from the mainland to attack them. The Unionists stood their ground; and, after brisk firing, the enemy retired. Federal loss, 14 killed, and 30 wounded; rebel loss not known.

———— A strong force of United States infantry, supported by artillery, was thrown forward in front of the position at Yorktown, for the purpose of clearing it of the rebel skirmishers and to gain a point where their works could be commanded. This was accomplished principally by Vermont volunteers, under Colonels Stoughton and Lord, of General Smith's brigade, assisted by Captain Ayres's battery. The Union troops charged into a rifle-pit and cleared it, amidst a heavy fire from the whole line of the enemy's works. Our loss in killed was 35; wounded, 120; missing, 4. The enemy subsequently admitted their loss to be "severe." After driving the rebels out of some of their works, they were strongly reinforced; and our troops fell back a portion of the distance, but retained a very eligible position.

———— 61 of Ashby's rebel cavalry, with 3 officers, were surprised by United States cavalry and the 46th Pennsylvania regiment, beyond Columbia Furnace, Virginia. They surrendered without resistance.

———— Operations commenced by the Western gunboat fleet, Commodore A. H. Foote, commanding, against Fort Pillow and Fort Wright, on the Mississippi River, above Memphis.

April 17.—Mount Jackson, Virginia, occupied by General Banks's troops, who saved from destruction, by the rapidity of their movements, two bridges, with locomotives, cars, &c., and took 60 prisoners of Ashby's cavalry.

April 17.—New Market, Virginia, occupied by General Banks.

———— A skirmish at Edisto Island, South Carolina, between 62 men from the Union gunboat fleet, and New York, Pennsylvania, and New Hampshire regiments, with 1 howitzer, and 200 rebel cavalry. The latter had no artillery, and could not stand the manner in which our gun was served with shell. After three desperate attempts to capture it by a charge, they broke and fled, losing 50 killed and wounded.

April 18.—The naval expedition against New Orleans, under command of Commodore D. C. Farragut, opened fire upon Forts Jackson and St. Philip, on the Mississippi River, below the city, from 20 bomb-ketches under direction of Commander D. D. Porter, U.S. Navy. The forts replied with spirit, and firing was kept up all day. Fire-rafts were sent down against the United States fleet; but proper receptions for these had been arranged by means of grapnels and ropes, by which they might be seized and towed away where they could do no harm. Buckets, axes, and other appliances were also ready, and the damage meditated by these means was avoided. This bombardment continued with terrific fury for five days.

———— The advance of General McDowell's armycorps occupied the banks of the Rappahannock River, opposite Fredericksburg, Virginia. There was skirmishing with the rebels upon the march, with losses on both sides. They burned the bridge across the river at Fredericksburg in order to stop the progress of McDowell. In the skirmishing previously upon the march, Lieutenant Decker, of the Ira Harris (New York) cavalry, was killed, with 4 others, and 16 were wounded. Several rebel prisoners were captured.

April 19.—An expedition, under General Reno, of Burnside's corps, with 2000 men, went to Elizabeth City, North Carolina, and thence to South Mills, or Camden, to attack a rebel force reported to be intrenching themselves there. The enemy opened with artillery upon the appearance of the Nationals, which was replied to with spirit. A charge was made upon the intrenchments, when the rebels broke and fled. They were about 1100 strong, with two batteries of artillery. Their loss was 60 killed and wounded; ours, 12 killed, and 48 wounded. After this, the object of the expedition—which was to destroy the locks of the Dismal Swamp Canal—was effected.

April 21.—The British ship Emily St. Pierre arrived at Liverpool. She had been captured by a United States gunboat, in an attempt to run the blockade. A prizemaster was put on board, with orders to take the ship into Philadelphia. During the voyage thither, the British crew rose upon the captors, put them in irons, and carried them into Liverpool. The United States afterward claimed a return of the vessel, the recapture being illegal; but the British Government refused to recognise the validity of the claim, and, while admitting that the capture would have been good if the vessel had been taken into an American port, maintained that it was the duty of the blockaders to put a sufficient force on board of the vessel to have made a recapture impossible.

April 22.—Luray, Virginia, occupied by General Banks. The Valley of Virginia was at this time entirely abandoned by "Stonewall" Jackson, who had retreated to Gordonsville.

———— Harrisonburg, Virginia, occupied by General Banks's troops, after a slight skirmish with the rebels.

April 23.—After the bombardment of Forts Jackson and St. Philip, on the Mississippi River, for five days, it was determined by Commodore D. C. Farragut to endeavor to pass them with his fleet and proceed to New Orleans. At two o'clock in the morning, the ships moved forward in three divisions. The steam-sloops Hartford, Brooklyn, and Richmond, gunboats Sciota, Iroquois, Kennebec, Pinola, Itasca, and Winona, under the direction of Commodore Farragut, were to operate against Fort Jackson. The steam-sloops Pensacola, Mississippi, Oneida, and Varuna, gunboats Katahdin,

Kineo, Wissahickon, and Cayuga, under Captain Bailey, of the Colorado, formed the second division, to engage Fort St. Philip. The gunboats Harriet Lane, Westfield, Owasco, Miami, Clifton, and Jackson comprised the third division, under Captain Porter, with directions to enfilade Fort Jackson with grape and shrapnel. These vessels were all of wood; but they had been ingeniously mailed by hanging iron cable down the sides,—which had a very useful effect in protecting them from the enemy's shots. The boilers and works of the steamers were also protected by barricades of hay, by storage of coal so as to receive line-shots in the direction of the boilers, and by other careful expedients. When the vessels moved up, the whole fleet of mortar-boats opened upon the forts with fury; the ships going into action added to the terrific nature of the scene; and the firing from the forts was swift and appalling. Through this terrific rain of shot and shell, the United States vessels succeeded in passing the two fortifications. When they had attained this success, they met the rebel fleet, consisting of 16 iron-clad rams and gunboats, and had to force their way through hulks and various obstructions, intended to keep a hostile fleet within range of the guns of the forts. A huge iron boom-chain was stretched across the river. These were all disposed of by running through, breaking them, or evading them. The attack of the rebel gunboats was furious. Their rams made desperate endeavors to run down the Federal ships: the latter received considerable damage. The United States gunboat Varuna, Commander Boggs, after disposing of six steamers and rams, was run into by a rebel ram, and injured so badly that it was impossible to keep the former afloat. As she was going down, she fired eight guns into the ram, with such destructive effect that both vessels sank together. The celebrated ram Manassas ("turtle" of Commodore Hollins) was sunk by the guns of the United States frigate Mississippi. In this remarkable engagement, the rebels lost 11 of their gunboats and rams, which were sunk and destroyed. The Union loss was the Varuna, and Maria J. Carlton (a mortar-boat). Among the rebel vessels thus disposed of were the William H. Webb, Palmetto, Phœnix, Jackson, and Morgan. The loss of the Federal ships in this memorable encounter was 36 killed, and 123 wounded. We captured a regiment above the forts, commanded by Colonel S. Zymanski.

April 24.—A reconnoissance made to Pea Ridge, Tennessee, by General A. J. Smith: 3000 rebels, drawn up in line of battle, decamped at the first fire of the artillery, leaving their tents, private baggage, &c. Tents enough to accommodate a division were taken and burned; 12 prisoners were captured.

April 25.—Major-General Charles F. Smith, U.S. Army, died at Savannah, Tennessee, of dysentery.

—————— An action between the United States gunboat New London, and the rebel steamers Oregon and Pamlico, at a distance of one thousand yards. The latter withdrew, after firing an hour and a half.

—————— New Orleans surrendered to the United States fleet, under Commodore D. C. Farragut, which arrived before the city the previous day.

April 26.—Major Hubbard, 1st Missouri volunteers, with 146 men, defeated Colonels Coffee and Stamright and 600 Indians, at Neosho, Missouri, killing and wounding 32, and capturing 62 prisoners, 76 horses, and a large quantity of arms.

—————— Fort Macon, North Carolina, surrendered to the United States land and naval forces, under General Parke and Commodore Goldsborough, after having sustained a bombardment of twenty-four hours, from shore-batteries, and the steam-gunboats Daylight, State of Georgia, Chippewa, and the bark Gemsbok, The Union loss was 1 killed, and 2 wounded; of the enemy, 8 killed, 20 wounded, and 155 prisoners, with Colonel White, their commander, who were allowed to march out upon parole. During the bombardment, 13 guns of the fort were dismounted. 50 heavy guns were taken, with 20,000 pounds of powder, shot, shell, and 400 stand of arms.

—————— A rebel lunette, on the bank of the Warwick River, near its head, was carried by assault by one company of the 1st Massachusetts regiment. It was guarded by two companies of infantry, and had a ditch six feet deep. 14 prisoners were taken, some killed and some wounded, and the work destroyed so as to be of no use for offensive purposes thereafter. Union loss, 3 killed, and 13 wounded.

April 26.—Ashby's rebel cavalry attacked the pickets of Colonel Donnelly's brigade, Banks's division, eight miles beyond Harrisonburg, Virginia, on the Gordonsville road. Reinforcements were brought up, and the rebels repulsed.

April 27.—Fort Livingston, below New Orleans, Louisiana, and above Forts Jackson and St. Philip, surrendered to the United States forces; also the "Terrible" (a small battery).

April 28.—Forts Jackson and St. Philip, below New Orleans, were surrendered to Commander D. D. Porter. Whilst the parties were signing the terms of capitulation, the officers of the rebel navy set fire to the formidable floating iron-plated ram and battery Louisiana, of 16 guns (one of the largest ever constructed), and sent it down against the Union fleet. Fortunately it exploded a short distance from the ships. After the surrender, the United States fleet went after two rebel steamers (all that was left of the Confederate navy which defended New Orleans). They surrendered unconditionally.

—————— Major-General Butler, U.S. Army, landed his troops below New Orleans, above Fort St. Philip, under the guns of two vessels of the squadron.

April 29.—A rebel battery on Grumball's plantation, South Carolina, taken by the United States gunboat Hale, Lieutenant Gillis, and destroyed, together with 2 guns.

April 30.—An expedition, under Major-General Mitchell, went to Bridgeport, Alabama, and dispersed 6800 rebels, under General E. Kirby Smith, who were guarding the bridge near that point. The enemy were driven across the stream; after which, Mitchell succeeded in getting in their rear and surprised them. They fled, after setting fire to the main bridge. They lost 63 killed and a large number wounded, 300 prisoners, and 2 guns.

—————— A reconnoissance from General Hallock's army, before Corinth, Mississippi, was made to Purdy, Tennessee. A rebel force of cavalry fled, Purdy was occupied, one locomotive and a train of cars with passengers were taken, and two bridges were burned.

May 1.—An expedition from General Mitchell's division advanced from Bridgeport, twelve miles toward Chattanooga, Georgia, and captured stores and the Southern mail.

May 2.—General Beauregard, at Corinth, issued an address to the "soldiers of Shiloh and Elkhorn," informing them that they were "about to meet once more in the shock of battle the invaders of our soil."

—————— The Union batteries at Yorktown opened upon a portion of the rebel fortifications at that place and at Gloucester, Virginia. Heavy firing ensued on both sides,—during which, a large gun in the rebel works exploded, killing many who were in the neighborhood of it.

May 3.—The rebel steamer Ella Warley (formerly the Isabel), captured, on a voyage to Charleston, South Carolina, by the United States gunboat Santiago de Cuba, arrived at New York.

—————— The prize steamer Nostro Signora de Regla, captured while attempting to run the blockade, by the United States gunboat Empire City, arrived at New York.

—————— The prize steamer Florida, captured by the United States bark Pursuit, April 4, in Tampa Bay, Florida, arrived at Philadelphia.

—————— The prize steamer Bermuda (English), captured by the United States gunboat Mercedite, Commander Stellwagen, with contraband of war, arrived at Philadelphia.

—————— General Paine's (Federal) division made a reconnoissance to Farmington, Tennessee, where it als, killing 30, wounding onors, with tents, camp-tilled, and 12 wounded. loucester, Virginia, were night. It was supposed had at this time 100,000 General McClellan for the was certain that the place buried torpedoes and ox-rts of the works, by which id wounded. There were artillery, spiked, at York-sition at Gloucester, with n as the evacuation was ry and infantry started in t, and the gunboats went

Merrimac came out from led herself at the mouth to prevent troops from attack the rebels retreat-

were taken at Pulaski, ry, under the rebel guer-s were killed, 3 wounded, oss was 6 killed, and 2

avalry were attacked at ral Dumont, with a force Vynkoop's (Pennsylvania) uted, losing many killed, mith and Woolford (Fede-

urg, Virginia, between a i's army, under Generals k, and the rear-guard of erals Joe Johnston, Long-to number 40,000. The is behind five redoubts, with artillery. General of these works with two in front, the other in the force in the woods, which, 'igade detailed for the lat-force and endeavored to n extricating themselves lists suffered considerable evere; they also lost three lded in the mud and could g killed. At this time the gainst the Unionists; but in the field, made such a ide of disaster was turned. by an assault made by and another by General it the Union troops occu-vorks, and remained there in the morning. Union 00 wounded. Among the iel John P. Vanleer, 6th cers. Rebel loss, killed, olonel Mott, Mississippi; fficers, and probably 400 y, General Raines, Colonel loin, and 800 men; taken l. een the Ira Harris (New shby's rebel cavalry, five g, Virginia. The latter iles of the town, losing 10 ; Union loss, 1 killed, and

Point, Virginia, between Franklin, General Dana, rebels (a portion of their own). The Federal troops and Pamunkey Rivers in he enemy was found to be derals endeavored to drive lid so under disadvantage,

being compelled in some parts of the line to fall back. The manœuvres were such that, in order to meet them, the rebels were compelled to take a position where they were in range with the United States gunboats lying in the Pamunkey. The latter opened upon them, and, aided by firing from the Union field-batteries, compelled them to fly. Union loss, 300 killed and wounded. The rebel loss is supposed to have been about the same.

May 8.—The United States frigates and gunboats Dacotah, San Jacinto, Susquehanna, Seminole, Monitor, and Naugatuck proceeded to Sewall's Point, Virginia, and shelled the rebel batteries there, aided by the Union battery on the Rip-Raps. The response was feeble, and it was evident that the works were held by a very small force. After firing for some time, the rebel steamer Merrimac came out from Norfolk; but there was no engagement with her further than firing at long range. The object of this demonstration by the vessels was to ascertain the condition of the rebel shore-batteries, in order to inform the President and military authorities as to the propriety of an attack upon Norfolk, Virginia.

——— A fight at McDowell, Western Virginia, between United States troops under General Milroy, and rebels under "Stonewall" Jackson. Milroy was reinforced by General Schenck. The enemy were defeated in attempting to plant a battery in a commanding position, and a bayonet-charge was made against them. The rebels being reinforced, Milroy and Schenck withdrew in the night, and fell back to Franklin. Union loss, 30 killed, and 200 wounded; rebel loss (by their own reports), 40 killed, and 200 wounded.

——— A reconnoissance, by General Paine, of Pope's division, United States volunteers, was made from Farmington,—being principally composed of United States cavalry. They were caught in ambush, but fought their way through, losing Major Applington, killed, with several others wounded. The rebels lost 49 killed, wounded, and missing,—among whom were a lieutenant-colonel and captain killed.

May 9.—Major-General Hunter, commanding the Department of the South, issued a proclamation, announcing that the three States of Georgia, Florida, and South Carolina were under martial law, that "slavery and martial law are altogether incompatible;" in pursuance of which, he proclaimed that persons within the States named, "heretofore held as slaves, are therefore declared forever free."

——— The United States steamer Shawsheen, with one company of the New York 9th, went up the Chowan River, North Carolina, to Gates county, and destroyed fifty thousand dollars' worth of provisions.

——— Pensacola, Florida, evacuated by the rebels, who first burned the navy-yard at Warrington, and the barracks, marine hospital, two steamboats, wooden buildings in the forts, and tore up the railroad, &c. General Arnold (Union) occupied the town on the 12th, with 3000 troops.

——— A skirmish in Virginia, at Slater's Mills, between McClellan's advance and the rebel rear-guard; 14 rebel cavalry were killed, and some taken prisoners; Union loss, 3 killed, 13 wounded, and 3 missing.

——— An attack was made, by 20,000 rebels, under Bragg and Van Dorn, upon a portion of Major-General Pope's command, under General Paine, at Farmington, Tennessee. Two brigades of the Union army held their position for five hours; after which, being heavily pressed, they withdrew across Seven-Mile Creek. Union loss, 200 killed and wounded.

May 10.—Six vessels of the United States flotilla, commanded by Captain C. H. Davis, upon the Mississippi River, lying above Fort Wright, were attacked by eight steamers, a rebel gunboat fleet, under Commodore Hollins. The principal work was done by the rebel iron-clad ram Mallory, which attempted to board the United States gunboat Cincinnati, and was twice repulsed by the use of hot water and steam. There was then a general action,—during which, two of the rebel gunboats were disabled and drifted away, and a third was shot through the boiler; the remainder then retired under the guns of Fort Wright. The United States gunboat Cincinnati afterward sunk, but was raised again and put in order.

May 10.—An engagement between the United States iron-clad frigate Galena, and rebel batteries, upon the James River. Two of the latter were shelled out, and the garrisons fled. The rebel gunboats Jefferson and Patrick Henry were under the guns of the second battery, but did not aid in its defence: they made their escape up the river as rapidly as possible.

———— Major-General Butler, in command at New Orleans, seized $800,000, in possession of the consul for the Netherlands, alleging that it was intended for the payment of interest upon Confederate bonds.

———— General Wool, U.S. Army, landed 5000 men at Willoughby Point, Virginia, and marched upon Norfolk. Slight skirmishing ensued, without hindering the movement. At five o'clock in the afternoon, a delegation of citizens of Norfolk met the United States troops, and the town was formally surrendered and occupied,—General Viele being appointed Military Governor. The same night, the rebels set fire to the buildings of the navy-yard at Gosport, and attempted to blow up the dry-dock,—in which they partially succeeded.

May 11.—About five o'clock in the morning, the iron-clad rebel steamer Merrimac, in Hampton Roads, Virginia, was blown up by her officers, and totally destroyed.

———— The armed rebel steamer Planter was navigated from Charleston, South Carolina, by Robert Small, a slave, with a crew of slaves and their families, and surrendered to the United States blockading fleet.

May 12.—The rebel steamer Governor A. Mouton captured in Berwick Bay, Georgia, by the United States gunboat Hatteras.

May 14.—The rebel steamer Alice captured in the Roanoke River, North Carolina, by the United States steamers Ceres and Lockwood. She was loaded with bacon and other articles for the use of the rebels.

May 15.—The United States iron-clad frigate Galena, the iron-clad Monitor, the Naugatuck, or Stevens battery, the Aroostook and Port Royal (gunboats), encountered a heavy battery on Drury's Bluffs, James River, called by the Federals "Fort Darling." The river was obstructed at this place, and the battery situated upon a high bank, from which plunging shot could be thrown upon hostile vessels coming up the river. The fort was engaged by the iron-clads. The Monitor could not elevate her guns sufficiently to bear on the battery. The Galena and the Naugatuck conducted the action, the wooden vessels keeping out of range. The result of the engagement was that the United States vessels failed in producing any impression on the fort. The big gun of the Naugatuck (100-pound Parrott) exploded, and the Galena withdrew after having nearly exhausted her ammunition. Loss on the Galena, 13 killed, and 11 wounded; Port Royal, 1 wounded; Naugatuck, 2 wounded. The rebels acknowledged a loss of 6 killed, and 7 wounded.

———— Suffolk, Virginia, taken by Union troops under Colonel Dodge.

May 16.—An attack upon 17 men of the 28th Pennsylvania regiment, Colonel Geary, by 300 rebel guerrillas, beyond Front Royal, Virginia, and 1 killed, 3 wounded, and 13 taken prisoners by the latter.

———— Princeton, Western Virginia, taken by the rebels under Humphrey Marshall.

May 17.—Princeton, Virginia, retaken by General Cox, U.S. Army.

———— A combined army and navy expedition, under Captain Murray, U.S. Navy, and Major Willard, went twenty-five miles up the Pamunkey River, and compelled the rebels to burn 2 steamboats and 20 schooners.

May 19.—A skirmish near Corinth, Mississippi, between General M. L. Smith's (Union) brigade, and three rebel regiments, with cavalry and artillery. Loss of the enemy, 30 killed, and several wounded: Federal loss, 12 killed, and 30 wounded.

———— A skirmish at Lacy, Arkansas, between 150 men of General Osterhouse's (Federal) division, and 600 rebels, under Colonels Coleman and Hicks. The latter were routed, with a loss of 150 killed, and a number wounded; Union loss, 15 killed, and 31 wounded.

May 19.—The President of the United States issued a proclamation, stating that General Hunter's proclamation of May 9, declaring that slaves in South Carolina, Georgia, and Florida were free, was issued without authority, and was void.

May 20.—A train of seventeen Government wagons, captured on the Springfield road, twenty miles from Rolla, Missouri, by rebel guerrillas, who burned the wagons, and carried off 86 horses and mules.

———— General Carleton's (Federal) brigade entered Arizona Territory, and took possession of Tucan without opposition. The rebels fled to the Rio Grande.

May 21.—Skirmishing along the whole line in front of Corinth. Union loss, 40 killed and wounded.

May 23.—The 1st Maryland regiment, Colonel Kenley, with three companies of the 29th Pennsylvania regiment, two companies of New York cavalry, and a section of Knapp's battery, were attacked at Front Royal, Virginia, by the advance of rebels, under "Stonewall" Jackson and Ewell, 22,000 strong. Kenley made a gallant stand, but was forced to retreat, destroying a bridge; but, being overwhelmed, he gave the command to his troops to save themselves by flight. Colonel Kenley was wounded and taken prisoner. The rebels captured the greater part of Kenley's force, and killed and wounded many.

———— Colonel Heth, with 3000 rebels, attacked Colonel Crook, having 1300 men, at Lewineville, Virginia, and was beaten back, losing 4 cannon, 200 stand of arms, and 100 prisoners,—including a lieutenant-colonel, a major, and several other officers. Union loss, 10 killed, and 40 wounded and missing.

———— Battle of Lewisburg, Virginia. 3000 rebels, under General Heath, with 13 rifled cannon, attacked a portion of General Fremont's corps, under Colonel Crook. After some sharp fighting, the enemy were routed by a bayonet-charge, which was followed up by cavalry-charges. Four of the enemy's guns were taken; 73 of their dead were found on the field; 125 rebel prisoners were taken, including one colonel, several captains, and other officers. Union loss, 14 killed, and 50 wounded.

May 24.—Steamship Stettin, of London, attempting to run the blockade at Charleston, South Carolina, was captured by the United States gunboat Bienville.

———— A skirmish at Mechanicsville, Virginia, from which place the rebels were driven, with severe loss. The Louisiana "Tigers" lost 50 killed, and 50 taken prisoners; Federal loss, 10 killed and wounded.

———— A skirmish near New Bridge, Virginia, between five companies of the 4th Michigan regiment, and four companies of the 5th Louisiana regiment. The latter were taken by surprise and thrown into a panic, losing 65 killed, 15 wounded, and 31 prisoners; Union loss, 2 killed, and 6 wounded.

———— A fight at Ellison's Mills, Virginia, between Stoneman's cavalry, with Davidson's brigade, and four rebel regiments, with 9 pieces of artillery, and some cavalry. There was brisk firing on both sides, and the rebels withdrew to the village at night.

May 25.—The fight at Ellison's Mills was renewed, and, after some time, the rebels retreated across the Chickahominy. Union loss, 2 killed, and 4 wounded.

———— General Negley's brigade engaged the rebel General Stewart's brigade, near Mechanicsville, Virginia. Union loss, 2 killed, and 6 wounded.

———— A skirmish before Corinth, Mississippi, between a reconnoitring-party of General Pope's command, and three rebel regiments. The latter were routed, losing blankets, knapsacks, and haversacks. Several were killed and wounded, and 6 prisoners were taken. Federal loss, 6 wounded.

———— Ewell and Jackson's (estimated at 22,000) troops attacked General Banks, at Winchester, Virginia. The latter made good resistance,—during which, a retreat was organized toward Martinsburg. Banks had but 4000 men,—the greater portion of his corps having been taken from him to reinforce McClellan and cDowell. He was followed by the rebels with much vigor, and engagements took place at Strasburg, Middletown, Newton, and other points along the route. Notwithstanding the manner in which he was pressed, General Banks saved 445 of his train of 500 wagons, by forced march of fifty-three miles (thirty-five of which were made in one day), subject to constant attacks in rout, rear, and flank. He succeeded in crossing the Potomac into Maryland. The rebels boasted that they took 4000 prisoners in the battles commencing at Front Royal, and only lost 100 killed and wounded. The Union loss was officially reported to have been estimated at 38 killed, 155 wounded, and 711 missing.

May 27.—Battle of Hanover Court-House, Virginia, between the division of Major-General Fitz-John Porter, U.S. Volunteers, and rebels under General Semmes. There were three separate engagements. The first, before noon, about three miles from the court-house, was between the advance under Colonel Johnson, and the enemy in the woods: the latter were driven from their cover, after brisk fighting for two hours. The second engagement was near Harris's house, with the rebels, gain in the woods, from which they were compelled to retreat. The third fight was at Kinney's house, the rebels also in the woods, from which the enemy were again driven by shot, shell, and musketry. Federal loss, 53 killed, and 326 wounded; rebel loss, over 100 killed, 500 wounded, and 500 prisoners.

—— British steamer Nassau, attempting to run the blockade, was captured off Wilmington, North Carolina, with a cargo of ammunition and Enfield rifles.

May 29.—Three strong reconnoitring columns advanced against Corinth, Mississippi. The enemy contested the ground, but were driven back at all points. Union loss in Pope's column, 25 killed and wounded. 0 dead rebels were found upon the field. A rebel battery was shelled by Pope's heavy batteries, and abandoned by the enemy.

May 30.—Colonel Elliott, 2d United States Cavalry, by forced marches from Corinth, reached Booneville, on the Mobile & Ohio Railroad. He destroyed the railroad-track, blew up culverts, burned the depôt, locomotives, and cars loaded with supplies, destroyed 10,000 stand of arms, with ammunition, and took 2000 sick and wounded prisoners in the hospitals and paroled them.

—— Corinth, Mississippi, having been abandoned by the rebels during the previous night, was occupied by the Union troops.

—— Front Royal, Virginia, recaptured from the rebels, by Rhode Island cavalry, under Colonel Nelson, who drove out Louisiana and Georgia troops, and captured 6 officers and 150 men, 2 locomotive engines, and 1 cars. Union loss, 8 killed, 5 wounded, and 1 missing.

—— Steamer Patras, of London, captured off Charleston, South Carolina, while attempting to run the blockade.

May 31.—A reconnoissance from Front Royal, Virginia, encountered a large force of rebels on the Winchester road, and drove them for some distance, taking gun, 12 wagons, several horses and mules, and recapturing 6 Union prisoners taken some days before. Union loss, 1 killed, and 2 wounded.

—— Battle of Fair Oaks, Virginia (called by the rebels "the battle of Seven Pines"). The rebels, in heavy force, under Generals Hill, Longstreet, Garland, Rhodes, Rains, Huger, Pryor, Bronk, and Howell Cobb, numbering 75,000, made a sudden attack upon the division of General Casey (the most advanced in the United States army), near Seven Pines,—the intention being to cut them off, the Chickahominy being in the rear, and the main body of the Federal troops on the other side. Casey had about 6000 men. The time chosen for the assault was during a severe thunder-storm, by which was supposed that the Chickahominy would be very much swollen. Casey's division, although composed principally of raw troops, contested every foot of the ground gallantly, and, by their courage and determination, kept the rebels back until reinforcements arrived, under Hooker and Kearney, from Heintzelman's division. The latter, going into action, drove the enemy partially back by bayonet-charges. At the close of the day, a portion of the field lost by Casey was regained; but the rebels still occupied a considerable portion of our camps, and had taken 19 guns from Casey.

June 1.—Second day's battle at Fair Oaks, Virginia. The rebels attempted to press forward, but were met by Sumner's and Heintzelman's corps, which checked their advance, compelled them to stop, and, after several hours' fighting, finally drove them, by bayonet-charges. in full speed to Richmond. The loss in the two days' battles was very heavy. On the Union side there were killed Colonel Bailey, chief of artillery, Colonel J. M. Brown, 100th New York, Colonel James Miller, 81st Pennsylvania, Colonel Rippey, 61st Pennsylvania, Colonel Riker, 62d New York, and other officers. The official statement of General McClellan was that the killed in the two days' battles were 890; wounded, 3627; missing, 1222,—grand total, 5739. The rebels lost severely:—General Pettigrew, South Carolina, Colonels Long, Lightfoot, Britton, John A. Winston, Alabama, were taken prisoners; General Hatton, of Tennessee, Colonel Davis, Colonel T. Lomax, Alabama, Colonel Champ, North Carolina, Colonel Davis, North Carolina, were killed; General Rhodes, Colonel Edmunds, Virginia, Colonel D. H. Christie, North Carolina, Colonel Coppen, Louisiana, Major-General Joseph E. Johnston, were wounded. Their semi-official reports stated that 85 regiments were engaged in the battle, and that their loss in killed, wounded, and missing was 5897 men: General Joseph E. Johnston subsequently declared that it was but 4283.

—— A skirmish, five miles from Strasburg, Virginia, between the advance of General Fremont's forces, and the rear-guard of General "Stonewall" Jackson, in retreat: 25 rebel prisoners were taken; Union loss, 7 wounded.

June 3.—By order of the rebel War Department, officers in the field of battle are permitted to wear a fatigue-dress without embroidery on the collar; mounted officers are ordered to dismount in time of action; "officers of all grades are reminded that unnecessary exposure in time of battle, on the part of commissioned officers, is not only unsoldierlike, but productive of great injury to the army and infinite peril to the country."

June 4.—A portion of the 1st Kentucky (Union) cavalry, 70 in number, under Captain Chilson, were attacked by Stearns's rebel cavalry, near Murfreesboro', Alabama, and defeated: 6 were killed, and the rest captured.

—— Two regiments (the 97th Pennsylvania and the 47th New York), with two companies of the 6th Connecticut regiment, attacked on James Island, South Carolina, by a large force of rebels, who were repulsed, after a fight of two hours, with a loss of 17 killed and left on the field, 30 wounded, and 6 prisoners; Federal loss, 3 killed, and 13 wounded.

—— A rebel battery on James Island, South Carolina, having 8 guns, was taken by assault by the New York 79th and 8th Michigan: 3 guns were taken off, and the rest destroyed.

—— Colonel Adams's (rebel) force surprised at Sweeden's Cove, Alabama, by General Lytle. The rebels fled, losing 6 men.

June 5.—Forts Wright and Randolph, Mississippi River, abandoned by the rebels, and taken possession of by Union troops.

—— A fight near Pocotaligo, North Carolina, between eight companies of the 24th Massachusetts regiment, with 2 guns, and Colonel Singletaries's North Carolina regiment, which was posted in ambush in a wood. After an action of forty-five minutes, the rebels were driven out. Union loss, 7 killed, and 9 wounded.

June 6.—65 men of the 9th Pennsylvania cavalry, under Captain McCullough, were attacked at Tompkinsville, Kentucky, by 100 of Morgan's men, under Captain Hamilton. Both commanders were killed, and 3 wounded on each side. The rebels were driven off.

—— Eight rebel rams and gunboats, lying at the levee, Memphis, were attacked by the United States ram-fleet, under Colonel Charles Ellet, Jr. Seven of the enemy's vessels—viz. the General Beauregard, General Sterling Price, Jeff Thompson, Sumter, Little Rebel, General Lovell, and General Bragg—were run down, blown up, and burned. One rebel gunboat—the Van Dorn—succeeded in escaping. The action took place in front of the city of Memphis; and, after it was over, the town surrendered to Colonel Ellet. Upon the ram-fleet the only person injured was Colonel Ellet, who afterward died from the effect of his wound.

June 7.—A fight, four miles beyond Harrisonburg, Virginia, between the advance of Fremont's corps and the rear-guard of "Stonewall" Jackson. The Federal cavalry, under Colonel Sir Percy Wyndham, were caught in a rebel ambush, and suffered severely,—Colonel Wyndham being taken prisoner, and many of his officers and men killed and wounded. In attempting to support them, 125 men of the Pennsylvania Bucktail regiment were overpowered by four rebel regiments. Their lieutenant-colonel (Kane) was taken prisoner, with many of his men. The Federal loss was 89 killed, wounded, and missing. The rebels lost General Turner Ashby (their cavalry officer), Major Green, and other officers, and probably 60 killed, wounded, and missing.

—— Union troops, under General James A. Negley, cannonaded the enemy at Chattanooga, Georgia, from the opposite side of the river, driving off the enemy from the town, and forcing him to abandon his works and evacuate the city. They burned several railroad-bridges, to prevent pursuit.

—— William B. Mumford was hung at New Orleans, by order of General Butler, for high treason, in tearing down the American flag.

June 8.—Battle of Cross Keys, Virginia, fought by General Fremont's corps, under Generals Milroy, Stahl, and Schenck, and the rebel army of "Stonewall" Jackson. The enemy, having been pursued from Winchester, Strasburg, and Front Royal, were found strongly posted in the woods, their position being concealed by the nature of the ground, and their troops being formed in masses. The battle began with artillery, about eleven o'clock in the morning, and lasted with great violence until four o'clock in the afternoon, with skirmishing and occasional cannonading until dark. The rebels were driven by bayonet-charges and a gradual advance. At night the Federal troops slept on the field of battle. Of Fremont's force, Colonel Von Gilsa, New York De Kalb regiment, and 125 others, were killed, and 500 wounded. 500 of the dead of the rebels were found in one field, and their loss is known to have been great. Their wounded, carried off, were many.

June 9.—"Stonewall" Jackson, retreating with the rebel army, after the battle of Cross Keys, Virginia, reached Port Republic. Here General Shields had been ordered to intercept him and cut off his flight. Only a portion of Shields's force were in the town, being one brigade, but 1600 strong, under Colonel Carrol. The latter, either by order or by some fatal error, determined that he would not burn the bridge, which was the only means by which Jackson could escape from Fremont, who was in pursuit. In the night, Jackson moved up his advance, quietly posted 20 guns to command the bridge, and opened upon Carrol at daylight. The latter lost several men, in a vain endeavor to set fire to the bridge, but was fired upon by so large a force that the Federals were compelled to withdraw. The enemy's cavalry then crossed the bridge, attacked the Union troops, and were followed by heavy columns of infantry. The Federals were driven from the field, and Jackson's troops had a clear road to Richmond. The rebels claimed to have taken 600 prisoners. The official report was 124 killed, 292 wounded, and 514 prisoners on the Federal side. Jackson's loss is not known.

June 13.—The rebel General Stuart, with 1500 rebel cavalry and 6 pieces of artillery, got in the rear of General McClellan's line at Garlick's Landing, Virginia, four miles above the White House, where they burned 2 schooners and several wagons, drove off mules, and killed some teamsters. They then proceeded to Tunstall's Station, fired into a passing railroad-train, wounded some passengers, destroyed stores, and then, by a circuit, escaped into their own lines.

June 15.—The Union tug Spitfire captured the rebel steamer Clara Dolson, loaded with 1000 bales of cotton, in Bayou Legreux, Arkansas.

—— The United States gunboat Tahoma, Lieutenant Howell, and the Somerset, Lieutenant English, captured a fort near the light-house, St. Mark's River, Florida, burned the buildings, and destroyed the works.

June 17.—Two United States gunboats bombarded rebel batteries erected on the banks of the Mississippi River, near Grand Gulf, Mississippi. The engagement was severe, the two boats being struck with forty-two shot. They retired, with the loss of 1 man killed, and 1 wounded.

—— An expedition, consisting of the United States gunboats Mound City, Captain A. H. Kilty, St. Louis, Captain McGunnigle, Conestoga, Captain G. W. Blodgett, Lexington, Captain J. W. Shirk, with the tug Spitfire and transports, with Colonel G. N. Fitch's 46th Indiana regiment, went up the White River, Arkansas, for the purpose of destroying rebel gunboats and transports which had been run up that stream. They encountered two batteries, one of which was silenced; the other threw shot from heavy guns. The gunboats answered with spirit. During the engagement, a 42-pound ball from the fort struck the Mound City, and exploded the steam-drum, causing a horrible destruction of life. There were 181 officers and sailors on board. Many jumped overboard, and, while struggling in the water, were fired upon from the lower battery, and by sharp-shooters, who also fired at the crews of the boats which went to rescue them. In the mean while, Colonel Fitch had landed his troops below, and, by a quick march, he surprised the second fortification, taking it in the rear by assault. Several rebels were killed. The commander, Captain Fry, was wounded, and about 30 taken prisoners. Rebel loss, about 200 killed and wounded,—the greater proportion being killed. There were scalded in the Mound City 154 officers and men,—the most of whom died.

June 18.—Commander Palmer dropped down with the United States squadron to the batteries at Grand Gulf, Mississippi, and shelled the town for an hour. The rebels deserted their batteries.

—— Cumberland Gap, Tennessee, taken by General George W. Morgan, U.S. Volunteers,—the rebels having evacuated it in consequence of the operations of General Morgan, which gave him the command of the Gap from the Pine and Cumberland Mountains.

June 20.—Holly Springs, Mississippi, occupied by a portion of General Sherman's (Union) troops, who destroyed trestle-work in various places on the Mississippi Central Railroad.

June 21.—A rebel camp at Simon's Bluff, South Carolina, was shelled by the United States gunboat Crusader. It was abandoned by the enemy, and destroyed.

June 23.—Battle of Secessionville, South Carolina; 12,000 Federals, commanded by General Benham, were directed, under Generals Wright, Stevens, and Williams, to assault a rebel battery on James Island. By some means, Stevens got into action before the other divisions came up: he had 4000 men; the rebels, 14,000. Stevens stormed the batteries three times, and was repulsed as often, losing very severely. The other divisions did not come up until an hour afterward. Federal loss, 863 killed, wounded, and missing.

June 24.—At 3 A.M., President Lincoln, who had come from Washington by express-trains, arrived at West Point, New York,—whither he had gone to consult Lieutenant-General Scott—it was supposed—upon matters of great moment. After a conference of some hours' duration, the President returned to Washington in eight hours and twenty minutes from West Point,—the fastest trip on record.

June 26.—The left wing of General McClellan's army before Richmond advanced their pickets, under Generals Kearney and Hooker, to Tavern Hill, near Richmond, and gained an advantageous position. Federal loss, 200 killed and wounded.

of Stuart's rebel cavalry
[Tunstall Station, in the
hich "raid" was afterward
 which justified the subse-
ls,—it was determined by
al troops to evacuate these
so that he could obtain his
ames River. This move-
, by despatching transports
e Pamunkey River, to the
'as designed to be the new
night of the same day, it
Iouse that the rebel corps
Ewell were approaching,
k on the White House, but
ck the right flank of the
e post until the evacuation
l States gunboats were so
as to command the land-
eleven miles from White
shown in loading cars and
ith rapidity.

:e rams Monarch and Lan-
utenant-Colonel Alfred M.
liver, Arkansas, after the
which escaped from Mem-
olk and Livingston. The
nt them adrift against the
g to involve the latter in
backed out, and the rebel

?arragut, U.S. Navy, with
d Vicksburg, under fire of
Commodore Davis's gun-
deral fleet, 4 were killed,

, Judge of the United States
, Middle, and Eastern Dis-
rved from his office by the
impeachment, trial, and
the rebellion.
resident, the forces under
nd McDowell were con-
called "the Army of Vir-
)mmand of Major-General
Fremont, the second under
IcDowell. Fremont with-
he ground that he should
 officer whose commission
1.
ille, Virginia (called by the
'am," and "Battle of Elly-
it of a series of engagements
me that General McClellan
is army and moving for a
James River. Whether the
s intention, or had planned
f his designs, is not now
was that during the whole
pon his force with eager-
d States troops with fury,
 commenced by a move-
an's division by the rebels
:stimated at 55,000), near
tly afterward, the real as-
l McCall's division of the
heavy forces. They were
and musketry, and driven
both sides. The engage-
ck in the afternoon until
st assailed were the Penn-
ket-duty, who fell back to
 of McCall's division held
il they were reinforced by
Porter's corps. The rebels
vier losses than the Union
:cted by their rifle-pits and
:illed on the Federal side
:kson, 11th Pennsylvania
, 11th Pennsylvania Re-

serves; among the prisoners, Colonel Gallagher, 11th Pennsylvania Reserves. The rebels were in three columns, commanded by Generals "Stonewall" Jackson, Branch, and A. P. Hill; under whom were General D. H. Hill, Brigadiers Pender, Ripley, &c.

June 27.—Battle of "Gaines' Hill," or "Gaines' Mill" (both of which names are given to it). General Porter's corps, after the fight of the previous day, was ordered to retire in good order toward the James River. The movement was covered by McCall's Pennsylvania Reserve division, with the artillery. The march commenced at three o'clock in the morning, and was slowly conducted,—bridges being destroyed, and such stores as could not be carried off being burned. The rebels followed in great force. Near Woodbury's Bridge, Porter's men made a stand. The country was open and suitable for a field-fight. At noon the action commenced, and was maintained with spirit until near dark. At this time the rebels were strongly reinforced; and Porter was reinforced by Generals Slocum, French, Meagher, and Palmer. These met the desperate onset of the rebels with determination; and, after severe fighting, they repulsed them twice by bayonet-charges, but were finally flanked, overwhelmed, and compelled to fall back. The rebels were the corps of Jackson, Ewell, Longstreet, and the two Hills, with Brigadiers Pryor, Wilcox, Featherstone, Hood, Whiting, and Pender. The Federals lost 26 guns and large quantities of small arms. But the retreat was so well managed that they spiked many guns, set fire to commissary-stores and camp-equipage, broke up wagons, and carried off most of the dead and wounded. There were killed upon the Federal side Colonel Samuel W. Black, 62d Pennsylvania; Colonel John W. McLane, 83d Pennsylvania; Lieutenant-Colonel Sweetser, 62d Pennsylvania; Colonel Gove, 22d Massachusetts; Colonel Roberts, 1st Michigan; Lieutenant-Colonel Skillen, 14th New York; Colonel Pratt, 18th New York; Major Russell, U.S. Regulars; Colonel Gosline, 95th Pennsylvania; Lieutenant-Colonel William H. Hatch, 4th New Jersey; Major William Birney, 4th New Jersey; Major Hubbs, 95th Pennsylvania; Major Neagle, 83d Pennsylvania; Colonel Tucker, 2d New Jersey; Lieutenant-Colonel Heth, 5th Maine; and Major Blitz, 12th New York.

—— A battle, on the left, at "Coal Harbor," or "Cold Harbor,"—a part of the same battle, but fought at some distance from the principal battle-field. In this engagement the rebels lost General Wheat,—a notorious filibuster and adventurer. This affair was under the direction, on the rebel side, of General Toombs. The troops which attempted to make the charge were the 7th and 8th Georgia regiments. They were repulsed, with loss,—confessing to 188 killed, wounded, and missing; among whom were Colonel Lamar, 8th Georgia, wounded and taken prisoner, and Lieutenant-Colonel Towers, 8th Georgia, prisoner. The Federal loss was trifling.

—— The work of evacuation and removal at the White House being concluded, and very little property of value remaining, that station was evacuated about nine o'clock in the evening. Every thing combustible had been before that time destroyed; the immense fleet of transports had gone off safely; the gunboats alone remained. The rebels appeared on the river-bank about nine o'clock in the evening: they were received by a heavy fire from the gunboats, which was kept up for some time. With this parting salute the post was abandoned, and the rebels gained nothing at the White House but ashes, embers, and rubbish.

—— By the advance of "Stonewall" Jackson upon Mechanicsville, two regiments (the 17th New York, and the 18th Massachusetts, under Colonel Lansing) were cut off from the main body of the army. They had been stationed at Old Church. General Stoneman's cavalry were also cut off. These troops repaired to White House station. The infantry were taken off by the transports; the cavalry proceeded down the peninsula to Williamsburg and Yorktown, and finally arrived safely at Fort Monroe.

June 28.—A fight at Garnett's farm, Virginia. The

retreat of General McClellan's army to the James River was continued. His whole force was now across the Chickahominy. The trains pressed on, protected by troops. The enemy also crossed the Chickahominy, and made an attack, at Garnett's farm, upon four companies of the 33d New York, and three of the 49th Pennsylvania,—not more than 500 men.

June 29.—110 men of the Louisville provost-guard, and a detachment of Captain Andrews's Michigan battery, under command of Captain John O. Daily, were surprised at Henderson, Kentucky. The enemy were routed. Lieutenant Andrews was killed, and Captain Daily wounded.

—— The British steamer Ann, which had run past the blockading fleet in the darkness of the previous night, was cut out from under the guns of Fort Morgan by the United States steamer Kanawha. An action took place between the United States steam-frigates Susquehanna and Kanawha and the fort,—during which the steamer was abandoned and went adrift. She was then taken possession of by a portion of the crew of the Kanawha, under a severe fire.

—— Battle of Peach Orchard, Virginia. The front of the Federal army which had menaced Richmond was ordered to fall back. The enemy discovered the movement, and followed cautiously. At daylight on the 29th, they attacked a portion of Sumner's corps and of Heintzelman's. They were allowed to approach within three hundred yards, when the whole force of artillery opened upon them. They fell back, standing this fire for half an hour; after that, they replied but feebly. The engagement lasted four hours, and was fought, on the Federal side, by Meagher, Richardson, and Sedgwick, with a loss of about 150 killed and wounded; a rebel loss of 1500. The rebels afterward attempted to charge through the brigades of Burns, Dana, and Gorman, but were repulsed. The victory here was a decided one on the Union side. Having held the position as long as was necessary, the Federal troops marched on to Savage's Station, in order to concentrate with other corps.

—— Battle of Savage's Station, Virginia. After the battle of Peach Orchard, in the morning, the enemy pressed on rapidly after the Federal army. At Savage's Station, Sedgwick's division and other troops were attacked, but fought their way until they reached White Oak Swamp, which they crossed after dark, after some fighting near the crossing. The enemy did not attempt the passage that night. During the battle, the railroad-bridge across the Chickahominy was destroyed, a train, with locomotive and twelve cars, was run overboard under a full head of steam, and large quantities of provisions and stores were burned. The United States hospital at Savage's Station was abandoned, and the sick and wounded—many of them in the battles of the previous days—were left behind and fell into the hands of the enemy. The rebel troops were McLaw's division, with Kershaw's, Semmes's, and Griffith's brigades of Magruder's division, and others. They were reinforced, toward the end of the engagement, by Magruder's division on the south side, and Stuart's cavalry on the north. The Federal troops engaged were the brigades of Martindale, Murell's and McCall's divisions. Heintzelman guarded the rear in the retreat, and had the principal command during the battle. Two guns were captured by Meagher's brigade. The Federal loss was estimated, at Savage's Station, at from 700 to 1000 killed and wounded,—besides the large number of Federal wounded concentrated there in hospitals from the previous actions, all of whom fell into the hands of the rebels. The Federals took 500 prisoners, whom they were also compelled to release. Wounded, Colonel Pierce, 29th Massachusetts (General Pierce at Big Bethel, three-months volunteers); killed, Colonel Hinks. Killed on the rebel side, General Griffith, and General Rhett, South Carolina.

June 30.—General Crawford, with a portion of his brigade, and cavalry under Colonel Tompkins, entered Luray, Virginia, driving in the rebel pickets and four companies of cavalry: 4 prisoners were taken, and some wounded. Federal loss, 1 killed, and 3 wounded.

June 30.—Battle of Wh man's corps, United Stat toward the James River, enemy being in pursuit, tl Oak Swamp and Four-Mi which was done by the eng were under Brigadiers Han others. The rebels were v with D. H. Hill, Whiting, a of the bridges hindered th Federal artillery was poste and the crossing. The bat a tremendous fire, during Mott's New York battery some desperate efforts to cr repulsed and kept back b whilst the main body of He toward the James River.

—— Battle of Charl rebels having been prevent Swamp in front, hope was be kept off at other points. appointed. About 5 P.M., I corps attacked Heintzelman fierceness. The fight comm the afternoon, and continue The ground was hotly cont rebels pressed in to muske heavy firing from the Fed was reinforced by Porter an efforts and severe losses, th field.

—— Battle of Glend Roads, Virginia. A portion withdrawn from the intre were followed up by the on sion took part in the battle greater part remained with On the 30th, the rebels be division, Pennsylvania R which had suffered seve Gaines' Mill, and was wor stood his ground bravely, being reinforced by Hooker rent of disaster. Late in Aroostook and Galena, i range of the masses of the mond, and opened upon th the direction in which the by the signal-corps. This rebels to waver. They vigorous charge, led by II they broke and fled. The rible. The Federal loss w wounded, and prisoners; t heavier. 1000 rebel prison killed on the Federal side Massachusetts; prisoners, vania Reserves, and Gener

July 1.—Battle of Mal rebel General Magruder at Federal forces. The Unit previous night reached the at Harrison's Landing, wh its occupation,—the large saved,—General McClella enemy a better reception t during the retreat. He a an attack, posted his artill as to command every aven fought furiously, and adva most destructive fire. Th terrible fierceness and wit damage upon the Federal more severely than in any sula, and, after vain ende retreated to Richmond. 7 by Longstreet, A. P. Hill, the brigades of Toombs, Armistead.

se battles of the peninsula
.anicsville to Malvern Hills
follows :—

Killed.	Wounded.	Missing.
170	1068	848
189	1051	833
69	507	201
573	3700	2779
245	1313	1179
...	2	21
19	60	97
1265	7701	5958

ebel loss was never officially
d at 18,000, but could not
he Federal army, in conse-
of the latter in artillery.
Federal side, during the six
nd Burns.
' eighteen loyal States pre-
ident of the United States,
an increase of the army.
ed to call out 300,000 men.
nts, numbering 4700 men,
nel Sheridan, commanding
ce-guard of Curtis's army
h of Booneville, Missouri.
ld in check for five hours,
al loss, 41 killed, wounded,
ft 65 dead on the field.
el) command in the Indian
rised by Union troops : 75
104 taken prisoners, 30
red mules and ponies, and
ts, equipage, &c. Federal

rdment was opened upon
the combined fleet of the
odore D. C. Farragut and
They were answered from
e the town, and the firing
ntil night. The bombard-
and continued many days ;
many operations,—among
the course of the Missi-
nal across a bend of land,
int above to a point below
ed entirely. The water of
ugh the canal.
at Teaser was captured on
ited States gunboat Mara-
with a balloon made of old
inflated for the purpose of
neral McClellan's camps at

Clellan, in camp at Harri-
lress to his troops, in which
or forces, and without hope
ucceeded in changing your
nk movement,—always re-
us of military operations.
birthday we declare to our
the best interests of man-
ater the capital of their so-

a rebels and General David-
s Landing, Virginia. The
me prisoners.
dela, attempting to run the
the United States gunboat
ida.
b, making a reconnoissance
with 4000 men, came sud-
f General Hindman's rebel
was a fight. Fitch was
reinforced by 400 more In-
ven from the field of battle.
ounded, and 40 taken pri-
, and 4 wounded. Colonel
aries.

July 7.—The British steamer Emily (formerly the William Seabrook) was captured off Bull's Bay, South Carolina, while attempting to run the blockade, by the United States steamer Flag and bark Restless.
——— Captain Charles Wilkes was appointed to the command of the James River flotilla.
——— A portion of Major-General Burnside's division arrived at Fort Monroe from North Carolina,—they being intended to assist General McClellan either by reinforcement or co-operation, as might be determined.
——— A battle near Cotton Plant, Arkansas, between the advance of General Curtis's army, under General Steele, and 6000 rebels. The latter were worsted, and fied toward Little Rock. 110 of the rebel enemy were found dead on the field. Union loss, 8 killed, and 32 wounded.
——— An engagement near Pleasant Hills, Missouri, between a company of State militia, and Quantrill's guerrilla band. The latter were repulsed, with a loss of 6 killed, and 5 wounded. The Federals had 9 killed, and 15 wounded.
July 8.—A rebel battery at Corpus Christi Bayou, Texas, abandoned by the rebels, was taken by Captain Kittridge, U.S. Navy, who raised the American flag.
July 9.—An engagement on Roanoke River, North Carolina, between the United States gunboats Commodore Perry, Ceres, and Shawsheen, with a company of Hawkins's New York Zouaves, and a regiment of rebel cavalry, supported by artillery. The gunboats intended to proceed to Hamilton. At a point six miles above Williamston they met with barricades, and were fired upon by infantry in ambush on shore. The latter were dispersed with shell. The barricades were then blown up, and the fleet proceeded, being fired upon frequently from masked batteries and by rebels on shore. At Hamilton there was a heavy fort, well manned, and a steamer loaded with sharp-shooters approached. The decks of the latter were swept by the cannon of the gunboats, a force was landed from the gunboats, the batteries were flanked, and the fort taken by a charge made by the United States soldiers and sailors. Hamilton was then occupied. There were captured the rebel steamer, a large number of vessels, commissary-stores, cotton, &c. Federal loss, 2 killed, and 12 wounded.
——— Colonel Williams's Pennsylvania cavalry, at Tompkinsville, Kentucky, was attacked by 1500 rebel cavalry, under Morgan, with 3 pieces of 4 artillery. The Federals were routed, with a loss of 4 killed, and 20 prisoners; the Federals lost 9 killed, and several wounded. Major Jordan was among the prisoners.
July 10.—Memphis, Missouri, was taken by guerrillas: 20 citizens were carried off as prisoners.
July 11.—450 rebel cavalry, commanded by Jack Allen, were encountered and defeated at New Hope, Nelson county, Kentucky, by a party of the 35th Ohio regiment, Lieutenant-Colonel Moore.
——— Lebanon, Kentucky, burned by Allen's guerrillas, who robbed two banks, and committed other outrages.
——— The army of General Curtis, after long and forced marches from Batesville, Arkansas, which they left June 24, arrived at Helena, Arkansas.
——— Major-General Henry W. Halleck appointed to the command of all the land-forces of the United States.
——— Excitement in Cincinnati, Ohio, in consequence of the rebel raid which threatened Lexington, Frankfort, and Louisville, Kentucky. Troops were sent forward to Lexington. The City Councils appropriated $5000 to equip them and send them forward.
July 13.—Culpepper, Virginia, occupied by General Hatch (Federal), who repulsed 100 rebel cavalry, wounding 5, and taking 11 prisoners.
——— Forrest's rebel cavalry (about 4000 in number) captured Murfreesboro', Tennessee. The 9th Michigan regiment, Colonel Parkhurst, was captured; also General T. T. Crittenden and Colonel Duffield (acting brigadier). The rebels destroyed the railroad-depôt, &c. There was a desperate fight. The 9th Pennsylvania

cavalry lost, in killed, wounded, and missing, 200 men. The Federal loss was 33 killed, and 62 wounded, besides 800 prisoners; rebel loss, 50 killed, and 100 wounded.

July 13.—A dash was made at Orange Court-House, Virginia, by Federal cavalry, who tore up the railroad, burned the bridge across the Rapidan, and destroyed stores and munitions of war.

July 14.—The long bridge on the Kentucky Central Railroad, between Cynthiana and Paris, destroyed by a portion of Morgan's rebel cavalry.

———— The President of the United States sent to Congress a message recommending the passage of a law guaranteeing compensation from the public treasury to any State which would abolish slavery. It was accompanied by the draft of a bill for that purpose.

———— Major-General Pope issued an address to the army of Virginia, in which he informed the troops that he was about to lead them against the foe,—adding, "In the mean time, I desire you to dismiss from your minds certain phrases which I am sorry to find much in vogue among you. I hear constantly of *taking strong positions* and holding them, of *lines of retreat* and *bases of supplies*. Let us discard such ideas. The strongest position a soldier should desire to occupy is one from which he can most easily advance against the enemy. Let us study the probable lines of retreat of our opponents, and leave our own to take care of themselves. Let us look before, and not behind. Success and glory are in the advance; disaster and shame lurk in the rear."

July 15.—1600 rebels, under Rains, Coffee, Hunter, Hawthorne, and Tracy, were attacked, at Fayetteville, Arkansas, by 600 Federal troops, with 2 guns, and dispersed, the main body being pursued for twelve miles.

———— The rebel ram Arkansas (iron-clad), Lieutenant Brown commanding, came out of the Yazoo River, Arkansas, and ran down the Mississippi through the whole Federal fleet above Vicksburg, receiving the fire of several of the vessels without apparent injury. Loss on the United States ships, 12 killed, and 15 wounded.

———— The United States fleet (Atlantic squadron), under command of Commodore D. C. Farragut, which had previously passed the rebel batteries at Vicksburg, Mississippi, and joined the river squadron under Captain Davis, again ran past Vicksburg, on a downward passage, amidst a heavy fire from the batteries and the iron-plated ram Arkansas. A shot from one of the United States vessels passed through the Arkansas, and killed 2 men, and wounded 3.

July 17.—Cynthiana, Kentucky, captured, after an hour's fight, by Morgan's rebel guerrillas.

———— Henderson, Kentucky, taken by rebel guerrillas.

———— Newburg, Indiana, taken by rebel guerrillas, who crossed the Ohio for the purpose: 1 Federal was killed, and 250 sick soldiers taken prisoners; there were also taken 250 stand of arms.

July 18.—Major-General Pope, commanding the army of Virginia, issued a General Order (No. 5), declaring that his troops "should subsist upon the country in which their operations are carried on." Also Order No. 6, in relation to the manner in which celerity of movement could be best obtained by the army. Also Order No. 7, notifying the people of the Valley of the Shenandoah, and throughout the region in which the army operated, that they would be held responsible for any injury done to railroad-tracks, bridges, telegraph-lines, or attacks upon trains or straggling soldiers, by guerrilla bands in their neighborhood; that, whenever any damage was done, the people within five miles of the place where the outrage occurred should be compelled to repair it, and that full assessments for all damages should be levied upon them by military force; individuals detected in outrages against property or persons would be shot, without waiting for civil process.

July 19.—General Green Clay Smith, with 1000 cavalry, attacked Morgan's guerrillas, on Garret Davis's farm, Kentucky, and put them to flight, with a loss of 14 killed, and 17 prisoners.

July 20.—A Federal cavalry expedition, under Colonel Mansfield Davies, New York Ira Harris cavalry, by a forced march from Fredericksburg, Virginia, reached the Virginia Central Railroad at Beaver-Dam Creek, twenty-five miles west of Hanover Junction, and thirty-five miles from Richmond. They destroyed the track for several miles, burned the railroad-depôt, exploded 40,000 rounds of musket-ammunition, with flour and other valuable property. The troops marched eighty miles in thirty hours, and returned safely.

———— Hon. John S. Phelps, of Missouri, appointed Military Governor of Arkansas by President Lincoln.

July 21.—Morgan's rebel cavalry were overtaken on the road to Owensville, Kentucky, and scattered, after a fight of an hour and a half. Some of their plunder taken at Cynthiana was recaptured. Rebel loss, 25 killed; Union loss, 20 killed.

———— 100 rebel cavalry, near Carmel Church, Virginia, were attacked by a cavalry expedition sent out by General King, U.S. Army, and scattered. Their camp was burned, and also six cars laden with corn. Afterward the Federals were attacked by Stuart's rebel cavalry, who were defeated and driven back, with loss, across the North Ann River. Our cavalry returned, after a march of seventy miles made in twenty-nine hours, in which they had two fights.

———— The rebel steamer Reliance, loaded with cotton, attempting to run the blockade, was captured near Doboy bar, Georgia, by the United States steamer Huntsville, Commander Rodgers.

July 22.—Rebel guerrillas entered Florence, Alabama, burned the United States warehouses for army-storage, burned a United States steamer, and took some of General Mitchel's troops prisoners. They then proceeded down the Tennessee River to Chickasaw, Waterloo, and Eastport, where they burned all the warehouses which contained cotton.

———— United States steamer Ceres (transport), Captain Mitchell, was fired into, below Vicksburg, from three pieces of artillery stationed on the shore. She received twenty-one shots, by which Captain Brooks, 1st Vermont, was killed. The boat finally escaped.

———— British steamer Ladona, endeavoring to run the blockade at Savannah, was captured by the United States gunboat Unadilla.

———— An unsuccessful attempt was made to destroy the rebel ram Arkansas, lying under the protection of the batteries at Vicksburg, Mississippi, by the United States gunboat Essex and the ram Queen of the West. They were to have been supported by the United States fleets above and below Vicksburg, which were to engage the upper and lower batteries. By some misunderstanding, this was not done, and the two boats had to stand all the fire of the batteries. The ram did not strike the Arkansas fairly, but grazed her side. Loss on the Arkansas, 7 killed by a ball which entered a port-hole.

———— A cartel of exchange for prisoners, taken by the Federal army and by the rebel forces, agreed upon at Haxall's Landing, James River, between Major-General John A. Dix, U.S. Army, and Major-General D. H. Hill, C.S. Army. By this agreement, arrangements were made for the future exchange and parole of prisoners on both sides,—the depôts for the exchange being at Aikin's Landing, James River, Virginia, and Vicksburg, Mississippi.

July 23.—Major-General Pope issued a General Order (No. 11), directing that disloyal male citizens within the lines of the army should be arrested unless they took the oath of allegiance to the United States and gave security for their good behavior. Persons who should take the oath of allegiance and violate it were notified that they would be shot.

July 24.—The British steamer Tubal-Cain, with contraband of war, was captured at sea by Captain D. D. Porter, in the United States gunboat Octorara.

July 25.—The President of the United States issued a proclamation, in pursuance of the Act of Congress July 17, 1862, entitled, "An Act to suppress insurrection, to punish treason and rebellion, to seize and confiscate the property of rebels, and for other purposes," warning all persons "to cease participating in aiding, countenancing, or abetting the existing rebellion or any rebellion against the Government of the United States, and to return to their allegiance to the United States, on pain of the forfeitures and seizures" as by the sixth section of the said law provided. This is generally called "the sixty-days proclamation."

July 25.—By orders of the War Department, the corps of the United States army commanded by General Porter is denominated the fifth army corps; by General Franklin, the sixth; the forces under General Dix to be denominated the seventh; those under General Wool, the eighth; those under General Burnside, the ninth.

July 26.—The 10th Ohio regiment, guarding the Memphis & Charleston Railroad, between Decatur and Courtland, Tennessee, was attacked by a large force of rebel guerrillas, under Starns and Ward: 30 or 40 of the regiment were killed.

——— Courtland, Alabama, was taken by the rebel General Armstrong, with cavalry. Union loss, 3 killed and wounded, 159 prisoners, 6 railroad-cars, wagons, horses, camp-equipage, baggage, &c.

July 27.—200 guerrillas were attacked, five miles south of Patten, Missouri, by one company of Missouri militia, Lieutenant Chaveux. They were dispersed, several being killed and wounded, and their leader (Captain Patterson) being taken prisoner.

July 29.—179 guerrillas demanded the surrender of Mount Sterling, Kentucky. They were repulsed by Home Guards. In their flight, they encountered a portion of the 8th Kentucky regiment, and were driven back to Sterling, where the Home Guards again attacked them. They were dispersed, with a loss of 8 killed, 100 prisoners, and all their horses were lost; Federal loss, 1 killed, and 3 wounded.

——— A fight at Moore's Mills, Missouri, between 700 Federals, under Colonel Guitar, and a rebel force (about 800 in number) under Porter and Cobb. After an engagement of three hours, the rebels were routed, with a loss of 52 killed, and 100 wounded; Union loss, 10 killed, and 30 wounded.

——— Major Lazear, with 120 men of the 12th Missouri regiment, attacked 180 rebels, under Major Tenley, near Bollinger's Mills, Missouri, killing 10, and wounding many, without losing a man on the Federal side.

July 30.—80 rebels, near Brownsville, Missouri, were attacked by Colonel Dollins's cavalry: 40 prisoners were taken. The rebels were afterward reinforced, and recaptured 29 men and 14 horses. Federal loss, 6 wounded; rebel loss, 7 wounded.

——— The President of the United States nominated rear-admirals in the United States navy, as follows:—On the *retired list*, Charles Stewart, George C. Read, William B. Shubrick, Joseph Smith, George W. Storer, Francis H. Gregory, Elie A. F. Lavalette, Silas H. Stringham, Hiram Paulding; on the *active list*, David G. Farragut, L. M. Goldsborough, Samuel F. Dupont, A. H. Foote.

July 31.—About midnight the rebels opened an artillery fire upon the shipping and the Federal encampments at Harrison's Landing, Virginia, from the opposite side of the James River. Some of the vessels were struck, 5 men were killed, and 2 wounded. After a time, Union artillery replied, and soon silenced the rebels.

——— The British steamer Memphis, loaded with cotton, which had run the blockade at Charleston, South Carolina, was captured at sea by the United States gunboat Magnolia.

August 1.—A retaliatory order was issued by Jeff Davis, referring to the general order of the Secretary of War of the United States, directing officers of the Federal army to seize and use the private property of rebels for public use, without compensation to the owners. Reference was made to General Pope's order for the arrest of disloyal citizens within the Union lines unless they should take the oath of allegiance, &c.; also to an order of General A. Steinwehr, U.S. Army, for the arrest of five citizens of Page county, Virginia, as hostages for Union soldiers, "to suffer death in case any of the said soldiers were shot by the bushwhackers." The order then asserted that the order of the United States War Department was issued after a cartel for exchange of prisoners had been signed,—which never would have been agreed to by the Confederate Government if the intention of the United States had been known,—that a just regard to humanity forbade the punishment of enlisted men in the army of the United States "who may have been unwilling instruments of the savage cruelty of their commanders, so long as there is hope that the excesses of the enemy may be checked or prevented by retribution on the commissioned officers who may have the power to avoid guilty acti n by refusing service under a Government which set s their aid in the perpetration of such infamous barbu-_ ties." It was therefore declared that Major-General Pope, Brigadier-General Steinwehr, and all commissioned officers who served under them, should *not* be entitled to be considered as soldiers, and therefore not entitled to the benefit of the cartel for parole of future prisoners of war; "that in event of the capture of Major-General Pope, Brigadier-General Steinwehr, or any commissioned officer serving under them, the captive so taken shall be held in close confinement as long as the order aforesaid shall remain in force;" and that in the event of the execution of any hostage, under the said orders, a number of the commissioned officers of the United States, equal to the rebel bushwhackers and spies who were executed, should be hung.

August 1.—A fight at Newark, Knox county, Missouri, between 1000 of Porter's guerrillas, and two companies of Missouri militia, under Captain Lair. The latter resisted gallantly, were driven into the town, where, after a struggle, they capitulated, losing 4 killed, and 4 wounded.

——— 600 United States troops crossed the James River, opposite Harrison's Landing, to the ground which had been occupied by the rebel artillery party the previous night. The woods, dwellings, and all places that could afford protection to a lurking foe, were destroyed.

August 2.—Colonel Lowther, with 125 rebels, attacked Captain Buck's company (96 men) at Ozark, Missouri. Buck, being apprized of the movement, had abandoned his camp and burned his tents. The enemy appeared and demanded a surrender, which was responded to with musketry. The rebels broke and ran. They were pursued by Buck, and attacked on the morning of the 4th: 3 were killed, 7 wounded, and 25 taken prisoners, with 25 horses, 20 guns, &c.

——— General Burnside's corps—which, after leaving North Carolina, was encamped at Newport News, Virginia—embarked in transports and went up the Potomac River to Acquia Creek.

——— A successful reconnoissance was made to Orangetown, Virginia, by United States cavalry, under General Crawford. They engaged two regiments of rebel cavalry, under General Robertson: 11 of the rebels were killed, and 52 taken prisoners; Union loss, 2 killed, and 3 wounded. The railroad and telegraph between Orange Court-House and Gordonsville were destroyed.

August 3.—McMinnville, Tennessee, occupied by General Nelson, U.S. Army. The rebel Forrest fled.

——— A reconnoissance of United States cavalry was made upon the south side of the James River. They advanced to within fourteen miles of Petersburg. At Cox's Mills, five miles from the river, they encountered the 13th Virginia cavalry, drawn up in line of battle. The latter were charged upon, when they broke and fled to their encampment at Sycamore Church, two and a half miles farther, where they again formed, but were routed, leaving their tents and stores, all of which were burned.

——— 90 United States troops were surprised by rebels, fifteen miles above Helena, Arkansas, and all but two killed and captured.

August 4.—By proclamation of the President of the United States, a draft was ordered for 300,000 militia, to be immediately called into service.

August 4.—Major-General Butler, in command at New Orleans, issued an order declaring that he had discovered that certain corporations and persons had, before the capture of the city, contributed $1,250,000 to a fund for the purpose of defending New Orleans against the Federal Government, to be disbursed by a "committee of safety." Also that certain cotton-brokers had, in October, 1861, published a manifesto advising the planters not to bring their produce to the city. It was therefore ordered that the subscribers to the million-and-a-quarter rebel loan-fund should be assessed at the rate of one-fourth of that subscription ($312,716) for the support of the poor of New Orleans, and upon the cotton-brokers the sum of $29,200,—all of which sums were to be collected by seizures of the property of the persons named, if they neglected or refused to pay the sums assessed.

August 5.—An expedition, under General Hooker, went to Malvern Hills, Virginia, where rebel infantry, with artillery, were encountered. After three hours' firing, principally by field-pieces, the rebels fled. The intention was that they should have been intercepted by Patterson's brigade; but this part of the plan failed. Union loss, 20 killed and wounded; 128 prisoners were taken, and 4 guns.

——— An engagement at Tazewell, near Cumberland Gap, Tennessee, between De Courcey's Federal brigade, and Stevenson's rebel division in force. The rebels lost 225 killed and wounded. Lieutenant-Colonel Gerdon Ellerult, of Tennessee, was taken prisoner. Union loss, 3 killed, 15 wounded, and 50 prisoners.

——— General John C. Breckinridge, with 5000 rebels and 14 field-pieces, made an attack upon Baton Rouge, Louisiana, which was defended by 2500 Union troops, under General Thomas Williams. The latter fought gallantly, and repulsed the charges made by the enemy,—using the artillery on the flank with great effect. The rebels made a desperate attempt here to turn the Federal rear, but were beaten back, after having for a period carried the camps of three regiments and destroyed a portion of the baggage. The rebels intended that their iron ram Arkansas should have co-operated; but that boat ran aground six miles above, and was *hors de combat*. In the battle, General Thomas Williams, U.S. Army, was killed by a rifle-ball through the head. Federal loss, 70 killed, and 215 wounded. The enemy left 300 dead and 70 wounded on the field; 30 were captured,—among the latter, Brigadier-General Charles Clarke and his aide-de-camp, Colonel Lovell, commanding a brigade, and Captain A. H. Todd (a brother of Mrs. Lincoln, wife of the President of the United States); wounded, Colonel Allen, 4th Louisiana, Colonel S. Boyd, Louisiana battalion, Colonel Charles Jones, Colonel A. P. Thompson, and Colonel Thomas H. Hart, 5th Kentucky.

August 6.—General Robert L. McCook, U.S. Army, sick, and riding in an ambulance near Salem, Tennessee, was murdered by a party of rebel guerrillas.

——— The rebel ram Arkansas, which was intended to participate in the attack on Baton Rouge, Louisiana, the previous day, was attacked by the United States iron-clad gunboat Essex, Commander W. D. Porter. His solid nine-inch shot made a breach in the bow of the Arkansas, and an incendiary shell set her on fire. Her crew fought her until the last; but, the flames gaining on them, they abandoned her, and, shortly after, the Arkansas blew up, leaving scarcely a floating vestige of this pride of the Western rebel navy. The Arkansas mounted 10 heavy guns, the Essex 7 guns. The Arkansas had a crew of 180 men; the Essex had but 40 men.

August 7.—A fight at Kirkville, Missouri, between Colonel Neill's Union troops (1000 strong) and 2500 of Porter's guerrillas. The latter were put to flight. 128 dead rebels were found on the field. Their entire loss in wounded and prisoners was estimated at 150 men; Federal loss, 8 killed, and 25 wounded. Among the prisoners taken were 16 men who had previously taken the oath of allegiance to the United States: they were tried by a drum-head court-martial and shot.

——— Captain Peck, with 53 men of the 6th Illinois cavalry, surprised Faulkner's rebel cavalry, near Humboldt, Tennessee: 35 were killed, and 55 horses and many arms captured; Union loss, 7 killed, and 2 wounded.

August 8.—Order of the United States War Department issued, declaring that no citizen liable to be drafted shall be allowed to go into a foreign country, or absent himself from his county or State, before the draft is made.

——— Order of the United States War Department, directing the arrest of all persons who may discourage volunteer enlistments.

——— A skirmish at Wolfstain, Virginia, between Union pickets and a body of rebel cavalry. The 2d Pennsylvania cavalry, Colonel R. Butler Price, charged upon the rebels and drove them beyond the Rapidan, killing 2, and wounding several; Federal loss, 1 killed.

August 9.—Battle of Tazewell, Tennessee, between Stevenson's rebel forces, numbering 12,000, and 3000 Federal troops, under Colonel De Courcey. After a brisk fight, the rebels were routed, with a loss of 250 killed and wounded, 213 wagons of forage, and 70 horses. The Federals lost 3 killed, 15 wounded, and 57 prisoners.

——— Battle of Cedar Mountain, Virginia (called by the rebels "the battle of Southwest Mountain"). "Stonewall" Jackson and Ewell, with a force of 24,913 rebels, attacked General Bayard's cavalry, in the advance of General Banks's corps. There was skirmishing for some time before Banks came up. The fight was then, and for some time afterward, wholly with artillery. The enemy had their batteries posted on the mountains, and they fired with deadly effect as our troops moved up. At six o'clock in the afternoon the infantry became engaged, and the rebels came upon them in force at all points. The latter were repulsed with vigor, and fell back, relying henceforth upon their batteries, which fired until midnight. The Federal troops were under arms all night. At nine o'clock at night, McDowell's men took the place of Banks's corps, and the latter moved to the rear. In this battle there were not more than 7000 Federal troops engaged; but their loss was heavy. The enemy sent in a flag of truce for permission to bury their dead, and afterward retreated across the Rapidan. On the Union side were killed Major Cook, 28th New York, Lieutenant-Colonel Stone, 5th Connecticut, Colonel Coggswell, 55th Ohio, Colonel Crane, 3d Wisconsin, and Colonel Chapman, 5th Massachusetts; wounded, General Augur, General Geary, and Colonel Creighton, 7th Ohio. Among the prisoners taken were General Prince, Captain Watkins, and 24 other officers. The Federal loss was about 1250 killed and wounded, and 250 prisoners. On the rebel side, General C. S. Winder was killed. Their loss in killed, wounded, and missing was supposed to have been heavier than that of the Federal troops.

——— Colonel Wynkoop's Pennsylvania cavalry attacked Colonel Forrest's rebel force, on Calf River, near Sparta, Tennessee, and killed 30 of them.

August 10.—The rebel steamer General Lee, which, under pretence of being a flag of truce, came down the Savannah River to reconnoitre Fort Pulaski, was chased and captured as soon as the fraud became apparent.

August 11.—A fight at Kinderhook, Kentucky, between McGowan's Federal cavalry (108 in number), and 175 guerrillas: 7 of the latter were killed and several wounded, and 27 were taken prisoners; Union loss, 3 killed.

——— Bayou Sara, Louisiana, taken possession of by United States forces.

——— Independence, Missouri, was captured by 600 rebels, under General Hughes and Quantrill. The United States troops, under Colonel Buell, lost 20 killed; the rest (230) surrendered, with large quantities of stores and munitions of war. General Hughes was killed.

August 12.—The rebel Morgan, with 1800 cavalry and 4 pieces of artillery, entered Gallatin, Tennessee, and captured Colonel Boone, commanding the post, with 300 men of the 28th Kentucky regiment, 60 horses, corn, oats, &c.

August 12.—A part of Morgan's rebel force at Gallatin, Tennessee, was surprised by Union troops under Colonel Miller: 6 rebels were killed, of whom 3 were officers. No loss on the Federal side.

August 13.—A collision on the Potomac River, off Ragged Point, between the steamers Peabody and West Point: the latter sunk. She was loaded with convalescent soldiers of Burnside's army, and 79 of the crew and passengers were drowned.

August 14.—Poindexter's guerrilla band was attacked at Muscle Fork, Missouri, by Colonel Guitar's Union troops, and scattered in all directions. They were pursued for sixteen miles, and lost 300 killed and wounded.

August 15.—United States gunboat Sumter (rebel prize) grounded near Bayou Sara, Louisiana. The captain and crew left her in a boat to obtain assistance. While they were away, rebel guerrillas boarded the steamer, which they fired and destroyed. For this act the village of Francisville, near by, was burned by the crews of Union gunboats.

August 16.—General McClellan succeeded in conveying and marching his whole army from head-quarters at Harrison's Landing, near James River, Virginia. Some of the troops were sent down in transports, but others marched by land, crossing the Chickahominy by a pontoon bridge, and passing through Williamsburg, Yorktown, and Newport News to Fortress Monroe. This movement was effected without any opposition on the part of the enemy. Thus, General McClellan's change of base from the Pamunkey and York Rivers to the James River was the forerunner of the movement of his entire army from the Peninsula to Alexandria and Washington, whither it was transported, the entire campaign and movement on Richmond by that route having proved a failure.

———— Captain Smith, with 70 (loyal) Kentucky Home Guards, pursuing Witcher's rebel band, overtook them near Warfield, Kentucky, they numbering 208. After a sharp fight, the latter fled, and were again pursued. Smith's force was then divided into detachments, which sought the enemy in different directions. One squad of 11 men, under Captain Smith, overtook 60 rebels at the Falls of Guyan, where a fight took place, lasting several hours, resulting in the defeat of the rebels, with 9 killed, 30 prisoners, 30 horses, and 40 muskets. Smith lost 2 men killed, and 4 wounded. For the numbers engaged on the Union side, this fight was one of the most gallant and successful during the war.

August 17.—Two bridges on the Kentucky and Edgefield Railroad, and one over Red River, Tennessee, were burned by rebels.

———— Beriah Magoffin (rebel sympathizer), Governor of Kentucky, resigned. James F. Robinson, Speaker of the Senate, became the acting Governor.

———— English steamer Columbia, loaded with Armstrong guns and Enfield rifles, was captured at sea by the United States gunboat Santiago de Cuba.

August 18.—Steamers Skylark and Callie burned by rebel guerrillas at the mouth of Duck Creek, Tennessee River. The Skylark was heavily loaded with Government stores.

———— General Pope's army, which after the battle of Cedar Mountain, Virginia, had advanced but little beyond that field, began a retrograde march in consequence of information of the movements of "Stonewall" Jackson and other rebel generals menacing Washington and Pope's flank and rear. The "line of retreat" was toward the Rappahannock.

———— General Braxton Bragg, commanding the rebel "army of the West," issued a proclamation at Glasgow, Kentucky, to the people of that State, in which he informed them that he had come among them to offer them "an opportunity to free themselves from the tyranny of a despotic ruler." He promised that he would not be a conqueror or despoiler, but would restore to them "the liberties of which they had been deprived by a cruel and relentless foe. . . . Kentuckians, we have come with joyous hopes. Let us not depart in sorrow, as we shall if we find you wedded in your choice to your present lot. If you prefer Union rule, show it by your frowns, and we shall return from whence we came."

August 19.—Union cavalry, under Captain Frank Moore, attacked a rebel camp at White Oak Ridge, Missouri, killed 4, and took 19 prisoners, among them three captains; 27 horses and 100 stand of arms were captured. On the Federal side 2 were wounded.

August 20.—1500 United States troops, under General Blunt, drove a large force of rebels across the Osage River, Missouri, with the loss of all their baggage, transportation, and equipments.

———— A skirmish, about ten o'clock in the morning, near Brandy Station, Virginia, between the New Jersey, New York, and Rhode Island cavalry, and Stuart's rebel cavalry, in which the latter were driven back with loss, and some loss upon the Federal side. Same afternoon, there was another skirmish, in which three or four companies 1st New Jersey cavalry were made prisoners.

———— The rebel steam war-vessel Florida, formerly the Ovieto, commanded by Captain Maffit, came into Cardenas, Cuba, and was ordered off by the authorities.

———— Captain Atkinson, of the 5th Tennessee Regiment, in a stockade at Edgefield Junction, with only 20 men, was attacked by about 1000 guerrillas. He held out bravely, and repulsed them three times, killing 8 of the rebels, and wounding 18.

———— Captain Mason, 71st Ohio, with 200 men and 2 cannon, intrenched at Clarksville, Tennessee, surrendered without resistance to 600 guerrillas under Johnson, Woodward, and Gurth. A large amount of property was taken by the rebels. This surrender has been esteemed one of the most cowardly acts during the war. Mason was cashiered by the Government for cowardice.

———— Colonel Wright, Federal, in pursuit of guerrillas under Coffee, Hayes, and Quantrell, attacked their rear-guard in Missouri, killing 12, and capturing 31, with guns, horses, &c.

August 21.—General Pope, having succeeded, in his retreat from Cedar Mountain, in crossing the Rappahannock, the rebels followed him to that river. There were skirmishes along the whole front of the Federal lines, fifteen miles in extent, during the whole time that the army held this position, in one of which skirmishes Brigadier-General Henry Bohlen was killed.

———— Rebel salt-works at Swansborough, North Carolina, were destroyed by an expedition from Newbern: 44 buildings were burned.

———— Captain Goodwin and one company of the 34th Indiana regiment were attacked near Bowling Green, Kentucky, by 500 of Woodward's rebel cavalry, with three guns. Goodwin resisted gallantly, but at length was compelled to surrender, having killed and wounded 25 of the assailants. Federal loss, 7 wounded.

August 22.—About half-past eight o'clock Colonel Stuart's and Lee's rebel cavalry, 3000 strong, made "a raid" upon Catlett's Station, Virginia, in the rear of General Pope's army, which was then guarding the line of the Rappahannock. They attacked a railroad-train, killing one fireman and a sick soldier. The engineer had put on steam before he jumped from the locomotive, and the train ran to Warrenton Station. The camp of the Bucktail Rifles (Colonel-Kane), near by, was attacked: most of the soldiers escaped after having fired one volley into the enemy, but Lieutenant-Colonel Kane, captured once before, was again a prisoner. 1 Bucktail was killed, and 15 wounded. The rebels captured General Pope's private baggage, his letters, official papers, dispatches, maps, and plans of the campaign, and his money: they destroyed army wagons and supplies. An attack was also made by them on the Purnell Legion, Maryland, Lieutenant-Colonel B. M. Simpson, and they captured two companies.

———— A fight at Edgefield Station, Virginia, between 400 of Morgan's rebel cavalry, under Lieutenant Jim Smith, and a small force under Captain Jackson, 50th Indiana, in stockade. The rebels were three times repulsed, losing 7 killed, and 20 wounded.

———— The rebel transport Fair Play, loaded with Enfield rifle-muskets, 4 field-guns, howitzers, ammunition, &c., was captured in Yazoo River, Arkansas, by a combined land and naval expedition under Colonel Woods and Captain C. H. Davis, U.S. Navy. The expedition also took a rebel battery, heavily mounted with 64-pounders and 42-pounders, and two field-pieces, and 1000 small arms, which had been abandoned; also a rebel camp, with tents, &c.

August 22.—General R. W. Johnson (Federal), with 800 Indiana, Pennsylvania, and Kentucky troops, attacked 1700 of Morgan's rebel cavalry near Gallatin, Tennessee, and were defeated, with a loss of 26 killed and 33 wounded, and 300 prisoners, including General Johnson. The remaining 441 escaped, and got safely to Nashville. Rebel loss, 13 killed and wounded.

August 23.—Rappahannock Station, Virginia, was abandoned by General Pope's troops. The bridge across the river was burned, and the abutments blown up. The depôt and railroad buildings were also burned.

———— United States steam frigate Adirondack, Commander Gansevoort, wrecked on Man-of-War Keys, Bahama group. She ran on a coral-reef. The battery was taken off and spiked, and buried, so as to be again recoverable. The stores were then removed to the mainland, and burned. The officers and crew, 204 in number, were saved.

———— A fight near Richmond, Kentucky. 400 Union troops, under Colonel L. Metcalf, were attacked by two rebel regiments, with three guns. 300 of Metcalf's men broke and fled early in the engagement, but 100 nobly stood their ground for an hour and a half, when they were compelled to fall back, with a loss of 10 killed, and 40 wounded and prisoners. Rebel loss, 25 killed and wounded.

August 24.—Colonel Garrard, with 560 men, attempting to force his way through the rebel lines surrounding General Morgan at Cumberland Gap, Kentucky, had a skirmish at Red Bend, Kentucky, with 150 rebel cavalry under Colonel Stearns: 3 of the latter were killed, and 2 wounded. The remainder fled.

———— Major Lippert, 13th Illinois cavalry, with 200 men, met 350 rebels near Cape Girardeau, Missouri, and after a short fight defeated them, with a loss of 30 killed, 50 wounded, and 15 prisoners, and horses, wagons, arms, &c.

———— A fight near Lamar, Missouri, between 60 men 6th Kansas, and Hays and Quantrell's guerrillas. The Federals were defeated: loss, 2 killed, and 21 wounded.

August 25.—White's rebel cavalry attacked Captain Mean's (Union) cavalry at Waterford, Virginia: most of the latter were killed or captured.

———— Major Lippert, 13th Illinois cavalry, with 130 men, attacked Hick's guerrilla band, 300 strong, 36 miles beyond Bloomfield, Missouri, and routed them, with a loss of 20 killed, 60 wounded, several prisoners, 60 horses, 70 stand of arms, and their camp-equipage.

———— An attack was made two miles from Henderson, Kentucky, by a party of guerrillas in ambush, upon Federal infantry and cavalry, commanded by Lieutenant-Colonel Johnson, 65th Indiana. The latter rallied, were reinforced, and attacked the enemy, who fled, losing 5 killed, several wounded, and 17 prisoners. Union loss, 2 killed, 4 wounded.

———— 200 guerrillas encamped on Shelby farm, near Danville, Kentucky, were surprised and attacked by 60 men of the Kentucky Home Guards, who killed 3, wounded 8, and put the rest to flight, also losing 30 horses. Union loss, 1 killed, and 2 wounded.

———— Colonel Woodward (rebel), with 800 infantry and cavalry, and two field-pieces, demanded the surrender of Fort Donelson, Tennessee, which was held by Major Hart with four companies of the 71st Ohio. The latter refused to comply with the summons, when Woodward attacked the fort, and was repulsed, with a loss of 30 killed and wounded.

August 26.—After the battle of Cedar Mountain, Virginia, the rebels apparently retreated from before General Pope's army; but the movement was really made for the purpose of assisting a strategic operation upon Washington by the right flank and in the rear of the Federal forces. The rebels who fought at Cedar Mountain left a sufficient force in front of Pope to menace his lines on the Rappahannock and keep his army active by frequent skirmishes. While they were thus engaged at Warrenton, the rebel generals Lee, Jackson, Ewell, Longstreet, Hill, Stuart, and Fitz-Hugh Lee massed a heavy army near the head-waters of the Rappahannock, at the base of the Blue Ridge, and by forced marches came through Thoroughfare Gap, back of Manassas. They first made their appearance on the evening of the 26th at Bristow Station, at which place a railroad-train was fired upon by dismounted cavalry on both sides of the road. The engineer did not stop, but let on all steam, and ran to Manassas Station. Here there were stores and supplies worth $500,000, with not more than 80 men as a guard. These made what disposition for defence they could; but in an hour the rebels were upon them in large force. The Federals resisted, but many were killed and wounded, and, the enemy being very strong, some surrendered, and some succeeded in escaping. The stores were then plundered, and what could not be immediately used by the rebels was destroyed, with the buildings and depôts. They captured seven trains laden with ammunition, provisions, &c., and ten locomotives. Same night, about 8 o'clock, the pickets at Manassas Junction were driven in, and three companies stationed there surprised and attacked by General Ewell's rebel division, 7000 to 10,000 strong, with cavalry and artillery. The Federals fled; some were killed, and some taken prisoners.

August 27.—The advance of the rebels from Manassas Junction was disputed by two Ohio regiments under Colonel Scammon, between the Junction and Bull Run. The fight lasted three hours, and was gallantly contested. At 12 o'clock Colonel Scammon found it impossible to resist the increasing reinforcements of the enemy, and was obliged to fall back in the direction of Alexandria.

———— Another body of the enemy, advancing by the Centreville road to Manassas, were met by General Taylor's New Jersey brigade, and gallantly resisted. Taylor was overpowered by superior numbers, and defeated, with considerable loss, being caught in a very disadvantageous position, in consequence of his not knowing the real strength of the force opposed to him. On the Federal side there were killed Lieutenant-Colonel Collet, 1st New Jersey; Captain Campbell, Major Titus, 12th Pennsylvania, Lieutenant J. H. Plum. Wounded, General Taylor; Colonel Buck, 2d New Jersey.

———— Battle of Kettle Run, Virginia. General Pope, having discovered the movement of the rebels upon his flank and rear, set off immediately from his head-quarters at Warrenton and Warrenton Springs, dividing his army into three columns. The first, under McDowell, with his own and Sigel's corps, to march upon Gainsville by the Warrenton and Alexandria pike. The second, under Reno, with one division of Heintzelman, to march on Greenwich. The third, with Porter's and Hooker's divisions, General Pope accompanying, to march to Manassas. McDowell was ordered to get between the forces of the enemy already at Manassas, and the main body which was following through Thoroughfare Gap. Hooker, of the third column, came upon the enemy near Kettle Run, about three o'clock in the afternoon. Kearney, of the second column, had advanced about the same distance from Greenwich. There was a sharp action, in which the rebels were worsted, and completely routed, with 300 killed and wounded, and the loss of their camps and baggage, small arms, and 700 prisoners. The loss on the Union side has been estimated at 50 killed, and 200 wounded; among the latter was Lieutenant-Colonel Porter, New York Excelsior Brigade. Among the rebel wounded, General Trimble, General Taliaferro.

August 28.—A fight near Woodbury, Tennessee, between Colonel Mundy's Kentucky cavalry and Forrest's guerrillas. The rebels lost 8 killed, 30 wounded, and 15 prisoners. Union loss, 1 killed, and 5 wounded.

———— General Schofield, commanding at St. Louis,

Missouri, assessed $500,000 upon the secessionists of St. Louis county for equipping the enrolled militia for the defence of the State, and the support of their destitute families.

August 28.—Fredericksburg, Virginia, was evacuated by General Burnside, who blew up the bridges and burned the iron-foundry, and then marched to Acquia Creek.

August 29.—Second battle of Bull Run, Virginia (first day). At daylight, Kearney's, Reno's, and Hooker's divisions of Heintzelman's corps were at Manassas, but the enemy had moved off. They were followed by Kearney by the Centreville road, crossing Bull Run. Near Centreville there was a skirmish with cavalry. The enemy's infantry advancing were met by skirmishers and driven back. Kearney advanced to Centreville, and occupied the works without further molestation. Hooker and Reno were near this place, and had encamped there the previous night; and Sigel's troops were in position, the right on the Leesburg road, the left on Bull Run. Kearney moved on, and formed a junction with Sigel,—Hooker and Reno in reserve. The rebels attacked Sigel's right, under Carl Shurz, at Groveton, about ten o'clock, and pressed them fiercely. Hooker was set upon in great force, and was compelled to fall back, his flank being exposed by Augur's brigade, which had previously fallen back. Kearney was exposed by these movements, but managed to hold his position until night, with the assistance of two regiments of Stevens's brigade. On the Union side there were killed, Colonel Cantwell, 82d Ohio; Colonel Brown, 20th Indiana; Colonel Roberts, 1st Michigan cavalry; Lieutenant-Colonel Thomas S. Martin, 11th Pennsylvania. Wounded, General Robert Schenck; Colonel Leasure, 100th Pennsylvania; Colonel Rosa, 46th New York; Colonel Soest, 29th New York; Major Henkin, 58th New York; Lieutenant-Colonel Potter, New York; Major C. H. Towne, 1st Michigan cavalry; Lieutenant-Colonel Thomas, 72d New York; Lieutenant-Colonel Henderson, 7th Pennsylvania Reserves; Colonel Hayes, 62d Pennsylvania; Colonel Champlin, 3d Michigan. Prisoners, Colonel Brodhead, 1st Michigan cavalry. Of the rebels there were killed, Colonel Neff, 33d Virginia; Major May, 12th Virginia; Lieutenant-Colonel Skinner, 1st Virginia. Among the rebel wounded were Generals Ewell, Jenkins, Taliaferro, Mahon, and Trimble; Colonels Benbon, Moore, McGowan; Major Del Kemper; Major Terry, Virginia; Major Lawson Botts, 22d Virginia; Colonel Rowan, Virginia; Majors Neulenbonseb, Scott.

—— Skirmish near Richmond, Kentucky. It was commenced by an attack by the rebels on the Federal cavalry in front. General Manson moved up with two regiments, and the enemy retreated, losing one gun.

August 30.—Battle of Richmond, Kentucky. General Manson remained during the preceding night on the field of the skirmish. In the morning he advanced. The enemy attempted to turn our left flank: sharp fighting ensued. The rebels succeeded in this effort, and Manson fell back three miles, and re-formed his line of battle. After two hours' fighting, the enemy turned the right flank of Manson, who again fell back. The men were again rallied and formed. General Nelson came up; but after another stand the Federals again retreated, leaving the rebels in possession of the field, and losing their guns and camp-equipage. The rebel force was from 15,000 to 20,000; Federal force, 9000. The latter retreated to Lexington. The rebels were commanded by General Kirby Smith. Killed, Lieutenant-Colonel Topping, 71st Indiana; Major Conklin, 71st Indiana; Colonel Linn, 12th Indiana; Lieutenant-Colonel Wolf. Wounded, General Nelson; Lieutenant-Colonel Stout, Colonel Warne, 18th Kentucky. The whole Federal loss was estimated at 250 killed, and 600 wounded.

—— Second day of the second battle of Bull Run, Virginia. The Federal army was reinforced by the arrival of McDowell's and Porter's divisions. Porter was sent to turn the enemy's right. At two o'clock Porter opened the attack, and the fight soon became general under Porter, Sigel, and Reno. After two hours, McDowell was forced back, and General Pope ordered a general falling back to form a new line in a better position. Here the artillery had full play. The enemy pressed forward, but were met by a destructive fire. They were driven back to the woods, but, again rallying, attacked Ricketts's division with masses of troops, and, falling furiously upon McDowell, again forced him back. A change of the whole Federal front was necessary, which was executed with success in face of the enemy. Ricketts rallied, and, with Kearney, Gribben, and Reno, disputed the field. Reno drove the rebels back on the left. Ricketts was ordered back by General Pope at seven o'clock. Reno followed at eight, and Kearney and Gribben, without support, were compelled to withdraw to the Centreville heights. The Federal troops lay upon their arms all night; but the enemy did not attack, and in the morning they were not present in force. On the Federal side were killed, Colonel John A. Koltes, 73d Pennsylvania; Colonel McConnell, 2d New Jersey; Colonel O'Connor, 2d Wisconsin; Colonel Fletcher Webster, 12th Massachusetts; Major Town, 1st Michigan; Major Barney, 24th New York; Major May, 19th Indiana; Colonel Connell, 82d Ohio; Colonel Thornton Brodhead, 1st Michigan cavalry (died of his wounds); Lieutenant-Colonel McLean, 88th Pennsylvania. Union killed, 500; wounded, 5000. Wounded, General Duryea, General Towers, General Hatch; Colonel Frisbie, 30th New York; Colonel Cutler, 6th Wisconsin; Colonel Robinson, 7th Wisconsin; Colonel Root, 14th New York; Colonel Farnsworth, 79th New York; Colonel George P. McLean, 88th Pennsylvania; Colonel Gavin, 7th Indiana; Colonel Thomas, 22d New York; Colonel Mott, 6th New Jersey; Lieutenant-Colonel George J. Tileston; Lieutenant-Colonel Ward, 8th New Jersey; Lieutenant-Colonel Fowler, 14th New York; Lieutenant-Colonel Beardsley, 24th New York; Lieutenant-Colonel Hamilton, 7th Wisconsin; Major Bell, 7th Wisconsin; Major Kirkwood, 63d Pennsylvania; Major Thomas, 21st New York; Major F. A. Lancaster, 115th Pennsylvania; Major D. M. Jones, 110th Pennsylvania. On the rebel side were killed, a large number of officers and men, names unknown; also, Colonels Means, Marshall, Gadberry, South Carolina, and others. In these battles, including Kettle Run, it was estimated that the Federals lost 4000 killed and wounded. It is said that 3600 dead rebels were found on the field,—which is probably an exaggeration. The rebel papers estimated their loss on the first day at 1000 killed and wounded. Their loss is represented to have been heavier than ours, and may be placed at 5000 killed and wounded in both battles.

August 30.—The rebel steamer Emma ran aground in the Savannah River, and was burned by the rebels to prevent her falling into the hands of the Unionists.

—— Colonel Leggett (Federal), with one regiment, six companies, and a section of artillery, had a fight with a large force of the enemy's cavalry near Bolivar, Tennessee, which continued, with skirmishing-operations, for seven hours. Union loss. 25 killed and wounded,—among them Lieutenant-Colonel Hogg, 2d Illinois cavalry, killed.

—— Buckhannon and Weston, Western Virginia, taken by guerrillas under Jenkins and Imboden. At the former place about 250 soldiers and citizens resisted them, but were defeated and fled.

August 31.—A fight at Morganfield, Kentucky, between a force of rebels, and Union troops under Colonel Shackelford. The latter were surprised, and fled, losing several killed, about 50 prisoners, 40 horses, &c.

September 1.—Battle of Chantilly, Virginia. Intelligence being received at the Federal head-quarters at Centreville, Virginia, that the rebel generals Hill and Longstreet were preparing to move on our right, to cut off our supply-trains, General Reno was despatched to Fairfax Court-House to intercept them, and it was determined that the entire Federal army should retire to the same position. At nine o'clock Reno led the march, McDowell's division following. At four P.M., Reno was attacked, about one mile and a half from Fairfax Court-House by a detachment from Hill's division. Stevens's division was the first engaged: Reno formed a junction with them. The enemy were concealed in the shrubbery in the woods. They were routed from this position by a general charge of bayonets, before which they fled with great slaughter. Kearney's artillery opened upon them, and completed the rout. There were killed on the Federal side, Major-General Philip Kearney, Brigadier-General Isaac L. Stevens, and other officers. The killed and wounded on the Union side were estimated at 1000: the enemy's loss was probably as large.

September 1.—Colonel Dennis, with 500 men, had an engagement near Medon, Tennessee, with seven regiments of rebel cavalry. The latter were defeated, losing 110 men left dead on the field, and over 300 wounded. Union loss, 5 killed, and 55 wounded.

—— Poindexter, the guerrilla leader, was caught on the North Missouri Railroad, twenty miles from Hudson, while asleep in a farm-house.

—— White's rebel cavalry, 1000 strong, were attacked twelve miles southeast of Pittman's Ferry, Missouri, by five companies of United States troops, under Major Lippert, and routed after an hour's fight, losing all their wagons and equipage, horses, mules, &c.

September 2.—300 Union soldiers, under command of Captain Hammell, at Plymouth, North Carolina, were attacked by 1400 rebels, commanded by Colonel Garret. Hammell and all his commissioned officers were sick or wounded, and the command devolved on Sergeant Green, who conducted the affair with gallantry and ability. After a fight of one hour's duration, the rebels were routed. Their colonel (Garret), one lieutenant, and 40 other prisoners, were captured, with 30 of their horses; 30 rebels were killed. Union loss, 3 killed.

—— Battle at Britton's Lane, Tennessee. Two Federal regiments of General Ross's command, under Colonel Dennis, attacked the rear of the rebels, under Villipique, then threatening Jackson, Mississippi, and routed them. Colonel Adams and 110 dead rebels were left on the field; their wounded was estimated at 250. Union loss, 5 killed, and 40 wounded.

—— In consequence of the threatening operations of the rebels in Kentucky, martial law was declared in Cincinnati, Ohio, and Newport and Covington, opposite, in Kentucky.

—— Lexington, Kentucky, occupied by the rebels under Kirby Smith.

—— Winchester, Virginia, was evacuated by Federal troops, under General Julius White. All the guns and ordnance stores, excepting four thirty-two pounders, were carried off; a large quantity of commissary stores, and the warehouses in which they were, destroyed; the magazine was exploded, and Fort Sigel blown up.

—— General McClellan was appointed to the command of the army for the defence of Washington, thus superseding General Pope.

—— A United States army train of 100 wagons was captured between Fairfax and Centreville by the rebels.

September 3.—United States transport-steamer W. Z. Terry, while aground in Tennessee River, near Duck River shoals, was captured by a party of rebel guerrillas, and burned: 17 officers and men of the boat were captured.

—— The rebel camp of Colonel Johnson, Geyer Lake, Kentucky, attacked by Colonel Shackelford (Federal), and taken possession of. The rebels, 600 strong, rallied and fired upon Shackelford. The latter dismounted his men, and they answered with their carbines, but were finally compelled to retreat. Before they did so, they burned the rebel camp and guns. Colonel Shackelford and 8 others were wounded.

—— The whole Federal army fell back, in front of defences at Washington, to Munson's Hill.

September 5.—The whole rebel army, under Lee, Jackson, Hill, and Longstreet, crossed the Potomac at several fords, and entered Maryland.

—— The rebel General Bragg entered Kentucky with his army at Albany, Clinton county.

September 6.—Clarksville, Tennessee, reoccupied by Colonel Lowe (Federal), who drove out 450 guerrillas and citizens.

September 6.—Frederick, Maryland, occupied by the rebel advance under General Hill.

—— Extensive steam salt-works, St. Joseph's Bay, Florida, were destroyed by an expedition from the United States gunboat Tahoma and steamer Somerset. All the buildings were burned, and twenty-eight steam-boilers destroyed.

—— Washington, North Carolina, in occupation of Union troops, 500 strong, was attacked by 1200 rebels, who were repulsed after a fight of two hours, the United States gunboat Louisiana, Captain Renshaw, assisting. During the fight the United States gunboat Picket, Captain Nichols, blew up from the accidental explosion of their magazine. Captain Nichols and 19 of his men were killed, and 6 wounded. Federal loss on shore, 7 killed, 47 wounded, and 4 missing. Rebel loss, 30 killed, several wounded, and 36 prisoners.

September 7.—Major-General Reno was appointed to the command of the third army corps, and General McDowell granted leave of absence.

—— 400 rebel cavalry attacked Martinsburg, Virginia, and were repulsed by General Julius White, in command at that place. Rebel loss, several killed and wounded, and 50 prisoners. Union loss, 2 killed, and 10 wounded.

—— Bloomfield, Missouri, attacked by rebels. It was defended by 1000 militia under Colonel Boyd. The rebels withdrew, and afterward shelled the town.

September 8.—The rebel commander-in-chief, Major-General R. E. Lee, issued a proclamation from the army of Virginia, near Frederick, in Maryland, addressed to the people of Maryland, in which he assured them, "The people of the Confederate States have long watched with the deepest sympathy the wrongs and outrages that have been inflicted upon the citizens of a commonwealth allied to the States of the South by the strongest social, political, and commercial ties. They have seen, with the profoundest indignation, their sister State deprived of every right and reduced to the condition of a conquered province. . . . Believing that the people of Maryland possessed a spirit too lofty to submit to such a government, the people of the South have long wished to aid you in throwing off this *foreign yoke*, to enable you to enjoy the inalienable rights of freemen, and restore independence and sovereignty to your State. In obedience to this wish, our army has come among you, and is prepared to assist you with the power of its arms in regaining the rights of which you have been despoiled. . . . It is for you to decide your destiny, freely, and without constraint. This army will respect your choice, whatever it may be, and, while the Southern people will rejoice to welcome you to your natural position among them, they will only welcome you when you come of your own free will."

—— A fight at Cochran's Cross-Roads, Missouri, between 370 Federal troops, under Colonel Greerson, and rebel cavalry and infantry, 800 strong. The rebels were well posted, but were driven back, losing 4 killed, and 10 wounded.

September 9.—One of Ashby's rebel cavalry regiments, at Poolesville, Maryland, with one piece of artillery, was routed by a force of cavalry under Colonel Farnsworth, with some infantry. Rebel loss, 7 killed, and 8 wounded, and 6 prisoners; Union loss, 1 killed, and 7 wounded.

—— Coldwater Bridge, Missouri, burned by the rebels, who fled upon Colonel Greerson's advance. Colonel Greerson entered Senatobia, where he burned the railroad depôt and cars.

—— Williamsburg, Virginia, held by the 5th Pennsylvania cavalry. Colonel Campbell was captured by 500 rebel cavalry under Colonel Shingles, with three pieces of artillery: 5 captains, 4 lieutenants, and a few privates were taken prisoners. Colonel Campbell, with 8 of his officers, and 9 men, were killed. In a short time the place was retaken by the Federal troops.

September 10.—5000 rebels, under General Loring, attacked parts of two regiments, about 1200 men, under

Colonel Siber, at Fayette, Western Virginia. The latter cut their way through, with a loss of 100 killed and wounded.

September 10.—Another column of the enemy approached Gauley Bridge, Virginia, and cut off one Federal regiment and three companies at Summerville. In consequence of these movements, Colonel Lightburn, commanding the Federal troops, evacuated Gauley, destroying all the Government property which he could not remove, estimated to be worth $500,000.

September 11.—Governor Curtin, of Pennsylvania, called out 50,000 citizens of the State for immediate service, to repel an expected advance of the rebel army, then in Maryland, to Pennsylvania; Chambersburg, Carlisle, and Harrisburg being threatened, and Hagerstown, Maryland, being occupied by rebel cavalry.

September 12.—Palmyra, Missouri, taken by Porter, guerrilla leader, who released 40 secession prisoners, and then retreated.

—— Attacks were made by guerrilla parties upon steamboats in the Ohio River, at Curlew, Battery Rock, Caseyville, and other points: some steamers were burned.

—— Hagerstown, Maryland, entered by the advance of the rebel army, about 2000 strong, who seized provisions, tore up the railroad-track, and plundered the stores of Union men.

—— General Burnside, with the advance of the Federal army, entered Frederick, Maryland, and was warmly welcomed by the inhabitants. 450 sick rebels had been left behind and were captured.

—— A rebel army under Major-General Kirby Smith, which threatened Cincinnati, Ohio, and occupied a large portion of the State of Kentucky, fell back along the whole line. In consequence, Governor Tod, of Ohio, discharged the State militia, which had been assembled for the defence of Cincinnati.

September 13.—Four squadrons 3d Indiana cavalry charged on a regiment of rebel cavalry, supported by artillery, on the road leading from Middleton to Harper's Ferry. Federal loss, 30 killed and wounded.

September 14.—Battle of Munfordsville, Kentucky, between a rebel force under General Duncan, and Union troops commanded by Colonel Wilder. The rebels had from 5000 to 7000 men, the Federals 2500. The latter were behind breastworks, with heavy guns. The rebels endeavored to carry the intrenchments by assault, but were five times repulsed with slaughter. Union loss, 8 killed, and 27 wounded; rebel loss, 500 killed and wounded, and two pieces of artillery.

—— Battle of South Mountain, Maryland (called by the rebels the battle of Boonsboro Gap), between the rebel army under Generals Longstreet, D. H. Hill, A. P. Hill, and Stuart, and others, estimated to be 40,000 strong, and the Federal army under Major-General McClellan. The latter was in pursuit of the rebels, and had caught up with their rear-guard at Middletown. On the morning of the 14th the movement was resumed by McClellan. The rebels retired slowly, contesting the advance in every available position. About three o'clock the rebels were discovered drawn up in line of battle in the mountain-ridges. Their left rested upon Turner's Gap, and their right extended to Crampton's Gap. The Federal troops were under General Hooker on the right, Burnside in the centre, and Franklin on the left, at Crampton's Gap. The engagement at once became general with musketry and artillery. For two hours this interchange continued, until the enemy showed signs of unsteadiness, having been crowded by Hooker on the right and threatened in flank. About five o'clock a general charge was ordered along the whole line, under pressure of which the rebels were driven over the ridges and down the slope toward Boonsboro. On the Federal side there were killed, General Jesse L. Reno; Colonel Childs, 4th Pennsylvania cavalry; Colonel Coleman, 11th Ohio; Colonel Paxon, 57th New York; Colonel Goodrich, 60th New York. Wounded, General Hatch; Colonel Willy, 36th Massachusetts; Colonel Whittington, 17th Michigan; Colonel Gallagher, 18th Pennsylvania Reserves; Lieutenant-Colonel Hays, 23d Ohio; Major Burey, 12th Ohio; Colonel Bollinger, 9th Pennsylvania Reserves; Colonel Sullivan, 24th New York; Colonel Beale, 19th Maine. The official report of General McClellan of the losses at this battle was, killed, 443; wounded, 1806; missing, 76. Total, 2325. The rebel killed have been estimated at 500; their wounded, probably 2000; prisoners, 1500. Total, 4000. On their side were killed, General Garland, North Carolina; Colonel Strong, 19th Virginia; Colonel James, South Carolina.

September 14.—A United States flotilla of three steamers having been fired upon by guerrillas on shore at Prentiss, Mississippi, and some men killed and wounded, that village was shelled and burned in retaliation.

September 15.—Colonel Lightburn, with Union troops, after the fights at Gauley and Charleston, Western Virginia, retreated to Ravenswood, which he reached, after a fatiguing march, in good order.

—— Harper's Ferry, Virginia, was surrendered to a rebel army under "Stonewall" Jackson and Hill, numbering about 35,000 men. The assailants were detached from Lee's main army in Maryland, and proceeded at once to Harper's Ferry. They appeared, September 12, in the rear of Maryland Heights, upon which they made an attack. They were resisted at some distance from the heights by two regiments, which were driven back. The large guns on the Maryland Heights then began to shell the woods, and the Union troops retreated to their fortifications. After the guns on Maryland Heights had been firing for five hours and a half, Colonel Ford, in command of Maryland Heights, gave orders to spike the guns and throw them down the mountain: this was done, and the troops retreated to Harper's Ferry. On Sunday the rebels appeared on Loudon Heights, on the Virginia side of Harper's Ferry, and opened a fire from Maryland Heights, Loudon Heights, and Sandy Hook on Harper's Ferry. They fired all day, without doing much damage. On Monday morning, the 15th, they opened again. At eight o'clock Colonel Dixon H. Miles, commanding the post, hoisted the white flag, met the rebel officers, arranged terms of surrender, and soon afterward was killed by the explosion of a shell. By this disgraceful act of cowardice were surrendered to the rebels 11,583 men: 2000 cavalry had cut their way out the night before, and reached McClellan's lines, capturing a rebel ammunition-train on their way. The enemy took 73 pieces of artillery, 11,000 stand of arms, 1800 horses, besides immense quantities of stores of all kinds. A court of inquiry afterward held in reference to this affair decided that Colonel Ford had conducted his operations without military ability, and showed such lack of capacity that he was disqualified for a command in the service; that Colonel Dixon H. Miles's incapacity amounted almost to imbecility; that the surrender was a shameful one: that General Wool was to blame for appointing him; and that General McClellan might have succored him if he had conducted his advance into Maryland with more energy. "Had the garrison been slower to surrender, or the army of the Potomac swifter to march, the enemy would have been forced to raise the siege, or would have been taken in detail, with the Potomac dividing his force." The loss on the Federal side during the siege of Harper's Ferry was small,—not 100 killed and wounded.

September 16.—A fight at Fricke's Lick, Missouri, between 75 militia under Captain Johnson, and a party of rebel guerrillas, who were dispersed, with a loss of 1 killed, and 3 wounded.

September 17.—Battle of Antietam, Maryland, called by the rebels the battle of Sharpsburg, between the entire rebel army, under Major-General Lee, 97,000 strong, and the entire Federal army, Major-General McClellan. The rebels were reinforced by "Stonewall" Jackson, who, after the capture of Harper's Ferry, abandoned it on the 16th and recrossed the Potomac at Williamsport to assist General Lee. At daylight on the 17th the battle was commenced in the centre by General Hooker, and on the right by General Sumner. After a sharp contest, the enemy were driven one mile. They rallied, howover, being reinforced, and regained the greater part of the ground, with terrible loss. General Sumner once more urged on his troops, and the rebels were again driven backward with great slaughter. He pushed the enemy a quarter of a mile farther than they had been driven in the morning. On the left, Generals Burnside and Porter drove the rebels from the line of Antietam Creek, on the Sharpsburg road, and crossed the creek. General Sykes's regulars, with the assistance of General Sumner, carried a ridge on the right side of the road, with considerable loss. On the left wing, the possession of a bridge over Antietam Creek was fought for with desperation on both sides. General Burnside's corps, after a repulse, carried it by a determined charge, and obtained the key of the position. The enemy left their killed and wounded on the field. The battle lasted fourteen hours, and was only ended by the coming on of the night. The next afternoon the rebels commenced moving off toward the Potomac, and by the morning of Saturday had crossed over in a body to Virginia, the plan to "liberate Maryland" having signally failed, from the indisposition of the inhabitants of that State to accept the advantages held out in flattering terms by General Lee's proclamation. At this battle the rebels were commanded on the left by General Jackson; centre, General Longstreet; right, General A. P. Hill. The official report of General McClellan gives the Federal loss in this battle as follows:—Killed, 2010; wounded, 9416; missing, 1043: total, 12,469. Among the Federal killed were Brigadier-General Mansfield, U.S. Army; Lieutenant-Colonel Parrisin, 14th Connecticut; Major Sedgwick, Colonel McNeil, Pennsylvania Bucktails; Colonel Samuel Croasdale, 128th Pennsylvania; Colonel Goodrich, 6th New York; Colonel Hinks, 19th Massachusetts; Colonel Coleman, 11th Ohio; Major Force, 108th New York; Major T. A. Smith, 1st Delaware; Lieutenant-Colonel R. A. Oakford, 132d Pennsylvania. Wounded, General Hooker, Major-General Rodman, General Dana, Major-General Richardson (died of his wounds), General Hartsuff, General Duryea, General Sedgwick, General Weber, General Meagher; Colonel Kingsbury, 11th Connecticut; Colonel Polk, 2d Sharpshooters; Colonel Stears, 4th Rhode Island; Major Gile, 88th Pennsylvania; Colonel Barlow, 61st New York; Major Dwight, 2d Massachusetts; Colonel Wistar, 71st Pennsylvania; Colonel Revere, U.S. Army; Colonel Palfrey, 20th Massachusetts; Lieutenant-Colonel Kuhn, 19th Indiana; Major Rice, 19th Massachusetts; Major Moon, 14th Indiana; Colonel Zinn, 115th Pennsylvania; Major Rodgers, 14th Connecticut; Colonel Post, 2d New York; Lieutenant-Colonel Bachman, 19th Indiana; Colonel James Kelly, 69th New York; Major Devoe, 15th New York; Major Burbank, 12th Massachusetts; Colonel Baxter, 7th Michigan; Major Dorsey, 69th Pennsylvania; Lieutenant-Colonel Hanneman, 128th Pennsylvania; Major Warner, 128th Pennsylvania; Colonel Palmer, 108th New York; Major Ardt, 10th New York; Major Bloomenburg, 5th Indiana; Major Karvera, 14th Indiana; Major Nice, 4th Pennsylvania; Lieutenant-Colonel Bull, 66th New York; Colonel Reall, 10th Pennsylvania Reserves; Colonel Anderson, 1st Delaware; Major McGannin, 3d Delaware; Lieutenant-Colonel Waldron, 10th Pennsylvania Reserves. On the rebel side were killed, General Starke, General Anderson, General Whiting, Colonel Branch, General Colquitt; Colonel John T. Thornton, Virginia. Wounded, Generals Ripley and Hayes; General Wright, Georgia; General Lawton, General Armistead, General Ransome; Colonel Alfred Cummings; Colonel Parker (died of his wounds); Colonel De Rossett, North Carolina (died of his wounds). The losses of the rebels in the battles of South Mountain and Antietam are not known. After the latter, 3000 of their dead were buried by the United States troops, and probably 500 by the enemy before their retreat. General McClellan, by his despatch to the War Department, estimates the rebel dead in both battles at 4000; wounded (in the same ratio as the Federal loss), 18,742; prisoners, 5000. Total killed, wounded, and prisoners, 25,542. The Federal army did not lose a single gun, but captured 13 guns, 7 caissons, 9 limbers, 15,000 small arms, 39 colors, and 1 signal-flag.

September 17.—Corpus Christi, Texas, was bombarded by Union gunboats, which continued for three days.

——— A rebel battery at St. John's Bluff, Florida, was shelled by the gunboats Paul Jones, Commander Steedman; Cimerone, Commander Woodbull; Uncas, and Patroon. The engagement lasted for five hours, after which the gunboats withdrew.

——— Munfordsville, Kentucky, was surrendered to the rebels under General Chalmers. By this capture they took 4500 prisoners, with heavy guns, small arms, &c. Colonel Wilder, who had gallantly repulsed a large force on the 13th, was now surrounded by the main body of Bragg's army, and the contest was hopeless. The enemy had 25,000 men, and 72 pieces of artillery. They lost severely before the surrender, their killed being 500, wounded 700. The loss in officers was very heavy.

September 18.—150 rebels, under Major Snyder, were attacked by Captain Snyder, Missouri militia, with 125 men, in Rolla county, Missouri. The former fled, losing in killed Major Snyder, and 15 wounded, all their tents, guns, blankets, &c. On the same day, Lieutenant Dillon, with a portion of his company, came up with the fugitives, and took 5 prisoners, 11 horses, guns, &c.

September 19.—Battle of Iuka, Mississippi. General Rosecrans, with 12,000 men, attacked the rebel general Sterling Price, with 17,000 men, in the afternoon, two hours before dark. The rebels were retreating from Iuka. It was planned that they should be attacked by Rosecrans on the right wing, and by General Ord on the left. This combined movement failed; but Rosecrans, with a portion of the Federal army, came upon the retreating party upon a road, where they formed in line of battle upon a ridge. From this they were driven by a bayonet-charge, but they rallied and drove back our troops, who again rallied and were successful in another charge. The contest was closed by darkness. The Federals bivouacked upon the ground, but during the night the rebels moved off, leaving all his dead and wounded upon the field. On the rebel side were killed General Little and other officers. Wounded, General Whitefield (prisoner), Colonel Gilmore, Colonel Mahoney. The Federal loss was 120 killed, and 200 wounded. 261 dead rebels were left on the field, and their loss was 800 killed and wounded.

——— Owensboro', Kentucky, attacked by 600 guerrillas. Colonel Miller, who resisted one of the parties, was slain, and 5 Federals were wounded; rebel loss, 5 killed.

September 20.—A skirmish at Ashby's Gap, Virginia, between a brigade of United States cavalry, under Colonel R. B. Price, 2d Pennsylvania cavalry, and the 5th regiment Virginia cavalry, Lieutenant-Colonel Green, who were driven back sixteen miles. 4 rebels were killed, 12 wounded, and 3 officers taken prisoners.

——— Lieutenant-Colonel Wood, with 450 Union troops, attacked and routed the rebels at Owensboro', under Colonel Martin: the latter lost 38 killed, and 25 wounded.

——— Commander George H. Preble, U.S. Navy, senior officer in command of blockading force off Mobile, was dismissed from the service for permitting the rebel steamer "Ovieto" to run the blockade.

——— A fight at Shirley's Ford, ten miles northwest of Carthage, Missouri. between 3d Indiana regiment, Colonel Ritchie, and 600 rebels. The latter were routed, with a loss of from 60 to 90 killed.

September 21.—Three regiments of Federal cavalry, under General A. McCook, captured Munfordsville, Kentucky, driving out 8000 rebels, who lost a colonel and lieutenant-colonel.

——— 120 Kentucky Home Guard cavalry, Captain Robt. Morris, surrendered to 200 rebel guerrillas, under George Jesseo, at Newcastle, Kentucky.

——— The rebel army under Lee, Longstreet, Jackson, and others, having crossed the Potomac into Virginia, and it being supposed that they had retreated, a reconnoissance was made on the Virginia side of the

Potomac, beyond Shepherdstown, by the 4th Michigan and portions of the 62d and 118th Pennsylvania regiments, with Griffin's battery. The troops crossed in face of the fire of four field-pieces which were manned by gunners but did not seem to be supported by infantry. The artillerists ran away upon the landing of the force, leaving their guns. No enemy was visible; and a Federal brigade, Colonel Barnes commanding, also crossed. After they were fairly landed, the enemy suddenly appeared from ambush, opened upon them with shot and shell, and soon came out of the woods in immense strength. The Federals stood their ground, but were finally overwhelmed, and retreated, crossing the river under fire. In this unfortunate affair the killed, wounded, and missing were probably 500. The 118th Pennsylvania (Corn Exchange) lost 45 killed, 121 wounded, 112 missing.

September 22.—Proclamation by the President of the United States, declaring that the slaves of persons in States which, on the 1st of January, 1863, should be in rebellion, "shall be thenceforth and forever free;"—also prohibiting army and naval officers of the United States from employing any portion of their forces for the capture or return of slaves who have escaped from their owners.

September 24.—The advance of General Buell's army in pursuit of Bragg entered Louisville, Ky.

——— A proclamation was issued by the President of the United States, declaring that during the continuance of the rebellion "all rebels and insurgents, their aiders and abettors in the United States, and all persons discouraging volunteer enlistments, resisting the militia-drafts, or guilty of disloyal practices, affording aid and comfort to the rebellion," shall be subject to martial law, and liable to trial and punishment by court-martial or military commission; also that "the writ of habeas corpus is suspended in respect to all persons arrested, or who are now or may be hereafter, during the rebellion, imprisoned in any fort, camp, arsenal, military prison, or any other place of confinement, by any military authority, or by the command of any court-martial or military commission."

——— The Governors of fourteen of the loyal States, and proxy representatives for three more, met at Altoona, Pa.. in consultation upon the condition of the country. They adopted an address to the President of the United States pledging the support of their respective States in all measures necessary to put down the rebellion. They signified their approval of the Emancipation proclamation, and congratulated the President and the country upon the splendid valor of the United States army.

September 25.—Brigadier-General Prince, U.S. Army, Colonel George D. Chapman, 5th Connecticut, and 92 other officers of Pope's army, captured at Bull Run and other battles in Virginia, arrived at Fort Monroe, having been exchanged by the rebel Government, notwithstanding the threat in Jeff Davis's proclamation that such officers should be held as felons, and not as prisoners of war. This change of policy was no doubt occasioned by the fears of retaliation upon the rebel officers captured at South Mountain and Antietam.

September 26.—Faulkner's rebel guerrillas having fired upon steamboats in the Mississippi River from the town of Randolph, Miss., that place was destroyed and burned by an expedition under Colonel Wolcott, 46th Ohio.

——— Harper's Ferry, Va., evacuated by the rebels, after an occupation of five days. During this time they removed very much of the property which they had captured, started off wagon-trains, attempted to blow up the piers of the railroad-bridge across the Potomac, destroyed the ponton-bridge, burned trestle-works, stables, workshops, and warehouses, and tore up the railroad-track.

September 27.—A British vessel which arrived at London reported that the British steamer "Alabama," or "290," fitted up as a rebel piratical craft by 290 English merchants, and sent out of an English port, had captured and burned at sea, off the Azores, the American vessels Ocmulgee, Almahan, Ocean Rover, Alert, Occola, Ocean Cruiser, Benj. Tucker, Weathergage, Admiral Blake, and schooner Starlight.

September 27.—500 rebel cavalry dashed into Augusta, Ky., drove out a small force of Union soldiers, and burned the village. Union killed, 15; rebel killed and wounded, 75. Among the latter was a son of George D. Prentice, of Louisville. The property destroyed was worth $100,000.

September 28.—Ten citizens of Missouri who had taken the oath of allegiance to the United States, and afterwards violated it, were shot at Hudson, Mo., in accordance with the sentence of a court-martial.

——— Major-General S. R. Anderson (rebel) demanded the surrender of Nashville, Tenn. General Negley, U.S. Volunteers, returned a reply that he was "prepared and determined to hold his position."

September 29.—Major-General William Nelson, U.S. Army, was killed at the Galt House, Louisville, Ky., by Brigadier-General Jefferson C. Davis, U.S. Army.

September 30.—A party of rebels at Russellville, Ky., who had burned a bridge, were routed by a Federal force sent against them, with a loss of 50 killed and wounded, and 15 prisoners.

——— Under the supposition that a rebel force in Newtonia, Mo., was about 500 strong, 600 United States troops were sent against them. The Federals charged into the town, where they discovered that the rebels, who had been previously reinforced, numbered about 7000, with 6 pieces of artillery. Our troops got out the best way they could, and were followed by the rebels. Three miles from Newtonia the United States troops were reinforced by 300 cavalry and 4 pieces of artillery, and drove the rebels back. At night the Federals fell back, were again followed, and again drove back the rebels. Union loss, 140 killed, wounded, and prisoners.

October 1.—The Western gunboat-fleet, which had hitherto been under the jurisdiction of the United States War Department, was transferred to the Navy Department. This fleet had been distinguished for brilliant and important services at Fort Henry, Fort Donelson, Columbus, Island No. 10, Pittsburg Landing, Memphis, Vicksburg, White River, Natchez, and Baton Rouge. It was manned by naval officers and men, but was under the control of the War Department.

——— Sabine Pass, Texas, taken by United States steamer Kensington, Captain Crocker, and schooners Seaman and Jones. They captured 1 fort, 2 camps, also 30 buildings and 10 rebel vessels, which were burned.

October 2.—President Lincoln visited Harper's Ferry, Va., and the next day crossed the Potomac and reviewed the army of General McClellan.

October 3.—General George W. Morgan, with the whole of his command,—10,000 men,—arrived at Greenupsburg, Ky., having evacuated Cumberland Gap and brought with him all his trains, 400 wagons, and 28 pieces of artillery. The march occupied sixteen days, through a wild portion of the country, in many parts of which roads had to be made, and in others obstructions to be overcome. Added to these were constant attacks by the rebel cavalry, which hung upon the flanks and rear. The men were almost without rations, gathering subsistence from the corn-fields. They were shoeless, hatless, and almost naked, but bore their hardships and fatigues with patience and cheerfulness.

——— A reconnoissance was made up Blackwater River, N.C., by three United States gunboats, commanded by Captains Flusser, Calhoun, and French. They were attacked near Franklin by 5 rebel regiments in ambuscade. They shelled the woods in return, causing immense loss to the rebels by firing grape and shell. The latter charged up to the boats by regiments, and gave favorable opportunities for the use of cannon. At another place the river was obstructed by trees thrown across it, and a desperate fight occurred at that point. The rebels lost 300 killed and 600 wounded; loss on the gunboats, 6 killed, and 13 wounded.

——— The ship Brilliant, of New York, was burned at sea by the British rebel privateer "Alabama," or "290," which had also shortly before captured and burned the whaling-vessels Virginia and Elisha Dunbar.

October 3.—Battle of Corinth, Miss. (first day). Early in the morning the outposts of General Rosecrans's corps, about six miles northeast of Corinth, were attacked by the rebels in force. The engagement became general by nine o'clock, the enemy hurling heavy masses of men against the weakest parts of the line. The United States troops were borne back by the pressure, the enemy being in superior force, continually threatening our flanks and attempting to get into our rear. As the Federals fell back, the rebels pressed on, until they were within the Federal breastworks, having captured 3 pieces of artillery. The coming on of night put an end to the contest, the rebels remaining in possession of the ground which they had won. They were 40,000 strong, and commanded by Price, Van Dorn, Villipique, Rust, Armstrong, and Maury, and were nearly double the Union force. On the Union side were killed Brigadier-General Hackleman; wounded, General Oglesby, Colonel J. L. Kirby Smith, Colonel Gilbert.

—— A fight at Blackwater, Suffolk county, Va., between 5000 rebels and the 11th Pennsylvania cavalry, Colonel Spear. The enemy, under the command of General Gustavus W. Smith, were routed, and pursued some distance.

October 4.—Battle of Corinth (second day). The rebels, holding the ground taken the night before, opened upon the town with shot and shell. They were replied to with spirit, during which 2 of their guns were disabled and a battery of 7 guns captured. After this the enemy made a desperate charge upon the town in heavy columns. This effort, although daring, was disastrous to them. They moved into the range of batteries in front and upon each side of them. They were mowed down by a withering fire, which thinned out their regiments with fearful slaughter. Notwithstanding their losses, they rushed on, and captured Fort Robinett, a small battery, causing a panic on the Union side. The rebels advanced into the streets of Corinth. New batteries opened upon them, and their advance was checked. They wavered, fell back, and soon fled. The captured battery Robinett was regained, and its guns joined in the work of destruction. The enemy then took to flight in disorder, after heavy losses, which on this day, in consequence of their exposure to the batteries, was immense in comparison with that on the Union side. 1423 dead rebels were found on the field. Their wounded must, according to the usual proportions, have exceeded 5000. They lost 2628 prisoners, among whom were 137 field-officers, captains, and subalterns, representing 60 regiments, 14 batteries, and 7 battalions. They also lost 3300 stand of small arms, 2 guns, and 14 colors. They were pursued 40 miles with infantry, and 60 miles with cavalry. Union loss, 315 killed, 1000 wounded. On the Union side, among the killed on the second day were Colonels Thrush, Baker, and Miles. Among the rebels killed and left on the field were General Rogers, New Orleans, General Martin, General Moore, Colonels Johnson, Ross, Morton, McLane, Major Lane, Colonel Wirt Adams, Miss., Colonel McFarland, Mo., Lieutenant-Colonel Lee, Major Vaugh; wounded, Colonels Danby and Pretch, General Cabell.

October 5.—Battle of Hatchie, Miss. The rebels under Price, Van Dorn, and Villipique, repulsed at Corinth, Miss., the previous day, were intercepted in their retreat by Generals Hurlbut and Ord. After a severe fight, the rebels were driven back across the river Hatchie and toward Corinth. They made a stand half a mile across the river, but were again defeated and took to flight. On the Federal side Colonel Davis, 46th Illinois, was wounded.

October 7.— The rebel steamer Blanche, formerly the General Rusk, was pursued by the United States gunboat Montgomery, near Havana, and run ashore, abandoned by her crew, and burned. The vessel was said to be English property and under the English flag; and the pursuit so near the coast of Cuba was considered an invasion of the sovereignty of Spain.

—— Anderson's rebel camp at Lavergne, Tenn., fifteen miles east of Nashville, was surprised by 2600 U.S. troops, under General Palmer and Colonel Miller. The enemy had 4000 men. They contested the attack, but were routed in thirty minutes, losing 175 prisoners, 80 killed and wounded, 3 guns, stores, provisions, tents, &c. Among the prisoners were Lieutenant-Colonel Maury, another lieutenant-colonel, and a number of line-officers. The rebel force was completely dispersed. Federal loss, 5 killed, 9 wounded, 4 missing.

October 8.—Battle of Chaplin Hills, at Perryville, Ky. Major-General A. D. McCook, of Buell's army, having under him Generals Rosseau and Jackson's divisions, with the brigades of Terrill, Starkweather, Webster, and Lytle, was attacked near the Chaplin River, about three miles from Perryville, by Bragg's army, under Generals Polk, Hardee, Cheatham, and Buckner, at two o'clock in the afternoon. The enemy brought up masses of troops, in their usual fashion, and made heavy attacks upon the exposed parts of the line. The attempt upon Rosseau's division on the right was made with charged bayonets; but the rebels were twice repulsed, suffering fearfully. They finally broke, and left that part of the field. On the left, affairs were not so successful. The rebels flanked and turned Terrill's brigade. That officer fell mortally wounded at the head of his men, while rallying them to recover the ground. His men fell back. Colonel Webster's brigade advanced to their support, General Jackson assisting. The enemy were driven back nearly to the extent of ground which they had gained, when General Jackson fell, mortally wounded; Colonel Webster, commanding the brigade, was also wounded. The parties struggled on until night. On this portion of the field the Federals lost 10 guns, 8 of which were retaken the next morning, with 2 of the enemy's to replace the balance. The Union troops remained at dark on the field, and during the night Bragg's army moved off, and continued its retreat without stopping until it got out of Kentucky. General McCook and General Bragg both agree in their official reports that the fighting was the most desperate which they had seen during the war. The Federal troops numbered 18,000. The rebels were the entire army of Bragg, who had planned the attack and was ready for it. They are supposed to have numbered at least 40,000. Among the rebels killed were Generals Wood, Cleborn, and Brown, Colonel Patterson, Lieutenant-Colonel Evans, Major W. Pryor. On the Federal side were killed General Jackson, General Terrill, General Lytle, Lieutenant-Colonel Jewett, 15th Kentucky cavalry, Major Campbell, 15th Pennsylvania cavalry, Colonel Webster, 98th Ohio; wounded, Colonel Pope, 15th Kentucky cavalry. General Buell stated the Federal loss in killed and wounded at 2300; and Bragg, in his official report, names his loss at 2500.

October 10.— 1800 rebel cavalry, with four pieces of artillery, under Generals Stuart and Hampton, having crossed the Potomac at McCoy's Ferry by rapid movements, passed through Maryland and entered Pennsylvania, occupying Mercersburg and appearing before Chambersburg, Pa., about eight o'clock in the evening of the 10th. They demanded a surrender of the town, and, there being no United States officers or troops there, the principal citizens agreed to their terms. The rebels remained in possession until the next morning. In the mean time they seized all the horses in the neighborhood, and appropriated a small quantity of clothing stored for the use of the United States soldiers, shoes, &c. Before they left, they burned the railroad-depôt and workshops and destroyed a portion of the railroad-track. They pushed rapidly for the Potomac, in a direction opposite to that by which they came, passing through Emmetsburg, Woodsboro', New Market, and crossed the Baltimore & Ohio Railroad at Monrovia, where they cut the telegraph-wire and tore up some rails. They succeeded in crossing the Potomac into Virginia at Conrad's and Edwards's Ferries. General Pleasanton, who was sent in pursuit, came up with their rear at the mouth of the Monocacy, where the rebels lost nine prisoners, but succeeded in getting to White's Ford, where they crossed the river and made their escape.

nnoissance was made to
eral Hancock's division.
h for two hours, when the
village. Federal loss, 1
loss, 9 prisoners.
Kansas, was partially
ler Quantrell. They de-
he town, killed 9 citizens,
hey could find.
gan, with 1500 guerillas,
ky, overpowering a small
ught him gallantly, losing
50 of the Federal cavalry
ward left the town. He
organ, 10 privates, and 15

nt, with 2500 men, met
en Versailles and Frank-
re engaged and routed.
was reoccupied by United

llas captured 80 Federal
ky, and burned them.
tuart, 10th Illinois, with
els under Colonel Dersey.
ld, Missouri. The latter
7 wounded, 15 prisoners.

ebel guerillas, who had
s of Nashville, Tennessee,
olonel Miller, and driven
A colonel and several

· Minho, which ran the
round near Fort Moultrie,

l March 30th, 1861, pre-
cott, describing the course
illy in the early stages of
chanan Administration to
he threatened outbreak of
ern States, was published
telligencer.
made towards Leesburg
ind artillery, under Gene-
ey encountered a force of
em, took 40 prisoners, and
loss, 1 killed, 3 wounded.
ry, foraging near Lovetts-
by United States cavalry
abels lost 15 killed and 32
d and 4 wounded.
ville, Arkansas, between
Blunt, and 7000 rebels.
tter were routed, losing 6
, transportation and camp
d through Maysville and
Mountain.
cked 200 Union soldiers,
nessee, and were repulsed,
l wounded, and 25 prison-
2 wounded.
organ's and Isett's rebel
Paint Lick and Big Hill,
McCook's cavalry, 500 in
were killed, and 33 taken

rangers were attacked by
ludd, seven miles west of
ptain was killed, 40 taken
a wagon-load of arms—

William S. Rosecrans was
e U.S. Army in Kentucky,
J. Buell, removed.
ces were attacked at Mor-

gantown, Kentucky, by Colonel Bruce's Union cavalry. The rebels lost 16 prisoners.

October 25.—Colonel Brown's rebel cavalry were attacked near Thomasville, Missouri, by Lieutenant-Colonel Lazear. The enemy were routed, losing 8 killed, 18 prisoners, 25 stand of arms, and 12 horses.

October 26.—The British steamer Anglia, attempting to run the blockade, was captured by the United States Bark Restless, Captain Conroy, on the coast of South Carolina.

—— Clarke's rebel guerillas, at Clarkson, Missouri, were routed by a force under Captain Rodgers, 2d Illinois. 12 rebels were killed. Colonel Clarke, and 7 other officers, with 37 men, were taken prisoners, together with 70 stand of arms, 42 horses, 13 mules, wagons, &c., and the barracks and magazines were burned.

—— General Burnside, with the advance of the U.S. Army, crossed the Potomac at Berlin, by a pontoon bridge, from Maryland into Virginia.

—— The British iron steamer Wachuta, attempting to run the blockade, was captured by the United States gunboat Memphis.

October 27.—The British steamer Scotia, attempting to run the blockade at Bull's Bay, South Carolina, was captured by the United States bark Restless, Captain Conroy.

—— 1500 rebels, at Putnam's Ferry, Missouri, were attacked by Colonel E. Lewis, 23d Iowa. The former lost several killed, and 40 prisoners.

—— The rebel army under Generals Echols, Floyd, and Jenkins, retreated from Charlestown, Western Virginia, thus giving up the Kanawha Valley.

—— General Pleasanton with cavalry, in advance of the U.S. Army, encountered a force of rebels at Snicker's Gap, Virginia, and drove them out, losing 1 killed and 2 wounded. He took 10 prisoners.

October 28.—The rebel steamer Caroline, loaded with arms and munitions of war, captured off Mobile by the United States gunboat Montgomery.

—— Battle of Pocotaligo Bridge, South Carolina. Eight United States gunboats, two armed steamers, and five transports, with 4448 troops—a combined expedition under Generals Brannan and Terry and Captain Steedman, U.S. Navy—engaged in operations against Pocotaligo and Coosawatchie, South Carolina, partially with a design to reconnoitre the Broad, Coosawatchie, Tulfinny, and Pocotaligo rivers, to ascertain the strength of the rebels on the mainland, and to destroy as much of the railroad leading from Charleston to Savannah as was possible. The troops were landed at Mackey's Point, eleven miles from Pocotaligo, and marched toward the latter village; about seven miles out the advance was encountered by field artillery, well served by the rebels. From this position the latter were beaten. They made a second stand, and were again driven. The third stand was made at an iron bridge across the Pocotaligo: the rebels had 12 guns, the Federals but 4 Parrots and 3 boat howitzers. The 4th New Hampshire volunteers and 47th Pennsylvania made a charge and drove the rebels across the bridge. This occurred at 6 o'clock, the fight having lasted from 12 o'clock. Meanwhile Beauregard had sent reinforcements from Charleston, and, night coming on, the Federals retired. The rebels were commanded by Colonel Walker. Federal loss, 15 killed, 106 wounded, 2 missing. The rebel papers say that their loss was 20 killed and 60 wounded.

—— While the United States troops were engaged in the battle of Pocotaligo, about 500 men, under Colonel Barton, 48th New York, went up the Coosawatchie, and landed near the village. They intercepted a train laden with troops, which they fired into. The town was shelled, the telegraph wires cut, and the railroad destroyed. In this expedition the only loss on the Federal side was 1 killed.

—— General Herron, U.S. Army, with 1000 men, attacked 3000 rebels under Colonel Cravens, four miles from Fayetteville, Arkansas, and routed them after an hour's engagement. Union loss, 1 killed, 6 wounded. The enemy left 8 dead on the field, with all their camp equipage, and a few wagons.

October 29.—The ship Alleghany, of New York, from Baltimore to London, loaded with guano, at anchor in the Chesapenke Bay, near the mouth of the Rappahannock, was boarded by 75 rebels, captured, pillaged, and burned.

——— The brig Baronda Castine, of Boston, Captain Saunders, was captured at sea, not far from the coast of the United States, by the British rebel privateer steamer "290," or "Alabama," commanded by Captain Raphael Semmes. She was released upon condition of taking as passengers to the United States the crews of the bark Lamplighter, ship Lafayette, schooner Crenshaw, and bark Lauretta, which had been previously taken and burned. Captain Saunders gave a ransom bond for $6000, payable to the President of the Confederate States "30 days after peace is declared." Semmes reported that he had also taken and burned the ship Manchester and brig Dunkirk. He put their crews as passengers on board the ship Tonawanda, also captured, and ransomed to take off the crews of the other ships, on bond for $80,000, payable as above.

October 30.—Major-General O. M. Mitchell, U.S. Army, commanding the Army of South Carolina, died at Beaufort, South Carolina, of yellow fever.

October 31.—Charlestown, Western Virginia, occupied by United States troops under Major-General Cox.

November 1.—Ex-President Buchanan published in the *National Intelligencer*, Washington, a defence of his conduct during the last months of his administration, in regard to the anticipated rebellion in the Cotton States, and in reply to the strictures of General Scott.

——— The prize steamers Alliance, William Curry, Susan, and Union, sold at Key West.

——— Burbridge's and Green's guerillas were attacked at Bollinger's Mills, Missouri, by Colonels Dewey and Lazear, and pursued fifteen miles, losing 236 killed, wounded, and prisoners. Federal loss, 1 killed and 7 wounded.

——— A skirmish at Phillimont, Virginia, between General Pleasanton's cavalry and Stuart's rebel cavalry, with 1 battery. It was carried on by artillery. The enemy retreated to Union. Federal loss, 1 killed, 14 wounded. 5 rebels are known to have been killed.

November 2.—General Pleasanton occupied Union, Virginia, after a skirmish in which he lost 1 killed, and 4 wounded.

——— An engagement in front of a rebel breastwork near Roanoke River, North Carolina, by General Foster's command (Federal) and 3000 rebel infantry, supported by 6 pieces of artillery. The latter lost 60 killed and wounded. Union loss, 10 killed and wounded.

November 3.—Upperville, Virginia, occupied by General Pleasanton, U.S. Army, after an engagement of 4 hours.

——— The rebels were driven out of Thoroughfare Gap, Virginia, by General Stahl's cavalry.

November 4.—Hamilton, North Carolina, taken by Union troops under General Foster, the enemy abandoning it.

November 5.—A skirmish at Barbus, Virginia, between Pleasanton's (Federal) and Stuart's (rebel) cavalry. The latter, 3000 strong, were driven off, one regiment being routed by a charge by Colonel Gregg's 8th Pennsylvania cavalry. 36 dead rebels were left on the field; many were wounded and carried off; 17 prisoners were taken. Federal loss, 5 killed, 10 wounded.

——— A skirmish near Nashville, Tennessee, between General Naglee's (Union) troops and rebels. The latter were beaten off, losing their dead and wounded taken off, and 19 prisoners. Federal loss, 26 wounded, 19 missing.

——— Rebels defeated at Piketon, Kentucky, by Colonel Dill's 39th Kentucky cavalry, losing 80 prisoners, muskets, tents, wagons, horses, mules, &c.

——— A battalion of Colonel Shackelford's 8th Kentucky cavalry was attacked by Fowler's guerillas, on Bird River, near Madisonville, Kentucky. The rebels were repulsed, losing, among the killed, Colonel Fowler and 7 others, a number of wounded and prisoners.

November 7.—An order of the United States War Department, dated November 5th, relieving Major-General McClellan from the command of the Army of the Potomac, was received at headquarters at 11 P.M. General McClellan was ordered to report at Trenton, New Jersey, and the command of the Army of the Potomac was turned over to Major-General Burnside.

November 8.—A skirmish near Warrenton, Virginia, between Pleasanton's (Federal) and Stuart's (rebel) cavalry. The latter lost 3 pieces of artillery and 7 prisoners.

——— Colonel Thomas .H. Ford, 32d Ohio, dismissed from the United States service, for his cowardly action in abandoning Maryland Heights, September 15th.

November 9.—Captain Ulric Dahlgren, of General Sigel's staff, with 60 of the 1st Indiana cavalry, made a dash into Fredericksburg, Virginia, which was occupied by 9 companies of rebel cavalry. Dahlgren took several prisoners at first, but was soon compelled to meet the enemy eight to one. He fought them gallantly, and succeeded in getting off with a loss of 1 killed and 3 missing, bringing off 39 prisoners, with their horses and accoutrements.

——— St. Mary's, Florida, shelled by United States gunboat Mohawk and burned; cause, the treacherous firing into a flag of truce by inhabitants of the town.

——— General Butler confiscated all the property within the district of Lafourche, La. Loyal citizens were to be confirmed in their rights, to hold their own property, but rebel property was held for the use of the United States.

November 10.—Imboden's rebel camp, 18 miles south of Mansfield, Western Virginia, was attacked by General Kelly, who routed the enemy, killing and wounding many, capturing his camp, horses, cattle, arms, &c., and 50 prisoners.

——— A general cartel of exchange for prisoners on both sides arranged at Aikin's Landing, Virginia, by which 926 United States officers were exchanged for 1596 rebel officers, and also 24,000 men, most of whom were on parole. This cartel left a balance of about 6000 privates due to the United States. The place of exchange in Virginia in future was changed from Aikin's Landing to City Point.

——— An expedition under General Ransom, U.S. Volunteers, came up with General Woodward's rebel force, 800 strong, near Garretsburg, Kentucky, and routed the latter after a short engagement, killing 16 and wounding 40, taking 20 prisoners, with 100 horses and mules, arms, equipments, tents, &c. Union loss, 3 killed and 7 wounded.

November 11.—Skirmish near La Grange, Tennessee. Rebel loss 16 killed, 134 prisoners; Union loss 2 wounded.

November 14.—The Army of the Potomac was organized as follows:—Right wing, 2d and 9th corps, to be commanded by General Sumner; left wing, 1st and 6th corps, General Franklin; centre, 3d and 5th corps, General Hooker; 11th corps (reserve) under General Sigel.

November 17.—The advance of General Burnside's troops arrived at Falmouth, opposite Fredericksburg, Virginia.

——— Jefferson Davis issued a proclamation declaring that if General McNeill, of the Missouri Militia, who hung ten guerillas accused of the murder of a Union citizen, was not delivered up to him, he would hang ten United States officers, who might fall into his hands.

——— Cavalry fight at Cove Creek, North Carolina: rebels driven from their position by flying artillery, and their barracks destroyed.

November 21.—General Sumner, United States Army, demanded the surrender of Fredericksburg, Virginia, in consequence of his troops being fired upon from the town, and threatened to shell the place after 16 hours' time.

——— Mayor Slaughter of Fredericksburg replied, that the firing was not by citizens but by troops, and asked for time to remove non-combatants.

November 22.—Upon a conference the threat to shell Fredericksburg was withdrawn by the United States officers.

——— Political prisoners of State arrested by the United

States military authorities, were discharged by order of the Secretary of War. Prisoners taken in arms were retained.

November 23.—The United States gunboat Ellis, Commander Cushing, was blown up near the mouth of New River, North Carolina, by her officers. The Ellis had been upon an expedition, captured the town of Onslow, destroyed salt works, and took prize schooners and boats. On the return the Ellis run aground, and was attacked by artillery from the shore. There being no means of escape for the gunboat, the crew were put on board one of the captured schooners, and the Ellis blown up.

November 25.—A rebel camp at Sinking Creek, West Virginia, surprised and captured by Colonel J. D. Paxton's Union Virginia cavalry. 118 prisoners taken, with horses, muskets, stores, &c.

—— A rebel raid upon Poolesville, Maryland, by cavalry which crossed the Potomac. But little damage was done.

November 28.—Marmaduke's rebel forces on the march for an invasion of Missouri, were overtaken by General Blunt's Union troops, at Cane Hill, Arkansas, and routed after a flying fight carried on over twelve miles of ground.

November 29.—Rebels at Snicker's Ferry, Virginia, were attacked by Stahl's Federal cavalry and dispersed, losing 50 killed and 40 wounded. 80 horses and cattle were also taken.

December 1.—The commencement of the third session of the 37th Congress. The President's message, among other things, recommended the passage of a law guaranteeing compensation to each loyal state, that would emancipate its slaves before the year 1900.

—— A skirmish at Franklin, Virginia, between Union troops sent from Suffolk, Virginia, by General Peck and rebel troops. "The Pittsburg battery," taken by the rebels during McClellan's battles on the Peninsula, was recaptured.

December 2.—A fight near Charlestown, Virginia, between Union troops under General Geary, and a force of rebels. The latter were routed, losing 70 killed and wounded, and 145 prisoners.

—— General Hovey, U.S. Army, occupied Grenada, Mississippi, with 20,000 men. The rebels abandoned the town, and burned 15 locomotives and 100 cars.

December 3.—The rebels abandoned Abbeville, Mississippi, at the approach of General Grant.

—— Winchester, Virginia, surrendered to General Geary.

December 6.—A large expedition of troops sailed from New York, under command of General Banks, destination not made public.

December 7.—Battle of Prairie Grove, Arkansas, between Union troops under Generals Blunt and Herron, and 28,000 rebels under General Hindman. The rebels were defeated and retreated during the night, losing 1500 killed and wounded. Union loss 495 killed and 500 wounded.

—— The Anglo-rebel steamer Alabama, Captain Semmes, captured the California steamer Ariel, off the coast of Cuba. The Ariel was released upon giving a ransom bond of $228,000, payable after the close of the war.

—— 300 rebels attacked 60 men of the 8th Pennsylvania cavalry at King George's Court House, Virginia, and killed and wounded 20. 40 of the cavalry escaped.

—— Three Federal regiments, the 104th Illinois, 106th, and 108th Ohio, and several soldiers of the 2d Indiana cavalry, captured at Hartsville, Tennessee, by Morgan's rebel cavalry, after a loss of 55 killed.

December 9.—Concordia, Arkansas, burned in retaliation for the seizure and burning of the United States steamer Lake City, the day before.

—— Plymouth, North Carolina, destroyed by rebels during a fight with United States troops.

December 11.—Leesburg, Virginia, occupied by General Geary.

—— Fredericksburg, Virginia, bombarded by United States troops, in order to cover the laying of pontoon bridges. Rebel sharpshooters resisted this movement. They were driven out by a force sent over in boats; afterwards the Union troops occupied the city.

December 13.—Battle of Fredericksburg, Virginia. The Federal troops were led in three columns, under Generals Sumner, Hooker, and Franklin. The rebel works were strongly placed, and stubbornly defended Several gallant charges were made by the Union troops, but they were repulsed each time with fearful slaughter; at night, although advanced positions were held, no important advantage had been gained. The next day there were no active hostilities. Finding the assault impossible, the Federal troops withdrew during the night of the 15th, and morning of the 16th, without being pursued, and took up their old position at Falmouth; of the United States troops Generals Bayard and Conrad F. Jackson were killed, and Generals Vinton, Gibbons, Kimball, Caldwell, and Meagher, wounded. General Burnside reported the Union loss 1512 killed, 6000 wounded, and 100 prisoners. The rebels lost Generals T. R. Cobb and Maxcy Gregg killed. They reported their loss in killed and wounded, to be 1800 only.

—— An expedition under General Foster, left Newbern, North Carolina, for Goldsborough. They met the rebels at Southwest Creek, and routed them; at Kinston they were again attacked, and after 5 hours' fighting, driven from their position, losing 11 guns and 400 prisoners.

—— The United States gunboat Cairo was blown up by a torpedo in the Yazoo River, and sunk in 15 minutes. The crew were not injured, and all were saved.

December 14.—A raid into Poolesville, Maryland, by 400 rebel cavalry. 1 Union soldier was killed and 17 wounded, the remainder, 21 in number, escaped. Rebel loss 2 killed.

—— The expedition under General Banks arrived at New Orleans, and Major-General Butler was superseded by the former.

December 16.—General Foster advanced to Whitehall, North Carolina, where the rebels were intrenched. After a fight of 3 hours they retreated to Goldsborough.

December 17.—General Foster reached Goldsborough, North Carolina, and routed the rebels after a short fight. The railroad bridge and track at that place were destroyed, after which, the Union troops repaired to Newbern without molestation.

—— General Grover took possession of Baton Rouge, Louisiana, which had been evacuated by the Federals in August 1862.

December 18.—A cavalry skirmish near Corinth, Mississippi, between United States cavalry under General Dodge, and Forrest the rebel guerilla.

—— Secretaries Seward and Chase tendered their resignations to the President from their positions in the Cabinet, in consequence of the action of certain Republican Senators, accusing them of being responsible for the disaster at Fredericksburg. The President held the resignations under advisement.

December 19.—Holly Springs, Mississippi, captured by rebel cavalry, who took and destroyed commissary stores, provisions, clothing, &c., worth $2,000,000, and captured 1950 officers and men.

—— Major-General A. E. Burnside addressed a letter to Major-General Halleck in relation to the battle of Fredericksburg, the disaster at which contest had, by partisan misrepresentations, been ascribed to the interference of members of the cabinet. In this letter he says, "For the failure in this attack I am responsible." The President decided not to accept the resignations of Messrs. Seward and Chase, the accusations of the Republican caucus not being founded on fact.

December 20.—Davis's Mill, Tennessee, attacked by Van Dorn. It was defended by 250 Federals. The rebels were repulsed, with a loss of 20 killed, 30 wounded and left on the field, and several prisoners.

December 21.—General Carter with 1000 horsemen left Loudon, Kentucky, for a raid upon the main rebel railroad route through East Tennessee. Two important bridges were burned, beside locomotives, cars, railroad tracks and trestlework. The expedition was one of the most dangerous, and for the great extent of ground travelled over, the most remarkable of the war up to that time.

December 22.—A company of Colonel R. Butler Price's 2d Pennsylvania cavalry surprised at Occoquan, Virginia, and taken prisoners, Captain Johnson killed.

——— Seven gunboats and 114 transport steamers, with the divisions of Generals Sherman, Hurlbut, McClernand, A. C. Smith, and G. W. Morgan, comprising 50,000 men, left Memphis bound for Vicksburg.

December 23.—Skirmish near Dumfries, Virginia, between a portion of Sigel's command and 4000 rebel cavalry. The latter were driven off with loss.

——— A proclamation issued by Jefferson Davis at Richmond, denouncing the conduct of General Butler at New Orleans, and the hanging of Mumford, and threatening to hang General Butler if caught, or any of his officers, also prohibiting any exchange of commissioned Federal officers taken prisoners thereafter.

December 26.—Major-General W. S. Rosecrans, being ready at all points for aggressive movements, commenced the march of his army from Nashville, Tenn., towards the rebel lines towards Nolinsville and Stewart's Creek.

December 27.—Skirmish at Elkford, Kentucky, between 175 men of the 10th Kentucky cavalry under Major Foley, and 350 rebels. The latter lost 17 killed and 57 prisoners, 80 horses and all their camp equipage.

——— Elizabethtown, Kentucky, defended by 250 Federal soldiers under Lieutenant Colonel Smith, was attacked by 2800 guerillas under Morgan, who captured the town after a gallant resistance by Colonel Smith's men.

——— Generals Blunt and Herron marched over Boston Mountain to Van Buren, Arkansas, drove the rebels across the Arkansas, killed and wounded some, took 6 steamboats loaded with provisions for the rebel army, camp equipage, and 100 prisoners.

——— General Sherman's expedition against Vicksburg was debarked on the Yazoo River and proceeded to attack the enemy's works upon the Chickasaw Bluffs, which were 6 miles from Vicksburg. The fleet and gunboats attacked the batteries at Haines's Bluff. The fight lasted five hours. The rebels were driven out of their advanced intrenchments.

December 28.—Thirty-eight Sioux Indians, convicted of murdering the inhabitants of Minnesota, were hanged at Mankato, Minnesota.

December 29.—General Sherman's troops employed against Vicksburg advanced. General Steel commanded the left wing, Generals Morgan and Blair the centre, and Generals A. L. and M. L. Smith the right; after heavy fighting, the rebel works opposite the centre were attempted by assault. After a desperate fight the United States troops were repulsed, leaving 500 killed and wounded on the field and losing 300 prisoners.

December 30.—A general advance was made by the troops under General Rosecrans in Tennessee. The rebels were pushed 7 or 8 miles. There were smart skirmishes near Nolinsville and Stewart's Creek.

December 31.—The rebels at Vicksburg being strongly reinforced, and amounting to 65,000 men, fell with fury upon Sherman's small force, which was within 2 miles of the city. There was desperate fighting on both sides, but Sherman was compelled to fall back and abandon the expedition. He re-embarked his troops and left the Yazoo January 4th 1863, having lost during the operations 600 killed, 1500 wounded, and 1000 missing. The rebels reported that their whole loss was 100 killed, wounded, and missing. Among the killed on the Federal side were Captain Gwyn, commanding United States gunboat Benton, General Morgan, Colonel J. B. Wyman. Wounded, Colonel Morgan L. Smith and many other officers.

——— The United States iron-clad steamer Monitor foundered at sea south of Cape Hatteras, losing 4 officers and 12 men, and 7 men of the steamer Rhode Island, who were trying to save the crew of the Monitor.

——— First day of the battle of Murfreesboro or Stone River, between the United States army under General W. S. Rosecrans, 45,000 strong, with 100 pieces of artillery, and the rebels under General Bragg. During the early part of the day the enemy were pressed forward in some parts of the field, but they massed their men for a furious attack upon the right wing, under General McCook, which, after severe fighting, was pressed back two miles. About the same time a heavy assault was made upon the Federal centre, which was withstood after a desperate contest. The same manœuvre was tried upon the left; the enemy crossed the river, but failing in the attack, withdrew. Rosecrans lost much of the ground which he held in the morning. After eleven hours' fighting both sides ceased their efforts. The Federal troops lost heavily in killed, wounded, stragglers, and prisoners, besides 28 pieces of artillery.

1863. *January 1.*—Second day of the battle of Murfreesboro or Stone River. The rebels made several demonstrations upon the Union lines, but being promptly met they were repulsed without heavy fighting.

——— The rebel guerilla Forrest was attacked at Hunt's Cross Roads, Tennessee, by General Sullivan with 6000 men, and routed with a loss of 1400 killed and wounded, 400 prisoners, 350 horses, 6 guns, and 1000 stand of arms. Union loss, 200 killed and wounded.

——— A land and water attack was made by rebels under Magruder upon the small Federal force holding Galveston, Texas. The United States steamer Harriet Lane was carried by boarding. The United States flagship Westfield, having run ashore, was blown up, and with it Commodore Renshaw and Lieutenants Green and Zimmerman. The United States troops, 300 in number, were commanded by Colonel Burrel. Federal loss in soldiers and sailors, 160 killed and 300 prisoners. Among the killed were Captain Wainwright of the Harriet Lane, and Lieutenants Edward Lea, James Pollock, John Hart, and Henry Newton, of the same ship.

——— The President of the United States issued a proclamation reciting the terms of the proclamation of September 22, 1862, and declaring that according to the terms of that proclamation, the slaves of the people of the States still in rebellion were free.

——— Morgan's guerilla force was defeated south of Lebanon, Kentucky, by Colonel Hoskins' Kentucky cavalry. He crossed the Cumberland River early in December, appeared in front of Munfordsville December 25, and visited Munfordsville, Elizabethtown, Muldraugh's Hill, and Rolling Fork, destroying railroads, bridges, and trestle-work as he went. He was attacked several times, and lost in the last engagement several killed, 90 prisoners, guns, caissons, &c., and fled precipitately.

——— Forrest, the rebel guerilla, was whipped at Spring Hill, Tennessee, and routed with a loss of all his artillery and 300 stand of arms. The rebel Colonel Napier was killed and Colonel De Shay taken prisoner.

——— Richard Yeadon, of Charleston, South Carolina, offers to pay $10,000 (Confederate currency) to any one who will capture and deliver Major-General Benjamin F. Butler, U.S. Army, *dead* or *alive*, to any rebel authority.

January 2.—Third day of the battle of Murfreesboro or Stone River. There was skirmishing in the morning along the entire lines. In the afternoon an attack was made by the rebels in strong force upon a single division, which was driven with a loss of 80 killed and 375 wounded. The rebels were repulsed by reinforcements and opened upon by the artillery. In forty minutes they fled, having lost 2000 men by the terrible rapidity of the Federal firing. They were pursued and lost 4 guns and colors.

January 3.—Fourth day of the battle of Murfreesboro or Stone River. There was light skirmishing on both sides. Provisions and ammunition were distributed in the morning. At night the rebels fled, abandoning Murfreesboro and all their sick and wounded. General Rosecrans fought the battle with 43,400 men, and lost in killed 1533, wounded 8778, prisoners 2800. The rebel force was estimated by General Rosecrans at 62,400, their loss in killed and wounded at 14,500. The Federals lost in killed General Sill, Colonels Shaffer, Milliken, Fornam, Jones, Carpenter, Roberts, Kell, Lieutenant-Colonels Garesche, Cotton, Jones, McKee, Majors Rosengarten, Carpenter, and many officers and men. Wounded, Generals E. M. Kirk, Willich, Wood, Van Cleve, Colonels Cassall, Miller, Blake, Moody, Larraby, Lieutenant-

ajors Slemmer, King, Foot, ginia" into a dismal mud, through which it was impos-
els lost in killed Generals sible to drag the artillery and heavy caissons, except by
Hanson, Colonels McNair, monstrous and fatiguing effort.
founded, Generals Clardon, *January* 21.—The United States blockading ship Morning Light and a schooner were captured by the rebels
oorfield, Western Virginia, off Sabine Pass, Texas, by an expedition sent from the
nent and 3000 rebel cavalry shore.
Federals fought coolly and —————— The President approved of the finding of a
he rebels were driven off. court-martial convened to try Major-General Fitz-John
isoners. Porter, dismissing him from the army, for disobedience
essage to the rebel Congress of the orders of General Pope, his superior officer, in the
at in retaliation for Presi- battles in Virginia, August 27 and 29, 1862, near Manas-
 proclamation he would sas, by which he was directed to reinforce General Pope
officers captured thereafter and to execute certain manœuvres which would have
horities, to be dealt with as inevitably caused the defeat of the rebels, all of which
 be neglected and refused to do.
rtsville, Missouri, between *January* 25.—The advance of the United States troops
ler Major Collins and 4000 landed opposite Vicksburg, Miss., on the Louisiana side.
with 5 pieces of cannon. *January* 26.—Major-General Joseph Hooker was ap-
nded. Rebel loss, 150. pointed commander of the Army of the Potomac, in the
House, Virginia, two sloops place of Major-General A. E. Burnside, resigned. Major-
c., were burned by United Generals Franklin and Sumner were also relieved from
 their commands.
erating against Vicksburg —————— By order of Secretary Stanton, Governor An-
th severo loss, and being drew, of Massachusetts, was permitted to recruit "per-
ects of the expedition, was sons of African descent" for military service, organized
lernand took command of into separate corps.
having been superseded. *January* 27.—The rebel Fort McAllister, at the mouth
luntoon's Mills, Tennessee. of the Ogechee River, was bombarded by the United
g 16 killed, 46 prisoners, 50 States iron-clad Montauk, without any perceptible effect.
 This bombardment and several which succeeded were
upon Springfield, Missouri, really made to test the power of the iron-clad ships.
aaduke, about 5000 strong, *January* 29.—A battle near Blackwater River, Virginia,
d 13 hours, and the rebels between United States troops under General Corcoran
losing 300 killed, wounded, and rebels under General Roger A. Pryor. The latter
as defended by 600 militia was routed. Killed on the Federal side, Captain Taylor,
 130th New York, Lieutenant Sawtelle, 6th Massachusetts.
xas, was bombarded by the Wounded, Colonel Knoderer, 167th Pennsylvania. Total
n, and gunboats New Lon- killed 24, wounded 80. The rebel loss was quite as
 heavy.
t, upon the Arkansas River, *January* 30.—The United States gunboat I. P. Smith,
ernand with the troops re- with 11 guns and 230 men, taken by the rebels in the
Commodore Porter, of the Stono River, South Carolina, having run aground.
ed by storm, and with them *January* 31.—The rebel iron-clad steamers Chicora
l, 4720 prisoners, and nine and Palmetto State, accompanied by three small steam-
ions of war, &c. The loss ers, made an attack on the United States blockading
small. In the navy there fleet off Charleston, South Carolina. The gunboat Mer-
. In the army, about 250 cedita was pierced by a shot, which exploded her boiler.
e rebels, about 200 killed The Keystone State was fired into. Commander Stel-
 wagen, believing that the Mercedita was sinking, sent a
rivateer Oreto, or Florida, boat to one of the rebel rams, offering to surrender, but
ng past nine ships of the the rebels did not take possession of the ship, and shortly
 afterward they returned to Charleston. 3 men of the
Pattersonville, Louisiana, Mercedita were killed, and of the Keystone State 23
ederal brigade, aided by the killed and 17 wounded. Both ships remained and were
un, and three gunboats and afterwards repaired. Beauregard issued a flaming pro-
vere driven from their In- clamation in consequence of this "victory," announcing
the expedition was to de- that two United States gunboats were sunk and the rest
iron-clad gunboat Cotton, driven off, and that the blockade of Charleston was
ral troops and blown up. raised. During the fight the blockade runner Princess
Thomas McKean Buchanan, Royal was captured by other vessels of the blockading
t Calhoun, was killed near squadron.
River, Louisiana, by a shot *February* 1.—Island No. 10, Mississippi River, was
 attacked by 3000 rebels in flatboats, who were beaten
l States steamer Hatteras off by the garrison of the island.
Texas, by the rebel priva- *February* 2.—The United States ram Queen of the
a gallant fight the Hatteras West ran past the rebel forts at Vicksburg, being under
were taken off, but 43 were fire for 45 minutes.
 —————— The United States troops commenced operations
eamer Tropic, formerly the for opening the Yazoo Pass, via the Coldwater and other
irleston, South Carolina, by channels to the Yazoo River, in the rear of Vicksburg.
g fleet and burned by the They cut the levee crossing the entrance of the pass,
 and let in the water of the Mississippi River, flooding a
ansas River, was taken by large region of country. The efforts to open a naviga-
River expedition. There tion through this pass continued for many weeks, and
uskets, and 150 prisoners. were prosecuted with prodigious labor to overcome the
the Potomac attempted to natural obstacles that were presented to the engineers.
rebels near the Rappahan- *February* 3.—A small force of United States troops
om accomplishing it by a under Colonel Harding, holding Fort Donelson, Tenn.,
ied "the sacred soil of Vir- were attacked by the rebel General Wheeler, with 4500

men and 8 pieces of artillery. The garrison were saved by United States gunboats, which arrived in the night and opened upon the rebels with immense effect, causing their precipitate flight, leaving 140 dead upon the field. Their wounded are estimated at 400, and 150 prisoners were taken. Union loss, 16 killed, 60 wounded, and 50 prisoners.

February 5.—The United States ram Queen of the West destroyed three steamers on the Mississippi below Vicksburg, laden with stores and munitions of war for the use of the rebel army.

——— By order of General Hooker, the Army of the Potomac is reorganized by assigning the following officers to commands:—*First Corps,* Major-General John F. Reynolds; *Second,* Major-General D. N. Couch; *Third,* Major-General Daniel E. Sickles; *Fifth,* Major-General George G. Meade; *Sixth,* Major-General John Sedgwick; *Eleventh,* Major-General Franz Sigel; *Twelfth,* Major-General H. W. Slocum. The cavalry to be consolidated under General Stoneman.

February 8.—Lebanon, Tennessee, was occupied by the Federals, and 600 rebels captured.

February 12.—Skirmish at Cainesville, Tennessee. 500 of Morgan's rebel cavalry were defeated by 250 United States cavalry under Colonel James Monroe, with a loss to the rebels of 20 killed, several wounded, 6 prisoners, and 50 horses. Union loss, 3 wounded.

February 13.—The United States iron-clad gunboat Indianola passed the rebel batteries at Vicksburg.

——— The American ship Jacob Bell, loaded with teas, cassia, camphor, silks, &c., valued at $1,500,000, all British property, was destroyed at sea by the rebel privateer steamer Florida, Captain Maffit.

February 17.—The United States ram Queen of the West was captured by the rebels in Red River, near Fort Taylor, having been run aground under the batteries, it is said, by the treachery of the pilot. The greater part of the crew jumped overboard and made their escape.

——— A skirmish near Helena, Arkansas, between Union infantry and Forrest's cavalry, the latter attempting to prevent the operations for the opening of a pass into the Coldwater. The rebels were beaten off and took to flight.

February 18.—The bombardment of Vicksburg was commenced by the forces under General Grant and Commodore Porter, U.S. Navy.

——— A convention of secessionists which attempted to assemble at Frankfort, Kentucky, was broken up and dispersed by United States soldiers under Colonel S A. Gilbert, acting by authority of General Q. A. Gilmore.

February 22.—Tuscumbia, Alabama, was taken by a force under Colonel Corwin, accompanied by five gunboats. Ferry-boats were destroyed by the United States troops, and an assessment levied on the people of the town.

February 24.—The United States iron-clad Indianola in the Mississippi River, below Vicksburg, was attacked by the rebel rams Webb and Queen of the West (the latter lately captured from the United States), and so injured that she surrendered, but sunk near the shore, the upper works being exposed.

February 25.—An expedition of steamers and gunboats loaded with troops left Moon Lake and went up the Coldwater River, and reached the head of the pass March 9. The object of this expedition was to find a means of reaching the Yazoo River in the flank of Vicksburg.

——— Stuart's and Fitz-Hugh Lee's rebel cavalry made a raid in the Federal lines north of Falmouth, killing 3 and taking 50 prisoners.

February 26.—The rebel privateer Retribution arrived at Nassau, from a cruise in which were captured and destroyed several commercial vessels belonging to citizens of the United States.

——— The bill "for calling out the national forces," commonly called "the Conscription Bill," was passed finally in Congress. It was signed by the President March 3.

February 27.—By proclamation of Jefferson Davis, March 26 is appointed as a day of fasting and prayer throughout the rebel States.

——— An expedition of gunboats and transports went up the Yazoo Pass from the Mississippi River, hoping to reach the Yazoo River by that course and flank the rebel batteries on the Yazoo at Haines's Bluff, above Vicksburg.

——— A skirmish at Bradyville, Tennessee. Rebel loss in prisoners, 8 officers and 62 men, 70 horses, with tents, &c. Federal loss, 1 killed, 10 wounded.

——— The rebel steamer Nashville, attempting to get to sea, ran aground near Fort McAllister, Georgia, and was cannonaded by the United States fleet, set on fire by an incendiary shell, and totally destroyed.

March 3.—The rebels blew up the iron-clad gunboat Indianola, being frightened by the approach of a wooden imitation of a gunboat rigged upon a flatboat, which they believed to be "a turreted monster." This sham monitor had been fitted up to send past the batteries at Vicksburg, in order to draw their fire, and ascertain the number and location of the guns.

——— An attack was made upon the rebel Fort McAllister, Georgia, by three United States iron-clads and one mortar boat. The bombardment was continued at intervals for several days, the principal object being to try the powers of the iron-clads and the force of their guns.

March 4.—A skirmish near Franklin, Tennessee, between Van Dorn's rebel advance and Federal troops. 23 of the latter were taken prisoners.

March 5.—Five regiments United States volunteers, with one battery and cavalry, under Colonel Coburn, were attacked and defeated at Spring Hill, Tennessee, by Van Dorn's men, who were present in great force. Union loss, 1200 officers and men taken prisoners, 400 killed and wounded. Rebel loss, 180 killed and 4((wounded. The rebel attacking force was 30,000 strong.

March 7.—Russel's rebel cavalry were defeated at Unionville, Tennessee, by Minty's Union cavalry. Rebel loss, 50 killed and 80 wounded, 58 prisoners, with horses, mules, tents, &c.

March 9.—General Stoughton, U.S. Army, and several men were captured by Moseby's guerillas, with horses, &c., at Fairfax Court House, Virginia.

——— Major-General Ed. V. Sumner was appointed to the command of the Department of the Missouri, *vice* Major-General S. R. Curtis, relieved.

——— British steamship Douro, loaded with cotton, and endeavoring to break the blockade, was captured off Cape Fear by the United States gunboat Quaker City.

March 10.—A proclamation was issued by President Lincoln, warning deserters from the army and navy to return to service, promising to all who did so before April 1, 1863, a remission of punishment, except pay and allowance during the time of their absence, and menacing the severest penalty of the law against those who did not return to duty.

——— Jacksonville, Florida, captured by United States colored troops under Colonel Higginson.

March 11.—The Yazoo Pass expedition, from Admiral Porter's fleet and General Grant's army before Vicksburg, having succeeded in passing through the Coldwater and Tallahatchie rivers, met with resistance from Fort Pemberton, at Greenwood, near the confluence of the Tallahatchie and Yallobusha rivers. A smart action took place between the iron-clads and the fort, during which the vessels suffered some damage. A battery was then constructed on shore with guns from the steamers.

March 13.—A fight at Greenwood, Mississippi, between the Union gunboats of the Yazoo Pass expedition and the shore battery erected by the soldiers and sailors of the Yazoo Pass expedition, and the rebels in Fort Pemberton. The engagement was spirited, but without any important advantage on either side. Operations for the reduction of the fort then commenced, and continued for many days.

March 14.—An attempt was made to pass the rebel batteries at Port Hudson, on the Mississippi, by Commodore Farragut, with eight gunboats and steamers

The vessels started on their perilous trip about 11 o'clock at night. The rebels discovered the movement and opened upon the ships. The frigate Mississippi ran aground, and was abandoned and burned. 65 of the crew were killed, drowned, or taken prisoners. The Hartford and Albatross passed the fort and went up the river; the other vessels were repulsed.

March 16.—Water was let into the Lake Providence Canal, 60 miles above Vicksburg, with the expectation of opening a communication via the Tensas, Red, and Black rivers, into the Mississippi River, 180 miles below Vicksburg.

—— The schooner Chapman, bought by rebel sympathizers and fitted out for a privateer, was seized in the harbor of San Francisco, when upon the point of sailing, with the intended crew, guns, &c.

March 17.—A fight near Kelly's Ford, Virginia, between Averill's United States cavalry and rebel sharpshooters and cavalry under Stuart and Fitzhugh Lee. Several dashing charges were made and the rebels were routed, losing 80 prisoners, besides killed and wounded. Union loss, 50 killed and wounded.

—— Colonel James B. Fry was appointed Provost Marshal of the United States, under the act for calling out the national forces.

—— A fight on the Blackwater, Virginia, between the 11th Pennsylvania cavalry, Colonel S. P. Spear, with artillery, and rebels intrenched behind breastworks. The Federals could not carry the works, and lost 17 wounded and missing.

March 18.—The rams Lancaster and Switzerland attempted to run past the rebel batteries at Vicksburg. They were fired upon. The Lancaster was sunk, and the Switzerland temporarily disabled.

March 20.—Colonel Hall's brigade was attacked while on a scout near Milton, Tennessee, by Morgan's and Breckenridge's cavalry, 1000 strong. The rebels were repulsed, losing 40 killed, 140 wounded, and 12 prisoners. Federal loss, 17 killed and 31 wounded.

March 21.—Major-General Ed. V. Sumner died at Syracuse, New York, of congestion of the lungs.

—— The Anglo-rebel blockade running steamer Nicholas I. was captured off Little River, North Carolina, by the United States gunboat Victoria; having on board Enfield rifles, powder, &c.

March 23.—Mount Sterling, Kentucky, was taken by the rebel Colonel Clarke with a strong force. The garrison, only 200 in number, fought gallantly from the houses in the town, but were finally compelled to surrender. The rebels then burned the village.

March 24.—The people of West Virginia voted upon the amendment to their constitution, proposing that all children of slaves born after July 4, 1863, should be free, that all slaves then under 10 years of age should be free at the age of 21 years, and that all slaves between 10 and 21 years of age should be free at the age of 25. This was known as "the Willey Amendment," and was carried by the following vote:—For the amendment, 23,318; against the amendment, 572; majority for the amendment, 22,746. In 10 of the 48 counties no election was held, in consequence of the rebel occupation.

March 25.—The Liverpool (Eng.) Emancipation Society presented a petition to the British House of Commons against the rebel privateer Alabama, as illegally fitted out in England and manned by Englishmen, and asking that the ship be treated as a public enemy, and that the fitting out of such vessels shall be stopped in future.

—— About 300 United States troops at Brentwood, Tennessee, were attacked by 5000 rebel cavalry under Wheeler, Forrest, and Wharton. They surrendered after a feeble resistance, giving up all the government property at that place. The rebels were pursued by General Green Clay Smith, and within 6 miles of Brentwood he retook all the wagons and ammunition, but, being beset by a superior force, destroyed them. Union loss, 16 killed, wounded, and missing. Rebel loss, 15 killed and wounded, and 50 prisoners.

—— Point Pleasant, Western Virginia, captured by 700 rebels under General Jenkins, and recaptured by United States troops the same day. The rebels burned several houses and several thousand bushels of corn.

March 30.—Cluke's rebel guerillas were defeated at Mount Sterling, Kentucky.

—— The rebels commenced the investment of Washington, North Carolina, which was held by United States troops. Major-General Foster had arrived there the day before, in order to make the proper defence. The town was soon surrounded by the rebel troops, rendering escape from it very dangerous. Skirmishing and artillery firing was carried on between the belligerents for many days.

—— The President of the United States issued a proclamation recommending the observance of the 30th of April, as a day of fasting and prayer.

March 31.—A fight at Somerset, Kentucky, between 2800 rebels under General Pegram and 1200 United States troops under General Gilmore. The rebels were driven towards the Cumberland River, where they succeeded in crossing, losing 50 killed, 200 wounded, and 40 prisoners. Union loss, 10 killed, 25 wounded.

April 1.—Palmyra, Tennessee, was burned in retaliation for firing into the gunboat St. Clair a few days before from that town.

—— The United States gunboat Diana was captured by the rebels at Pattersonville, Louisiana. Captain Peterson, of the Diana, was killed, and several officers and men of the crew wounded and taken prisoners, with about 100 soldiers.

—— A rebel camp at Woodbury, Tennessee, was broken up by Ohio cavalry. 1200 rebels were dispersed, with severe loss to them.

—— A serious bread riot in Richmond, Virginia, by a mob composed of women, estimated three thousand in number, armed with clubs, guns, and stones. They broke open the government stores and private stores, and took from them bread, clothing, provisions, &c. Jeff Davis made them a speech, and the militia were called out to put down the disturbance.

April 2.—An iron steamship, bearing the name of the "Japan," which was ostensibly built "for the Emperor of China," left Greenock, Scotland, and proceeded to a creek on the coast of France, at which point were taken on board 12 Whitworth guns, with powder, shot, shell, &c. The vessel then hoisted the rebel flag, and started upon a career of piracy and destruction, under the name of the "Georgia."

—— A skirmish at Snowhill, Kentucky, between United States troops under General Stanley and Morgan's and Wharton's cavalry. Rebel loss, 20 killed, several wounded, and 60 prisoners.

April 6.—A rebel camp at Greenhill, Tennessee, was broken up by General Mitchell, with Federal cavalry.

—— Governor Tod, of Ohio, was arrested in Fairfield, upon a charge of kidnapping Dr. Olds, a political prisoner, who had been arrested some time previously by order of the United States government.

April 7.—The United States gunboat Barataria struck a snag in the Amite River, Louisiana, and was burned by her officers.

—— The United States fleet of eight iron-clad Monitors and the frigate New Ironsides, under command of Admiral Dupont, made an attack upon Fort Sumter, in Charleston harbor, opening fire at the distance of 1700 yards. The Ironsides ran aground and became unmanageable—the other ships went into action. The rebel forts and batteries responded vigorously. The Keokuk, which was within 600 yards of Fort Sumter, was struck ninety times in half an hour by shot from rifled cannon of heavy calibre. Many of these shot went through the ship, and the next morning it was found to be in a sinking condition; the crew escaped, and shortly after the Keokuk sank. The engagement was kept up from 1 until 4 o'clock, when the fleet retired, having accomplished nothing of importance. The rebels reported their entire loss at 2 killed and 5 wounded.

—— An expedition of cavalry under Colonel A. D. Straight left Murfreesboro, Tennessee, for an incursion through Alabama and Georgia. They proceeded down the Cumberland and up the Tennessee rivers, and joined the forces of General Dodge. They then moved rapidly and accomplished serious damage by destroying bridges, railroads, &c. They were pursued by Forrest's cavalry, and were attacked at Dayton's Gap, Town Creek, Bluntsville, Gadsden, and Cedar Bluff, twenty-six miles from Rome, Georgia, which latter town was the object of the expedition. By this time they were reduced by constant fighting and fatigue, and surrendered, 1700 in number, to Forrest's forces.

April 7.—800 soldiers of Spinola's brigade left Newbern, North Carolina, by way of Tar River, to reinforce General Foster, who with 1200 men were besieged at Washington, North Carolina, by a large rebel force under Generals Hill and Pettigrew, reported to be 27,000. strong. Meeting a number of batteries on Tar River, the expedition was forced to return.

April 8.—The United States gunboat Washington was destroyed in Broad River, near Port Royal Ferry, South Carolina; a shot from a rebel field battery on shore struck the magazine, and caused the destruction of the boat. 12 men were killed and 8 wounded.

—— Colonel Wilder's expedition returned to Murfreesboro, Tennessee, after having passed through Lebanon and Carthage, in which there were skirmishes with the rebels, and destruction of their wheat, tobacco, and stores, and the capture of 80 prisoners, 100 horses, and 150 negroes.

—— 1200 rebels under Woodward, with 2 pieces of artillery, captured and burned the steamers Saxonia and Lovell, near Clarksville, Tennessee. They were pursued by a force under Colonel Boone, and lost some men in killed and wounded.

—— The Yazoo Pass expedition returned to Helena, having left Fort Pemberton on the 5th, the siege being abandoned. On its return the expedition was attacked several times by guerillas concealed in the canebrakes, by whose fire several soldiers were killed and wounded. The attempt to get into the Yazoo River by that course, after assiduous effort and prodigious labor and hard fighting with forts and batteries, was abandoned.

—— A force of United States troops sent out from Newbern, North Carolina, to reinforce General Foster at Washington, had several skirmishes and found the enemy in front in such force, that it was compelled to return to Newbern.

April 9.—Pascagoula, Louisiana, was taken by Colonel Daniels with 180 United States colored troops. He was attacked by 300 rebel cavalry, who were repulsed with a loss of 20 killed and 50 wounded. The same day the place was abandoned by Colonel Daniels.

April 10.—Van Dorn's whole rebel force, 15,000 strong, attacked General Granger at Franklin, Tennessee. After a fight of 2 hours the rebels were repulsed, and retreated, leaving 300 of their dead upon the field. Union loss, 100. 2 guns were captured from the rebels.

April 11.—The Anglo-rebel blockade running steamer Stonewall Jackson, formerly the Leopard, laden with munitions of war, attempting to run into the harbor of Charleston, was fired into by the United States fleet and run ashore, being there burned by the crew.

April 12.—Lieutenant-Colonel Kimball, 9th New York Zouaves, was shot dead by Brigadier-General Michael Corcoran, near Suffolk, Virginia. Kimball was endeavoring at the time without authority to stop the progress of General Corcoran, proceeding to the front of the army under orders.

—— An attack was made by General Wise upon the camp of the 5th Pennsylvania cavalry, near Williamsburg, Virginia. The camp was burned, but the rebels were repulsed by the fire from Fort Magruder and fell back with some loss, but they held possession of Williamsburg.

—— The entire United States iron-clad fleet left Charleston, South Carolina, and went to Port Royal.

April 13.—The ram Queen of the West, captured by the rebels from the United States, was attacked on Grand Lake, Louisiana, by the Federal gunboats Calhoun, Estrella, and Arizona, under Commodore Cook. The Queen was set on fire by an incendiary shell from the Calhoun, and blown up when the flames reached her magazine. Rebel loss, 130 killed, wounded, and prisoners. No loss on the Federal side.

April 13.—Major-General A. E. Burnside at Cincinnati, issued an order No. 38 denouncing the penalty of death against all persons found guilty of aiding the rebels, and declaring that persons sympathizing with the rebels should be arrested and sent beyond the lines.

—— A riot at New York; Irish laborers attacked the negroes.

—— Skirmishing which had taken place for two days near Suffolk, Virginia, was continued. The Union troops under General Peck were assisted by gunboats, which shelled the woods and kept back the enemy.

—— General Steele's expedition returned to Greenville, Mississippi, 170 miles above Vicksburg, having been absent six days, in which time damage was done in the rebel region amounting to $3,000,000 in property seized and destroyed. Rebel guerillas were also attacked and dispersed. The expedition was fitted out to punish the people of that section for their participation in guerilla operations.

—— The United States troops under General Weitzel, operating in the Teche country, Louisiana, captured the rebel intrenchments at New Iberia, which were abandoned. 2 guns remained, with a large number of small arms. The steamer Cornie was captured at this place. The rebels burned seven large steamers and two of their gunboats, the Diana (captured from the United States) and Hart, the latter iron-clad.

—— United States troops under General Grover, operating in conjunction with those under General Weitzel, met the enemy at Irish Bend, Louisiana. A smart action ensued, and the rebels were defeated.

April 14.—The rebels with field artillery opened upon the disabled steamer Mount Washington, on the Nansemond River, but were repulsed by the Stepping Stones. Federal loss, 5 killed and 18 wounded.

—— The skirmish at Suffolk, Virginia, continued.

April 15.—200 Indians intrenched south of Salt Lake City, Utah Territory, were routed by United States troops under Colonel Evans, and 30 of them killed. Loss on our side, 1 killed and 2 wounded.

April 16.—The steamer Escort arrived at Newbern, North Carolina, from Washington, having gallantly run the rebel batteries at Rodman's Farm and Hill's Point under a heavy fire. General Foster and his aids were passengers on the boat.

—— The United States gunboats Benton, Tuscumbia, Lafayette, Pittsburg, Carondelet, Mound City, and General Price, with three transports, ran past the rebel batteries at Vicksburg in the night. The transport Henry Clay caught fire opposite the city and was burned. The other vessels received no material damage.

—— General Stoneman, with a force of Federal cavalry, infantry, and artillery, left the Army of the Potomac, near Falmouth, for a grand expedition through the rebel lines in Virginia.

April 17.—Battle at Vermillion Bayou, Louisiana, between a large rebel force and Union troops under General Grover. After a heavy fight the rebels were routed and fled, first burning the bridge over the bayou.

—— The rebels under General Hill, who were besieging Washington, North Carolina, abandoned their works, and left that portion of the state.

—— Colonel Grierson, with 1000 cavalry, left Lagrange, Mississippi, for an extensive raid through Georgia and Alabama. They burned the rebel depot and stores at Okalona, and the depot, locomotive, and cars at Newton. They exploded an ordnance train containing 3000 shells, and intended for the rebel batteries at Vicksburg. They burned all the bridges between Newton and Meridian, and the rebel ordnance works at Enterprise, and then returned to Newton. From thence they went to Jackson, burning all the bridges on their route, and the great bridge over Pearl River. They followed the Jackson and New Orleans Railroad to the Louisiana line, and evaded a force of 5000 rebels at Clinton. Finally they reached the Union lines at Baton Rouge, Louisiana, May the 1st, having captured on their route 500 rebel prisoners, with numerous horses, and bringing in with them 300 negroes. They cut every railroad in Mississippi, and did immense damage.

April 17.—J. L. Barrol, editor of the *Conservator* newspaper, published at Chestertown, Maryland, and James Downe, editor of the Leonardstown, Maryland, *Beacon*, were sent South by order of General Schenck, for the publication of disloyal articles.

April 18.—A Federal expedition sent to Celina, Tennessee, under Colonel Graham, broke up a rebel camp and destroyed a very large amount of stores collected there for the use of the rebel army, with 40 transports. Rebel loss, over 100 killed and wounded. Union loss, 101 killed, wounded, and missing.

———— Fayetteville, Arkansas, was attacked by 3000 rebels with 4 pieces of artillery under General Cobell. The Union forces under Colonel Harrison were 2000, but they succeeded in repulsing the enemy, who retreated in disorder.

———— A skirmish near Noncona, Tennessee, with Blythe's rebel cavalry.

A_p 'l 19.—Blythe's rebel cavalry were again attacked near Noncona; 20 killed, 40 wounded, 80 and captured. They retreated across the Coldwater.

———— A rebel battery at West Branch, on the Nansemond River, was stormed by United States troops under General Getty. 5 pieces of artillery were captured and 161 rebels taken prisoners. The troops were supported by the flotilla under Lieutenant Lamson.

———— General Grover occupied Opelousas, Louisiana.

———— Skirmishes at Creelsboro, Tennessee, and on the south bank of the Cumberland River. The rebels were attacked and beaten at each place.

April 20.—Bute La Rose, Louisiana, was captured by 4 Union gunboats, being surrendered without a fight.

———— Skirmish at Piketon, Tennessee. 78 rebels were captured, with their horses, arms, &c.

April 21.—The President of the United States issued a proclamation, declaring that the State of West Virginia was admitted into the Union.

———— McMinnville, Tennessee, was occupied by General Reynolds, U.S. Army, capturing two trains of cars, a train of wagons, and some prisoners.

———— Six transports ran the rebel batteries at Vicksburg with but little damage, although they were fired upon without intermission as long as they were within range.

April 22.—Upon the trial of the information laid by the United States against the British steamer Peterhoff, at New York, which ship was supposed to have been intended to run the blockade with contraband of war, the mail bag of the steamer was given up to the British Consul without examination, in pursuance of orders of Wm. H. Seward, Secretary of State.

April 23.—Tuscumbia, Alabama, was recaptured by General Dodge, who attacked the rebel General Chalmers, then holding the town. Federal loss, 100.

April 25.—Greenland Gap, West Virginia, was successfully defended by 75 men under Captain Wallace, 23d Illinois regiment, against 1500 rebel raiders under General Jones, from 5 P.M. until after dark, when the rebels fired a church in which the Federal troops were, and compelled them to surrender. The rebel killed and wounded exceeded 80, among whom were one colonel and several line officers. Union loss, 2 killed and 4 wounded. General Kelly, in his dispatches, characterized this as one of the most gallant defences of the war.

April 26.—8000 rebels, under Marmaduke and Burbridge, attacked General McNeil at Cape Girardeau, Missouri, and were repulsed after 3 hours' fighting. The same day the attack was renewed, and they were again repulsed. They then retreated. Federal loss, 20 killed and wounded. Rebel loss, 50 killed, 200 wounded. The same night the retreating rebels were met by United States troops under General Vanderver and severely punished.

———— Raids made by small parties of Imboden's, Jenkins's, and Harper's cavalry, upon several towns and villages in Western Virginia, viz. Piedmont, Cranberry Summit, Oakland, Rowlesburg, and Altamont, which were generally supposed to be reconnoissances to ascertain the feasibility of a grand advance by Lee's army upon Pittsburgh.

April 27.—Morgantown, West Virginia, was captured by Imboden's and Jenkins's cavalry, about 2000 in number. Great excitement followed in Pittsburgh and Wheeling, which were supposed to be in danger. The rebels stole without restriction whatever they wanted, and carried off a large number of horses.

———— The camp of the 1st Texas legion, on Carter's Creek, Pike, Kentucky, was broken up by Watkin's Kentucky cavalry. 128 rebels were taken prisoners, with horses, mules, tents, &c. 8 wagon-loads of arms were burned.

———— The United States sloop of war Preble took fire accidentally at Pensacola, Florida, was burned, and finally blown up.

April 28.—The 76th Ohio regiment, Colonel Wood, returned to Milliken's Bend, Mississippi, from an expedition into the interior of the State, during which they destroyed 350,000 bushels of corn and 30 cotton-gins and grist-mills.

April 29.—The rebel batteries at Grand Gulf, Louisiana, were attacked by the United States fleet under Admiral David D. Porter, comprising four gunboats. The lower batteries were silenced after a fight of 5 hours and 30 minutes, but the upper batteries were difficult to reach by the artillery of the boats. At 6 o'clock in the evening all the gunboats passed by the batteries. Federal loss, 24 killed, 56 wounded. On the rebel side, the commander of the forts, Colonel Wade, was killed, and several more were killed and wounded.

———— Fairmount, West Virginia, was captured by rebel cavalry under General Jones, 5000 strong. It was defended by 300 Federal soldiers, who made a good fight, but being surrounded were compelled to surrender. The rebels destroyed the suspension bridge over the Monongahela, one of the finest structures of the kind in the United States.

———— The Army of the Potomac under Major-General Hooker and the corps commanders, Generals Howard, Slocum, and Meade, crossed the Rappahannock at Kelly's Ford. The cavalry force under General Stoneman also crossed. The corps of Generals Reynolds, Sickles, and Sedgwick also crossed the river four miles below Fredericksburg. There was some resistance by the rebel pickets and skirmishers, which was soon overcome. Upon the right, the corps of Meade, in the advance, marched to Chancellorsville, ten miles south-west of Fredericksburg and in the rear of that town, and held it as a point for the concentration of the great body of the Federal troops.

May 1.—Major-General U. S. Grant, who had anded his troops at Boulinsburg, Mississippi, the day before, met the rebels 11,000 strong, and after a battle of some hours' duration routed them, with a loss of 1000 killed and wounded, and 500 prisoners. Among the killed were General Tracy and Lieutenant-Colonel Pettus. Federal loss, 100 killed and 500 wounded. The rebels retreated towards Vicksburg, destroying two bridges over Bayou Pierre, which were rebuilt and the pursuit continued.

———— Port Gibson, Mississippi, was taken by Union troops under Generals McClernand, Carr, Osterhaus, Smith, and Hovey, after a severe field fight. Rebel loss, 400 killed and 750 wounded. Federal loss, 350 killed and 700 wounded.

———— Monticello, Kentucky, was captured by General Carter, U.S. Army, with 5000 men.

May 2.—General Sedgwick, with three of the army corps, having made a feint below Fredericksburg, and having occupied the ground on the south side of the river, withdrew his troops to the north side of the river, and then recrossed. In the meanwhile the 3d and 2d corps had been sent to reinforce the main body of the army under Hooker, and General Sedgwick was left with the 6th corps and one division of the 2d corps. With this force General Sedgwick again crossed the Rappahannock, and took possession of Fredericksburg.

———— First day of the battle of Chancellorsville, Virginia, called by the rebels "The Battle of the Wilderness."

Skirmishing had been going on along the lines since the crossing of the Rappahannock by the Federal troops. The position taken by General Hooker in the flank and rear of the strong rebel works at Fredericksburg had a tendency to cause the withdrawal of the main body of Lee's forces from Fredericksburg. The latter organized a strong attack upon the right wing of the United States troops. This movement was executed by "Stonewall" Jackson with 40,000 men, who surprised the 11th army corps under General Howard on the extreme right. A swift and furious assault was made upon this corps. A portion of it gave way disgracefully and fled, bearing down in their flight upon the troops massed behind them, and occasioning a panic and confusion throughout the army. Another portion of the 11th, the brigades of Bushbeck and McLean, held their own, and prevented the disaster from becoming a complete rout of Hooker's troops. By this disaster, the corps of Sickles and Slocum, which had been pushing forward on the centre of the line, were in great danger. A night attack upon the rebels was resolved upon to restore the Federal lines. This movement was commenced at 11 o'clock, and was entirely successful.

May 3.—Second day of the battle of Chancellorsville, Virginia. The contest was resumed, the object upon the part of the Federals being to repair the disasters occasioned by "Stonewall" Jackson's success against the right wing, and to drive the rebels from the rear of our army. The battle lasted for six hours, at the expiration of which time the rebels were driven back, and the United States troops repossessed themselves of the intrenchments previously thrown up, with the rebels between them and Fredericksburg.

———— Battle of Marye's Hill, Virginia. Major-General Sedgwick's force in possession of Fredericksburg, Virginia, moved against the strong intrenchments of the rebels in the rear of the town, before which Burnside's army had been repulsed at the first battle of Fredericksburg. After heavy skirmishing and severe losses, an assault was made upon Marye's Hill, the centre of the enemy's works. This position was attacked by the 61st Pennsylvania, Colonel Spear, 43d New York, Colonel Baker, supported by the 1st Long Island, Colonel Cross, and 82d Pennsylvania, Major Bassett, forming the column on the right. On the left the column was composed of the 7th Massachusetts, Colonel Johns, 36th New York, Colonel Welsh, supported by the 6th Maine and 5th Wisconsin. The enemy opened upon the forlorn hope a terrible fire, in which officers and men fell thick and fast, but the storming party persevered and finally carried the hill, capturing 8 guns and 800 prisoners. In this assault there were killed on the Federal side, Colonel Spear, 61st Pennsylvania, Major Haycock, 6th Maine, Major Faxon, 6th New York, and other officers and men; wounded, Major Healy, New York, Major Bassett, 82d Pennsylvania, and other officers and men.

———— General Averill with his cavalry command returned to United States Ford, Virginia, having been out 23 days, and having gone as far south as Rapidan Station, on the Orange and Alexandria Railroad. Fitzhugh Lee's and W. H. Lee's rebel cavalry were driven out of Culpeper Court House, where a lot of flour was burned. At Rapidan Station the rebels lost Colonel Rosse, killed, and several prisoners.

———— The fleet under Admiral Porter made preparations for a new attack upon the rebel batteries at Grand Gulf, Louisiana, but before the gunboats were arranged in line of battle, the rebels abandoned the works, blowing up their ammunition and spiking their guns.

———— A strong reconnoissance in force was made on the right bank of the Nansemond River, by Union troops under General Getty. The rebels contested the advance, and there was spirited fighting. Killed, Colonel Ringgold, 103d New York, and killed, wounded, and missing, about 70 on our side.

———— An attack was made by Moseby's rebel guerillas upon Heintzelman's troops near Warrenton Junction, Virginia. The enemy was repulsed with heavy loss.

May 4.—General Hooker finding himself hardly pressed by the rebels, and being without the reinforcement of Sedgwick's division, withstood constant skirmishing attacks during the day. At night, upon consultation with the corps commanders, it was decided to abandon the field and recross the Rappahannock. About midnight the troops began to cross by pontoon bridges, which, were in great danger in consequence of a storm and the swollen condition of the river. They succeeded in doing so without being discovered by the rebels, and left their dead and many of their wounded on the field to the tender mercies of the enemy. In these battles the Federal loss was at least 15,000. General Hooker estimated the rebel loss at 18,000 men *hors du combat*, including 5000 prisoners, with 15 colors and 7 guns. Among the killed on the Federal side were Generals Berry and A. W. Whipple; Colonels McKnight, 105th Pennsylvania; Riley, 75th Ohio; Lancaster, 175th Pennsylvania; Stainrook, 109th Pennsylvania; Stevens, New York; Miles, 61st New York; Town, 95th Pennsylvania; Collet, 1st New Jersey; Lieutenant-Colonels Scott, 3d Wisconsin; Chapin, 86th New York; Majors Keenan, 8th Pennsylvania cavalry; Strouse, 46th Pennsylvania; Faxon, 88th New York; Joseph R. Chandler, 114th Pennsylvania; Chapman, 28th Pennsylvania, and many other line officers and men. Among the wounded were Major-Generals Howard, Couch, and Sickles; Brigadier-Generals Devens, Mott, Greene, Ward, and Geary; Colonels Willets, 12th New Jersey; Pierson, 1st New York; Parks, 2d New York; Burling, 6th New Jersey; Potter, 12th New Hampshire; Ramsey, 8th New Jersey; Gregory, 91st Pennsylvania; Hayman, 37th New York; Sewell, 5th New Jersey; Hecker, 82d Illinois; Noble, 17th Connecticut; Von Vegesack, 20th New York; Johns, 7th Massachusetts; Brown, 36th New York; Richardson, 25th New York; Von Gilsa, New York; Ross, 20th Connecticut; Deaver, 148th Pennsylvania; Buck, 2d New Jersey; Irwin, 140th Pennsylvania; Lieutenant-Colonels Cook, 145th New York; Lounsberry, New York; Collins, New York; Knight, 24th New Jersey; Norton, 126th New York; Avery; Majors Angell, 5th New Jersey; Willoughby, 137th New York; Higgins, 86th New York; Woodal, 1st Delaware; Thomas, 16th New Jersey; Anthony, 129th Pennsylvania; Town, 95th Pennsylvania; Cress, 5th New Hampshire. Prisoners: General Hayes, Colonels Matthew, 128th Pennsylvania; Bostwick; 27th Connecticut; Glautz, 103d Pennsylvania; Packer, 5th Connecticut. On the rebel side there are known to have been killed, Major-General T. J. ("Stonewall") Jackson (shot by his own men and died from the effects of an amputation), General Paxton; Colonels T. S. Garnett, Mallory, Virginia; Lieutenant-Colonels L. W. Walker, Stafford, Louisiana; Majors Stover, Price, Virginia. Wounded, Generals A. P. Hill, McGowan, Heth, Nichols, Maluney, Ransom, McLaws; Colonels Edmundson, Virginia; Warren, Virginia; Monagan, Louisiana; Major Selden.

———— Fort de Russy, at the mouth of the Red River, Louisiana, was taken possession of by the United States Mississippi squadron, under Admiral Porter.

———— The Federal troops on the Nansemond advanced in three columns upon the rebel intrenchments, under the command of General Corcornn, General Terry, and General Getty. The rebels had retreated during the night. They were pursued for some distance, but not overtaken.

May 5.—Clement L. Vallandigham, of Ohio, was arrested at his residence at Dayton, Ohio, by United States soldiers acting under command of Major-General Burnside. An attempt was made to rescue him, but it failed. At night a mob set fire to the office of the *Journal*, and several houses adjoining were destroyed. Troops from Cincinnati were sent for and restored order.

May 6.—Alexandria, Louisiana, was taken possession of by the fleet under Admiral Porter. General Banks arrived on the 7th, and the command was turned over to him.

———— C. L. Vallandigham was brought before a court-martial at Cincinnati. He refused to plead to the charges against him, which were founded upon disloyal sentiments uttered in a speech made by him at Mount Vernon, Ohio.

May 7.—A force under Major-General E. A. Keyes was sent forward to Whitehouse, Virginia, accompanied by gunboats.

——— The rebel General Van Dorn was killed at Spring Hill, in Tennessee, by Dr. Peters, whose wife he had seduced.

——— Colonel Kilpatrick, of Stoneman's command, arrived at Gloucester Point, Va.

——— Rebel batteries at Warrenton, Mississippi, were destroyed by United States gunboats, the shells of which set the works, of log' covered with cotton bales, on fire.

May 8.—Port Hudson, Louisiana, was bombarded by the Union fleet, which operation was continued for several days following.

——— Colonel Clayton, with United States cavalry, left Helena, Mississippi, for a raid into Arkansas. He was gone 10 days and returned safely, having destroyed 200,000 bushels of corn, several storehouses, mills, &c.

——— General Stoneman, with the main body of his column, arrived at the Rappahannock and crossed at Kelly's Ford, joining Hooker. During the extensive raid made by his command, the whole country in the rear of Lee's army was traversed by the cavalry. He divided his force into three columns: one, under General Averill, crossed the Rappahannock at Kelly's Ford and proceeded direct to Culpeper; a column under General Buford marched to Gordonsville; the third column, under General Stoneman, proceeded direct to Richmond and went within two miles of that city. Here a portion under Kilpatrick were detached, and went down the Peninsula to Gloucester Point. Stoneman made a circuit, and crossed the Rappahannock in safety. The damage done by this expedition was immense; they destroyed railroads, bridges, and depots, and railroad trains and locomotives, and factories, mills, and forges, with grain, provisions, ammunition, &c., taking 500 prisoners, and throwing the people of Southern Virginia into a panic. The whole of Lee's railroad communications with Richmond were for a time cut off. The expedition executed this daring circuit and damage with very slight loss.

——— A proclamation was issued by the President of the United States, giving notice of his intention to put the national militia law in force, and giving notice to all aliens who had declared their intentions of becoming citizens of the United States, that if they remained in the country after 65 days they would be held to be liable to enrolment and draft.

May 10.—The blockade-running steamer West Florida was destroyed at sea by the United States gunboats Owasco, Lieutenant John Madigan, and the Katahdin, Lieutenant P. C. Johnson.

——— The rebel General Morgan, with 4000 men, was defeated at Horse Shoe and Bottom Narrows, Kentucky, losing 90 killed. The Union troops, under Colonel Jacob, lost 42 men.

May 11.—Crystal Springs, Mississippi, destroyed by General Grant's cavalry.

May 12.—The 1st Texas (U.S.) cavalry under Colonel Davis left Amite River, Louisiana, for a raid along the Jackson Railroad into Mississippi. They defeated the rebels at Tiefaw and pursued them to Camp Moore, where a depot and a railroad bridge over the Tangipaho River were burned, and cars and railroad property destroyed. At Independence, Hammond Station, and Ponchatoula similar destruction was effected. The expedition returned safely.

——— Raymond, Mississippi, was taken by General McPherson, of Grant's army, after a brisk fight of more than 2 hours. Union loss, 51 killed and 180 wounded; rebel loss, 800 killed, wounded, and prisoners.

May 14.—Jackson, Mississippi, captured by General Grant, after a fight of 3 hours with rebel forces under Joseph E. Johnston. The enemy retreated northward, having lost 400 killed and wounded, and 17 guns. Union loss, 70 killed and 200 wounded. Jackson was held for 3 days. Before it was abandoned, General Grant burned depots, factories, foundries, Confederate offices and works, and two bridges.

May 16.—Battle of Champion Hills or Baker's Creek or Edwards's Station, by all of which names it has been designated. General Grant attacked General Pemberton's rebel army near the Big Black River, and after 5 hours' fighting compelled it to fall back beyond the river. The rebels lost 4000 men and 29 guns. Their general, Tilghman, was killed. Federal loss, 1700 killed and wounded.

——— Clement L. Vallandigham was found guilty of expressing disloyal sentiments by the court-martial at Cincinnati, and ordered by General Burnside to be closely confined in Fort Warren, Boston Harbor. On the 22d of May the President changed the sentence to transportation to the South across the enemy's lines.

May 17.—Battle of the Big Black Bridge, Mississippi, between General Grant and the rebels under General Pemberton. The latter was defeated, and lost 3000 killed and wounded, 3000 prisoners, and 29 pieces of artillery. He retreated to Vicksburg, and was followed closely by General Grant.

——— The rebel steamer Cuba was burned at sea by her crew, being chased by the United States gunboat De Soto, and hardly pressed.

May 18.—General Grant's army crossed the Big Black River in the rear of Vicksburg, upon pontoon bridges, and immediately proceeded to invest every avenue of approach to the city.

——— The rebels evacuated their works at Haines's Bluff, near Vicksburg, Mississippi, in consequence of the vigorous proceedings of General Grant. The navy under Admiral Porter took possession of the bluffs and 14 forts, and then moved down and shelled Vicksburg.

May 20.—A force of rebels under Price, Steele, and Cooper, was defeated by Colonel Phillips, near Fort Gibson, Arkansas. Union loss, 26 killed and 20 wounded. Rebel loss estimated heavier.

——— General Schofield assumed the command of the Department of Missouri, in place of General Curtis, relieved.

May 21.—A general assault was made upon the rebel works at Vicksburg, and the Union troops were repulsed at all parts of the line, with a loss of 2000 killed and wounded, after a contest of 9 hours.

——— An expedition sent by Admiral Porter up the Yazoo River went to Yazoo City, under Lieutenant-Commander Walker, and destroyed three powerful steam rams, one of them iron-plated, a navy yard, with machine shops, saw-mills, blacksmith's shops, &c.; the property thus disposed of was worth $2,000,000.

——— The rebel batteries at Walnut Hills and Snyder's Bluff were taken by General Steele, of Grant's army, after a fight of 5 hours.

May 22.—A second assault was made by Grant's troops upon the rebel batteries at Vicksburg. The United States forces were repulsed with heavy losses, estimated at 2000 killed and wounded. The officers suffered severely.

——— A rebel encampment at Gum Swamp, North Carolina, was captured, destroyed, and the troops dispersed by an expedition under command of Colonel J. Richter Jones, 58th Pennsylvania volunteers. On the return the Federal soldiers were pursued by the rebels, and skirmishing ensued. Colonel Jones was killed inside of our own lines. Federal loss, 1 killed, 7 wounded, and 60 missing. Rebel loss, 2 killed, 5 wounded, and 195 taken prisoners.

May 23.—General Steele, of General Grant's army, carried the rifle pits on the north of Vicksburg, Mississippi.

May 24.—Clement L. Vallandigham was delivered over to the rebel pickets, near Shelbyville, Tennessee, protesting that he was a citizen of the United States, and had been sent there against his will.

——— Austin, Mississippi, was burned by Colonel Ellet, of the Marine Brigade, as a punishment for a guerilla attack at that point upon one of his steamboats the day before.

——— Lieutenant-Commander Walker left the Mississippi squadron near Vicksburg, upon a second expedition up the Yazoo River. He was successful in destroying nine rebel steamers, worth $700,000, a saw-mill, and other property.

May 26.—The United States gunboat Cincinnati was sunk near Vicksburg, Mississippi, by the fire from the rebel batteries. She went down with her flags flying. 25 of the crew were killed and wounded, and 15 were drowned.

May 27.—The rebel fortifications at Port Hudson, which had been closely invested by Major-General Banks, were assaulted along the whole line by the divisions of Weitzel, Emory, Grover, Augur, and Sherman; the artillery under command of General Arnold. Weitzel took a six gun battery. Sherman, after hard fighting, was driven back from the right. On the centre there was a desperate struggle for the ground, and some advantages were gained on the Federal side. Some of the outer works were carried, but the principal fortifications were untaken. The Union loss was about 1000 killed and wounded. Among the killed were Colonel Daniel S. Cowles, 128th New York regiment; Colonel Clark, 8th Michigan; Colonel Paine, 2d Louisiana regiment. Wounded, General T. W. Sherman, General Neal Dow, Lieutenant-Colonel Smith, 2d Zouaves. Rebel loss not known. In this assault the native negro troops, 1st Louisiana regiment, were placed in the front. General Banks reported of them, "They answered every expectation—no troops could be more determined or daring." During the assault the enemy's works were bombarded by the fleet under Admiral Farragut.

May 28.—Bluffton, South Carolina, was destroyed by an expedition under Colonel Barton, sent out from Hilton Head, South Carolina.

May 30.—Colonel Kilpatrick, with that part of Stoneman's cavalry which had gone to Gloucester Point, Virginia, left that place to join General Hooker. He crossed the Dragon River at Saluta, and thence proceeded through Middlesex county to Urbanna, on the Rappahannock, crossing that river at Union Point, and reporting at headquarters. This completed the operations of the Stoneman raid.

—— An immense caravan arrived at New Orleans with spoils from the Teche country, Louisiana. It consisted of 600 wagons, 6000 negroes, 3000 mules, and 1508 head of cattle.

June 1.—The United States gunboat Alert caught fire at the Norfolk Navy Yard and was blown up.

June 2.—A cavalry expedition under General Blair, U.S. Army, returned to Walnut Hills from the Yazoo country, having destroyed several bridges, grist-mills, cotton-gins, and cotton, between the Big Black and the Yazoo.

June 3.—The steamers John Adams and Harriet A. Weed returned to Beaufort from an expedition up the Combahee River, South Carolina, with 300 men of the 2d South Carolina (colored) volunteers under command of Colonel Montgomery. A rebel pontoon bridge was destroyed, with cotton, rice, and other property worth $1,000,000. 725 negroes were brought back, with horses, &c.

—— The ship Tacony, of Philadelphia, was taken by the rebel pirate Florida No. 2, formerly the Clarence II. Haldeman, of Baltimore, which had been taken by the steam privateer Florida and fitted out as a tender under the command of Lieutenant Charles W. Reed. Several other American vessels had been captured by the Florida No. 2, but upon the capture of the Tacony, the Clarence was abandoned and set on fire, and the rebel flag hoisted upon the Tacony.

June 4.—A fight at Saluria, Mississippi, between United States troops, 3000 in number, under Colonel Kimball, and a rebel force under Wirt Adams. The latter was routed, losing 100 prisoners and some killed and wounded. Union loss, 1 killed and 17 wounded.

—— A rebel foundry, mills, &c., were destroyed at Aylett's Station, Va., by the crews of 3 United States gunboats and transports sent up the Mattapony River.

—— Colonel Cornyn, who had left Corinth 2 days before upon a raiding expedition, reached Florence, Alabama, and surprised the rebels there, who fled. Shops, factories, mills, and machine shops were destroyed, with corn, bacon, &c. 100 rebels were taken prisoners, and 500 horses and mules captured, and 150 negroes. Federal loss, 2 killed and 3 wounded.

June 4.—A fight at Franklin, Tennessee, between rebels under Forrest, and Colonel Faulkner's Kentucky (Union) cavalry. The rebels were driven from the town.

June 5.—The Isaac Smith, formerly a Union gunboat, and captured by the rebels in the Stono River, South Carolina—attempting to run out of Charleston harbor, was sunk by the United States blockading fleet.

—— Howe's division of Hooker's army crossed the Rappahannock one mile below Fredericksburg on pontoons, drove the rebel skirmishers out of their rifle pits, and took some prisoners. The troops held their positions during the night, and returned next morning without molestation. The object of the reconnoissance was to ascertain whether a strong force of rebels still remained in the neighborhood of Fredericksburg.

June 8.—2500 rebels under McCullough attacked the 23d Iowa regiment and 600 colored troops at Milliken's Bend, Louisiana. The enemy was repulsed—the blacks acting with great determination; they lost 100 out of 184 killed. The wounded on the Union side were about 150. The rebels left 120 dead on the field, and took away many wounded. Federal loss, 110 killed and 200 wounded.

June 9.—9000 United States cavalry of Pleasanton's command, under Generals Buford and Gregg, and a brigade of infantry, crossed the Rappahannock between Culpeper Court House and Beverly Ford, and attacked Stuart's rebel cavalry under General Fitzhugh Lee. The fight lasted from 5 o'clock in the morning until 3 o'clock in the afternoon, by which time the whole of Stuart's cavalry, consisting of 12,000 horsemen with 16 pieces of artillery, were driven back 3 miles on the right and 5 on the left. The engagement was generally with sabres. Killed on the Federal side, Colonel B. F. Davis, 8th New York regiment; Lieutenant-Colonel Irven, 10th New York. Wounded, Colonel Wyndham, 1st New Jersey; Lieutenant-Colonel Broderick, 1st New York; Major Morris, 6th Pennsylvania; Major Stillwire, 1st New Jersey. This bold attack retarded for a time the rebel invasion of Maryland and Pennsylvania.

—— Colonel Lawrence William Orton, of the rebel service, formerly Lawrence Williams, United States cavalry, and Lieutenant Dunlop, of the rebel army, were arrested within the United States lines at Franklin, Tennessee, clothed in full Federal uniforms and pretending to be inspectors of the United States army, having with them forged orders and passes purporting to be by Adjutant-General E. D. Townsend, U.S. Army, countersigned by General W. S. Rosecrans. They were tried by court-martial, found to be spies, and hung.

June 10.—The British steamer Havelock, attempting to run into the harbor of Charleston, was chased by the blockading fleet, run ashore, and set on fire.

June 11.—An attack was made upon Triune, Tennessee, by Forrest, with 5000 rebel cavalry and 12 guns. They were beaten off by General R. B. Mitchell, in command, losing 21 killed, 65 wounded, and 10 prisoners. Union loss, 6 killed.

—— The state of Pennsylvania was divided into two military departments, for the purposes of defence. The Western District, west of Johnstown and the Laurel Ridge Mountains, to be called "The Department of the Monongahela," and to be commanded by Major-General Brooks, headquarters, Pittsburgh; "The Department of the Susquehanna," under the command of Major-General D. N. Couch, headquarters, Chambersburg.

—— 250 rebel cavalry crossed the Potomac and made a dash into Poolesville, Maryland, burned a small camp, and retreated.

—— Darien, Georgia, burned and destroyed by United States troops, Colonel Montgomery.

—— Clement L. Vallandigham was nominated as the Democratic candidate for Governor of Ohio, by a convention assembled at Columbus.

June 12.—Governor Morton of Indiana issued a proclamation to the people of that state, warning them

States militia law or the
uties.
of Pennsylvania issued a
War Department had re-
ge rebel force of cavalry,
ry had been prepared for
d into Pennsylvania, and
e State to volunteer for its
the "general orders" of
) mode of organization, &c.
uincy A. Gilmore assumed
of the South, vice Major-
id.
s steamer Somerset, Lieu-
man, destroyed the exten-
gator Harbor, Florida—8
200 bushels of salt.
rell's rebel troops, 20,000
ral pickets at Front Royal,
lriven in, and resistance
them was overcome. By
o Winchester were in the

was made by the Union
) at Port Hudson, Louisi-
to the divisions of Gene-
Jeneral Paine, and feints
General Augur. The ob-
were so many, that it was
ifications, and after a des-
ates troops were repulsed
wounded.
ice during the greater part
ginia. At 5 o'clock in the
) eight gun batteries west
) outworks by a charge at
:harge was then made by
as repulsed with slaughter.
roy, who was in command,
it was decided to abandon
fore daybreak, thus giving
y and siege guns, with 18
iunition, horses, mules, &c.
with a rebel brigade, and
re repulsed, and retreated
)idly as they could, having
nissing. Milroy had 7000
the time when the rebels

ia, was captured by the
ok several cannon, stores,

the United States issued a
he invasion of Maryland,
breatened, and calling for
50,000 from Pennsylvania,
nd 30,000 from Ohio, for

. Curtin, of Pennsylvania,
the people of the State to

s rebel army in Maryland
by a regiment of infantry
ght them for an hour and
surrendered.
, under General Jenkins,
ylvania.
marine brigade, Colonel
mond, Mississippi, drove
prisoners, and burned the

into Indiana by 200 rebel
io River at Flint Rock.
s and villages of Leavens-
aoli, and Orleans. They
Orleans, and other places
ley attempted to return by
ney had crossed, but were
boat, and troops on land.
aptured.

June 17.—A force of rebel cavalry captured a train on the Baltimore & Ohio Railroad at Point-of-Rocks, Mary- land, destroying the locomotive and 23 cars, with their contents.

—— The rebel iron-clad frigate Chattahoochie, 6 guns, Lieutenant Guthrie, burst a boiler and was blown up at Chattahoochie, Florida.

—— The rebel iron-clad steamer Atlanta, formerly the British steamer Fingal, carrying 7 guns, was cap- tured by the United States Monitor Weehawken, Cap- tain John Rodgers, in Warsaw Sound, Georgia. After firing six shots, the Atlanta surrendered, having in fifteen minutes been penetrated by three shots from the Wee- hawken. The Atlanta was fully equipped for a destruc- tive attack upon the United States vessels of the block- ading fleet, and was accompanied to Warsaw Sound by rebel steamers from Savannah filled with ladies and gentlemen, who expected to see the Yankees easily whipped.

June 18.—Jenkins's rebel cavalry withdrew from Chambersburg, Pennsylvania.

—— A cavalry fight at Aldie, Virginia, between United States cavalry under General Kilpatrick and General Fitzhugh Lee's rebel cavalry. Several despe- rate charges were made, and the fight lasted over 3 hours. The rebels were routed and 100 prisoners taken. Colonel Doughty, of the Maine cavalry, was killed, and Colonel De Cesnola taken prisoner.

June 19.—100 rebel cavalry crossed the Ohio River for a raid into Indiana.

—— A portion of Rhodes's rebel cavalry entered McConnelsburg, Pennsylvania, and sacked the town.

June 20.—An attack was made upon the bridge at Lafourche Crossing, Louisiana, by 4 rebel regiments, which made a charge, but were repulsed, losing a lieu- tenant-colonel, 53 dead on the field, and 50 prisoners. Union loss, 8 killed and 16 wounded.

June 21.—General Pleasonton, with the Federal cav- alry, fought Stuart's rebel cavalry, and drove them from beyond Middleburg through Upperville and Ashby's Gap, a distance of 8 miles. Frequent charges were made. The rebels lost 2 guns and 4 caissons, and 100 killed and wounded, among whom were Colonels Williams and Hampton, killed, and General Fitzhugh Lee and Colonel Butler, wounded.

June 22.—Clement L. Vallandigham arrived at Nassau, N. P., having run the blockade in the rebel steamer Lady Davis.

June 23.—The rebel advance in force reoccupied Chambersburg, Pennsylvania. The Union troops at the town fell back.

—— An expedition under Colonel S. H. Sanders arrived at Boston, Kentucky, having penetrated East Tennessee as far as Massey's Creek, and having torn up the railroad, burned three important bridges, and taken guns, ammunition, horses, stores, &c., besides destroying mills, saltpetre works, and other property.

June 24.—The Army of the Cumberland, under Major- General Rosecrans, commenced its march from Murfrees- boro, Tennessee, toward the rebel lines. There was a skirmish at Guy's Gap, between McCook's division in the advance and a rebel brigade. Federal loss, 225 killed and wounded. Also at Liberty Gap, between Willich's division and rebel troops, with a loss of 50 killed and wounded. Also at Hanover Gap, by Colonel Wilder, who drove the rebels, losing 50 killed and wounded. On the 25th, at the same place, Federal loss, 40 killed and 100 wounded.

June 25.—Pennsylvania cavalry under Colonel S. P. Spear penetrated within 6 miles of Richmond, Virginia, having left White House for the purpose of a raid. They destroyed grain, stores, bridges, railroads, &c., and took 150 prisoners, among them General William H. Fitzhugh Lee, son of the rebel commander- in-chief, Lieutenant-Colonel Hargrave, and 7 company officers.

—— An assault was made by McPherson's corps upon the rebel works at Vicksburg. A terrible struggle took place in a breach which was made in one of the rebel forts by the explosion of a mine. Seven Federal regiments were in the fight, which was mostly carried on by hand grenades. Lieutenant-Colonel Melancthon Smith and Major Fisk were killed, and many wounded. Union loss, 100. Rebel loss supposed to be greater. The fort was held by the assailants.

June 25.—The Pembroke, an American merchant steamer, was fired upon, on the coast of Japan, by armed vessels belonging to the Prince of Nogato, one of the nobles of Japan hostile to foreigners. The Pembroke managed to escape without sustaining much damage. On the 16th of July the United States ship Wyoming went to the place and destroyed the steamer, sunk the brig, and had a brisk fight with six shore batteries.

June 26.—The rebel advance reached Carlisle, Pennsylvania. General Knipe, commanding the Federal militia, abandoned the town.

———— Gettysburg, Pennsylvania, was occupied by General Early, of Longstreet's corps.

———— Governor Curtin of Pennsylvania issued a proclamation, calling for 60,000 men for three months or for the emergency.

———— Brashear City, Louisiana, was captured by the rebels. They took 1000 Federal prisoners, 600 negroes, 20 guns, with an immense quantity of stores, &c., of all sorts, ammunition, &c., the value of which was probably $2,000,000.

———— The rebels by a flank movement were compelled to abandon their works at Beech Grove, Tennessee, and were pursued by General Rosseau, of Rosecrans's army, to Fairfield.

———— Liberty Gap, Tennessee, was taken from Cleburn's division by Rosecrans's army. Union loss, 300 killed and wounded. Colonel Gavan, 2d Arkansas, and Major Claybrook (rebels) were killed.

———— Manchester, Tennessee, was occupied by General Reynolds, of Rosecrans's army.

———— General Stanley's United States cavalry made a dash into Shelbyville, Tennessee, drove the rebels first into and then from their fortifications, and then into and across the Duck River, in which 100 of them were drowned. 60 officers and 700 prisoners were taken. Union loss, 6 killed and 40 wounded.

———— Rear-Admiral Andrew H. Foote, U.S. Navy, died at the Astor House, in the city of New York. Admiral Foote had been out of service for some months, in consequence of a wound received in the discharge of his duty at Fort Donelson. He was appointed to the navy in 1822.

June 27.—Major-General George G. Meade was appointed to the command of the Army of the Potomac, in place of General Hooker, relieved.

———— York, Pennsylvania, was surrendered to the rebels by the chief burgess, David Strong, and "a committee of safety."

———— The rebel forces advancing towards Wrightsville, on the Susquehanna, Pennsylvania, opposite Columbia, were skirmished with by a regiment of militia under Colonel Frick. The latter then retreated to Columbia and set fire to the bridge across the Susquehanna, which was totally destroyed.

———— The Archer, a schooner captured by the rebel pirate Tacony or Florida No. 2, Lieutenant Charles W. Reed, came into Portland, Maine, with the whole crew of the privateer on board. They had shifted their flag from the Tacony to the Archer, and burned the Tacony. The latter was the object of pursuit by several armed Federal vessels, and they hoped to elude the pursuers by this trick. In the harbor of Portland, in the night, they boarded and captured the United States cutter Caleb Cushing, and put out to sea. They were discovered and chased by steamers, on board of which field artillery was placed. Failing in their efforts to escape with the vessel, they set fire to her and took to their boats. The latter were captured with all the rebels, but the Cushing was blown up.

———— The rebel General Greene made an assault upon Donaldsonville, Louisiana, and was repulsed after a fight of 3 hours, losing 100 killed and left on the field, 300 wounded, and 120 prisoners. Federal loss, 6 killed and 14 wounded.

June 28.—A skirmish at Oyster Point, 4 miles from Harrisburg, between the rebel advance and the 71st New York regiment and Captain E. S. Miller's battery of Philadelphia.

June 29.—The rebel force at Carlisle and York, Pennsylvania, fell back, to concentrate, in consequence of the advance of the Army of the Potomac under General Meade. Whilst in occupation of York, a demand was made by General Early upon the citizens of the town, that they should furnish for the use of the rebel army $100,000 in cash, and clothing, provisions, &c., estimated to be worth $200,000 more.

———— A skirmish at McConnelsville, Pennsylvania; between Pierce's Federal cavalry and Imboden's guerillas. The latter were driven from the town, losing 2 killed and 33 prisoners. The Federals had 2 wounded.

June 30.—Battle at Hanover Junction, Pennsylvania, between General Pleasanton's cavalry and the rebel cavalry.

———— Colonel Wilder's cavalry returned to Manchester, Tennessee, having penetrated in the rear of Bragg's lines as far as Hillsboro and Dechard, destroying property, railroads, bridges, &c., and taking prisoners. The expedition travelled 126 miles in two days and a half.

———— Martial law was declared in Baltimore, Maryland, by Major-General Schenck.

July 1.—Tullahoma, Tennessee, was occupied by General Rosecrans, the rebels having abandoned it and retreated.

———— The Board of Officers, U.S. Army, sitting at Washington, decided the following as the order of rank of the major-generals of volunteers, the commissions all bearing the same date: 1. George B. McClellan; 2. John C. Fremont; 3. Nathaniel P. Banks; 4. John A. Dix; 5. Benjamin F. Butler.

———— General Getty, with 10,000 men, left White House, Virginia, for the purpose of destroying the remaining bridges across the South Anna River. He met a large force of rebels at Baltimore Cross Roads, near the bridges, and after skirmishing, retired, having lost 2 killed and 5 wounded. He tore up some miles of railroad track, destroyed a depot, and returned.

———— Carlisle, Pennsylvania, was occupied by Union militia under General Smith. In the afternoon, a force of rebels returned and demanded the surrender of the town, which was refused. The enemy bombarded the town, and managed to set fire to the United States Barracks, which were at some distance from it. The gasworks and some other buildings were destroyed. Federal loss, 1 killed and 16 wounded.

———— First day of the battle of Gettysburg, Pennsylvania. The 1st army (United States) corps, Major-General Reynolds, marching north, encountered the rebel commands of Longstreet and Hill posted advantageously. The latter were driven through Gettysburg, but rallying with reinforcements, the Federal troops fell back in good order, during which movement they managed to take prisoners General Archer and a whole reb' brigade. During these operations General Reynolds was killed. The 11th corps, Major-General Howard, now came up and went into the battle, which raged all day and with such disadvantage to the Federal troops that they retired to a strong position south of Gettysburg. In this day's battle, the Federal troops engaged numbered 22,000. The rebels were estimated at 50,000.

July 2.—Second day of the battle of Gettysburg. The United States army took advantageously posted on a series of hills in horse-shoe form, south of Gettysburg. On this position, after skirmishing all day, the rebels made a furious attack about 4 o'clock in the afternoon, opening with a heavy artillery fire, under cover of which they made several attempts to carry the left flank of the Federal lines by assault in heavy column. These were repulsed with effect at 8½ o'clock in the evening, and the enemy withdrew from the field.?

July 3.—Third day of the battle of Gettysburg. Artillery firing in the morning, and an assault upon the right wing of the Federal army, which was repulsed. The enemy then concentrated all his artillery, 150 pieces, upon the left centre of General Meade's lines, and opened ck in the afternoon. This three hours, during which e upon the same position, lomely, with a loss of 3000 lemy, among them General and officers of lesser rank. preparations to retreat, and rable portion of his troops dead and the greater part d. Upon the Federal side John F. Reynolds; Briga-;; Colonels W. W. Dudley, ampshire; Dennis O'Kane, berts, 140th Pennsylvania; ils; Ward, 15th Massachu- liles, Pennsylvania Buck- ennsylvania; Majors A. J. Lowere, 62d Pennsylvania. ckles, Hancock, and But- Barlow, Gibbons, Graham, s R. R. Cummings, 142d 5th Pennsylvania; George aircbild, 2d Wisconsin; A. A. Morrow, 34th Michigan; artung, 74th Pennsylvania; ; J. J. Lockman, 119th New 2d Ohio; Colville, 1st Min- A. Mitzel, 74th Pennsyl- 'ork; Miles, 3d Pennsylva- nsylvania; Majors George Kearney, 11th New Jersey. as taken prisoner. Of the rals Barksdale, Mississippi; and; Armistead, Garnett, Avery, North Carolina; Mississippi; Smith, North ; De Saussure, South Caro- nes, Georgia; Carrington, Williams, Virginia; Allen, rginia. Wounded, Major- ner) and Hood; Brigadier-), Pickett, Kemper, Scales, Jenkins; Colonels Bennet, gia; Kennedy, South Caro- ippi; Gantt, Hunton, Stu- Mississippi, Lightfoot, Ala- nly, Mississippi; Lieuten- ia; Heiser, McElroy, Mis- losely, Mississippi; Majors sissippi; Berkley, Wilson, ; Blair, Mississippi. The General Meade to be 5000 isoners, 3000 deserters; to- ss has been estimated at wounded, and missing. vacuated Tullahoma, Ten- tanooga.

Arkansas. 10,000 rebels , and Marmaduke, attacked by General Prentiss with unboat Tyler. The rebels a heavy fire, before which They finally retreated, hav- d, 1500 wounded, and 1200 Federal loss, 230 killed ebels killed were Generals l colonels, and officers of

Torpedo, formerly the Dra- River, Virginia, having on l, Vice-President of the so- nt. By flag of truce it was the bearer of a letter from Lincoln, and he requested on in the Torpedo, to pre- Lincoln in person. This President and Cabinet, but ould be communicated, the gs and proceeded up the ; for an answer.

July 4.—Vicksburg was surrendered to the United States troops under General Grant. There were captured 1 lieutenant-general (Pemberton), 4 major-generals, 13 brigadiers, 31,263 men, 200 pieces of artillery, including 60 siege guns, 66,000 small arms, a heavy stock of am- munition, a large supply of army clothing, and a much heavier stock of provisions than was expected. The prisoners were paroled and sent into the rebel lines. During the siege 2 brigadier-generals were killed in the town and 1 wounded. It has been estimated that in the campaign of 64 days, ending with the capture of Vicks- burg, the rebel losses were 48,700 killed, wounded, and prisoners, 71,000 small arms, and 230 pieces of artillery. The Federal losses were as follows:—

	Killed.	Wounded.	Missing.
Port Gibson	130	718	5
14 mile Creek	4	24	
Raymond	69	341	32
Jackson	40	240	6
Champion Hills	426	1342	189
Big Black Bridge	29	242	2
Vicksburg	545	3688	303
	1243	6595	537

Total, 8375.

July 5.—General Kilpatrick with Federal cavalry cap- tured a rebel train at Smithburg, Maryland, and took 160 ambulances and wagons, which were destroyed. He also took 2 guns and 167 prisoners.

——— The 20th Kentucky regiment, 400 strong, sur- rendered Lebanon, Kentucky, to John Morgan's rebel cavalry, 4000 in number. The latter burned the railroad depot and some houses.

July 6.—Captain H. W. Sawyer, 1st New Jersey cav- alry, and Captain John Flynn, 1st Indiana, were desig- nated, by lots drawn at the Libby Prison, Richmond, to be shot in retaliation for the shooting of Captain W. F. Corbin and T. J. McGraw, rebel spies caught recruiting for the rebel army within the Union lines, and executed by order of General Burnside at Sandusky, Ohio, May 15th.

——— General Pierce, U.S. Army, occupied Green- castle, Maryland, and captured 500 prisoners, 3 guns, and 10 wagons of the enemy.

——— An expedition under General Ransom left Vicksburg for Natchez, where were captured 18 guns, a large quantity of ammunition, 5000 beef cattle, and 9000 hogsheads of sugar, intended for the use of the rebel army.

July 8.—A fight near Funkstown, Maryland, between Kilpatrick's United States cavalry and a large rebel force. Federal loss, 50 killed and wounded. Rebel loss, 100 killed and wounded, and 50 prisoners.

——— Eleven rebel regiments of cavalry, with 10 pieces of horse artillery, commanded by General John Morgan, numbering 5000 men, crossed the Ohio River at Brandenburg, for the purpose of making a raid through Indiana. They went at first to Corydon, then to Salem (July 9), where they burned a railroad depot and took 500 prisoners. They successively occupied various towns and villages, burning bridges, railroad depots, tearing up tracks, and stealing everything valuable that came in their way. They pursued an irregular course through Indiana, being headed off and pursued by the Union troops. 65,000 men volunteered for the purpose of meeting the invaders in two days, a large number of whom were accepted and armed. Morgan made several attempts to get near the Ohio River for the purpose of recrossing, but was turned back by fear of the heavy forces in front of him. He finally crossed the lines and entered the State of Ohio.

July 9.—Port Hudson, Louisiana, was surrendered by the rebel General Gardner to Major-General Banks, U.S. Army, with 31 field pieces, 20 siege guns, 5000 small arms, a large supply of ammunition, and 5500 men, 1 major-general, 1 brigadier, and 5 colonels and other officers.

July 10.—General Gilmore's United States troops sur- prised the rebel forces in their fortifications on the south end of Morris Island, Charleston Harbor, South Carolina, and after a brisk fight routed the enemy and took possession of their intrenchments and 11 heavy guns. The assaulting column was led by General Strong, and the movement was assisted by four Monitors under command of Admiral Dahlgren. This left the rebels only in possession of Fort Wagner and Battery Gregg on that island.

July 11.—An attempt was made to carry the rebel Battery Wagner on Morris Island, Charleston Harbor, which failed. The Union troops were repulsed. Total of losses on the Federal side by operations on Morris Island, including the assault on Fort Wagner, 290 killed, wounded, and missing up to this time.

——— Fort Powhatan, on the James River, Virginia, was bombarded by United States gunboats, and captured after a short siege.

July 12.—Hagerstown, Maryland, was taken by General Kilpatrick's cavalry.

July 13.—A riot commenced in the city of New York, ostensibly in opposition to the draft for a militia, under the law of the United States, commonly called "the conscription law." The mob burned the provost marshal's office for one of the drafting districts. The provost guard was beaten off, several houses were burned, and brutal attacks were made upon citizens, soldiers, and particularly upon negroes, who were beaten and some hung. Attacks were made upon newspaper offices, stores, and dwelling-houses, and much valuable property was stolen.

——— Rebel cavalry were defeated at Jackson, Tennessee, by troops under Colonel Hatch. Rebel loss, 700 killed, wounded, and prisoners, with horses, mules, &c.

——— Lee's rebel army crossed the Potomac at Williamsport and Falling Waters, during the night and the morning of the next day, by means of a pontoon bridge and scows.

——— Yazoo City, held by about 800 rebels, was captured by General Herron. 250 prisoners were taken. The rebels burned 4 transport steamers below the city. The United States gunboat De Kalb was blown up by torpedoes. The rebels burned 14 large steamers up the Yazoo, to prevent their capture.

July 14.—Colonel Kilpatrick occupied Williamsport, Maryland, which he found abandoned by the rebels. He then crossed to Falling Waters, where he attacked the rebel rear guard and took 2500 prisoners. Their general, Pettigrew, was killed, and 2 guns and caissons, and 2 battle flags were taken.

——— Second day of the riot at New York. The mob continued its ferocious demonstrations, burning down buildings, robbing and assaulting negroes and white persons. The military now endeavored to repress them. There were several fights between the mob and the soldiers, in which ball and bayonets were freely used by the latter. Colonel O'Brien, a volunteer militia officer in command of 250 men, was captured by the rioters, beaten, and then hung to a lamp post.

——— A mob gathered in Boston and broke open some gun-shops, and were about to proceed to other outrages, but the military being promptly on hand, fired upon them and put down the riot, after killing 5 men and wounding 12.

——— Rioting on Staten Island, New York. A railroad depot was set on fire and some dwellings.

——— The Federal troops under General Parke advancing on Jackson, Mississippi, had a skirmish with a portion of the rebel forces. After half an hour's fight, the latter retreated with a loss of 300.

July 15.—The rebels abandoned Jackson, Mississippi, and retreated, after setting fire to their storehouses holding provisions for the army. The flames spread, and burned about 40 houses.

——— The rebel General W. Fitzhugh Lee and Captain Winder, prisoners at Fort Monroe, were ordered to be held as hostages for the safety of Captains Sawyer and Flynn, condemned to death by the rebel authorities at Richmond.

——— The President of the United States issued a proclamation recommending that the 6th of August be celebrated as a day of thanksgiving, praise, and prayer, for the recent victories of the Union troops.

——— Third day of the N violent demonstrations in va were dealt with by grape, Negro houses in various pa and burned, and the unfortu brutal ferocity.

July 16.—The rebel Gener uated Jackson, Mississippi, of by General Grant's troo Over 40 locomotive engines loss to the rebels.

——— Fourth day of the orders were generally quelle breaks during the day and ev met by the police and milita 150 persons were killed, a was estimated at $2,000,000

——— Rioting at Brookly docks were attacked, and ar and other damage done.

——— Colonel De Bussy brigade of infantry, left Jacl in the same State. They b the rebels, burned a depot, t and considerable cotton. The in which the rebels were and a forge and foundry for ed, with 13 machine-shops locomotives, 50 cars, 100,0 bales of cotton. The railro and a pontoon bridge were work, railroad tracks, &c. having lost only 20 men, an railroad was rendered useles

——— A fight at Elk Cre Blunt's troops and rebels u latter were routed, losing 1 and 100 prisoners. Federal ed. Cooper retreated.

July 18.—An expedition Newbern, North Carolina, fo North Carolina. They were they destroyed a rebel gunbe a cotton factory in working munitions of war, worth abo

——— An expedition se ana, under Lieutenant-Com to Vicksburg. Four steam expedition, together with a l provisions, &c., collected fo

——— A heavy bombar Wagner, Morris Island, Cha lina, by the United States t and the iron-clad fleet. A tempt was made to carry Fo was made by ten regiments eral Strong and Colonel Put in the face of a dreadful fi mounting the parapet, whe necticut were planted. The lading fires. The 54th Mas over the parapet, but were numbers of the rebels, wh with wild passion. The res troops were beaten back. Federal side Colonel Putna sachusetts, (colored), Lieu New York. Wounded, Ger mour, Major Filleo.

July 19.—Colonel Dick M Morgan's rebel raiding part ton, Ohio.

——— The rebel Morgan' to cross the Ohio river near vented by a gunboat, losin and 1000 prisoners. Morg and made off in the directio

July 20.—General Shack men of Morgan's guerillas Morgan escaped.

a proclamation ordering a
ng white population of the
of 18 and 45 years of age.
e over Tar River, North
, cavalry expedition sent
:. The depot at Rocky
ton factory and 5000 bales
.rs.
was captured by United
Powell and Toland, who
ad 700 muskets. Colonel
Powell wounded, and 63
Rebel loss 75 killed and
e railroad was destroyed,.
en fired upon from houses

nassas Gap, Virginia, be-
ade, 800 strong, and about
lerson. Notwithstanding
ederals made a determined
them to flight with a loss
Federal loss 28 killed, 106

Mound, Dakotah Territory,
under General Sibley and
re routed with heavy loss

General John H. Morgan,
to of the command, 400 in
New Lisbon, Ohio. Mor-
t to the penitentiary, and
ment of Colonel Straight
the rebels\as prisoners of

ake, Dakotah Territory.

, the rebel leader who de-
rt and precipitate the Cot-
died at Montgomery, Ala-

uffalo Lake, Dakota Ter-
ain routed, and retreated
rritory across the Missouri

d Pegram's troops attacked
ntucky, and were repulsed.
cked the main rebel force
they retreated.
issued a proclamation de-
will protect its troops of
dered that a rebel soldier
oldier of the United States
s of nations, and that for
emy or sold into slavery,
ed at hard labor on the
ntil the other shall be re-
ent due to a prisoner of

im's rebels were attacked
ost 20 killed and 100 pri-

inder Major Ransom went
Natchez, and destroyed 5
ned a cotton factory and

ih steamer was condemned
l States Prize Court, for
the time of capture.
Brandy Station, between
h infantry supports, and a

ram's rebel troops crossed
ndoned Kentucky, having
their expedition.
sed the order of July 15,
iths' service, the exigency

alette (Union) was elected
62 majority.
l pirate steamer Alabama

put into Table Bay, Cape of Good Hope, capturing an American ship in full sight of land. This vessel was reported to be the fifty-sixth American vessel captured by the Alabama since she was permitted to leave England. The greater number of these and their cargoes were burned at sea.

August 8.—The rebel privateer ship Tuscaloosa, formerly the United States merchant bark Conrad, put into Simon's Bay, Cape of Good Hope.

August 13.—A skirmish at Pineville, Missouri. A rebel attack was repulsed, the enemy losing 30 killed and wounded, with horses, wagons, stores, &c.

—— An expedition started from Lagrange, Tennessee, for Grenada, Mississippi. It was commanded by Lieutenant-Colonel Phillips. They reached Grenada on the 17th, drove 2000 rebels out of it, and destroyed 57 locomotives, 400 cars, depot buildings, machine shops, blacksmith shops, and ordnance stores. Before they completed their operations they were joined by Colonel Winslow of General Grant's army, with a force sent from below.

August 16.—The Anglo-rebel pirate steamer Georgia put into Simon's Bay, Cape of Good Hope, having captured 15 vessels since she entered upon her career.

August 17.—A grand attack was made on Fort Sumter, Charleston Harbor, South Carolina, by General Gilmore's land batteries, and the iron-clad fleet of 7 ships and 7 wooden gunboats. The firing was heavy and effective. The rebel forts and batteries replied vigorously. Fleet-Captain George W. Rodgers, commanding the Catskill, was killed. Fort Sumter was very much damaged.

August 20.—Lawrence, Kansas, was invaded by the rebel chief Quantrell, with 800 guerillas, who killed and wounded 100 unarmed citizens, many of the women, and set fire to the town, destroying property valued at $2,000,000.

August 21.—General Rosecrans's army appeared before Chattanooga, Georgia, and opened fire on the city. One steamboat was sunk and another disabled by the artillery fire.

—— The United States brig Bainbridge foundered in a gale off Cape Hatteras. 79 of the crew were lost—only one sailor was saved.

—— General Gilmore having breached Fort Sumter and rendered it untenable as a fortification, demanded the surrender of that fort and Morris Island in 4 hours, threatening to shell Charleston in 24 hours if the demand was not complied with. No attention was paid to this demand.

August 22.—General Gilmore threw heavy rifled shells into Charleston, South Carolina, from a 280-pounder gun nicknamed "the Swamp Angel," mounted on a battery located in a marsh, and distant 5 miles from the city—a range before that time never attained by any piece of artillery in the world.

—— In compliance with complaints of the British and Spanish consuls at Charleston, South Carolina, of the shortness of time for the removal of non-combatants, women, and children, General Gilmore agreed to suspend the bombardment for two days.

—— The rebel Generals Steele and Cooper, with 11,000 men, retreated from a force of 4500 men, offering battle near the Arkansas River, Arkansas, and were pursued to Perryville, 100 miles south of the Arkansas.

August 23.—General Gilmore threw more rifled shells into Charleston, South Carolina, loaded with an incendiary composition, commonly called "Greek fire."

—— Six deserting substitutes attached to the 119th Pennsylvania regiment, were ordered to be shot on the 26th inst., which sentence was carried into effect against five of them.

August 24.—Major-General Q. A. Gilmore reported to General Halleck, that after seven days' bombardment, Fort Sumter was "a shapeless and harmless mass of ruins." The breaching batteries were between 3330 and 4240 yards from the fort. The rebels reported that 9551 shot had been fired at Sumter, 3945 struck inside and 2130 outside. The flag was shot away 14 times.

August 25.—The United States gunboat Satellite and tug Reliance were captured near the mouth of the Rappahannock River, by parties coming from the shore, who boarded them in boats. With these vessels they captured 2 schooners, and then went up the Rappahannock for safety.

——— A committee of the Liverpool (Eng.) Emancipation Society memorialized Earl Russell to stop the departure of two iron steam rams built on the river Mersey for the use of the rebel government.

August 26.—General Davidson, U.S. Army, drove Marmaduke's rebel cavalry out of Brownesville, Arkansas, capturing a colonel and some men.

——— The rebel General Jeff Thompson, with 100 guerillas, was captured by Colonel Woodson's Federal cavalry, at Pocahontas, Arkansas.

——— The rifle pits of the rebels at Vinegar Hill, Morris Island, in front of Fort Wagner, were carried by General Gilmore's troops, with a loss of 10 killed and 17 wounded. Hand grenades and cohorns or small mortars were used on both sides.

August 27.—A battle at Rocky Gap, West Virginia, between 3000 United States cavalry under General Averill and rebels under General Jones. Averill had been sent out by General Kelly, and had destroyed the rebel saltpetre works at Pendleton. In the action at the springs he lost about 100 killed and wounded, and retired after two days of fighting.

August 28.—General Davidson with 8000 men engaged 7000 rebels at Bayou Metoe, Arkansas. There was artillery firing with slight losses on both sides.

August 29.—Battle of Bayou Metoe, Arkansas. General Davidson by his artillery dislodged the rebels, who after a brisk fight fled, first setting fire to a bridge which it had been their principal object to defend. The rebels lost 100 killed and wounded, and 300 prisoners. Federal loss, 39 killed and wounded.

August 31.—The rebel steamer supposed to be the Gibraltar or Sumter, was sunk in the harbor of Charleston, South Carolina, by the guns of a battery on Sullivan's Island, the garrison supposing it to be a Federal steamer or gunboat. The Gibraltar or Sumter had a number of rebel soldiers on board, many of whom were drowned.

——— Fort Smith, Arkansas, was captured by General Blunt, U.S. Volunteers.

September 1.—Fort Moultrie, Charleston Harbor, was bombarded by the United States fleet. Fleet-Captain O. C. Badger was severely wounded and afterwards died.

September 2.—General Gilmore's saps having advanced so near Fort Wagner on Morris Island, South Carolina, that it was in danger of successful assault, and Beauregard believing that it was impossible to hold it much longer, the batteries Wagner and Gregg, and the whole of Morris Island, Charleston Harbor, were abandoned in the night to the United States troops, the guns, 19 in number, being spiked.

——— Major-General Burnside took Kingston, Tenn., moving in co-operation with General Rosecrans on the flank.

——— General Kilpatrick with cavalry went to Port Conway, on the Rappahannock, and opened fire on the gunboats Satellite and Reliance, captured by the rebels August 25. The Satellite was sunk, and the Reliance so damaged as to be useless.

September 4.—A bread riot took place at Mobile, Ala., by women. A regiment of soldiers refused to quell it. A company of cadets which attempted to quell the disturbance, were put to rout by the female rioters.

September 7.—Admiral Dahlgren demanded the surrender of Fort Sumter, Charleston Harbor, from the rebel General Beauregard. The latter answered that he "could have the fort when he could take it and hold it."

September 8.—Thirty launches loaded with sailors and marines made an attempt to enter the ruins of Fort Sumter, Charleston Harbor, by assault. The difficulties were much greater than expected. The attacking party was repulsed, losing 80 killed and wounded, and 113 prisoners.

——— General Sully, U.S. Army, attacked over 400 lodges of hostile Indians near White Stone Hill, N. W. Territory, fought and dispersed them with a loss of over 100 warriors killed.

September 8.—Six iron-clads engaged Fort Moultrie, Charleston Harbor, for 7 hours, during which time one of the magazines of that fort was exploded by a shell.

September 9.—The United States gunboats Clifton and Sachem were captured by the rebels at Sabine Pass, La. They were riddled by the fire from the fortifications on shore. They were operating for the landing of a column of United States troops under Major-General Franklin, to be employed in a movement against Louisiana and Texas. In consequence of the failure at this point, the movement was abandoned.

——— Cumberland Gap, Tennessee, was taken by General Shackelford, of Burnside's army. The rebel General Frazier, with 2000 men and 14 pieces of artillery, were captured.

——— Lieutenant-Colonel Hays, with 300 men of the 18th Ohio regiment, surrendered at Tilford, Tennessee, to 1800 rebels under Jackson, after a fight of 2 hours.

——— The rebels having evacuated Chattanooga, Georgia, it was taken possession of by Major-General Rosecrans and his army.

——— Colonel Cloud defeated 1000 rebels under Colonel Steerman, at Damonville, Arkansas, and captured their camp.

September 10.—Little Rock, Arkansas, was occupied by Major-General Steele.

September 15.—The President of the United States issued a proclamation, suspending the writ of habeas corpus in all cases of a military nature, concerning soldiers, sailors, spies, deserters, prisoners of war, civil officers of the United States, persons charged with resisting the draft, and of persons charged with military or naval offences.

September 19.—First day of the battle of Chickamauga, Georgia. The rebels made a heavy attack, in mass, upon the extreme left of General Rosecrans's lines, held by General Brannan's division. After a severe contest, five Federal brigades were routed and two divisions were attacked. The latter resisted stoutly, and with the aid of well-posted batteries checked the advance. A rally was made, the rebels were beaten back, and the lost ground recovered, under the skilful management of Major-General Thomas, who recovered several guns that had been captured, and took 500 prisoners. The rebel troops here engaged were Buckner's and Longstreet's corps. About the time that the attack on the Federal left was repulsed, the rebels made a strong movement against the centre. This portion of the line yielded, was reinforced, and yielded again; another rally was made, and another break followed. The rebel success was checked by reinforcements sent by General Rosecrans, and they fell back. The original Federal lines were then regained upon the whole field. After night a new attack was made upon the Union lines, which was again repulsed.

September 20.—Second day of the battle of Chickamauga, Georgia. The rebels commenced with a desperate attack upon the extreme left of the Federal lines, held by Major-General Thomas. Several charges were made upon the breastworks by Longstreet's, D. H. Hill's, and Buckner's corps. The ground was held for some time, but finally the United States troops gave way, being greatly outnumbered, but rallied again. Meanwhile heavy demonstrations had been made against the centre of the line, which was cut in two by the terrific force of the enemy. McCook's and Crittenden's divisions did not hold their ground. General Thomas, who was now separated from the line of the army, re-formed his shattered brigades. The rebels again turned their united strength against this gallant remnant. They stood their ground, and were saved by reinforcements under General Granger, who met the rebels before they had reached Thomas, and by a brilliant charge drove them from a hill. A desperate effort was made to take this position, but it failed. The rebels fell back to reorganize and reinforce for a new attack. This was attempted with greater violence than ever, but Thomas was firm, and his men poured into the enemy a terrific fire from artillery and musketry. All the efforts of the rebels were vain, and the battle was concluded by a splendid charge ich the rebels fell back and nflicted heavy loss upon the verely themselves, but having for which the battle was tianooga. At night, Geneville, and concentrated his army. General Rosecrans nd prepared himself to hold reinforced. In this battle ifantry force of Rosecrans's killed, 9342 wounded, and ; total, 15,682. With the hat the total will be 16,000. had captured 25 colors and f arms. Their own papers it is believed to have been idams of Texas, and 1200 a first day. On the Federal eral Lytle; Colonels Key, inois. Wounded, General ley, Jones, 36th Ohio; Carth Kentucky; Frankhouse, rson, 6th Ohio; Armstrong, iels Hunt, 4th Kentucky; 11th Michigan; Tripp, 6th i; Vaughan, 7th Kentucky; Vauntan, Weldman, 18th Illinois; Dawson, 19th Infs. On the rebel side there Hood; Brigadier-Generals 'olfford, Georgia; Waltham, ntucky; Desbler; Colonels nd, South Carolina; Ould, Alabama; Harper, Haid, iol Inge, Alabama; Majors d, Major-Generals Gregg, r-Generals Daniel Adams, n, John Helm, —— Brown; jor Haskel, Tennessee. on, the rebel commissioner ussell at London that his nd that he was ordered to

lent of the United States ing the blockade against

neral Dana's (U.S.) brigade wered near Morganza, La.,

rson's Cross Roads, Tenn. savalry attacked Wheeler's iem, killing 120, taking 87 d States Government proken by Wheeler a few days

oln issued a proclamation ember as a day of general

essee, captured by Wheeler's a the garrison, a Federal ailants burned a train of depot, &c. They also detheir march to the place. le upon the rear of General rebel cavalry. They burned irfreesboro.
was made to blow up the igate Ironsides, in Charles. orpedo. The instrument of m the bow of a small cigarriven against the Ironsides explosion followed, which n the deck of the Ironsides, to the vessel. Lieutenant he rebel steamer, was taken n overboard by the force of Ironsides, Ensign Charles skot-shot fired by Glassett, ng the frigate.
ima, was bombarded by the rebels from Lookout Mountain, without any important effect.

October 7.—The rebel steamers General Taylor and Fulton were destroyed in the Red River, Louisiana, by an expedition under Lieutenant Couthong, U.S. Navy.

October 9.—Two iron-plated rams built on the Mersey, England, by the Lairds for the use of the rebel government, were seized by order of the British government, upon a charge of an intention to evade the neutrality laws.

——— An expedition under General I. J. Wistar, which had been sent to Matthews county, Virginia, to suppress guerillas and naval parties, returned, having taken some prisoners, with 100 cattle, horses, arms, &c., and destroyed 150 sloops and boats which had been employed in contraband trade on the Chesapeake Bay.

October 10.—A fight at Madison Court House, Virginia, between Kilpatrick's (Federal) and Stuart's (rebel) cavalry. The latter were successful in driving the former back to their infantry supports, and a considerable number of prisoners were taken. Most of these were recaptured by an infantry charge.

——— Battle at Blue Springs, Kentucky, between Burnside's troops and the rebels. The latter were defeated and driven to Zollicoffer and Bristol. Six bridges were burned by the Federal troops, 3 locomotives, and 35 cars. Federal loss, 100 killed and wounded. Rebel loss supposed to be greater.

——— Rebels at Bible Ridge, Tennessee, were defeated by Union cavalry. They were followed to Henderson and Zollicoffer, and routed at each place, losing in both days' fight 300 killed and wounded.

——— Battle at Farmington's Farm, Tenn. Wheeler's rebel cavalry were defeated by Union troops under General George Crook. The rebels lost 4 guns, 1000 muskets, 240 prisoners, and a considerable number of killed and wounded. They retreated across the Tennessee River, having lost during their raid in the rear of Rosecrans's lines, 2000 killed, wounded, and prisoners.

October 11.—The Anglo-rebel blockade-runner steamer Douro was chased and run ashore off New Inlet, N. C., abandoned, and totally destroyed. The Douro had been captured once before, but being sold was purchased by parties who transferred her to the rebels.

October 12.—A fight at Merril's Crossing of Salt Fork, Missouri, between 1600 Federal troops under General E. B. Brown and 2000 rebels under Shelby, who had made an incursion into the State. The fight was commenced near night, in the midst of a rain, and continued as long as the parties could see. It was resumed in the morning, the enemy being on the retreat. They were routed, with the loss of 1 gun. Federal loss, 30 killed and wounded. Rebel loss, 53 killed, over 70 wounded, and several prisoners.

October 14.—Battle at Bristoe Station, Va. General Lee formed the plan of getting between the forces of General Meade at the Rapidan, and Washington, by sending a portion of his troops through Thoroughfare Gap to Manassas and Centreville, Va. General Meade, penetrating the plan, fell back rapidly towards Washington, crossing the Rappahannock and marching northwardly. His activity frustrated the rebel designs. At Bristoe Station a portion of the 5th corps and the 2d corps under General Warren, marching by the flank, were attacked by a portion of the rebels of Hill's corps, under General Heth. A spirited fight ensued, in which the rebels were beaten and forced to retreat, with a loss of 5 guns, 2 colors, and 450 prisoners. On the Federal side there were killed, Colonel Mallon, 42d New York (Tammany) regiment, and several line officers, and about 200 killed and wounded. The rebels lost General Cooke, Colonel Ruffin, 1st North Carolina, Colonel Thompson. 5th North Carolina cavalry, and 500 killed and wounded. The defeat of Lee in this battle, and of his attempt to get into the rear of Meade, caused the former to retreat as rapidly as he had advanced. Meade followed him closely until he recrossed the Rappahannock.

October 15.—Canton, Mississippi, was captured by General McPherson, U.S. Army, after a fight in which the rebels lost 200 prisoners.

1863. *October* 17.—Proclamation of the President of the United States for 300,000 men to serve for 3 years or the war; a draft to be made for deficiencies. January 5, 1864.

October 18.—Union troops at Charlestown, Virginia, were surprised and captured by a superior rebel force under Imboden, losing 434 men, 500 stand of arms, &c.

October 19.—The main body of Lee's rebel army, which had been advancing towards Washington and Maryland, retraced its course and crossed the Rappahannock, leaving Stuart's rebel cavalry on this side of that stream.

October 20.—Stuart's rebel cavalry was driven out of Gainesville, Virginia, by Kilpatrick's union cavalry. Union loss, 200 men.

———— Morrison's and Dibbord's rebel cavalry captured 700 prisoners, 50 wagons, 6 guns, &c., from Federal troops, at Philadelphia, Tennessee.

———— Major-General Grant succeeded Major-General Rosecrans in command of the armies of the Cumberland, and of Ohio and Kentucky.

October 21.—Opelousas, Louisiana, occupied by Major-General Franklin and U.S. troops. Vermillion Bayou occupied by General Dana.

October 24.—Rebel cavalry crossed the Rappahannock and engaged Gregg's Federal cavalry. Of the latter, Major Charles F. Taggart, 2d Pennsylvania cavalry, was killed.

October 25.—Battle of Pine-Bluff, Ark. 4000 rebel cavalry, under Marmaduke and Cobbett, attacked 700 Federal infantry under Colonel Clayton fortified in the town. Several charges were made by the rebels, who were repulsed each time, and finally retreated, leaving 300 killed and wounded in our hands. Federal loss, 11 killed and 53 wounded.

———— The blockade runner Venus was destroyed by shots from the U.S. Gunboat Nansemond off Wilmington, North Carolina.

October 27.—Rebels at Brown's Ferry, Tennessee, were surprised by Union troops under General W. F. Smith, who floated down 50 pontoons and drove the rebels from the ridge.

———— Rebels on Lookout Mountain, Tennessee, were attacked by Hazen's brigade and driven back. Union loss, 5 killed, 15 wounded.

———— General Hooker was attacked at Brown's Ferry, Tennessee, by the rebels, commencing at midnight and fighting until 4 o'clock in the morning. The enemy was repulsed in several charges.

———— Charleston, South Carolina, bombarded from Gilmore's batteries, and heavy firing upon Forts Sumter, Johnson, and Moultrie. 1215 shots alone were discharged against Fort Sumter.

———— Skirmish near Bealeton Station, Virginia, between Federal and rebel troops; damage to the parties about equal.

October 28.—Battle of Wauhatchie, Lookout Mountain, Tennessee, was taken by U.S. troops under General Hooker with but little loss. The rebels lost 107 prisoners, and 350 killed and wounded, and 1000 small arms.

October 29.—The barque Saxon was captured on the west coast of Africa, 400 miles north of the Cape of Good Hope by the United States steamer Vanderbilt; she had a board part of the cargo of the barque Conrad—afterwards turned into a rebel privateer, by the title of the Tuscaloosa.

October 30.—Hawkins's guerrillas were attacked near Piney Factory, Tennessee, by Lieutenant-Colonel Shively with infantry, and were routed, losing 20 killed and 60 prisoners.

November 1.—Three days' cavalry skirmishing and fighting below Loudon, Tennessee, were ended by driving back the rebels—with a Union loss of 483 killed, wounded, and missing, 24 wagons and 6 guns. Rebel loss, 700 men.

November 2.—An expedition fitted out by General Banks landed some troops at Brazos Santiago, Texas.

During the voyage from Union foundered—the cre' schooners were also sunk.

November 3.—Cavalry Tennessee. 120 Michigan bon defeated 400 rebel ca and taking 24 prisoners.

———— Battle of Collier: under Chalmers were repul and 13 of his staff were ca and wounded and 50 priso:

———— The rear guard army corps, retreating fr attacked by the rebels at ana, and cut off from the and wounded and 550 pris ing, the enemy were drive

November 4.—Burbridge was attacked at Bayou C rebels under Walker and M loss, 700 and 1 gun. Rebe Federals retreated to Vern

November 5.—Brownsvill of by General Banks. It rebel garrison, after a sh secessionists and unionists

November 6.—4000 rebe Echols defeated at Droop's and Federal troops, with a l 100 prisoners, three gun: Federal loss, 100 killed an

———— Rodgerville, Ten who took 506 prisoners, 2 ; horses and mules.

November 7.—Battles of Kelly's Ford, Virginia. M the rebels rom the statio prisoners, and 4 guns. Mn Ford took 400 prisoners. by both columns. The reb pahannock. Union losses i wounded.

November 8.—Fight near Buford's Federal cavalry a rebel corps. Union loss, 5

———— The rebels crosse themselves on the south si

November 10.—Lord Ly nicated to the United State of a plot agreed by seces the rebel prisoners on J Measures to prevent the ec immediately taken.

November 14.—Longstree see river on the road to attacked by General Burns him.

November 15.—Longstree the Tennessee, he attacked fell back to Denver.

November 16.—General advance of Longstreet, evn delivered at Campbell's S some hours. The Federal (tion of their batteries, whic effect and checked their ad river; a second battle was continued until nightfall, I sion of the ground. Loss o killed and wounded. Li Michigan, was killed. The killed and wounded.

November 17.—The reb made efforts against the fee upon the Loudon and Clin ing continued all day. T

l back; after which they
ling the Federal troops to
. General Sykes, of the
ed. The Federal loss was
and wounded.
er Joseph L. Gerity, on a
New York with a cargo of
is seized by the latter, who
w; and after keeping them
it them adrift at sea in a
utually landed on the coast
d captain were put in the
rebel flag and fired a salute
hey would carry vessel and
them.
ear Mount Jackson, West
and rebels under Gillmore
defeated, losing 27 prison-
al loss, 2 killed, 6 wounded

e upon the Union positions
Knoxville, Tennessee, by a
gstreet. General Sanders,
ras severely wounded, and
is, 100 killed and wounded.
back towards the town.
el blockade runner steamer
ited States steamers Dela-
gton, North Carolina.
the operations of the battle
pits of the rebels between
ck were carried by Federal
ias, taking 109 prisoners.

r of the battle of Chatta-
ive along the whole line.
ntain and drove the enemy
the east end of Missionary
iomas held the position in
the previous day.
f the battle of Chattanooga.
dge from Rossville to the
the Federal troops. The
and withdrew in the night.
ided, and missing, reported
)00 prisoners, exclusive of
His loss in killed and
to our own. We took 42
tand of arms. This battle
ilo among the achievements
the strength of the rebel
ins. It was also most im-
from communication with
the latter to abandon the
'ederal troops were under
neral U. S. Grant, and the
s of Sherman, Thomas, and
iward, Granger, Sheridan,
r, and Osterhaus. On the
Colonels Putnam, 23d Ohio;
9th Illinois; Heath, 100th
nois; Lieutenant-Colonels
143d New York; Majors
2d New York; Glass, 23d
Wounded. Brigadier-Gene-
Smith, Giles A. Smith, W.
)0th Illinois: Avery, 102d
5th Kentucky; Markdale,
Ohio; Gilmore, 26th Ohio;
ennnt-Colonels Espy, 68th
iis; Boynton, 85th Ohio;
rs McCawley, 10th Iowa;
b, 56th Illinois; Innis, 6th
l Missouri; McAlone, 27th
)l side there were killed,
arolina; Colonels Porcher,
Georgia; Bullock, Florida.
m and Maney; Colonels
nnessee. The Union losses
800 killed, 3000 wounded,

700 prisoners; total 4500. Rebel killed and buried by Federal troops, 640; wounded, 2560; prisoners, 7300; total 10,500, with 47 guns and 13,000 small arms.

November 25.—The army of General Meade crossed the Rapidan at Culpeper and Germania Ford and Jacobs' Mill Bridge. There was skirmishing between Meade's and Lee's armies at Oak Woods, south of the Rapidan. The rebels fell back.

November 27.—Battle of Mine Run, Virginia. Skirmishing and artillery firing between the Federal and rebel armies during the greater part of the day, the enemy falling back gradually. Federal loss, 100 killed and 325 wounded. Killed, Lieutenant-Colonel Theodore Hesser, 72d Pennsylvania. Among the wounded were Colonel McClellan and Colonel Higgins, 86th Pennsylvania. Rebel wounded, General Jones, Stuart, Lieutenant-Colonel Nelligan, 1st Louisiana.

——— The rebel General John H. Morgan and six of his officers escaped from the penitentiary, at Columbus, Ohio.

——— Battle at Ringgold, Georgia. General Hooker pursuing Bragg was turned upon by the latter, who inflicted upon him considerable loss. Colonel Creighton and Lieutenant-Colonel Crane, 7th Ohio, were killed.

November 28.—Cavalry fight at Louisville, Tennessee. 300 rebels were dispersed by 225 men, under Major Bears, 6th Illinois cavalry, losing 21 killed, 10 wounded, and 21 prisoners.

November 29.—General Meade withdrew the Army of the Potomac from before the works of the rebels on Mine Run, being convinced that they could not be taken without a great loss of life. He retired and crossed the Rapidan, taking position on the north side.

——— Rebel steamer Robert E. Lee, from Nova Scotia, to Wilmington, North Carolina, captured off Cape Lookout by the U.S. gunboat James Adger.

November 30.—Three brigades of Longstreet's corps made a desperate assault upon Fort Sanders, at Knoxville, Tennessee, but were repulsed by discharges of grape and cannister, before which the storming party melted away, losing 700 killed, wounded, and prisoners. Union loss, 25. The rebels lost Colonels Ruff, McElroy, and Lieutenant-Colonel Thomas, commanding the storming party, who were killed: Colonel Fisher wounded.

——— Fort Esperanza, Matagorda Bay, Texas, abandoned by the rebels and partially destroyed, was taken possession of by Major-General Washburne.

——— The rebel blockade runner Chatham was captured off Altamaha River, by the U.S. gunboat Huron.

December 2.—Fight at Walker's Ford, 20 miles from Cumberland Gap, Tennessee, between Union forces under General Foster and Longstreet's Cavalry. The rebels lost 4 guns. Federal loss, 50.

——— Chalmers's rebel cavalry, 4000 strong, made a desperate attack on Wolf River Bridge, Tennessee, and were defeated by Colonel Hatch's small command, with heavy loss.

——— Three rebel salt works on St. Andrew's Sound, Florida, were destroyed by the crew of the U.S. bark Restless.

December 4.—Longstreet abandoned the siege of Knoxville and commenced to retreat towards Virginia. This was caused as well by the Union victory at Chattanooga, as by the advance of large reinforcements under General Granger.

December 6.—British blockade runner steamer Ceres captured off Wilmington, North Carolina, by the U.S. gunboat Aries. The Ceres was destroyed.

December 7.—The steamer Chesapeake, Captain Willets, on the passage from New York to Portland, Maine, was seized by sixteen rebels, who were on board in the character of passengers. They rose on the crew, killed the engineer, and wounded the assistant engineer and mate. They put the other passengers on shore at Partridge Island, and ran away with the ship.

——— The U.S. monitor Weehauken sunk during a storm in Charleston harbor, South Carolina. Several officers and the crew perished with her.

December 8.—President Lincoln in his message to Congress appended a proclamation of amnesty, offering a full pardon and restoration of all rights of property, except slaves, to all rebels who should take the oath of allegiance to the United States, excepting all civil or diplomatic officers of the so-called Confederate Government; all military and naval officers above the rank of colonel in the army, or lieutenant in the navy; all who have left judicial stations in the United States to aid the rebellion; all who resigned their commissions in the United States Army or Navy and afterwards aided the rebellion; and all who have engaged in any way in maltreating colored persons, or white persons in charge of such, otherwise than as lawful prisoners of war—thus declaring, that whenever in the states of Arkansas, Texas, Louisiana, Mississippi, Tennessee, Alabama, Georgia, Florida, South Carolina, and North Carolina, a number of persons, not less than one-tenth in number of the voters at the Presidential election in 1860, each having taken the oath, and not having since violated it, and being a qualified voter under the election law of the state before secession, shall establish a state government, republican in character, such shall be recognised as the true government, &c., provided the said constitution shall recognise the acts of Congress with reference to slaves, unless the same shall be declared unconstitutional by the Supreme Court.

December 9.—English blockade runner Minna captured by the United States steamer Circassian off Charleston.

———— Charles City Court House, Virginia, taken by an expedition sent out from Fort Munroe by General I. J. Wistar, with a loss to the rebels of 90 men, 55 horses, tents, arms, ammunitions, &c. Union loss, 1 killed and 4 wounded.

December 10.—Major-General Burnside was relieved of the command of Knoxville, Tennessee, by Major-General J. G. Foster.

December 11.—Extensive rebel salt works on West Bay, Florida, with salt, implements, &c., were destroyed by an expedition from the United States armed vessels Restless and Bloomer. They were the rebel government works, three quarters of a mile square, and one hundred and ninety-nine salt works belonging to companies and private individuals, with 507 boilers, kettles, &c., the whole worth three millions of dollars.

December 14.—Battle at Bean's Station, Tennessee, between Federal troops under General Shackelford and Longstreet's command retreating from Knoxville. The Unionists were repulsed with a loss of 700. On the rebel side the confessed loss was 900. General Gracier was wounded.

December 16.—General Averill cut the Virginia and Tennessee Railroad at Salem, West Virginia, and destroyed three depots containing 100,000 bushels corn, 50,000 bushels oats, 10,000 bushels wheat, 2000 barrels meat, besides large quantities of leather, salt, clothing, cotton, and warlike equipments; the railroad was destroyed, with 5 bridges and culverts. On the return the rebels under Early, Jones, Fitz-Lee, Imboden, Jackson, Echols, and McClausland, made desperate efforts to intercept Averill upon six different roads, but were foiled by the superior strategy and fertile resources of General Averill, whose loss was 6 killed, 11 wounded, 94 missing. He captured 294 prisoners and 150 horses.

December 17.—An attack by 800 rebel cavalry under Stuart upon a company of the 155th New York regiment, on the Orange and Alexandria Railroad, was successful in capturing the company after a brave resistance.

———— Fort Gibson, Arkansas, was attacked by 1600 rebels under Standwaite, who were repulsed.

———— The steamer Chesapeake was captured in Sambro Harbor, Nova Scotia, by the United States steamer Ellie and Annie, Lieutenant Nickels. Three of the crew were taken, the others escaped.

December 19.—The steamer Chesapeake, in charge of the United States gunboat Ellie and Annie, arrived at Halifax. It was intended to hand over the prisoners to the British authorities, to be held as pirates, but this intention was frustrated by the efforts of a mob, who seized the prisoners from the boat's crew which had them in charge, and hurried them away.

December 20.—The rebel steamer Little Leila was destroyed in the Suwanee] States schooner Fox.

December 21.—The rebel erly the Conrad of Philad bama, was seized at St. Sim by British officers, upon a laws.

December 25.—The Unite lying at anchor off Lega opened upon by two mask Marblehead replied with lasted until the gunboat batteries and driven out th and wounded. Two of th with caissons, shovels, &c. killed and 4 wounded. Lo

———— Reeves' guerilla county, Missouri, by Feder 35 rebels were killed and horses, arms, &c. A comp prisoners were also recaptu

December 28.—Skirmish wassee River, Tennessee, cavalry and Wheeler's rebe driven off. Rebel loss, 12(wounded. Federal loss, 1:

———— A supply train u army, was attacked by W strong, near Calhoun, Te forced, the rebels were bea and wounded, and 121 pris

December 29.—Battle in tween the whole of Longs of infantry, and the cava fight continued for more were finally repulsed, and killed and wounded.

1864. *January 3.*—280 I Baens were captured near of 4000 men under the reb eight hours' fight, in whic and 30 wounded. Two gu

January 4.—Major Coles Ferry, were attacked by M in the morning. The latt of 4 killed and 3 wounde 13 wounded.

January 8.—The rebel b was run ashore near Wilm pursued by the United Sta crews of the United Stat Aries.

January 10.—United S tempting to tow off the b ashore near the batteries d mington, North Carolina, off. She was under the was afterwards blown up.

January 11.—British blo was beached and burned North Carolina. Same d Vesta was beached and b that the latter was the tw destroyed within six mont

———— Major-General] ana, issued a proclamation an election, Feb'' ary 22d, officers, according to the I tion, where one-tenth or m of allegiance.

January 14.—Rebel ste ner, captured south of T States steamer Union.

———— The rebel Gener a raid towards Tunisville, pursuing party commande

January 15.—General advanced to Dandridge, T ville, and drove out the re

January 17.—A despe

Sturgis's troops at Dandridge, Tennessee, by Hood's and Bushrod Johnson's divisions and the Hampton Cavalry. A complete defeat was prevented by a charge made upon the enemy by McCook's cavalry. Our loss was 150. Same day, Sturgis fell back to Strawberry Plains, 6 miles from Knoxville.

January 18.—Steamer Laura, blockade runner, captured in St. Mark's Bay, Florida, by the United States steamer Stars and Stripes.

January 19.—Sturgis crossed the Holston River, hoping to intercept Longstreet at Seviersville. The bridge over the Holston was burned, in order to prevent the expected advance of Longstreet against Knoxville.

January 20.—The provisional government of Arkansas was inaugurated at Little Rock by authority of the state convention. Isaac Murphy was chosen provisional governor. The new constitution adopted by the convention provided for the freedom of male negroes at 21 years of age, and of females at 18.

—— Blockade runner steamer A. D. Vance was beached near Fort Caswell, in attempting to enter the port of Wilmington, North Carolina.

January 21.—An expedition sent by order of General Graham, U.S. Army, up the Chuckituck River, Virginia, consisting of 90 men under Captain Lee with 1 gun, was encountered by a stronger force of rebels and compelled to retreat. The armed transport Smith Briggs was sent for, to relieve the troops. Captain Lee intrenched himself, and was attacked by 500 rebels with 4 guns. On the arrival of the Smith Briggs at Smithland, Lee retreated with his men to the vessel; a heavy fire of artillery was then opened upon the boat; a shot was sent through the boiler, and the engineer was killed. Lee and a portion of his men escaped by swimming, others were captured; the Smith Briggs was taken, and shortly afterwards blown up.

January 25.—An expedition under command of Brigadier-General Graham, sent out by Major-General Butler, landed on the James River, 7 miles below Fort Powhattan, and captured 22 soldiers, 99 negroes, pork, oats, iron, and 2 sloops loaded with tobacco.

—— Corinth was evacuated by the Federal troops, which concentrated at Memphis.

—— The rebels, 600 strong, attacked the Union garrison at Athens, Tennessee, about 100 strong, and were repulsed after a fight of two hours. Federal loss, 20. Rebel loss, greater.

January 26.—A raid was made by order of General Palmer to Jones and Onslow counties, North Carolina. The Federal troops destroyed over 150,000 barrels of pork, with beef, tobacco, &c., and captured a number of horses and mules, and returned in safety.

January 27.—A skirmish near Florence, Alabama. Federal loss, 15 killed and 25 wounded.

January 28.—Battle at Fair Gardens, Tennessee. General Sturgis and McCook drove Longstreet's cavalry in a running fight of 9 hours, finally routing them in a sabre charge, capturing 3 steel guns, 100 prisoners, with a heavy loss, 65 being killed in the charge alone.

—— Roddy's rebel cavalry were driven from the north side of the Tennessee River by Federal troops under Colonel Phillips, with a loss of cattle, sheep, horses, &c.

—— A train of 80 wagons loaded with commissary stores, on the way from New Creek to Petersburg, West Virginia, was attacked near Williamsport by 2000 rebels. The guard under command of Colonel J. W. Snyder, numbering 800, gallantly resisted and fought for more than 4 hours, but were finally overcome by superior numbers, and the train captured. Union loss, about 80 killed and wounded. Rebel loss, equally heavy.

—— British steamer Rosita, blockade runner, was captured at sea by the U.S. steamship Western Metropolis.

—— Scottsville, Ky., defended by 150 men, was captured by 500 rebels under Colonel Hamilton, who burned the court-house, robbed the stores, &c.

January 29.—James A. Bayard of Delaware resigned his seat in the United States Senate, after having taken the oath of allegiance to the United States, which he had hitherto refused and neglected to do, although it had been taken by every other Senator. George Read Riddle was elected U.S. Senator in his stead.

—— General Palmer, with General Davis's division of Federal troops, advanced towards Tunnel Hill, Georgia. The rebels were found to have evacuated the position during the night.

February 1.—President Lincoln issued a proclamation ordering a draft for 500,000 men, to serve for 3 years or during the war, to be made on the 10th day of March.

—— The United States gunboat Underwriter, lying in the Neuse River, North Carolina, was captured by several boat-loads of rebels, who took her by surprise. The crew escaped. The rebels set fire to the boat, and she was blown up.

—— The Federal outposts at Bachelor's Creek, North Carolina, were attacked by rebels represented to be Hoke's brigade, and Pickett's division, about 15,000 strong. The Federal pickets were driven in, and their camps destroyed, with a loss of 75 men, 2 guns, and camp equipage.

February 2.—British steamer Presto, blockade runner, was beached on Ludman's Island, Charleston harbor, and destroyed by the guns of our ships of war.

—— The British blockade runner, steamer Wild Dayrell, was run ashore at New Topsail Inlet, South Carolina, and destroyed.

—— Rosser's rebel cavalry attacked the guards at Patterson's Creek and North Branch, Virginia, on the Baltimore and Ohio Railroad, drove them off and burned the bridges. The rebels were pursued by General Averill's cavalry, and a fight took place at Springfield, from which place the enemy were driven several miles.

February 3.—Major-General Sherman, with the 16th and 17th army corps under Generals Hurlbut and McPherson, left Vicksburg with 25,000 infantry, 1200 cavalry, and 40 guns, in light marching order, upon an extensive raid in Mississippi. The route of the army was crossing the Pearl River, through Brandon, Morton, and Meridian, which latter place was reached February 14. The rebel Lieutenant-General Polk having a railroad to assist him in his retreat, escaped across the Tombigbee on the 17th. At Meridian this force stayed a week waiting for the junction of General William S. Smith's cavalry expedition, which left Memphis to join Sherman by February 10th. While at Meridian parties were sent out to destroy railroads, &c., which accomplished immense destruction. There were destroyed 150 miles of railroad, 67 bridges, 7000 trestles, 20 locomotives, 28 cars, 1000 bales of cotton, several steam-mills, and over 2,000,000 bushels of corn: about 4500 negroes and 1200 mules came in with the columns. Total Federal loss, in killed, wounded, and missing, 170 men. General Sherman returned to Vicksburg, February 27th, having marched 400 miles in 24 days, including stoppages.

February 4.—The rebel General Early was driven from Moorfield, West Virginia, after six hours' hard fighting, by Federal troops under Colonel Mulligan, who afterwards engaged Rosser on the South Fork.

—— The blockade runner Nutfield was destroyed by United States gunboat Sassacus, off Wilmington, North Carolina.

February 5.—The blockade runner Dee was destroyed by the United States gunboat Cambridge, off Wilmington, North Carolina.

—— The 16th army corps, General Hurlbut, and 17th corps, General McPherson, under orders of Major-General Sherman, entered Jackson, Mississippi, the enemy offering but little resistance. This was one of the initial movements in the grand south-western campaign.

—— Fight at Salatia, Yazoo River, between 3000 rebels on shore and gunboats of Foster's and Sherman's expeditions. The rebels made the attack with artillery, but were driven off. Their loss not known. Ours was 5 killed and 30 wounded.

—— An attack was made by Ross and Richardson, rebel leaders, on Yazoo City, defended by negro troops. The latter were driven out of a portion of the town, but, reinforced by the gunboats the rebels were repulsed.

February 5.—The English blockade running steamer Cumberland was captured off Mobile by the United States gunboat De Soto.

——— General Sherman's army, on the advance towards Georgia, entered Jackson, Mississippi, after some skirmishing, in which the rebels were worsted.

February 6.—An attempt was made to surprise Richmond by a force sent up the peninsula with great celerity by General Butler, the idea being to make a dash and release the Federal prisoners at Belle Isle. This project was revealed to the rebels by a deserter, and they prepared for it by felling trees, obstructing the roads, &c. The force under General Wistar penetrated to Bottom's Bridge, 12 miles from Richmond, and drove in the pickets, but, finding that their coming was anticipated, withdrew. Great excitement was occasioned in Richmond, which was at the time defended by few troops.

——— English blockade running steamer Pet was captured by United States gunboat Montgomery, off Wilmington, North Carolina.

——— English blockade running steamer Spunkie ran ashore below Wilmington, North Carolina, and went to pieces.

——— The 1st, 2d, and 3d corps of the United States army crossed the Rapidan, and advanced in the direction of the enemy. The 2d corps (Warren's), under command of General Caldwell, became engaged with the rebels, and there was skirmishing all day. The Federal troops retired at night. Loss, 200 killed and wounded. The movement was a reconnoissance in force, and it developed strong fortifications in front and that the rebels were also in force.

February 7.—An expedition sent from Knoxville to Quallatown, North Carolina, against a band of whites and Indians there, commanded by Thomas, returned completely successful, having killed and wounded 215, took 50 prisoners, and dispersed the remainder of the gang. Federal loss, 2 killed and 6 wounded.

——— A portion of General Gilmore's troops, under command of Brigadier-General Truman Seymour, landed at Jacksonville, Florida. The advance then pushed on, passing Vinegar Hill, and capturing at Camp Finegan a rebel battery. 8 guns and 100 prisoners were captured, and the rebels also burned a steamboat.

February 10.—The United States gunboat Conestoga was sunk on the Mississippi, below Natchez, from the effect of a collision with the General Price.

——— Federal officers escaped from the Libby Prison, Richmond, Virginia. Among them were Colonels A. D. Streight, J. F. Boyd, W. G. Ely, P. Kendrick, W. B. McCreary, Thomas E. Rose, J. R. Spofford, C. W. Felden, F. S. West. D. Miles, and also 7 majors, 32 captains, and 59 lieutenants, making in all 109. Colonels Spofford, Miles, and 46 others of those who escaped were recaptured by the rebels and returned to prison. The escape was accomplished by tunnelling under the walls of the prison, after a labor of fifty-one days.

——— The British blockade running steamers Emily and the Fannie and Jennie (the latter formerly the Scotia, once captured, condemned, sold, and put again in the trade), were destroyed by the United States gunboat Florida.

February 11.—A passenger train on the Baltimore and Ohio Railroad, going west, was stopped at Kearneysville, Virginia, by obstructions on the track. The cars were then entered by guerillas, who robbed the passengers of watches, money, and other valuables, worth in the aggregate a large amount, after securing which they made off.

——— A cavalry expedition under Generals W. Long, Smith, and Grierson, left Memphis.

——— Preparations by the rebels to attack the United States gunboats Nipsic and Housatonic, with a cigar-shaped torpedo-boat, were suspended in consequence of the sudden sinking of the infernal machine, with some of her crew on board.

February 14.—Gainesville, Florida, taken by United States troops under Captain Marshall, with 49 men, which he held for fifty-six hours, despite all efforts to take it by a force double his own number. Rebel stores worth $1,500,000 were captured and distributed among the people of the town.

February 15.—Judge Stewart, of the Provincial Court of Admiralty, Nova Scotia, gave judgment that the capture of the Chesapeake was an act of piracy, and ordered restitution of the vessel and cargo to the original owners.

——— The case of Vallandigham, who had petitioned the United States Supreme Court at Washington for a writ of certiorari and revision of the proceedings of the military court which sentenced him to transportation across the lines, was decided by Judge Wayne, who refused the writ, upon the ground that there was no authority in the Court to grant relief in that mode, and that there is no appeal or proceeding to the nature of an appeal, from a military commission to the Supreme Court.

February 17.—An expedition from the United States steamer Tahoma destroyed extensive salt works near St. Marks, Florida, occupying some 7 miles in extent. The work continued 3 days and 2 nights. Among the property were 390 salt kettles of the average capacity of 100 gallons each, 52 boilers, with furnaces, pumps, well apparatus, storehouses, &c., the whole worth $2,000,000.

——— An expedition from the United States bark Restless destroyed the rebel government salt works, on West Bay, Florida, with 26 boilers, 19 kettles, salt, &c., the whole costing to the rebels about $200,000.

February 18.—An expedition from the United States bark Restless destroyed sixteen rebel salt-work establishments at East Bay, Florida, with 5 boilers and 28 kettles, salt vats, tanks, and apparatus.

——— Major-General Sherman arrived at Quitman, Mississippi, on the Ohio and Mobile Railroad, having torn up railroad tracks and burned bridges as he went on. It was supposed by the rebels that he intended to attack Mobile.

——— By proclamation of the President of the United States, the port of Brownsville, Texas, is opened to commerce, with the exception of contraband of war.

——— The United States wooden corvette Housatonic, Captain C. W. Pickering, was destroyed in the harbor of Charleston, South Carolina, by a torpedo brought out by the rebel torpedo-boat Davis; the same which had unsuccessfully attacked the new Ironsides some months previously. The Housatonic sunk, losing 2 officers and 3 men; the rest of the crew were rescued. The torpedo-boat "Davis," and all on board, were destroyed by the same explosion.

February 19.—General A. J. Smith's expedition reached Egypt Station on the Mobile and Ohio Railroad, where they captured and destroyed a vast quantity of corn and provisions.

——— Another column of Smith's expedition, under Grierson, advanced to Aberdeen, Mississippi, and after some skirmishing destroyed 100,000 bushels of corn and some cotton.

February 20.—The rebel General Longstreet commenced his retreat from Strawberry Plains, Tennessee, toward Bull's Gap, destroying the bridge after crossing French Broad River.

——— Battle of Olustee, or Ocean Pond, Florida. General T. Seymour, advancing with about 5000 men, came upon the rebels, in force over 10,000 strong, posted in the woods under General T. Finnegan, who engaged the Federal troops at once. The latter were defeated and compelled to retreat to Jackson, 53 miles distant, which movement was forthwith undertaken. The United States lost 5 guns, nearly 600 stand of small arms, all the horses of its batteries, and about 1200 killed and wounded, most of whom were left on the field. During the retreat a large number of military stores were destroyed. Rebel loss, 935 killed and wounded (official). Killed, Colonel Fribley, 8th United States colored troops, Lieutenant-Colonel Reed, 1st North Carolina colored troops; wounded, Major Loran Burrit, Colonel Sammons, 115th New York, Colonel Henry Moore, 47th New York.

February 21.—Battle at West Point, Mississippi, between General A. J. Smith's expeditionary force and rebels under Forrest, Lee, Chalmers, and Roddy. The rebels tried to cut the column in two, without success. There were heavy movements on each flank. Smith lost 3 guns and 40 killed and wounded. Smith fell back slowly, ambushing the rebels wherever practicable.

February 22.—General A. J. Smith resumed his retreat followed by the rebels, and fighting heavily all day, with ambushing on our side, and occasional charges by the rebels. The rebel design was to prevent Smith from crossing the Tallahatchie, but he forced marches he got across safely. In one of these skirmishes at Joy's Farm, the rebel Colonel William Forrest was killed.

—— The National Executive Committee of the National Union Party, appointed by the Chicago Convention in 1860, met at Washington, and resolved that the National Convention should meet at Baltimore, June 7th, to make nominations for President and Vice-President of the United States.

—— 11th Tennessee cavalry were surrounded five miles east of Cumberland Gap, by a large rebel force of cavalry and infantry. Two officers and about 60 men cut their way through and escaped. The rest were killed, wounded, and taken prisoners.

February 23.—General Palmer, skirmishing with the enemy, drove him to Tunnel Hill, Georgia, capturing about 300 prisoners. Federal loss, 75 killed and wounded.

—— Fort Powell, below Mobile, was bombarded by the United States fleet under Admiral Farragut.

February 24.—A police magistrate at St. Johns, New Brunswick, ordered the Chesapeake pirates to be committed to be surrendered to the United States, upon charges of robbery, piracy, and murder.

February 25.—General A. J. Smith's expedition arrived at Memphis, having destroyed many miles of the track of the Memphis and Ohio Railroad, burned bridges and trestle work, destroyed over a million bushels of corn, captured and brought in 1500 mules, 2000 negroes, and 300 prisoners. On the way back the enemy harassed his flanks, and made frequent attacks. The expedition had been intended to join that of General Sherman, but failed to do so, in consequence of the dilatory motions of a portion of the troops in obeying orders, which occasioned the loss of a week's time. The total loss of the expedition was about 150 men. Rebel loss supposed to be 800.

February 26.—The United States army under General Thomas advanced towards Dalton, making a reconnoissance in force. They found the rebels strongly posted, and the latter made fierce attacks upon some parts of the line. In these skirmishes 42 were killed and 200 wounded on the Federal side. 500 rebel prisoners were taken. This movement was a diversion intended to assist the grand movement of General Sherman in Georgia. It had the effect to bring Cleburne's rebel division back to Dalton, and prevent him from reinforcing Polk.

—— Moseby, the rebel guerilla, made an attack upon Federal cavalry at Upperville, Virginia, and accomplished a slight success.

—— Lieutenant-Colonel Maxwell and command went to Bertie, North Carolina, and destroyed 200,000 pounds of pork, tobacco, &c. Horses, mules, and wagons were brought away.

—— An expedition from United States ship Tahoma destroyed rebel salt works on Goose Creek, Florida, 165 kettles, 53 boilers, &c., with numerous other articles.

February 28.—Moseby, the guerilla, attacked 180 Union soldiers at Drainesville, Virginia, and routed them, killing 15, wounding several, and taking 70 prisoners. His own loss, 1 killed and 4 wounded.

—— General Custer, of the United States cavalry, left the headquarters of the army for a raiding expedition, which was continued until he reached Stannardsville. He was opposed by the rebels at Charlottesville, where he charged and drove Stuart's rebel cavalry, captured and destroyed a camp, and destroyed six caissons. At Ravenna he burned the bridge, flouring-mills, &c., and returned safely, having ridden over a hundred miles in forty-eight hours, bringing in 50 prisoners, a large number of negroes, and 300 horses, not having lost a single man, 5 being wounded.

February 28.—Michael Hahn was elected Governor of Louisiana upon the free state ticket.

—— General Kilpatrick, with 5200 Federal cavalry, left Culpeper, Virginia, for the purpose, if possible, of surprising the city of Richmond, Virginia, and releasing the Union prisoners there. After the troops were at some distance on their way they were divided into two columns, the command of one of which was given to Colonel Ulric Dahlgren, which was to proceed east and then south towards Richmond. All the bridges and roads in the course of Kilpatrick were destroyed. On the 1st of March the expedition came within sight of Richmond. Kilpatrick took the rebel outworks and the second line, and the troops approached within two miles of the city. The inner line was found to be well defended, and after an attack was made upon them, Kilpatrick was compelled to retire. Dahlgren did not fare any better. His men were misled by a guide, whose treachery being discovered, he was hung without ceremony. The mistake, however, prevented the success of the movements which had been concerted with Kilpatrick. A retreat was necessary, and this being begun, the rebels followed, harassing and attacking the troops wherever it was possible. A force having been sent out by General Butler to co-operate with Kilpatrick, advanced until the column under Kilpatrick joined them. Colonel Dahlgren was not so fortunate. Retiring by way of King's and Queen's county, he was ambushed (March 4th) by a force of Virginia cavalry. Dahlgren was shot dead while riding at the head of his men, by a volley from the unseen foe. Some of his men were taken prisoners. The rebels pretend that they found on Colonel Dahlgren's body a paper, in which the purpose of the expedition was said to be the capture of Richmond, the release of the Federal prisoners, and that then they would kill Jeff Davis and his cabinet, and burn the city. Dahlgren's body was stripped and horribly mutilated, and buried secretly, so that all attempts to recover it would be in vain.

March 1.—General Ulysses S. Grant was nominated to the United States Senate by the President for the office of Lieutenant-General, and confirmed the next day.

March 2.—General Kilpatrick, with a large force of Federal cavalry, arrived safely within the Union lines upon the peninsula, near Yorktown, Virginia.

March 4.—The English blockade running steamer Don was captured off Wilmington, North Carolina, by the United States steamer Pequot.

—— The United States gunboat Bombshell, from Plymouth, going down the Chowan River, North Carolina, was fired upon from batteries on the bank. The gunboats Southfield, Whitehead, and Massasoit came to her assistance, and shelled out the rebels.

March 6.—English blockade running steamer Mary Ann captured off Wilmington, North Carolina, by the United States steamer Grand Gulf.

—— The United States steamer Peterhoff was sunk off Wilmington, North Carolina, by collision with the United States steamer Monticello.

March 7.—The United States steam-tug Titan, captured by the rebels at Cherry Stone, Virginia was destroyed in the Piankatank River.

March 9.—Suffolk, Virginia, captured by colored troops under Colonel Cole. Rebel loss, 65 killed. Union loss, 20 killed, wounded, and missing.

—— 47 officers and 660 exchanged prisoners arrived at Annapolis, having been sent from Richmond on the previous day.

March 10.—Justice Acbel, of St. Johns, New Brunswick, delivered an opinion in the habeas corpus cases of the Chesapeake pirates, refusing a warrant of extradition to the United States, upon points of technical law, and because, the offence being against the law of nations, the prisoners could be tried as well in New Brunswick as in the United States. N.B.—They never were tried in New Brunswick nor at any other place.

—— Pilatka, Florida, was taken possession of b Union troops.

March 11.—Major-General Banks issued an order for an election for delegates to a constitutional convention of the state of Louisiana, to be held March 28th; the convention to meet in New Orleans, April 6th.

March 12.—By official order of the President of the United States, Lieutenant-General U. S. Grant is assigned to the command of the armies of the United States; Major-General W. T. Sherman to the command of the military division of the Mississippi, composed of the departments of the Ohio, the Cumberland, the Tennessee, and the Arkansas; Major-General McPherson is assigned to the department and the command of the Army of the Tennessee; Major-General Halleck is relieved from duty as General-in-chief, and is assigned to duty in Washington as chief of the staff of the army.

March 14.—Rebels at Henderson's Hill, Louisiana, were surprised and routed by an expedition under General Mower, 282 prisoners taken, 4 guns with caissons, and horses.

———— Skirmishing at Cheek's Cross Roads, Tennessee, between Colonel Garrard's Federal cavalry and Colonel Giltner's rebel troops. The rebels were repulsed.

———— A call made by the President for 200,000 men, in addition to the call for 500,000, February 1. The draft to take place April 15th, or as soon thereafter as possible. Bounties to be paid until April 15th.

March 15.—Captains Sawyer and Flynn, who had been long held at Libby Prison, under sentence of death, in retaliation for the execution of two rebel spies, hung in Kentucky by General Burnside, were released and arrived at Fortress Monroe. They were exchanged for General W. F. Lee and Captain Winder, who were held by the United States as personal hostages for their safety.

———— Fort De Russy, with 10 guns, on the Red River, Louisiana, below Alexandria, was captured by the United States forces under General A. J. Smith, defeating the rebel General Dick Taylor, who attempted to intercept the Federal forces. The United States fleet, under Admiral Porter, co-operated with the land forces. 325 prisoners were taken by the United States troops. Federal loss, 46 killed and wounded.

March 17.— The bill to authorize the Secretary of the Treasury to anticipate interest becoming due on the national loans and payable in gold, or to sell surplus gold at his discretion, passed finally. Gold on that day was selling at $160.50 and $161 in paper per $100 in gold.

March 18.—Steamer Sumter captured on Lake George, Florida, by United States steamer Columbine. The Sumter was then sent to Lake Harney, where another steamer, the "Hattie Brock," was captured. Both boats were brought off safely.

March 21.—Natchitoches, Louisiana, captured by Federal troops under General Mower, with 200 prisoners and 4 cannon.

———— The steamer Chesapeake, surrendered by the authorities of New Brunswick, arrived at Portland.

———— The rebel steamer Clifton, formerly the United States gunboat of that name, attempting to run the blockade at Sabine Pass, got ashore, and was destroyed by the rebels, who burnt her, and a full cargo of cotton.

March 23.—By order of Lieutenant-General Grant, the corps of the Army of the Potomac are reduced to three: viz., the 2d, 5th, and 6th corps. The 1st and 3d are temporarily reorganized and distributed among the 2d, 5th, and 6th. Major-General G. K. Warren is assigned to the command of the 5th corps, General W. S. Hancock continues to command the 2d corps, and Major-General Sedgwick the 6th.

March 24.—1000 rebels under Forrest having crossed the Obion River, advanced to Union City, Kentucky. Colonel Hawkins, who held the place with 400 men, surrendered the post. The rebels burned the buildings and marched off with their prisoners. Hawkins's surrender was considered a disgraceful act.

March 25.—Forrest, the rebel commander, attacked Paducah, Kentucky, with burned a part of the town, was held by Colonel Hicks were made upon the fort, United States gunboats on the enemy, and fired 600 ro driven out. Federal loss, Rebel loss, 300 killed and le among whom was General buildings in the town were

March 26.—The main bo lin's troops arrived at Alex a junction with Major-Ge which had reached that to rebels retreated to Shrevepo

———— President Lincoln plaining that the amnesty to civil, military, or naval only to those persons who arrest, or confinement, and v and take the oath; also tha civil or military officer of th

March 28.—A riot at C certain citizens professing " States soldiers. The latter many of whom during the from the surrounding cour affray commenced by a citiz arms were then used on bc reinforced by their comrad strong. There were killed wounded, 6 soldiers, 4 citi were taken prisoners.

———— Admiral Farrag Powell and threatened Mo of General Sherman's oper drew the greater part of movement having been effec

———— Battle at Cane General A. J. Smith's Fede Generals Mower and Dudl forces, 12,000 in number.

March 29.—A rebel sign tured near Chuckatuck Cre the United States gunboat (

March 30.—A fight at Mc Federal troops under Colon eral Dickens, rebels. The of over 100 killed and wou &c. Federal loss, 15 killed, expedition had previously and captured 35 wagons an

———— Colonel Robert (exchange, arrived at Fortre consultation with Major-Ge of exchange of prisoners.

March 31.—The army of undertook the siege of Kn tered in the mountains of T toward Virginia, and evacu

April 1.— The United Sta destroyed in the St. Johns Four persons were drowne passengers, mostly soldiers,

April 6.—An election wa mine whether a State Con the purpose of proposing an of the state. The question jority.

———— Rossville, Missour under General Gans, who The rebels were afterwards

———— By order of the Pr dan is assigned to the com the Army of the Potomac. the consolidated 11th and the 1st. Major-General H corps. Major-General Sch

———— The British Hous

of the Alexandra, affirming the decision of the court below, which, although upon a technical ground, was substantially against the United States.

April 7.—Union cavalry of Banks's expedition, advancing in Louisiana, skirmishing with the rebels and driving them forward, were checked two miles beyond Pleasant Hill by Greene's rebel cavalry. The Federal troops charged and drove them off the field, with a loss of 40 killed and wounded upon the Union side.

April 8.—Battle of Sabine's Cross Roads, or Mansfield, Louisiana. One brigade of Union troops, under Colonel Gandrum, advancing with cavalry, were confronted by the rebel army under Generals Kirby Smith, Dick Taylor, Mouton, Green, and Price, with from 18,000 to 22,000 men. The rebels came up in great force, charging desperately; the Union troops now being well up under Generals Banks, Ransom, Stone, and Lee and Franklin's divisions were sent for, but before they came the Federal losses had been heavy, the whole force being driven back three miles. 16 guns were taken by the rebels, and the killed and wounded were many. On the Federal side were killed, Colonel Webb, 77th Illinois. Wounded, General Ransom, Colonel Vance, 96th Ohio, left on field. On the rebel side, killed, General Mouton.

April 9.—Battle of Pleasant Hill, Louisiana. At the close of the battle of Mansfield, on the previous day, a council of war was held by General Banks, and it was determined to withdraw the Federal army to Pleasant Hill, as a better place to give battle than that which the troops occupied at the close of the previous day, and also with the intention of joining General A. J. Smith's division at that place. The withdrawal commenced at 10 o'clock at night. The rebels did not discover it until morning. They followed promptly, and there was some skirmishing, but they did not attack until 5 o'clock in the afternoon, when they advanced in three lines of battle. Emory's division was so hardly pressed that it fell back, the fighting being very close and hand to hand. The rebels took a battery at this time, which was afterwards recaptured. Emory fell back towards A. J. Smith's 16th corps, which was in reserve, posted behind the crest of a hill, and concealed from the enemy by the rise of the ground. When the rebels were near enough, the whole of Smith's corps gave them a hot volley of grape, canister, and musketry, and charged. The rebels gave way at once; took to flight, and were dispersed. They were followed until dark. The Federal troops recovered the battery taken from Emory, and retook 2 guns lost on the previous day, and another gun, and they took 500 prisoners, 3 battle-flags, and a large number of small arms. On the Federal side were killed, Colonels Benedict, 162d New York; Mix, New York; Lieutenant-Colonels Newman; Lindsey, 48th Ohio. Wounded, Colonels Orne, 165th New York; Robinson, 1st Louisiana cavalry; Lieutenant-Colonels Green; Carr, 165th New York; Majors Mann, 19th Kentucky; Whiteman. On the rebel side, killed, Major Muller. This battle and that of the preceding day put an end to the Louisiana campaign of General Banks, who, from the time he left New Orleans, is estimated to have lost 20 guns, 3000 men, a large quantity of small arms, 130 baggage-wagons, and 1200 horses and mules. He fell back immediately after this battle to Grand Ecore, 55 miles from Mansfield and 35 miles from Pleasant Hill. The rebel loss has been estimated as low as 1000 and as high as 10,000 killed, wounded, and missing.

—— An attempt was made to blow up the United States steam frigate Minnesota, upon the James River, by a torpedo fixed under her side. The missile exploded, jarring the vessel violently, but failing in the object of destroying or even seriously injuring the ship. The torpedo was brought down by a torpedo-boat, which escaped in the darkness.

—— Speaker Colfax, of the United States House of Representatives, offered a resolution for the expulsion of Alexander Long, a representative from Ohio, "for declaring that he was in favor of recognising the independent nationality of the so-called Confederacy, now in arms against the Union." In the course of the debate, Benjamin G. Harris, of Maryland, said that "he endorsed every word that the gentleman from Ohio (Mr. Long) had uttered, and would stand by him for weal or woe." He also said, "The South asked you to let them live in peace, but no, you said you would bring them into subjection. That is not done yet, and God Almighty grant that it never may be. I hope that you will never subjugate the South." In consequence of this language, a motion was made to expel Mr. Harris from his seat, which received 81 yeas and 51 nays; but two-thirds being required to expel a member, the motion failed. A resolution to censure Mr. Harris was then introduced and carried, 92 yeas to 18 nays. The vote on the resolutions to expel Mr. Long was reached April 14. They were laid on the table, but resolutions of censure were passed. Yeas 80, nays 70.

April 12.—The rebel Forrest with 6000 men attacked Fort Pillow, below Paducah, Kentucky, previously demanding its surrender, which was refused by Major Booth, commanding United States colored troops. Three flags were sent in by the rebels, and at each time they took advantage of the delay to move up nearer to the fort; when, being sufficiently near, they made a great rush, swarmed over the parapets, and carried the works. The United States troops then surrendered, when an indiscriminate butchery of the unarmed white and black troops took place. Those who begged for quarter were shot down or bayoneted; those who were wounded were stabbed and shot again. Even dead bodies were horribly mutilated. Men, women, and children were also killed and wounded. The whole affair was one of the most ferocious massacres known in American history. Of 600 soldiers in the fort at the time of the surrender, only 200 escaped with their lives. After they had satiated their thirst for blood, the rebels took away the guns and abandoned the fort.

—— Paintsville, Kentucky, defended by Colonel Gillespie's United States soldiers, was attacked by Hedge's rebel brigade. The latter were repulsed and followed, and on the 14th their camp at Half Mountain was taken, with the loss to them of 200 horses' equipments, 300 small arms and a wagon train, and 85 killed and wounded. Federal loss, 1 killed and 4 wounded.

—— English blockade running steamer Alliance captured near Dawfuskie Island, Savannah River, with a valuable cargo for the use of the rebel government.

April 13.—Colonel Gallup, commanding United States troops at Painesville, Kentucky, was attacked by a large force of rebels under General William E. Jones. The rebels were repulsed.

April 14.—The Federal transports Clara Bell and Rob Roy, proceeding up the Red River, Louisiana, were fired upon by mounted infantry upon shore. The 19th corps being on hand, attacked and dispersed them, and captured 2 guns. The rebels left 164 dead on the field. The rebel General Green was killed.

April 16.—The United States steamer General Hunter was blown up by a torpedo, on St. Johns River, Florida, in the same place where the Maple Leaf was blown up a few days before. One person was killed, and the cargo of quartermaster's stores, a valuable one, was destroyed.

—— The bill to punish frauds in the sale of gold was passed by the United States Senate. The highest price of gold on that day was 175.

April 17.—Battle at Prairie D'Ana, Arkansas, between General Steele with Federal troops and Stirling Price's rebel force. The latter, although protected by strong works, were enfiladed, and they abandoned the position. The rebels were pursued towards Washington, Price supposing that Steele was marching for Shreveport, but Steele suddenly turned and marched for Camden.

—— Fort Gray, near Plymouth, North Carolina, held by United States troops, was attacked by a force of 10,000 men under General Pickett, having a battery with 6 field guns. The fort and town were assisted by Federal gunboats. The enemy attempted to assault the fort, but was repulsed.

April 18.—The rebel iron-clad ram Albemarle attacked 3 vessels of the United States, lying near Plymouth, North Carolina. The Southfield was sunk. Lieutenant Commander Flusser, of the Miami, was killed by the recoil of a shell, which he had fired against the iron sides of the ram, and which rebounded. The United States gunboat Bombshell sunk at the wharf at Fort Gray. The Albemarle soon retired.

—— A rebel torpedo-boat was sunk by a round shot fired from the United States frigate Wabash, in Charleston harbor, against which ship an attempt was intended to be made.

April 19.—Camden, Arkansas, entered by General Steele and nine forts captured. There was a race for this place between Steele's troops and those under Price, Marmaduke, and Dockery, and fighting along the whole route.

April 20.—Plymouth, North Carolina, was captured by the rebels under General R. F. Hoke, with the commander, General Wessels, 1600 men, 25 guns, stores, &c. The rebels were aided by the ram Albemarle and the armed steamer Cotton Plant. Several assaults by the rebels were repulsed by General Wessels, but the rebels being 15,000 strong, and there being no hope of reinforcement, a surrender was necessary. The Federal loss was 100 killed and wounded. The rebel loss was very heavy, as they stormed the forts and batteries from three to seven times, and were repulsed with slaughter: their killed and wounded were estimated at 1700.

—— Madison Court House, Virginia, was burned by a Federal reconnoitering party, who were fired upon from the houses in that town.

April 23.—An attack was made upon the Union pickets at Nickajack Trace. The latter were overpowered, losing 9 killed, 3 wounded, and 19 prisoners. Several of the latter were afterwards murdered by the rebels.

—— The United States gunboat Petrel was boarded by Wirt Adams's rebel cavalry, 2 miles above Yazoo City, and burned. A portion of the crew were taken prisoners. The latter defended the boat until a ball pierced the boiler.

April 25.—A train of 240 wagons, with an escort of United States troops and 4 guns, were captured by rebels near Pine Bluff, Arkansas.

April 26.—General Steele abandoned Camden, Arkansas, and retreated to Little Rock, Arkansas, harassed by the rebels on the march.

April 29.—General Crooks with 22,000 Federal troops left Charleston, West-Virginia, for some point unknown, supposed to be Lynchburg.

—— Cavalry skirmish at Tiger Creek, Georgia. The rebels were dispersed by Kilpatrick's horsemen.

April 30.—The steamer Harriet Lane and 3 blockade running steamers made their escape from Galveston, Texas.

—— Little Washington, North Carolina, was evacuated by the Federal troops, guns being spiked, and property destroyed.

May 2.—The cavalry of the rebel Forrest were defeated by the cavalry of General Sturgis, near Bolivar, Tennessee. They retreated, burning the bridge over the Hatchie River.

May 3.—An expedition sent out by General Butler passed up the peninsula of Virginia, as far as New Kent Court House and Bottom's Bridge, the intention being to lead the rebels to believe that the troops of Major-General Butler would attempt to march towards Richmond by that route.

—— Same day, transports on the James River began to take troops on board at Yorktown, on the York River, which operation took two days.

May 4.—A raid was made from Portsmouth, Virginia, by Union cavalry under Colonel S. P. Spear, 11th Pennsylvania cavalry. In the course of their expedition they captured a rebel camp near Jarrat's Station, on the Weldon and Petersburg Railroad, killed and wounded 281, and took 164 prisoners. Those who had escaped were reinforced and attacked Spear, but were repulsed after a hard fight, in which they suffered heavily. Depots and storehouses at Jarrat's Station were set on fire and totally destroyed; value $500,000. Nottoway bridge was also burned on the same day.

—— The Army of the Potomac, under the command of Generals Meade and Grant, crossed the Rapidan in a movement against Richmond. The crossing was at Jacobs', Culpeper, Germania, and United States Fords, and was effected without any serious opposition. Sheridan's cavalry in the advance drove Stuart's rebel cavalry on the road to Orange Court House, with heavy fighting.

May 5.—General Kautz with 3000 United States cavalry, co-operating with General Butler, left Suffolk, Virginia, and destroyed the bridge at Stony Creek, on the Weldon Railroad.

—— The United States transports City Belle, Emma, and Warner, in passing a battery 12 miles below Alexandria, on the Red River, Louisiana, were destroyed, and also the gunboats Signal and Covington.

—— An engagement took place on Albemarle Sound, at the mouth of Roanoke River, North Carolina, between the rebel ram Albemarle and the United States gunboat Sassacus. The latter, a wooden vessel, tried to run the Albemarle down, and there was considerable firing between them. The steamer Bombshell, sunk at Plymouth but raised again by the rebels and put in commission, was captured by the Sassacus. The latter received a shot through her boiler, killing and scalding 16 men. The Albemarle was injured in the fight, and with her tender, the Cotton Plant, withdrew. Other United States gunboats had come into action, and the losses on the Federal side were 36 killed and wounded.

—— Major-General Butler, after having loaded his transports with troops at Yorktown, Virginia, apparently for an advance to West Point and White House, by York and Pamunkey Rivers, suddenly changed the destination of his forces, and went down the York and up the James River, landing at City Point this day, without opposition, the movement not being anticipated by the enemy. General Butler intrenched himself at Bermuda Hundred, and destroyed several miles of the Petersburg and Weldon Railroad. A large fleet of iron-clads and other vessels accompanied him, under command of Admiral Sam Phillips Lee.

—— Colonel West with 1800 men, partly colored troops, left Williamsburg, crossed the Chickahominy at Jones's Ford, and captured the camp of the 46th Virginia regiment, killing 30 rebels, capturing horses, &c. These troops pressed through to the James River, and joined General Butler's column.

—— Battle of the Wilderness, Virginia. The rebel General Lee prepared during the previous night to resist the advance of Grant and Meade. The Federal army continued its march; at noon General Wilson's cavalry became engaged at Shady Grove Church with a large body of rebel cavalry, who gradually forced him back upon the 2d corps, which latter was driven back and only saved by the gallantry of Colonel Carroll's brigade, which came to its support. The real intention of Lee was to cut the Federal centre, on discovering which General Warren was directed to attack him at once. After a fight of an hour and a half the rebels were driven off. Lee then tried to penetrate between the corps of Warren and Hancock, but was prevented by reinforcements from Birney, Gibbon, and Getty; this fight occupied several hours, and was hotly contested until after dark.

May 6.—The United States gunboat Commodore Jones was blown up by a torpedo and totally destroyed, in the James River, near Turkey Bend. The man who discharged the torpedo by apparatus on the shore was killed, and a map of all the torpedoes in the James River found upon him—a most fortunate and valuable discovery.

—— Second day of the battle of the Wilderness, Virginia. The fight commenced at daylight, and it was maintained under very unequal conditions upon various parts of the line. Hancock was most sorely pressed by the rebels, but drove them and was driven himself. The fighting was desperate, but Hancock was relieved by the reinforcement of Burnside's 9th corps. Later in the day on the right, Sedgwick was attacked stubbornly, and his brestworks taken. But they were subsequently retaken, and the rebels ejected. This was late in the afternoon, the battle having ceased on other parts of the line. By the impetus of the rebels the right wing was outflanked and broken. Generals Seymour and Shaler, and a large number of men were taken prisoners. At 11 o'clock at night a very heavy assault was made upon Warren's corps, the 5th. His lines were broken through, and his men driven from their breastworks. The rebels held what they took, but the 6th corps fell back to a line parallel with that where the 5th rested. The estimate of the operations for the three days, since the crossing of the Rapidan was, that the Federals had lost about 12,000 killed, wounded, and prisoners, and had taken about 3500 prisoners. The battles of the Wilderness were fought in a thickly wooded country, which concealed the movements of the enemy, and prevented the use of artillery. The musket, sabre and the bayonet, were the only weapons that could be used. Killed in these battles, Brigadier-General Alexander Hayes; Brigadier-General Wadsworth; Colonel Carrol, 95th Pennsylvania; Colonel Woodward, 83d Pennsylvania; Colonel Stone, 2d Vermont; Colonel Barney, 6th Vermont: Chapman, 1st division, 2d corps; Staples, Bolanger, 7th Pennsylvania Reserves; Colonels Patterson, 102d Pennsylvania; Hays, 18th Massachusetts; Hudson. Wounded, General Getty, General Webb, Generals Bartlett, Baxter, Gregg; Colonel Gwinn, 118th Pennsylvania; Lombard, 4th Michigan; Guiney, 9th Massachusetts; Foster, 4th Vermont; Colonels Lewis, 5th Vermont; Carrol; Von Sickel, 4th New Jersey; Baxter, 72d Pennsylvania; Banks, 63d Pennsylvania; Colonels Sides, 57th Pennsylvania; Shurtliff, 10th Massachusetts; Ayres, 10th Pennsylvania Reserves; McCandless, 2d Pennsylvania Reserves; Locke, 5th corps; Lieutenant-Colonel Davies, 12th United States; Cartwright, Irish brigade; Kochersperger, 71st Pennsylvania; Major Koet, 14th Connecticut.

May 6.—The rebel ram North Carolina came out of Wilmington, North Carolina, during the night, and made an attack upon the United States gunboat Nansemond, which failed; several other United States vessels took part in the action, and the North Carolina withdrew after daylight.

———— Generals Heckman and Brooks, commanding a portion of the troops under General Butler, had a skirmish with rebel troops on the line of the Richmond and Petersburg Railroad. Beauregard was said to be in command of the rebels who had been brought up from South Carolina. By these movements the Federal troops succeeded in tearing up about a mile of the railroad.

———— Major-General Sherman was ready to commence effective movements in the grand campaign in Alabama and Georgia. His force being as follows: Army of the Cumberland, Major-General Thomas commanding, stationed at or near Ringgold, Georgia, 60,773 officers and men, and 130 guns; Army of the Tennessee, Major-General McPherson commanding, stationed at Gordon's Mill, on the Chickamauga, 24,465 officers and men, and 96 guns; Army of the Ohio, Major-General Schofield commanding, stationed near Red Clay, on the Georgia line, near Dalton, 13,559 officers and men, and 28 guns: grand total, 98,797 men and 254 guns. 'This strength was kept up nearly at the same figure during the whole campaign, despite losses, by effective reinforcement. The rebel army on the 6th of May concentrated at Dalton, under General Joseph Johnston, was estimated at about 60,000 men.

May 7.—Skirmishing at Todd's Tavern, Virginia, between a portion of the Federal cavalry, and rebel cavalry under Fitzhugh Lee. The rebels were driven back by Torbert, Custer, Gregg, and Merrit, about 4 miles. In the afternoon the rebels being reinforced rallied, and made a furious attack upon the Union cavalry.

———— A skirmish at Tazewell salt works, Virginia, between Averill's Federal cavalry, and Sam Jones and Morgan's rebel troops. A slight loss on both sides.

———— The British blockade runner steamer Young Republic, was captured off Nassau, by the United States gunboat Grand Gulf.

———— General Grant commenced a flanking movement, withdrawing from the battle field of the Wilderness, and passing down the road towards Spottsylvania Court House. Lee, discovering the movement, commenced to fall back on roads parallel to those marched over by the army of the United States.

May 7.—General Thomas's wing occupied Tunnel Hill, Georgia, the remainder of the army moving by the flank.

May 8.—United States gunboat Shawsheen was sunk in the James River, by an artillery fire from the shore.

———— There was considerable skirmishing and fighting all day, between the Federal army advancing on Spottsylvania Court House, and the rebel army which was opposing that movement. Some ground was won by the Union troops, who approached within 2 miles of the Court House. Major-General Robinson was wounded in this engagement.

———— A portion of General Sherman's forces in front of Rocky Face Ridge threatening the rebel position.

May 9.—General McPherson's command passed through Snake Creek Gap, after a sharp fight, Sherman's army skirmishing.

———— The transport Harriet A. Weed was blown up by the explosion of a torpedo in St. Johns River, Florida. The boat was loaded with quartermasters' stores.

———— Battle of Cloyd Mountain, West Virginia, between General Crook's Federal troops and rebels under Jenkins and McCausland. The rebels were defeated and pressed through Dublin to New River Bridge, with a loss on their side of 900 killed, wounded, and prisoners, among whom was General Jenkins. Federal loss, about 500.

———— General Sheridan, in command of the Federal cavalry, cut the enemy's lines north of Richmond, Virginia, tore up eight or ten miles of railroad, captured two locomotive trains heavily loaded with supplies for Lee's army, and a depot of supplies at Beaver Dam, containing 1,500,000 rations, and recaptured 378 Federal prisoners.

———— Major-General John Sedgwick was killed by a sharpshooter, while riding near the front of the army, no battle being in progress. There was a sharp fight towards evening between rebel troops and Sedgwick's and Warren's corps, during which Hancock's corps were pushed across the River Po. The command of Sedgwick's corps was given to Major-General Wright.

May 10.—Battle at New River Bridge, West Virginia, principally between artillery of Crook's and John H. Morgan's forces. The firing was kept up until night, when the rebels withdrew.

———— Battle of Cove Mountain Gap, near Wytheville, Virginia, between Federal troops under General Averill and rebel troops under General Sam Jones. The rebels were fought for four hours, after which they retreated in the darkness. Federal loss, 129 killed and wounded, none missing.

———— General Sheridan's cavalry crossed the South Anna River.

———— First day of the battle of Spottsylvania Court House, Virginia. There was skirmishing all the morning. About noon the rebels made the attack in heavy force against Hancock and Warren, and were repulsed. About half past three o'clock the rebels, being massed for the purpose, made a terrific charge against the right centre. They were received by Birney's, Cutter's, Gibbon's, and Barlow's divisions, with a heavy fire, under which the assaulting force gave way and fell back. Hancock then advanced and fell upon Heth's division of Longstreet's corps, with heavy slaughter to the latter. Just before sunset Wright and Burnside attacked the rebels, and carried their rifle-pits. Killed on the Federal side, Generals Rice and Stevenson. Wounded, Generals Morris and Ward; Lieutenant-Colonel Pierson, 39th Massachusetts. Prisoner, General Crawford. Rebel wounded, Colonels Golliard, South Carolina; Kennedy; Herbert, Alabama; Houller; Jones, North Carolina; Sheffield; Whitehead, Georgia; Board, Virginia; Winston, North Carolina; Lane, North Carolina; Sanders, North Carolina; Fullum, Georgia; Miller, South Carolina.

———— The United States gunboat Brewster was blown up on the Appomattox River, Virginia, by a shot from a rebel battery on shore.

May 11.—General Sheridan's cavalry captured Ashland Station, Virginia, and destroyed a locomotive, cars, engine-house, &c., six miles of railroad, six culverts, and two bridges. Marching on he encountered the rebel Stuart's cavalry at Yellow Tavern. There was a fight there, in which the rebel Major-General J. E. B. Stuart was killed. The rebels lost two guns at that point, and many officers and men.

—————— Second day of the battle of Spottsylvania Court House. At an early hour in the morning, General Hancock attacked the enemy's lines, capturing 30 guns, and between 3000 and 4000 prisoners, including Major-General Edward Johnson and Brigadier-General Stewart.

—————— Lieutenant-General Grant writing to Secretary Stanton, says: "We have now ended the sixth day of very heavy fighting. The result is to this time very much in our favor. Our losses have been heavy, as well as those of the enemy. I think the loss of the enemy must be greater. We have taken over 5000 prisoners by battle, whilst he has taken from us but few except stragglers. *I propose to fight it out on this line if it takes all summer.*"

May 12.—Third day of the battle of Spottsylvania Court House. The fighting continued all day. Hancock's corps took two lines of the rebel breastworks, a large number of guns, reported to be 39 in number, with 30 stand of colors. During the night the rebels retreated, thus ending the contest at this point. Killed, Colonels D. C. Striker, 2d Delaware; J. C. Coons, 14th Indiana; Hewlings, 49th Pennsylvania; Lieutenant-Colonels Davis, 12th New Jersey; Miles, 49th Pennsylvania; Merriam, 16th Massachusetts; J. W. Greenwalt, 106th Pennsylvania; Major Truefitt, 119th Pennsylvania. Wounded, General Webb; Colonels Sawyer, 8th Ohio; Pearce, 3d Michigan; Smyth, 1st Delaware; Carroll; A. C. Craig, 105th Pennsylvania; Lieutenant-Colonels J. H. Lockwood, 7th Virginia; Rogers, 110th Pennsylvania; Majors Fletcher, 40th New York; Bradley, 64th New York; Lynch, 145th Pennsylvania; Totten, 5th Wisconsin; Winslow, 8th Ohio. Prisoners, Generals Seymour and Shaler. Rebels killed, Generals S. M. Jones, Jenkins, and L. A. Stafford; Colonels Nances, South Carolina; Grice; G. H. Forney; W. W. Randolph; Finney; Carter; Avery, North Carolina; Lamar, Florida; Hartsfield, Georgia; Holt, Georgia; Willis, Louisiana; Hodges, Georgia; Willett, Louisiana. Wounded, Lieutenant-General Longstreet, Colonels Peislier, Jenner, Pegram, and Benning.

—————— General Sheridan, finding the enemy's works near Richmond too strong for him, recrossed the Chickahominy at Meadow Bridge. There was a fight at that point.

May 13.—Fighting between the Federal army advancing in Virginia, and the rear guard of Lee's army. The latter falling back, there was no general engagement.

—————— The Union fleet of gunboats, transports, &c., in the Red River, which had been caught while assisting in the movements of General Banks in West Louisiana, by the falling of the water, were extricated from their perilous position, by damming up the river; an expedient in engineering suggested by Lieutenant-Colonel Bailey, acting engineer of the 19th army corps, and executed under his supervision.

—————— General Sherman's army deployed in Sugar Valley, before Resaca. General Kilpatrick was wounded while operating with his cavalry in the advance. Howard threatened Dalton on the left.

May 14.—General Sheridan's cavalry reached Turkey Bend, on the James River, and made a junction with the forces of Major-General Butler, having destroyed several bridges on the route.

—————— General Sherman's flank movement compelled the evacuation of Dalton.

—————— First day of the battle of Resaca. Skirmishing commenced at daylight, and the battle continued the whole day. Howard joined Sherman on the left. The rebels attempted to turn the Union left, but, by a movement of Hooker's corps to that portion of the line, their object was frustrated.

May 14.—General Burnham's brigade charged upon the rebel works in front of General Butler's position on the James River, and took them, line by line, and section by section. The rebels fell back under the earthworks at Fort Darling. Federal loss, 150 men. 180 prisoners were taken from the rebels.

May 15.—Second day of the battle of Resaca. General Hooker charged the rebel works on the left about 1 P. M., but was not able to hold them. A general advance was then made along the whole line, and the first series of intrenchments were occupied. The rebels evacuated Resaca during the night. General Sherman captured 8 guns and 1000 prisoners. Generals Hooker, Kilpatrick, Manson, and Willich were wounded. The Federals lost 2400 killed and wounded, and 1100 missing. Rebel loss estimated at 2000 killed and wounded, and 1600 prisoners and 12 guns.

—————— Battle of Newmarket, Virginia. General Sigel, commanding Union troops advancing up the valley to carry out the plans of General Grant, was defeated by Breckenridge, Echols, and Imboden. Sigel lost 600 killed and wounded, 50 prisoners, and 5 pieces of artillery. He was very much encumbered with baggage trains, which prevented him from bringing all his men into the fight. He retreated to Strasburg, without the loss of any of his wagons.

May 16.—Battle of Avoyelles Prairie, Louisiana. Rebels endeavoring to prevent the retirement of Banks from Western Louisiana, were defeated with considerable loss.

—————— Battle of Port Walthal, Virginia. The advance of General Butler's forces, which were making a heavy demonstration on Fort Darling, was attacked in heavy masses by Beauregard's rebel troops during a fog, surprised, and defeated. General Heckman, who commanded the force which was first attacked, was taken prisoner. The battle was continued until night, when the Federal troops abandoned the field. The Federal loss was 2500 killed and wounded, 4 guns, and 1000 prisoners. The rebel loss, about 2000 killed and wounded, and 600 prisoners. The rebel General Corse was killed in this battle, also Colonel Richard Maury.

May 17.—A night attack was made upon General Butler's lines by the rebels, who were warmly received.

May 18.—Battle of Yellow Bayou, Louisiana, between a portion of Banks troops, and rebels under General Prince Polignac. The rebels were driven off the field with a loss of 500 killed and wounded, and 300 prisoners. Union loss, 150 killed and wounded.

—————— General Kautz, commanding Federal cavalry, returned to City Point, Virginia, after a raid on the rebel lines of railroad upon the Petersburg and Richmond, Weldon and Danville Railroads, and Richmond and Lynchburg roads. Great destruction was done at Walthal Junction, and at various stations, and depots, and bridges. No less than 4 railroads were seriously damaged, and an immense quantity of property was destroyed. The expedition was out several days, and lost 6 killed, and 50 wounded and missing.

—————— A fraudulent paper, pretending to be a proclamation of the President of the United States for 400,000 men, was published in the New York World and Journal of Commerce, in consequence of which the offices of those papers were seized by General Dix, commanding at New York, and guards put over the establishments. It was afterwards discovered that the forgery was perpetrated by persons named Howard and —————— Mallison, in order to profit in gold speculations, by the effect of the proclamation on the market. They were arrested and sent to Fort Lafayette.

—————— A fierce attack was made upon the rebel lines at Spottsylvania Court House, by Wright's 6th, and a portion of Burnside's corps. The rebels were well prepared for the attempt, and they opened with heavy discharges of artillery and musketry on the advancing forces. The first line of rifle-pits was carried, but it was impossible to advance further, and the attempt was abandoned, and the troops withdrawn.

—————— General Sherman's advance forces occupied Kingston and Rome, Georgia. With the capture of

Rome General Sherman secured 7 fine iron works, a quantity of machinery, and a large supply of stores.

May 18.—General Howard's corps, of General Sherman's army, defeated the rebels at Adairsville, Georgia.

———— General Johnston's rebel forces retreated across the Etowah River.

———— General Edward McCook's cavalry captured the bridge across the Etowah River, Georgia, and held it against the rebel cavalry.

May 19.—General Sherman's advance skirmished with the enemy from a point 2 miles beyond Kingston to a point beyond Cassville, the rebels being on the retreat. The rebels made a sortie after dark from Cassville, but were handsomely repulsed. Before daylight Cassville was occupied.

———— The corps of Ewell attempted to turn the right wing of the Federal army, but were repulsed by Birney's and Tyler's divisions. 450 prisoners were taken from the enemy, and his loss was fully equal to the Union losses, which were 150 killed and 600 wounded and missing.

May 20.—An attack was made on General Butler's lines at Bermuda Hundred by a heavy rebel force. It was repulsed. The rebel General Walker was taken prisoner, being badly wounded. Union loss, 180 killed, wounded, and missing.

———— General Grant commenced a flank movement to compel Lee to abandon his position at Spottsylvania Court House. The rebels in consequence left those works and marched south, falling behind the North Anna River. The Federal army occupied successively Guiney Station, Milford Station, and the country on that line south of the Mattapony.

———— Major-General Hunter replaces General Sigel in the command of the army of West Virginia and the Shenandoah Valley.

May 21.—A skirmish at Milford Station, Virginia, between the 2d corps under Hancock, marching to the flank, and a portion of Pickett's rebel division. The latter were taken in rear and routed.

———— A very heavy night attack was made by the rebels, under Beauregard, upon the lines of General Butler at Bermuda Hundred. The assailants were hurled in masses against the works. The attack being anticipated was properly prepared for, and the advancing crowds were swept away by a terrible fire. Several charges were subsequently attempted and were defeated. Federal loss, 10 killed and 50 wounded. Rebel loss, about 1400 killed, wounded, and missing.

May 22.—The advance of General Grant's army arrived at the North Anna River. The rebels made some show of resisting the advance, but were driven out of their positions by the different corps of the Federal army, with a loss of about 550 killed and wounded; the rebel losses being probably in the same proportion.

———— General Johnston established his rebel lines along the Allatoona Mountains, Georgia, with part of General Sherman's forces in his front. His headquarters were at Marietta, several miles further south.

———— General Gustavus W. Smith's iron works at Etowah, Georgia, were burned by General Sherman's forces. The works had been used for casting shot, shell, and ordnance, for the rebel army.

May 23.—General Sherman's army commenced a flank movement to the right of Allatoona range.

———— The United States steam-tug Columbine was captured on the St. Johns River, Florida, being disabled by a rebel battery.

———— Battle of the North Anna, Virginia. The rebels resisted the advance of the Federal troops near the railroad bridge and county bridge. The head of the line of the latter was taken by Eakin and Pierce's brigades of Birney's division, one of which then waded the river, and with musket and bayonet put McLaw's division of Longstreet's corps to flight. Warren's corps was over the river before night. Federal losses, 365 killed and wounded. Rebel loss equally heavy, with many prisoners.

May 24.—The United States steamers Granite City and Wave were captured at Sabine Pass, Texas, by rebel forces operating with artillery from the shore.

May 24.—Fitzhugh Lee, with 2000 rebel cavalry, made an attack upon the position at Wilson's Wharf, or Fort Powhatan, on the James River, which was defended by General Wild and colored troops. The latter defeated the assailants, who lost 250 killed and wounded. Federal loss, 2 killed and 40 wounded.

———— A cavalry fight took place near Taylorsville, Georgia, without any apparent result.

———— General Wheeler's rebel cavalry made a dash upon and destroyed part of the trains of a wing of General Sherman's army.

May 25.—General Hooker's forces engaged the rebels at a bridge over the Pumpkinvine Creek and drove them from it. The remainder of the army moved into position.

———— United States steamer Boston destroyed on the Ashepoo River, Florida, by rebel batteries.

May 26.—Demonstrations, by General Grant's army, upon the rebel lines and intrenchments on the north side of the South Anna River, Virginia, making it certain that they were too strong to be taken, except at an immense loss of life. General Grant decided to flank them, and crossing his troops to the north side of the North Anna, marched them off towards Hanover Junction.

May 27.—The United States transport Lebanon was captured near Gaines's Landing, Arkansas, by boarding.

May 28.—The battle of Dallas. The engagement near Dallas, sometimes called the "battle of Pumpkinvine Creek," or the "battle of New Hope Church," was fought between the armies of General Sherman and those under General Johnston. After three separate attacks the rebel commander ordered his forces back to their intrenchments, the Union troops holding their ground.

———— Battle of Hawes's Shop, Virginia. Upon the line of General Grant's advance the troops were under command of General Sheridan. The rebels were driven about a mile. Union loss, 48 killed, 304 wounded, and 15 missing. 100 prisoners were taken from the rebels. 126 of their dead were left on the field, many were taken away, and their entire loss was estimated at 600.

May 29.—General McPherson's corps drove back the rebels with a loss of 2500 killed and left in our hands, and about 300 prisoners; McPherson's losses not being 300 in all.

———— A column of General Butler's troops at Bermuda Hundred, under command of General W. F. (Baldy) Smith, left that place and went in transports to White House on the Pamunkey River, at which place they landed May 31, and were put in communication with Generals Grant and Meade.

May 30.—Battle of Bethesda Church, Virginia. General Warren, on the left wing of Grant's army, was attacked by Ewell's corps. The latter was repulsed, after a sharp action. Warren was then within seven miles of Richmond. Upon the attack being made upon Warren, Wright and Hancock were ordered to attack the enemy, which they did after night. Colonels Tyroll and Willis, rebel officers, were killed. 60 dead rebels were buried on the field, their wounded were estimated at 300, and they lost 81 prisoners.

———— An attack made upon Butler's lines by the rebels was repulsed. Several unsuccessful charges were made by the enemy.

———— Dardanelles, Arkansas, taken by the rebel Marmaduke, with 200 prisoners.

———— An attack upon cavalry pickets on the road between Cold Harbor and Old Church Tavern, led to a considerable fight, and the repulse of the rebels. Union loss, 70 killed and wounded. Rebel loss, 100 killed and wounded.

May 31.—Battle of Cold Harbor, Virginia. General Sheridan, of Grant's army, attacked and routed Fitzhugh Lee's rebel cavalry and Clingman's infantry, which latter was brought up to its support.

———— Battle at Tolopotomy Creek, Virginia. Birney's division took a breastwork held by Breckenridge's corps in a strong position. Federal loss, 25 killed. 50 rebel prisoners were taken.

———— A convention of the Radical Democracy was held at Cleveland. Major-General John Charles Fremont was nominated for President, and General John Cochrane for Vice-President, of the United States.

June 1.—Second day of the battle of Cold Harbor, Virginia. The rebel lines were attacked by the 6th corps, under General Wright. The first line of works was carried, and also the first line in front of General W. F. Smith.

—————— Fight on the James River, between a rebel iron-clad vessel and United States Monitors. The former withdrew.

—————— General McPherson's wing of General Sherman's army advanced to the front of the rebel position at New Hope Church, Georgia.

—————— General Sturgis's command, consisting of infantry and cavalry, left Memphis on an expedition against Forrest's rebel forces.

June 2.—The United States steamer Water Witch was captured by boarding, near Ossabaw Sound, Georgia, after a hard fight, in which the rebel Lieutenant Pelot, leader of the boarders, was killed.

—————— An attack was made upon the left wing of General Butler's lines at Bermuda Hundred. The rebels were repulsed.

—————— Generals Hooker's and Schofield's corps, of General Sherman's army, pushed towards Marietta, Georgia.

—————— Generals Stoneman and Garrard, with their cavalry, captured Allatoona Pass.

—————— General Rousseau assigned by General Sherman to the command of the "District of the Tennessee," embracing nearly all that state east of that river to Lookout Creek, a few miles north of Chattanooga.

—————— General Steedman placed by General Sherman in command of the "District of the Etowah," embracing all the country from Bridgeport to Allatoona, including Cleveland, Rome, and all the country east as far as controlled by the Union troops.

June 3.—Battle of Cold Harbor, third day. General Grant's troops attacked the enemy's lines by assault at all points, without gaining any decided advantage. 300 prisoners were taken by the Federal troops. Union loss estimated at 2000 killed, wounded, and missing. Killed, Colonels Haskell, 36th Wisconsin; Porter, 8th New York heavy artillery; Morris, 66th New York; Drake, and Townsend, 106th New York; Lieutenant-Colonel McConnough. Wounded, General R. O. Tyler, Colonels McMahan, 164th New York; Byrnes, 28th Massachusetts; Brooks, 53d Pennsylvania; Truix, 14th New Jersey.

—————— After the attack upon the rebel lines at Cold Harbor, and the repulse of the Federal troops, the rebels made an attack in force upon Smith's brigade of Gibbon's division. The attack was repulsed with heavy loss to the rebels, and Wilson's (Federal) cavalry then fell upon the rear of a brigade of Heth's division sent to attack General Burnside, and drove them from their rifle-pits. In this action there was killed, Colonel Preston, 1st Vermont cavalry. Wounded, Brigadier-General Stannard, 18th corps; Colonel Benjamin, 8th New York cavalry. General Grant estimated the entire loss at Cold Harbor during those three days at 7500 men.

—————— The British blockade runner steamer Rose was destroyed by the United States gunboat Wamsutta, at Georgetown, South Carolina.

June 4.—The rebels under Lee made an attack upon the corps of Hancock, Wright, and Smith, but were everywhere repulsed, with a loss of 300 killed, and over 1000 wounded and prisoners.

June 5.—Battle of Piedmont, or Mount Crawford, Virginia, between United States troops under Major-General Hunter and rebels commanded by General W. E. Jones. The latter was killed and his army defeated, after a ten hours' fight. The rebels lost 1500 prisoners, 3000 small arms, 3 guns, stores, &c.

—————— The rebels in General Sherman's front abandoned their works and retreated.

—————— General Sturgis's cavalry, after several skirmishes, passed through Ripley, Mississippi.

June 6.—General Sherman occupied Ackworth Station, Georgia, with his advance within six miles of Marietta.

June 6.—British blockade running steamer Donegal captured off the coast of Florida, by United States gunboat Metacomet.

—————— Staunton, Virginia, was occupied by General Hunter's Union troops.

—————— A fight at Columbia, Arkansas, between Union troops under General A. J. Smith and rebels under Marmaduke. The rebels were driven from their lines. Federal loss, 20 killed and 70 wounded. Rebel loss, about the same.

June 7.—An attack was made at midnight by the rebel troops under Lee upon the lines of General Burnside, which movement was repulsed.

—————— General Sturgis's co-operating cavalry destroyed the railroad depot at Rienzi, Mississippi.

June 8.—General Sturgis's cavalry joined his infantry column near Ripley, Mississippi.

—————— The rebel General John H. Morgan's forces, which had entered Kentucky with the double intention of a raid and of drawing off forces intended to recruit General Sherman's army, attacked the United States post at Mount Sterling, Kentucky, and routed the garrison.

—————— Same day, a part of General John H. Morgan's force took possession of Paris, Kentucky, and destroyed a trestle work.

—————— The Union National Convention held at Baltimore, Maryland, nominated Abraham Lincoln for President, and Andrew Johnson, of Tennessee, for Vice-President, of the United States.

June 9.—The rebels having shifted their line in front of General Sherman, it was found to be this day extended from Kenesaw Mountain to Lost Mountain.

—————— General Blair's corps joined General Sherman, and went into line on the right of General McPherson's army, north of Allatoona Creek, Georgia.

—————— General Sturgis's main column passed through Ripley, moving south-west.

—————— General Hunter left Staunton, Virginia, for Lynchburg, after having destroyed factories, foundries, &c., and property worth $3,000,000. A cavalry force was sent to Waynesburg, and destroyed several bridges and tore up the track.

June 10.—General Kautz with Federal cavalry charged the rebel works at Petersburg, Virginia, penetrating into the town, but not being supported by General Gilmore, as was expected, he was compelled to fall back. Kautz took 40 prisoners and 1 gun.

—————— General Morgan, commanding the rebel raiding party in Kentucky, was defeated at Mount Sterling by General Burbridge, who had pursued him from Beaver Creek, West Virginia, whence Morgan had struck into Kentucky. Burbridge's troops marched ninety miles in twenty-four hours.

—————— A portion of John Morgan's raiders made an attack upon Frankfort, Kentucky, with 1200 men. Demands made to the United States troops to surrender were refused, and, after ineffectual attempts to capture the Federal works, the rebels withdrew.

—————— Battle of Guntown, Tennessee, called by the rebels the battle of Tishamingo Creek. General Sturgis was attacked by the combined forces of Forrest, Lee, and Roddy, and defeated, with the loss of 200 wagons, 14 guns, and 2240 killed, wounded, and prisoners. He left his dead and wounded on the field, and retreated to Ripley. Rebel loss, 400 killed and wounded. General Sturgis's forces were to co-operate with the right of General Sherman's main army, and prevent Forrest from committing depredations upon General Sherman's communications or in his rear. His failure in this movement caused his removal.

June 11.—Battle of Trevillian Station, Virginia, between Sheridan's Federal cavalry, upon a raiding expedition against the Virginia Central Railroad, and rebel cavalry. Torbert's division and Gregg's brigade drove the enemy from successive lines of breastworks upon Trevillian Station, where Custer attacked him in the tear, producing a complete rout, the rebels losing 520 officers and men, 300 horses, Colonel McAllister killed, and Brigadier-General Rosser and Colonels Aken and Cutter wounded. The railroad was then broken up and burned, for a distance of several miles. Federal loss, 85 killed, 490 wounded.

June 11.—United States gunboat Lavender ran aground on Cape Lookout Shoals, North Carolina, and was totally lost. 9 of the crew died, the remainder were rescued.

June 12.—General Grant withdrew his troops from before the rebel lines at Cold Harbor and Gaines's Mills. General Smith's corps were sent to White House, where they embarked in transports, and went down the Pamunkey and York Rivers, and up the James. Wright's and Burnside's corps crossed the Chickahominy at Jones's Bridge, Hancock's and Warren's at Long Bridge, whence they marched to the James River, which they crossed to the south side of the James River, at Powhatan Point. The movement was effected with no other interruption from the rebels than slight cavalry attacks.

—— General Sturgis arrived with his expedition at White's Station, Tennessee, and reported his losses to be 223 killed, 394 wounded, missing and prisoners 2623.

—— Unsuccessful attempts were made upon the rebel lines near Gordonsville, Virginia, by Sheridan's cavalry—a portion of them were taken, but retaken by the enemy: after some demonstrations, finding that they were too strong, General Sheridan withdrew his forces. The whole loss of Sheridan at this battle and at Trevillian Station, was 85 killed, 490 wounded, and 160 prisoners. The rebels suffered to as great a degree.

—— The expedition of Federal troops under Crooks and Averill captured Lexington, Virginia. The Virginia Military Institute was burned.

—— General Hobson's command at Cynthiana, Kentucky, was attacked by the rebel John Morgan, who took 2 Union regiments prisoners after a severe fight. Federal loss, 15 killed, 50 wounded, and 1500 prisoners.

June 13.—Battle at Cynthiana, Kentucky. John Morgan's raiders were defeated by General Burbridge, who killed 300, wounded 300, took 400 prisoners, and recaptured all General Hobson's command, and over 1000 horses.

June 14.—General Sherman's forces advance on the rebels at Kenesaw. During the artillery contest arising from the movement, the rebel Lieutenant-General Polk was killed by a cannon-ball.

—— General Sturgis superseded by General A. J. Smith.

June 15.—Skirmishing along the lines of General Sherman's army and change of front, resulting in the contest known as Pine Mountain or Golgotha. During the movement 18 rebel officers and nearly 400 enlisted men were captured by General Harrow.

—— General W. F. ("Baldy") Smith made an attack upon Petersburg, Virginia, with 15,000 men. He carried the first line of the rebel works, with 16 cannon, small arms, stand of colors, and between 300 and 400 prisoners.

—— The United States gunboat General Bragg, going up the Mississippi River, was attacked by a battery of rebels on shore at Tunica Bend. The Bragg opened upon them and drove them off.

—— Clement C. Vallandigham, who had been sent across the lines into the rebel dominions, made his appearance at Dayton, Ohio, having ventured to come from Canada, where he had been staying for some time.

—— G. C. Memminger, the rebel Secretary of the Treasury, resigns, alleging the want of confidence in his financial ability among the rebels. George F. Trenholm was appointed in his stead.

June 16.—Major-General Samuel Jones, commanding rebel forces at Charleston, South Carolina, apprised General Foster, commanding United States troops at Charleston, that 5 general officers and 45 field officers of the United States, prisoners of war, had been brought to that city and placed within the range of the guns of the United States batteries. The United States War Department issued a retaliatory order, transferring to General Foster an equal number of rebel general officers, to be treated in the manner proposed, as long as our officers are exposed in Charleston.

June 17.—The amount of $41,000,000 of the $75,000,000 loan of 1881, was awarded by the Secretary of the Treasury to bidders at 104 and upwards. The balance was withdrawn, although bid for at par and up to 101.

—— The President of the United States approved the bill to prevent frauds in the sale of gold. On that day the highest price of gold was 196⅜. On the day that it was announced that he had signed the bill it rose to 198¾; and on the next day to 205 and 210. On June 22, it went up to 235, and later to 270 and beyond.

—— Two redoubts in front of Petersburg were taken by Burnside's 9th corps, with 450 prisoners, 4 guns, and 3 battle flags.

—— A battle at Quaker Church, 4 miles from Lynchburg, Virginia, between Union troops of Hunter's army, under Crooks and Averill, and Imboden's rebel cavalry. The latter gave way under a charge, but the pursuit was checked by the rebel infantry. The result of the demonstration satisfied the Federal commander that it would be impossible to take Lynchburg, without a heavier loss than could be afforded by the army. The rebels estimated Hunter's loss at 300 killed and wounded.

June 18.—Bardstown, Kentucky, was captured by a small gang of guerrillas, who moved down the railroad and destroyed a bridge and water station.

—— Successive attempts were made to carry the rebel lines near Petersburg, Virginia, but they failed. The losses on the Union side were heavy.

—— A freight train for Sherman's army was captured, on the the railroad between Kingston and Dalton, by the rebel General Wharton.

—— Demonstrations against the rebel lines in front of Lynchburg, Virginia, were made by General Hunter. It was found that the enemy had been reinforced during the night by the arrival of Early's troops, and Hunter withdrew, marching for West Virginia, having destroyed railroads in various places, the James River Canal, &c.

June 19.—The rebel pirate steamer Alabama, Captain Raphael Semmes, was sunk off Cherbourg, on the coast of France, by the United States gunboat Kearsarge, Captain Winslow, after an action of two hours. The Alabama sunk after she had surrendered, and before the prisoners could be secured. A portion of the crew of the latter, including Semmes the captain, were taken up by the English yacht Deerhound, belonging to John Lancaster, and carried into Southampton, England, where they were released. On the Alabama 6 were killed, 17 wounded, 2 drowned; 68 were picked up by the boats of the Kearsarge, 40 by the yacht Deerhound, and 10 by a French pilot-boat. On the Kearsarge none were killed, and but 3 wounded.

June 20.—The bombardment of Petersburg, Virginia, was opened by guns of Birney's division, at a range of 1200 yards.

—— The rebel Generals Fitzhugh Lee and Hampton made an attack upon the Federal troops intrenched at White House, Virginia, and commanded by General Abercrombie. The United States gunboats there opened upon them, and they were driven back. The intention of the enemy was to capture the post before Sheridan's cavalry, which were expected there after their raid towards Staunton, should arrive. In this they were mistaken, and Sheridan arrived the same day.

—— General engagement along Sherman's line at Kenesaw Mountain, ending without definite results.

June 21.—General Geary, of General Sherman's army, made a demonstration in his front, driving back the rebel lines. General Hood's rebel corps withdrew from the front of General McPherson's lines.

—— A reconnoissance was made to Kinston, North Carolina, by the 132d New York volunteers, Colonel Classen. They took a number of prisoners, and killed and wounded about 35 of the enemy.

June 22.—Battle of Jerusalem Plank Road. A portion of the 2d corps in the army operating against Petersburg, Virginia, being in advance of other parts of the line, were fiercely attacked by the enemy under Hill, and driven back nearly a mile to their intrenchments, losing severely. The rebels reported that they had taken 2000 prisoners, 4 guns, and stand of colors. A whole brigade was captured.

June 22.—Marmaduke's troops, 600 strong, were repulsed at White River, Arkansas, by two companies of the 12th Iowa infantry. Rebel loss, 24 killed and wounded. Union loss, 1 killed and 5 wounded. The arrival of the gunboat Tyler turned the scale against the invaders.

―――― General Wilson, with 6000 cavalry, set out from Prince George Court House, Virginia, on an extensive raid against the rebel railroad communications. They crossed the Petersburg and Weldon Railroad at Ream's Station, struck the Southside Railroad at Ford's Station, from thence went to Burksville, on the Danville Railroad. South of this point the destruction was very complete, as much as 60 miles of railroad being destroyed, with bridges, depots, locomotives, and cars. On the 26th the rebel cavalry of W. H. F. Lee appeared on their right flank, and travelled with them on roads parallel, with frequent skirmishes. At Ream's Station a very heavy force of Lee's army was posted to receive the raiding party. Finding themselves in danger of being surrounded, the efforts of Wilson, Kautz, and the other commanders, were turned to the means of escape. In this endeavor they lost 13 of their guns, and a wagon and ambulance train. Wilson's troops began to arrive in the Union lines July 2d. Estimate of Federal loss, 750 to 1000 men killed, wounded, and missing.

―――― Battle at Culp Farm, Georgia. General Sherman's forces heavily engaged with Johnson's rebel army during the passage of Nose's Creek. The contest began at 4 o'clock in the morning. The rebels resolutely advanced, but were driven back in disorder after a hard fight. An attempt to flank the Union troops was also repulsed with slaughter.

June 23.—General Wright with a portion of the 6th corps made a movement on the Weldon Railroad, below Petersburg, and destroyed about 5 miles of track: but before he had completed the work the rebels attacked him in heavy force, but were beaten off.

June 24.—A heavy artillery fire was opened upon the 18th corps, in front of Petersburg, by rebel batteries, under cover of which 400 men of Hoke's rebel brigade attempted to storm the position of Stannard's division. They were allowed to approach near enough to be in full range, and then were opened upon with a fierce fire. The result was that the whole party were killed, wounded, or taken prisoners.

―――― Battle of St. Mary's Church, Virginia, between Federal cavalry under Gregg and Wade Hampton's rebel cavalry. The latter attacked the wagon trains in their way from White House to Harrison's Landing, and endeavored to capture a part of the wagons. They were defeated after a sharp action, in which were killed, Colonel George Covode, 4th Pennsylvania cavalry; Colonel Huey, 8th Pennsylvania; and Colonel Smith, 1st Maine, wounded.

―――― United States steamer Queen City was captured at Columbia, on White River, by guerrillas, 200 in number. The boat was soon afterwards burned, upon the appearance of United States gunboats.

―――― The Maryland State Convention, in session at Annapolis, passed an amendment to the Constitution of the State, abolishing slavery.

June 25.—McPherson's wing of General Sherman's army engaged with the rebels near Big Shanty, Georgia.

June 26.—Sharp skirmishing along the front of General Sherman's army; the columns on the right and left moving by the flank.

―――― Lafayette, Tennessee, was attacked by the rebel General Pillow, with 3000 men. After a spirited defence by Colonel Watkins, with 400 men, the invaders were driven off. leaving 100 killed and wounded on the field. Union loss, 100 killed and wounded.

June 27.—A general assault was made upon the front of the rebel position at Kenesaw by General Sherman's army, but was repulsed with great slaughter. General C. G. Harker was mortally wounded, and died the next day. Federal loss at Kenesaw, 3000; the damage to the rebels, slight.

June 28 & 29.—Movement of General Sherman's army on the right, for the purpose of flanking the rebel position at Kenesaw Mountain.

June 30.—The rebels began to evacuate their position at Kenesaw Mountain, and to fall back upon other lines and on the Chattahoochee River, for the purpose of covering Marietta.

―――― Hon. Salmon P. Chase, Secretary of the Treasury, resigned. His situation was filled by the appointment of Hon. W. P. Fessenden, of Maine.

July 1.—General Hunter, with the army which had moved down the Shenandoah Valley, and made demonstrations against Lynchburg, arrived at Charleston, West Virginia, having marched 500 miles.

―――― A British blockade running steamer ―――― was beached near Mobile, by the United States steamer Glasgow, and destroyed by a boat expedition from the fleet of Admiral Farragut.

July 2.—British blockade running steamer Rouen was captured off Beaufort, South Carolina, by the United States gunboat Keystone State.

―――― An expedition of United States troops from Hilton Head, South Carolina, landed on Johns Island, Charleston Harbor, South Carolina.

―――― General Sherman's cavalry struck the Chattahoochee, and was followed by General McPherson's wing of Sherman's army.

―――― General Howard's column moved close up to the works at Kenesaw Mountain, and found they were evacuated.

―――― Same day a portion of the troops under General William Birney went up the Edisto River, landed at White Point, and attacked a battery with 2 guns which he did not take.

―――― An attempt was made to capture Fort Johnson on James's Island, Charleston Harbor. They captured an outer battery with 2 guns, which they held for a time, and then fell back. At night an attempt was made to take Fort Johnson by troops landed from boats; a portion of them took battery Simpkins, but being unsupported were all taken prisoners by the rebels, being 143 in number.

July 3.—An expedition of Major-General Slocum's troops left Black River, Mississippi, and marched for Jackson, under command of General Dennis. The latter place was taken on the 6th, after a small skirmish.

―――― Martinsburg, Virginia, was evacuated by General Sigel's troops, upon the approach of a strong rebel force down the Valley of Virginia, under the command of Early and Breckinridge.

―――― General Sherman's army occupied Kenesaw, Georgia, at daylight, and Marietta at half-past 8 o'clock A. M. General Thomas's wing moved down the main road to the Chattahoochee, marching towards the mouth of the Nickajack Creek and the Sandtown Road.

―――― During the past three days General Sherman captured over 2000 prisoners.

July 5.—General Bradley T. Johnson, with a force of rebels about 3000 strong, crossed the Potomac into Maryland.

―――― 250 rebel cavalry attacked a small Federal force at Hagerstown, Maryland, and were handsomely repulsed. Shortly afterwards the rebels being reinforced retook the town.

July 6.—A portion of the rebel advance under Early entered Maryland, crossing the Potomac near Antietam.

―――― A rebel force under Bradley Johnson entered Hagerstown, Maryland.

―――― Governor Curtin of Pennsylvania issued a proclamation for 12,000 volunteers to serve for 100 days in Pennsylvania, Maryland, and Washington, and its vicinity.

July 7.—Skirmishing at Canton, Mississippi, between United States troops under General Dennis, who had evacuated Jackson, and rebel cavalry.

―――― A fight at Ripley, Mississippi, between General A. J. Smith's expeditionary troops and rebels strongly posted. .The latter were dislodged and retreated.

―――― The rebel force which occupied Hagerstown, Maryland, retired, after having levied on the town and received 1500 outfits of clothing and $20,000 in United States currency.

July 7.—Heavy skirmishing near Frederick, Maryland, between rebels under Bradley Johnson and Union troops under Colonel Gilpin, in which the latter was successful in driving back the enemy.

—— Middletown, Maryland, taken by Early's rebel troops.

July 8.—British blockade running steamer Little Ada was captured by United States gunboat Gettysburg.

—— British blockade runner steamer Boston captured by United States steamer Fort Jackson off Wilmington, North Carolina.

—— The rebel force invading Maryland entered Frederick. General Lew Wallace, commanding Federal forces falling back before them, and retiring across the Monocacy River burned the bridge.

—— The rebel pirate Florida appeared off the coast of the United States, between Cape Henry and Cape May, and captured the barks Greenland, General Berry, Golconda, Zelinda, and schooner Margaret W. Davis. The vessels were burned, and the crews placed on board the pilot-boat Howard, of New York, which was also captured and bonded. The latter landed them at Cape May.

—— Major-General Rousseau, U.S. Army, with 2000 cavalry and infantry, left Nashville, Tennessee, upon a raiding expedition towards Selma, Alabama.

—— General Sherman's troops crossed the Chattahoochee River. The rebels began their retrograde movement towards Atlanta.

July 9.—Battle of Monocacy. The rebels, under Breckinridge and Johnson, advanced against the Union troops on the east side of the creek. The firing was for several hours across the river. The force of Wallace was small in comparison to that of the rebels, and late in the day it was flanked by six regiments and a battery, which got across the river from below. The Union troops were forced to retire, having lost 121 killed, 190 wounded, and 400 prisoners; total, 711. This battle, although resulting in a defeat to the Federals, was really a success, as it disconcerted the rebel plans, and probably saved Baltimore. Rebel loss, 300 killed, and 430 wounded and left behind.

—— The Federal troops on Johns Island, South Carolina, were attacked by rebels under General Bev. H. Robinson, and compelled to retire. Later in the day they abandoned the island. Rebel loss, 17 killed and 93 wounded.

—— Governor Joseph E. Brown, of Georgia, orders out the reserve militia of the state, which is composed of men between the ages of 50 and 55 years, and boys between 16 and 17 years. Georgia " being left to her own resources to supply reinforcements for General Johnston's army, all free white males between the ages of 17 and 50, who are exempt from Confederate conscription, are also ordered to come forward."

July 10.—The steamship Electric Spark, from New York to New Orleans, was captured by the pirate Florida, about 60 miles south of Cape Henlopen.

—— General Garrard's cavalry destroyed the factories at Rosewell, Georgia. The balance of General Sherman's main army began crossing the Chattahoochee River, and the line was established south-east of that stream.

—— General McPherson changed front, and took up a position on the extreme left of Sherman's army.

—— General Rousseau started from Decatur, Alabama, on his raid.

July 11.—Pontotoc, Mississippi, occupied by General A J. Smith's troops.

—— A portion of the rebel forces which had appeared in Maryland, approached Washington, D. C., by the Rockville Road, and were skirmished with in advance of Tenallytown.

—— The mansion of Governor Bradford, of Maryland, four miles from Baltimore, was burned, being set on fire by a small detachment of rebels sent forward for the purpose, as a retaliation for the burning of Ex-Governor John Letcher's house by General Hunter.

July 11.—Two passenger trains on the Baltimore and Philadelphia Railroad, at Magnolia Station, were captured by a rebel raiding party commanded by Major Harry Gilmore. Major-General Franklin, U.S. Army, who was a passenger, was taken a prisoner, and carried off. The rebels robbed the passengers, set fire to the trains, and ran the blazing cars upon the bridge over the Gunpowder River, which was partially destroyed.

—— The rear guard of the rebel army was driven out of Frederick, Maryland, by Cole's Maryland cavalry.

July 12.—The rebel advance approaching Fort Stevens, near Washington, D. C., was opened upon from Fort Stevens. They retreated, losing 300 killed and wounded, leaving their dead on the field, and 200 wounded behind them. During the night they retreated. On the Federal side the killed and wounded were 200. During the rebel retreat they burned the house of Montgomery Blair, Postmaster-General, at Silver Spring. Their line of march was for Edwards' Ferry.

—— Messrs. C. C. Clay, of Alabama, Professor J. B. Holcombe, of Virginia, and George N. Sanders, at Niagara Falls, New York, sent a letter to Horace Greeley, of New York, asking leave to visit Washington, D. C., under a protection, to consult upon the possibility of peace.

July 13.—Battle at Tupelo, Mississippi, between Federal troops under General A. J. Smith and rebels under Generals S. D. Lee and Forrest. The latter were defeated with very severe loss.

—— In the evening there was another battle. The rebels attacked the Union troops behind breastworks, and were again defeated.

July 14.—Major-General Franklin having escaped from the rebels, who captured him on the Baltimore Railroad train, arrived in Baltimore.

July 15.—The 6th army corps, under Major-General Wright, crossed the Potomac, at White's Ford, in pursuit of the army of Early and Breckinridge.

—— Battle between General A. J. Smith's and Forrest's troops. The latter led three desperate charges upon our lines, and failed in all of them.

July 16.—General A. J. Smith's expedition started upon its return, being reduced to the last ration. An attack by rebel cavalry was repulsed.

—— General Rousseau's forces reported by the rebels to be at Talladega, en route for the Montgomery Railroad.

July 17.—Lieutenant-General J. E. Johnston was removed from the command of the rebel army of the Tennessee, and the command turned over to Lieutenant-General J. B. Hood.

—— Battle at Grand Gulf, Louisiana, between General Slocum's expeditionary troops and rebels under Wirt Adams.

—— General Sherman's whole army advanced to within five miles of Atlanta, the left occupying Decatur, Georgia.

—— General Rousseau reported to have cut the railroad at Notasulga, and to have destroyed communication between Montgomery and Atlanta.

July 18.—General Sherman's lines still further extended, so as to flank Atlanta on the south-east, with a tendency to move further south.

—— A fight at Snicker's Gap, Virginia, between Crooks's United States troops and rebels of Early and Breckinridge's forces. The latter were defeated, and lost 300 wagons.

—— A Proclamation was issued by the President of the United States, calling for 500,000 volunteers within 50 days—drafts to be made in the districts which do not furnish their quota on the 5th of September.

—— Mr. Greeley, understanding that Messrs. Clay, Holcombe, and Thompson were accredited agents of Jefferson Davis, bearing propositions from Richmond looking to peace, tendered them the safe conduct of President Lincoln. They replied that they were not accredited with such propositions, but were in the confidential employ of their government, and felt authorized to declare that they would be invested with full powers if necessary. The President replied as follows :—

"EXECUTIVE MANSION,
"WASHINGTON, July 18, 1864.
" To whom it may concern :—
" Any proposition which embraces the restoration of peace, the integrity of the Union, and the abandonment of slavery, and which comes by and with authority that can control the armies now at war against the United States, will be received and considered by the Executive Government of the United States, and will be met by liberal terms on other substantial and collateral points, and the bearers thereof shall have safe conduct both ways.
"ABRAHAM LINCOLN."

Messrs. Holcombe and Clay refused to prosecute the affair further, alleging that these terms precluded all negotiation and hope of settlement.

July 18.—Battle of Island Ford, Virginia, between General Wright's and Crooks's troops, and Early's forces. Union loss, 300 killed and wounded. Rebel loss, 500.

July 19.—Major-General Wright crossed the Shenandoah, and advanced to Berryville, Virginia, but being informed (falsely) that Early had retreated, took up the line of march according to orders upon return, and went to Leesburg. General Crooks returned towards Harper's Ferry.

July 20.—Battle of Winchester, Virginia. General Averill attacked the rebel troops at Winchester, Virginia, defeating them, killing and wounding 300, capturing 200 prisoners, 4 guns, and several hundred small arms. General Lilley (rebel) was wounded and taken prisoner, and Colonel Board, 58th Virginia, killed.

—— Camp Gonzales, Florida, captured by Union troops under General Asboth.

—— The English blockade running steamer Ida was captured by United States steamer Sonoma.

—— Colonel James F. Jacques, 73d Illinois volunteers, and James R. Gilmore, "Edmund Kirke," returned to Washington, D. C., from Richmond, Virginia, at which city they consulted with Jefferson Davis and members of his cabinet as to the possibility of peace.

—— General A. J. Smith's expedition reached La Grange, Mississippi, having during the journey lost only 300 men, and not having lost a wagon. The rebel loss was not less than 2500.

—— The rebel army moved out from Atlanta and attacked the left wing of Sherman's army at Decatur. The assault was made with great vigor and desperation, but met with a bloody repulse. The rebels lost from 600 to 800 killed, and 4000 wounded and prisoners. Our forces held the field. Union loss before Atlanta, 1500 killed, wounded, and missing.

July 21.—The enemy driven by the Union troops, with small loss, to the works immediately around Atlanta.

July 22.—Part of General Sherman's forces occupied the outskirts of Atlanta. A severe battle took place in the vicinity of Atlanta, and great loss inflicted upon the enemy. General James B. McPherson killed by a rebel sharpshooter. Federal loss, 3722 killed, wounded, and prisoners. Rebel loss, 3240 killed and left on the field, 1000 prisoners, and 8000 wounded.

July 24.—Battle at Winchester, Virginia. Generals Crooks's and Averill's troops were defeated by rebels under General Early, and retreated to Harper's Ferry. Colonel Mulligan, Illinois volunteers, commanding a brigade, was killed. Federal loss, 1000 killed, wounded, and prisoners, and 4 guns.

July 25.—Skirmishing at Martinsburg, Virginia, between Early's forces and those of Crooks and Averill, who were falling back.

—— A fight at Big Creek, near Helena, Arkansas, between 280 Federal troops under Colonel Brooks and 1500 rebels. The latter were held in check until the United States troops got to a place of safety, with a loss of 50 killed and wounded. Rebel loss, 50 killed and over 100 wounded. Colonel Brooks was killed.

July 26.—Major-General Rousseau with his troops arrived at Marietta, Georgia. He lost 5 killed and 13 wounded in his expedition. He captured and paroled 2000 rebels, killed and wounded 200, captured 800 horses and mules, and 800 negroe round, and 13 depots, with s

July 28.—Battle of Hax corps, United States army, Petersburg, Virginia, cros Deep Bottom, and attacke a mile from the river. A captured, with a loss of 1(Federal side.

July 27.—Major-General of the Army of the Tenne death of General McPhers

—— Two bodies of ca man and McCook, left Sh around Atlanta.

July 28.—Battle of Four Sheridan's Federal cavalry of the rebels, which made latter were defeated, wit wounded. Federal loss, 2!

—— The British bloc was run ashore below M rebels rescued the cargo.

—— Detachments of Williamsport, Cherry Run and Shepherdstown. The under McCausland, marche burg.

—— Martinsburg, Virg States troops under Gener

—— The Army of the ' front from the extreme left man's army, was attacked march. The battle lasted the Union forces holding tiring within their works at dead in our hands; whole whole loss, killed and wou 600, our troops being prote

—— Palmetto Station 25 miles from Atlanta, d five miles of track, &c., McCook. During the nigh and pushed on to Fayettev

July 29.—Before daylig Fayetteville, 40 miles fro rebel government property pied the place. Portions destroyed.

July 30.—At Petersbur ploded beneath a rebel bat 15 guns. A South Caroli blown up. A heavy bor upon the rebel works, from under cover of which an portion of the enemy's wo the fort which had been t of a delay in sending forw an opportunity to recover sion, and to bring up troop exposed to a terrible fire but could not be held. Th wounded, and missing, inc prisoner. Rebel loss, 250

—— Chambersburg, I a force of 500 rebels, unde defenceless. McCausland backs, or $100,000 in gol yond the means of the inh even if they had been di given to burn the town. different parts of the plac destroyed. Various house troops. Property estimate and $2,000,000 was destroy destroyed was 260. Abou rebels retreated from the ill's cavalry.

—— General Hooke

of the 20th corps, and was succeeded by General Slocum.

July 30.—General McCook's forces, while returning from their raid, were attacked by the rebels at Newnan, on the West Point Railroad. A heavy fight occurred and the Union forces were scattered, but afterwards came into camp in detachments.

——— General Stoneman's forces arrived near Macon, but finding the rebels had removed the Union prisoners, returned after skirmishing with the enemy.

July 31.—General Stoneman's command, when between Clinton and Hillsboro, and about 15 miles from Macon, was attacked by the rebels in great force, and, after a fight of some hours, was compelled to surrender.

August 2.—An election was held in Pennsylvania on amendments to the constitution. The principal one, to extend the right of voting to soldiers in the army, was carried by a majority of 94,607. For the amendment, 199,959; against it, 105,352. Two other amendments were carried by majorities exceeding 75,000 each.

August 3.—The rebels, during the morning, attacked General Logan's works before Atlanta in force and drove him therefrom. In the evening he not only retook the works, but captured all the rebels who occupied them. He also advanced his lines 300 yards.

August 4.—New Creek, Virginia, was attacked by rebel troops under Bradley Johnson and McCausland. The post was well defended by Colonel Stevenson, and the enemy retreated during the night. Federal loss, 25 killed and 50 wounded. The rebel loss much heavier.

August 5.—Governor A. G. Curtin, of Pennsylvania, announcing that the rebel army had crossed the Potomac and occupied Hagerstown, issued a proclamation calling for 30,000 volunteer militia.

——— A mine excavated by the rebels in front of Petersburg was exploded near the position of the 8th corps, doing no damage. A sharp musketry fire followed, in which Colonel Steadman, 11th Connecticut regiment, was killed, and a few men wounded.

——— A skirmish near the Jerusalem Plank Road, Virginia, between Gregg's Federal cavalry and South Carolina troops under General Butler. The latter were driven from the ground. Rebel loss, 75 killed and wounded.

——— 500 rebels with 12 guns, under Cooper, Garvey, and Standthwaite, moving up to attack Fort Smith, Arkansas, were met outside of the fortifications by General Thayer, and defeated.

——— Admiral Farragut, with 32 war vessels, mounting 231 guns, passed between the rebel Forts Morgan and Gaines, below Mobile, Alabama. Inside the bay they encountered the rebel fleet, consisting of the ironclad ram Tennessee, and the gunboats Selma, Gaines, and Morgan. The Tennessee was attacked and rammed by the Monongahela, Lackawanna, and Hartford. After a short contest, the Tennessee surrendered. The commander, Admiral Buchanan, was wounded and taken prisoner. The Selma was captured, and the Gaines and Morgan escaped. The United States Monitor Tecumseh, Captain Craven, while going in, was struck by a torpedo and instantly sunk, with all on board. The total Federal loss, including the crew of the Tecumseh, was 41 killed, 82 wounded, and 120 drowned. 230 rebel officers and men were captured. The United States dispatch-boat St. Phillippe was sunk. The United States gunboat Oneida received a shot through her boiler, which exploded, scalding many.

August 6.—Fort Powell, in Mobile Harbor, held by the rebels, was abandoned. The garrison withdrew to Cedar Point. The guns, 18 in number, fell into the hands of the Federal troops under General Granger.

August 7.—English blockade running steamer Prince Albert sunk in Charleston Harbor, South Carolina.

——— Battle of Tah-kah-o-kuty Mountain, on the Little Missouri, between 6000 Indians and General Sully's little army of 2200 men. The latter were successful, and the Indians were put to flight.

——— Battle of Moorfield, Virginia, between Union troops under General Averill and the combined forces of McCausland, Johnson, Gilmore, and McNeill. The rebels were routed, losing all their artillery, 4 pieces, a large quantity of small arms, 400 horses, and 420 prisoners, with 100 killed and wounded. Union loss, 7 killed and 51 wounded.

August 7.—Major-General P. H. Sheridan was appointed to the command of the Army of Northern Virginia, in place of Major-General David Hunter, superseded.

——— 50 Federal officers, prisoners of war, who had been brought to Charleston, South Carolina, and placed under fire of the United States batteries, were exchanged for 50 rebel officers of the same rank brought down and placed under fire of the rebel batteries by way of retaliation.

August 8.—Fort Gaines, below Mobile, held by the rebel Colonel Anderson, surrendered, with 56 officers, 818 men, and 26 guns.

——— A Union blockhouse at Old Town, Virginia, defended by Colonel Stough and 450 men, was surrendered to the rebel Brigadier-General Bradley Johnson, with 6 guns. Union loss, 2 killed and 3 wounded. Rebel loss, 20 killed and 40 wounded.

August 9.—Atlanta shelled on all parts of the line.

August 10.—Terrific bombardment of Atlanta during the night.

——— Wheeler's rebel cavalry started from East Point on a raid within the Union lines.

——— A fight near Abbeville, Mississippi, between Union cavalry under General Hatch and 2000 rebels under Chalmers.

——— An ordnance-boat loaded with shot, shell, and powder, exploded at City Point, Virginia, killing 43 persons, wounding 126, and destroying sheds, storehouses, &c. The cause of the disaster is unknown.

August 11.—The United States merchant brigs Estelle, Sarah Boyce, Richard, bark Bay State, schooner Atlantic, and pilot-boat James Funk, were captured off Fire Island by the rebel privateer steamer Tallahassee, Captain John Taylor Wood, and burned.

——— The last of Early's forces left Winchester, Virginia. Union cavalry entered immediately afterwards.

——— Pilot-boat William Bell was captured 90 miles south-east of Sandy Hook, by the rebel pirate Tallahassee.

August 12.—The ship Adriatic was captured off Montauk by the rebel privateer Tallahassee, and burned.

August 13.—A Federal supply train of 75 loaded wagons, with 550 horses and mules, 200 cattle, and 200 prisoners, was taken by Moseby's guerrilla cavalry, near Berryville, Virginia.

——— The bark Glenalvon was destroyed by the pirate Tallahassee, off Nantucket.

——— Forrest's rebel cavalry were attacked at Hurricane Creek, Mississippi, by General A. J. Smith, and dislodged from their fortifications, leaving 50 dead on the field. Federal loss, 40 killed and wounded.

——— The rebel works at Atlanta again assaulted.

August 14.—Major-General Burnside was relieved from the command of the 5th corps in the Army of the Potomac.

——— Hancock's corps crossed the James River and reached Deep Bottom, near Dutch Gap, at night. Turner's, Terry's, and Foster's divisions were advanced by General Birney.

August 15.—Battle of Deep Bottom, Virginia. The whole force that had moved the day before advanced, overcame the rebel skirmishers, and attacked the rebel works, which were carried by Birney's division, capturing 6 guns and 2 mortars. The line gained was 10 miles from Richmond.

August 16.—Battle at Deep Run, Virginia, called by the rebels the battle of White Tavern. The rebel Generals Chambliss and Gherardie were killed. The rebels lost 400 prisoners. The rebel losses up to this time in killed and wounded equalled the Union loss, viz. 1000 killed and wounded. The Union lines were very considerably advanced towards Richmond.

August 16.—General Merrit's division of cavalry was attacked at Front Royal, Virginia, by Kershaw's, Wickham's, and Lomax's rebel brigades, the two latter of cavalry. After a handsome cavalry fight the rebels were beaten back, losing 308 prisoners, 2 stand of colors, and about 40 killed. Union loss, 31 killed and wounded.

—— 5000 rebel cavalry and infantry under Wheeler demanded the surrender of Dalton, Georgia. Colonel Siebold, with 600 men, who commanded the works, refused to capitulate. The rebels made several attempts to carry the works, but were repulsed. Next day reinforcements arrived under General Steadman, who engaged the rebels at once, and whipped them off.

August 18.—A peace convention met at Syracuse, New York, and adopted resolutions in favor of an immediate cessation of hostilities. It was addressed by Fernando Wood, Vallandigham, and others.

—— Major-General Sheridan with his army fell back to Berryville, Virginia, to foil a force sent up through Front Royal to flank him.

—— A strong attack was made at night upon General Birney's lines north of the James River, by the rebels, who came up in strong force. They were repulsed, with a loss of 1000 killed and wounded.

—— The 5th corps of General Grant's army, under command of Major-General Warren, left the lines before Petersburg, and marched to Ream's Station, on the Petersburg and Weldon Railroad, where the track was torn up for several miles. In the afternoon Hill's rebel corps made an attack upon this force, and, after heavy fighting, were repulsed. Union loss, 300.

—— The rebel pirate Tallahassee arrived at Halifax, having evaded the United States vessels sent in pursuit.

—— General Kilpatrick's command rendezvousing at Sandtown for a special raid.

August 19.—General Kilpatrick, at the head of about 5000 mounted men, started from Sandtown on his raid around the enemy's position at Atlanta; arrived at Fairburn, on the West Point Railroad, where he met the enemy and drove them from the ground; crossed Flint River; pushed on to Jonesboro and destroyed the place, and rested for the night near Lovejoy's. The Macon Railroad torn up for three miles, and a train of loaded cars destroyed during the day.

—— General Dodge, while locating advanced works, was seriously wounded by a bullet from a rebel sharpshooter.

—— The rebel pirate Tallahassee, having taken in a small supply of coal, was ordered off from Halifax by Admiral Hope.

—— The rebels made a heavy attack upon the right of Warren at Ream's Station, Virginia, and by getting between the 5th and 9th corps, and the connecting lines, achieved considerable success. Two divisions of Warren's corps were driven back, and General Hays and 2200 prisoners taken from them. Warren's lines were, after hard fighting, re-established. 300 prisoners were taken from the rebels. Union loss estimated at 3000, including prisoners.

—— Martinsburg, Virginia, was reoccupied by the rebels under Early.

August 20.—Kilpatrick's command attacked in force before daybreak by the rebels at Lovejoy's, and surrounded. The 2d division, under Colonel Minty, cut its way through the enemy, and the Union troops pushed on. Loss about 300.

—— Wheeler's rebel cavalry operating along the East Tennessee Railroad and Stewart's Landing, where he captured and murdered part of the garrison.

—— The pirate Tallahassee left Halifax, Nova Scotia. During its previous trip this vessel captured and destroyed 3 ships, 3 barks, 1 brig, 16 schooners, 2 pilot-boats, and bonded 6 vessels.

August 21.—An attack was made upon General Sheridan's lines near the Potomac. The pickets were driven in, and there was artillery firing and musketry at long range during the greater part of the day. The attempts of the rebels were repulsed. At night our troops remained on the ground. Union loss, 1200 killed and wounded. Rebel loss equally heavy.

August 21.—The rebel General Forrest, with 3000 cavalry, made a dash into Memphis, expecting to capture several Union field officers. In this they were mistaken, and they were soon beaten out, losing 30 killed and 100 wounded. They got some plunder and a few prisoners, but failed in the important object of the expedition.

—— General Sheridan advanced his forces and formed in line of battle in front of Halltown, Virginia, and offered battle to Early. The latter deemed it prudent not to attack.

—— The rebels in force made a strong effort to dislodge Warren from his line on the Weldon Railroad. They formed in three lines of battle and charged three times, but were repulsed by heavy discharges of grape, canister, and musketry, losing 500 prisoners and several stand of colors. Federal loss, 150 killed and wounded, and 100 skirmishers prisoners. Rebel loss, 600 killed, 1100 prisoners, and the rebel Generals Hayward and Sanders killed.

—— Kilpatrick's command crossed Cotton River at 1 A. M., and South River at 6 A. M., reaching Lithonia, on the Georgia Railroad, east of Atlanta, in the evening. The troops then went into camp, after their fatiguing raid.

August 22.—General Kilpatrick's command arrived at the main army encampment, after passing completely around Atlanta.

—— Wheeler's rebel cavalry, after cutting the East Tennessee Railroad, approached Knoxville.

August 23.—A fight near the Weldon Railroad, Virginia, between Gregg's and Kautz's Union cavalry and Hampton's rebel cavalry. Union loss, 10 killed and 60 wounded. Rebel loss, 150 killed and wounded.

—— Fort Morgan, in Mobile Harbor, surrendered to the United States fleet under Admiral Furragut and the army under General Granger. The bombardment commenced on the 14th by a portion of the fleet. On the 22d the whole fleet opened on the fort, and fired so heavily that the fort had but little opportunity to reply. By the surrender there were given up 60 guns and ammunition, and 600 prisoners, including General R. L. Page, commander. The latter was accused of having spiked the guns and mutilated the property after the surrender, but was acquitted of the charge by a court of inquiry.

August 24.—The steamship Georgia, formerly the rebel privateer of that name, was captured by the United States frigate Niagara. The Georgia had been dismantled and sold in Liverpool. The capture was made upon the ground that the sale of ships of war in the port of a neutral violates the law of nations.

August 25.—The rebel ram Nashville, unfinished, was blown up in Mobile Harbor, by the crew of the United States gunboat Metacomet.

—— A fight near Leetown, Virginia, between Torbert's Federal cavalry and infantry of Early's corps. Federal loss, 150 killed and wounded.

—— A very heavy attack was made by the rebels under General A. P. Hill, upon the 2d army corps, General Hancock, at Ream's Station. Three desperate assaults were made by the rebels, and some advantages were gained by them, one line of breastworks having been carried, but they were afterwards beaten back at all points. The rebels captured 9 pieces of artillery. After night Hancock withdrew, and took position nearer the main body of the army. The Union loss was estimated at 2000 killed and wounded.

August 26.—Early's army retired from Sheridan' front, falling back to Smithfield and Middleburg.

—— Sherman's main army, with the exception of the 20th corps, moved by the right flank to the rear of the rebel defences of Atlanta.

August 27.—The rebel privateer Tallahassee ran into the harbor of Wilmington, North Carolina, despite the vigilance of the blockading fleet.

August 29.—Wheeler's cavalry reported advancing upon Nashville via McMinville and Murfreesboro.

August 29.—The National Democratic Convention assembled at Chicago, Illinois.

August 30.—The Democratic Convention at Chicago adopted a platform of principles, the principal "plank" of which was as follows:—

"*Resolved*, That this Convention does explicitly declare, as the sense of the American people, that, after four years of failure to restore the Union by the experiment of war, during which, under the pretence of a military necessity of war power higher than the Constitution, the Constitution itself has been disregarded in every part, and public liberty and private right alike trodden down, and the material prosperity of the country essentially impaired, justice, humanity, liberty, and the public welfare demand that immediate efforts be made for a cessation of hostilities, with a view to an ultimate convention of all the States, or other peaceable means, to the end that at the earliest practical moment peace may be restored on the basis of the Federal Union of the States."

August 31.—Wheeler's rebel cavalry appeared upon the line of the Great Western Railroad, between Nashville and the Tennessee River, and commenced to destroy it. General Rousseau marched against him from Nashville, and met him three miles from Lagrange, and drove him forward.

——— The Chicago Democratic Convention nominated George B. McClellan, of New Jersey, for President, and George H. Pendleton, of Ohio, for Vice-President. The vote on the first ballot was for George B. McClellan, 202¼; for Thomas H. Seymour, of Connecticut, 23½. The nomination of McClellan was subsequently made unanimous.

——— Major-General Sherman's main army having, by a flank movement, withdrawn from before Atlanta, leaving only one corps in position, reached Jonesboro, Georgia, where Lee and Hardee attacked General Howard's corps, and were defeated, losing 400 dead on the field, and 2500 wounded.

September 1.—Second day of the battle of Jonesboro. The rebel lines were assaulted. Govan's rebel brigade were taken prisoners, with 8 guns. The rebels were driven into Jonesboro, and retreated during the night.

September 2.—General Slocum entered Atlanta, Georgia, the rebel General Hood having retreated during the night, after blowing up storehouses, cars, locomotives, and destroying property. Thus ended this memorable campaign. The following estimate of the losses on the Union side, from Chattanooga to Atlanta, is believed to be as nearly correct as possible to make it. It includes killed, wounded, and missing :—

Skirmishing from Chattanooga to Resaca	1,500
Battle of Resaca	3,500
Skirmishing from Resaca to the Allatoona Range	500
Battles at and near Dallas	2,000
Repulse at New Hope Church	2,000
Skirmishing near and battle at Lost Mountain	2,000
Skirmishing in front of Kenesaw before and after the defeat of the 27th	2,000
Unsuccessful assault upon Kenesaw	3,500
Heavy skirmishing near Marietta	1,000
Crossing the Chattahoochee	400
Skirmishing at Peach Tree Creek	700
Battle of the 20th of July	2,400
Battle of the 22d of July	5,800
Battle of the 28th of July	1,500
Skirmishing in front of Atlanta from the 28th of July to the 28th of August, including the unsuccessful assaults of Schofield on the 6th, and a portion of the 14th corps on the 7th ultimo	2,500
Total national loss from Chattanooga to Atlanta	31,300

In the above is embraced the cavalry losses, including the loss of portions of Stoneman's and McCook's forces around Atlanta, which has been reduced to less than 1000. Our loss in cannon was 15 ; 10 at the battle of the 22d July, 3 taken from Stoneman, and 2 abandoned by McCook. Our loss in colors is far inferior to the enemy's.

Up to the battle of Peachtree Creek, with the exception of the series of fights near Dallas, our losses exceeded that of the rebels, as a general thing. In all skirmishes the losses upon both sides were about the same. Rebel loss in all skirmishes from Chattanooga to

Atlanta	10,200
Battle at Resaca	3,000
Battles at Dallas	4,000
Battle of New Hope Church	1,000
Battle of Kenesaw Mountain	1,000
Battle of the 20th of July	6,000
Battle of the 22d of July	13,000
Battle of the 28th of July	5,500
Total rebel loss	43,700

Their loss in cannon exceeded 30, including 8 sixty-four pounders, while at least 20,000 stand of small arms have been left by them upon the field, and come into our possession otherwise. In two battles they lost 23 stand of colors, which were for a time in the possession of Generals Hooker and Frank Blair.

September 2.—The blockade running steamer Mary Bowers (British) was run ashore near Long Island, South Carolina, and totally lost.

September 3.—The United States ship Brandywine was burned in Hampton Roads, Virginia, being used at the time as a storeship.

——— The President of the United States issued a proclamation, alluding to the late successes of the Union arms, and recommending that the next Sunday should be observed as a day of thanksgiving. Also proclamations returning thanks to Admiral Farragut, General Canby, General Granger, and General Sherman, their officers and men, for the recent victories at Mobile and Atlanta.

September 4.—Reports reached Memphis, Tennessee, that the United States gunboats Hastings and Naumkeag had been captured by rebels on the White River.

——— General Sherman issued an order declaring that the city of Atlanta was to be held exclusively for warlike purposes, and ordering all the inhabitants to remove to the North or South, as they might desire. A proposition was sent to General Hood for a truce for ten days, to complete the evacuation. The latter acceded, protesting that the measure was inhuman.

——— Battle at Berryville, Virginia, between Union troops of Crooks's command and part of Early's forces. The latter made a strong attack, but were repulsed in every charge, losing 500 killed and wounded, and 50 prisoners. Union loss about 100 killed and wounded.

——— The rebel General John H. Morgan was surprised at Greenville, Tennessee, by General A. C. Gillem. The rebel force was dispersed, losing over 50 killed, 75 prisoners, and 1 gun. Morgan was killed.

September 7.—Dibrell's rebel brigade, 2000 strong, was surprised by Colonel Jorden, 9th Pennsylvania cavalry, with 230 men, near Readyville, Tennessee, who took 130 prisoners, and killed and wounded many. Union loss, 10 killed, wounded, and missing.

September 8.—The rebel General Price crossed the Arkansas River at Dardanelles, for the invasion of Missouri.

——— General McClellan addressed a letter of acceptance from Orange, New Jersey, to the committee appointed by the Chicago Convention to apprise him of his nomination.

September 9.—Rebel rifle-pits near the Jerusalem Plank Road, Virginia, were captured by three regiments under General De Trobriand, who took 90 prisoners.

——— The rebels made a strong attack upon the skirmish line in front of the 2d corps at Petersburg, and were repulsed.

September 10.—English blockade runner steamer Matagorda, alias "Alice," captured by United States steamer Magnolia.

——— Blockade runner steamer Habana captured off Yucatan Banks.

——— An expedition returned to Fort Morgan, Alabama, which had been sent out to burn and destroy rebel salt-works at Bonsecour Bay. 15 salt-houses, capable of making 1125 bushels of salt per day, were destroyed.

September 13.—A reconnoissance near Winchester by Sheridan's cavalry, under Generals Getty, Wilson, and McIntosh. The 8th South Carolina regiment was captured entire, 17 officers, 145 men, and 1 battle flag.

September 16.—5000 rebel cavalry, under Wade Hampton, made a dash upon the cattle-pens of the Army of the Potomac, overcame the guards, and ran off 2485 beeves, besides capturing 300 prisoners, and some horses and mules. The raiders were pursued, but ineffectually.

September 18.—Battle of Opequan, Virginia. The Union army under General P. H. Sheridan attacked Early's rebel troops. The battle commenced at daylight and lasted until 7 o'clock in the evening. The rebels were defeated, losing 4200 prisoners, 5 guns, 9 battle flags, 6000 small arms, and 4000 killed and wounded. The rebels lost Generals Rhodes and Godwin killed, and Carter and York wounded. Brigadier-General David Russell, Union, was killed at the head of his brigade. Wounded, Generals Chapman, McIntosh, and Upton. Entire Federal loss estimated at 4000. On the 28th of September it was officially announced that the number of rebel prisoners taken thus far at Opequan and Fisher's Hill was 8000, including the wounded. The total loss of the rebels in both battles estimated at 10,000.

September 19.—The merchant steamers Island Queen and Parsons were seized on Lake Erie by secessionists, who went on board the first named in the guise of passengers. The enterprise failed. The Island Queen sunk and the Parsons was abandoned. The whole party was captured by the United States gunboat Michigan, and several American citizens, inhabitants of Sandusky, who were in the plot, were arrested.

—— A train of 200 wagons was captured at Cabin Creek, Kansas, by 1500 rebels under Sturdivant. The value of the train was $1,000,000.

September 21.—John C. Fremont and John Cochrane, nominated for President and Vice-President of the United States by the Radical Democracy, withdrew their names from the contest.

September 22.—Battle of Fisher's Hill, Virginia. General Sheridan, pursuing Early's army in retreat, found them strongly posted. But the position was turned by Crook's cavalry, who drove the rebels, whilst the 6th and 19th corps attacked them in front. They were soon put to the rout, losing 21 pieces of artillery, 1100 small arms, and 2400 prisoners, besides killed and wounded, probably 1500. Federal losses estimated at 700 killed, wounded, and missing.

—— Alexander H. Stephens, the rebel Vice-President, wrote a letter to the citizens of Charlottesville, in which he avowed himself in favor of an armistice and peace, provided that the states went into the convention as acknowledged independent sovereignties. He said, "The action of the Chicago Convention, so far as its principle and platform goes, presents, as I have said on another occasion, a ray of light which under Providence may prove the dawn of the day to this long and cheerless night—the first ray of light I have seen from the North since the war began."

September 23.—4000 men of Forrest's forces crossed the Tennessee River at Bates's Landing. They attacked Athens, Alabama, and captured it, after a fight of two hours.

—— Hon. Montgomery Blair, Postmaster-General, tendered his resignation of that office to the President, which was accepted, and —— Dennison, of Ohio, appointed in his stead.

September 24.—Fredericktown, 20 miles east of Pilot Knob, Missouri, was occupied by Shelby's rebel cavalry.

—— A cavalry fight near Luray Court House, Virginia, between Torbert's Union horsemen and Wickham's rebel force. The rebels were defeated, losing several hundred killed and wounded, and 70 prisoners.

September 25.—English blockade running steamer Lynx run ashore on the coast of North Carolina, and burned.

September 26.—Staunton, Virginia, was entered by General Torbert, with Union cavalry, who destroyed a large quantity of rebel property, provisions, &c., and then proceeded to Waynesboro, where similar destruction was effected.

September 26.—Skirmishing took place all day near Pulaski, Tennessee, between Forrest's and Rousseau's troops. Forrest retired towards Lafayette, and Rousseau went back to Nashville.

—— Henry W. Allen, "Governor" of Louisiana, wrote a letter to the rebel Secretary of War, in which he says "the time has come for us to put into the army every able-bodied negro as a soldier."

September 27.—21 soldiers, most of them discharged veterans, returning home from Atlanta, were captured on a railroad train by Price's guerrillas, at Centralia. They were shot, and their bodies horribly mutilated. 4 citizens were also wounded, and the train was set on fire and started off at full speed. About an hour afterwards, Major Johnson, with 150 militia, arrived at Centralia, and started in pursuit. His men were ambushed, and 91 of their number, including the Major, were killed.

—— Jeff Davis, the rebel President, made a speech at the headquarters of General Hood, in which, turning to Cheatham's division of Tennesseeans, he said, "Be of good cheer, for within a short time your faces will be turned homeward and your feet pressing Tennessee soil."

—— Marianna, Florida, was taken by an expedition under General Asboth, with 81 prisoners, including a brigadier-general, horses, mules, cattle, &c. Federal loss, 32 killed and wounded.

September 28.—Fort Hodson, Florida, taken by assault by United States colored troops, under General Asboth.

September 29.—Hood's rebel army commenced its march for the purpose of executing a grand flanking movement on Sherman, getting in his rear, and driving him out of Atlanta.

—— The United States steam packet Roanoke, Captain Drew, left Havana for New York. Going out of the port the vessel was boarded by three boats, containing persons represented to be passengers, who were taken on board. The same evening the latter attacked the officers and crew, killed the carpenter, and announced that the steamer was captured by the authority of the Confederate States. The leader was Lieutenant Braine, conspicuous in a similar transaction with the steamer Chesapeake. The passengers were put on board a vessel passing by, and the Roanoke stood out to sea. Being out of coal the rebels set her on fire, and went into Bermuda in boats.

—— Battle of Chaffin's Farm, Virginia. General Ord, in command of the 18th corps, the night before crossed the James River, and in the morning carried the very strong intrenchments and long line of fortifications below Chaffin's Farm, with 16 pieces of artillery and 350 prisoners. General Birney, at the same time, advanced from Deep Bottom, and carried the Newmarket Road and intrenchments. General Ord and General Stannard were wounded. General Burnham killed. About the same time, General Kautz, with the cavalry, made a reconnoissance, and went within two miles of Richmond.

—— After the capture of the first line of works by the 10th corps, which was done with the bayonet, a second line at some distance was taken by a rapid march. A demonstration against a lunette three-quarters of a mile further on failed after three assaults, in which the colored troops suffered severely.

—— The rebel General Price, with his whole force, made an attack upon the fort at Ironton, or Pilot Knob, Missouri, which was defended by General Thomas Ewing: They made an attempt to carry the fort by assault, but were repulsed, with a loss of 1000 killed and wounded. Federal loss, 9 killed and 60 wounded. In the night General Ewing blew up the fort and evacuated Pilot Knob, bringing away his whole command safely.

—— English blockade running steamer Night Hawk run ashore and destroyed, off Chew Inlet, North Carolina.

September 30.—Major-General Warren, of the Army of the Potomac, made an attack upon the rebel works at Peeble's Farm, on the extreme right, and captured two lines of earthworks, with prisoners.

do moved from his left and
Poplar Springs Church,
re captured, a mile and a
50 prisoners. Union loss,
Total loss of Meade and
d, wounded, and missing.
d 9th corps and flanked a

attack in three strong
near Chaffin's Farm, Virision of the 18th corps.
y heavy fire, which swept

aughn was driven out of
on, Tennessee, by General

r steamer Condor beached
n, North Carolina. Mrs.
was drowned.
dge, with 2500 mounted
south-west Virginia, and
ers, and several horses.
ngly defended by Echols
rew. Federal loss, 350

ole force of cavalry, apbama, and demanded its

rgia, captured by Hood's
nt up from lower Georgia
aring Sherman's line of
g in his rear.
made upon Allatoona,
00 strong, under General
ntry. The garrison, 1700
sponded bravely, and the
oss of 300 killed, and 1000
loss, 600 killed, wounded,
f Allatoona was the turnget in the rear of Sher-

inner steamer Constance,
eston harbor, was sunk.
War Department revokes
18 and 45 years of age,
army.
Enquirer published an
iption of negro slaves as

orrest escaped from Geneing him, by crossing the
above and below Florence,

y, Georgia. Union troops
ttacked the rebels under

Price attempted to cross
Rock, Missouri, and was
he opposite side.
under General Price ap-
Missouri.
ian reported that he had
irginia, having made the
Ridge to North Mountain
He destroyed over 2000
and farming implements,
and wheat, and took over
ep. The destruction em-
lo Fort Valley, and Main

attack upon the Union
irginia, and drove Kautz's
nts. They then advanced
e severely repulsed. The
the Federal troops, and
captured. The rebels lost
200 prisoners. Kautz lost
regg was killed, and Gen.
l loss, 300 killed, wounded,

October 7.—The rebel privateer Florida, lying in Bahia Bay, off San Salvador, was run into by the United States gunboat Wachusett, Commander Collins. The Florida was summoned to surrender, which was done. The Wachusett then towed out the Florida. 12 officers and 58 men were captured. 5 officers and the rest of the crew were on shore.

October 8.—Hopkinsville, Kentucky, attacked by 700 rebels, who were repulsed.

——— An attack was made on Jefferson City, Missouri, by Price's troops, who were repulsed, and followed for 7 miles.

October 9.—Battle of Round Top Mountain, or Tom Brook, Virginia. The rebel cavalry general, Rosser, following General Sheridan to Strasburg, Virginia, was attacked by the latter and defeated by Torbert, Custer, and Merrit, in a cavalry fight. The rebels lost 11 guns, 330 prisoners, 47 wagons, and killed and wounded, and were raced back 26 miles.

——— California, Missouri, was entered by Price's rebels, who burned the depot and cars. A short time afterwards the rebels were driven out, with a loss of 100 killed and wounded.

October 10.—The English blockade runner steamer Bat, a steel-built vessel, was captured by the United States steamer Montgomery, at sea.

——— Colonel Hoge, with 1300 United States soldiers and a battery of 4 guns, on board of three transports, convoyed by three gunboats, was repulsed at East Point, Tennessee, by Forrest's forces, losing 20 killed, and 26 wounded and missing.

October 11.—An election to determine whether the new Constitution of Maryland should be adopted, was held in that state. Among other reforms, this instrument provided for the abolition of slavery. The Constitution was adopted by the following vote: for the constitution, 31,174 votes; against it, 29,199 votes.

October 12.—Minty's brigade of Union cavalry drove the rebel Roddy's command out of Rome, Georgia, taking all his artillery.

——— An English blockade runner steamer was sunk in Charleston Harbor.

——— Roger B. Taney, Chief Justice of the United States, died in Washington, D. C.

——— The rebels demanded the surrender of Resaca, Georgia, which was defended by Colonel Weaver and the 8th Ohio regiment. The demand was refused, and after some skirmishing the rebels withdrew.

——— Major-General Butler having information to the effect that 110 United States colored soldiers, prisoners of war, had been put to work upon the rebel fortifications in front of their lines, exposed to the fire of the Union batteries, ordered an equal number of Virginia prisoners to be set to work upon the canal at Dutch Gap, exposed to the rebel fire. The order was executed two days afterwards, and in a short time produced the effect of removing the negroes from the rebel fortifications.

October 13.—Dalton, Mississippi, was disgracefully surrendered by Colonel Johnson, 8th United States colored troops, without firing a gun. It was believed that he could have held it successfully until reinforced.

——— A railroad train on the Baltimore and Ohio Railroad was stopped near Kearneysville, Virginia, by the removal of a rail from the track. Moseby's guerrillas then appeared, and robbed the passengers of their money, about $160,000, watches, and effects, after which they ordered the passengers out of the cars, and burned the train.

October 14.—The headquarters of Price's rebel army were reported to be at Booneville, Missouri, at which place Price made a speech, stating that "he came to Missouri to redeem the people of that state. It was the last effort in their behalf, and if they would rally to his standard all would be well, and he would remain with them. If not, the Confederacy would not again offer them an opportunity for redemption from their woes."

——— Moseby's camp, near Piedmont, Virginia, was captured by Colonel Gansevoort, 13th New York cavalry, with 4 guns, and a large number of prisoners and horses.

October 14.—Poolesville, Maryland, was entered by a small guerrilla force of Moseby's men, who robbed the citizens, and then retreated.

—— Glasgow, Missouri, was captured by a rebel force of 6000 men, under Generals Clark and Shelby. The place was bravely defended by six companies of the 43d Missouri, Colonel Harding, for five hours. The rebels lost about 250 killed and wounded. Union loss, 35 killed and wounded, and 800 prisoners.

October 15.—Sedalia, Missouri, was captured by a force of 2000 rebels, under Jeff Thompson.

—— Ringgold, Georgia, was reoccupied by Union troops.

October 16.—Bridge at Mossy Creek, Virginia, burned y Breckinridge's forces.

—— Advices from General Sherman were received, o the effect that Hood, after having struck the railroad in the neighborhood of Dalton and Resaca, had fallen back before Sherman without fighting, thus abandoning the great flank movement to get in Sherman's rear, cut him off from the railroad, and invade Tennessee. About 15 miles of railroad were destroyed by the rebels, which were restored in a few days.

—— Ship's Gap, Georgia, taken by General Sherman, following the retreat of Hood's army.

October 17.—The rebel General Peter G. Toutant Beauregard assumes command of "the military division of the west," comprising the armies of Hood, Dick Taylor, and Price, which remain under their respective commanders.

—— The governors of the states of Virginia, North Carolina, South Carolina, Georgia, Alabama, and Mississippi, held a meeting at Augusta, Georgia, and resolved that there was nothing to abate their zeal in the military situation of the South; also, that the rebel army ought to be strengthened by the addition of every man that could be obtained, and that slaves ought to be put in military service, if required.

—— Ten or twelve of the principal commercial houses of Baltimore, Maryland, were closed, and the proprietors arrested upon charges of holding contraband trade with the rebels.

October 18.—A fair for the benefit of rebel soldiers was opened at St. George's Hall, Liverpool, England, by the Countess of Chester, Countess Dampierre, Lady Wharncliffe, and secession women.

—— The Union troops evacuated Bull's Gap, and retired to Knoxville.

—— Colonel Minty's brigade of cavalry met the rebels in force in Georgia, and, after a severe fight, routed them, taking General Young prisoner.

October 19.—25 armed men came from Canada to St. Albans, Vermont, and robbed the banks there of $223,000. They shot five citizens. Several of the party were arrested in Canada. They professed to be rebel soldiers.

—— General Blunt, with 2000 Union cavalry, was attacked by Price at Lexington, Missouri, who drove him out with loss. Blunt fell back to the Little Blue River, fighting all the way. Skirmishing continued for two days following, Blunt falling back. Federal loss, 400 killed and wounded.

—— Battle of Cedar Creek, Virginia. Early's army, by a bold flank movement through the mountains, succeeded in reaching the left of the lines of Sheridan's army, about daylight. They attacked with great impetuosity, and drove the Union troops back four miles in great confusion, with the loss of 24 pieces of artillery and many killed, wounded, and prisoners. The day seemed to be lost, and the Union army badly defeated. General Sheridan, who was absent, arrived on the field about noon. His presence reanimated the soldiers. His lines were re-formed, and at 3 o'clock the rebels were attacked with great vigor. The disasters of the morning were retrieved, the enemy were routed and driven in great confusion, losing all the artillery captured by them in the morning, besides others, in all 57, with caissons, wagon trains, 12,000 small arms, and 10 battle flags and ambulances. On the Federal side, killed, General Bidwell and Colonel Thoburn, commanding a division; wounded, Generals Wright, Grover, and Ricketts, Colonel J. H. Kitchen, and Colonel ing brigade. The rebel Ge wounded. General Rams prisoner, and afterwards prisoners, and were pursue whole loss in killed, wou mated at 10,000 men.

October 21.—The Englis Nando, alias Let-her-rip, ca Carolina, by the United St

October 22.—The Engli Hope was captured by Uni Charleston, South Carolina

October 23.—The Engli Florinae, attempting to run line, was chased ashore an

—— The rebel fleet on Gap, were driven from thei opened upon them from tw

—— British blockad sunk in Charleston Harbor

October 25.—Battle of th rebel army in Missouri wa by Union forces pressing l eral Marmaduke and Br taken prisoners. The ret south, and were followed vi who captured 15 pieces of nearly all the rebel wagon

October 26.—Witcher's g Winfield, Virginia, and we

—— Brigadier-Gener tured in the valley of Virg

October 27.—Three rebe Chickamauga, and Olustee, Carolina, despite the vigil They caused great destr commercial vessels on the

—— The rebel ram A the Roanoke River, North torpedo worked from a command of Lieutenant The force of the explosi Cushing and one seaman s rest of the crew, eleven captured.

—— Ferry and arrested in Baltimore, a Washington, D. C., charg plot to send forward to mense number of fraudu soldiers, living and dead, the Presidential election, N hue were tried by court-ma to imprisonment for life.

—— Lieutenant-Gene sance in force along his advanced to the Boydtwn and Armstrong's Mill. strongly posted, and his l soners were taken from th 1500, of whom 800 were p

October 28.—The rebel was defeated at Norristow lem, who captured 500 pri

—— Battle of Newt army were defeated by F of Blunt's division. Uni with two colonels capture

October 29.—Governor I declaring that the new C adopted, and would go int

—— Decatur, Alaban General Hood, who was Granger, who captured 6

—— The Union garri attacked by 350 rebels o repulsed with a loss of 1 large number wounded, Major Hill. Union loss,

1864. *October 7.*—The rebel privateer Florida was captured in the port of Bahia, Brazil, by the United States sloop of war Wachusetts, Captain Collins, while lying in the midst of the Brazilian fleet and under the guns of two forts. Captain Collins immediately got up steam, and towed out the Florida under fire of Brazilian ships and batteries. 12 officers and 58 men were taken prisoners, the captain and part of the crew being on shore.

October 9.—The British steamer Sea King, Captain Peter S. Corbett, left London in ballast, cleared for Bombay.

——— Same day, or about the same day, the British steamer Laurel left Liverpool, laden with cannon, muskets, swords, powder, shells, balls, and other warlike articles, ostensibly bound to Nassau to run the blockade.

October 18.—The British steamer Sea King appeared off Madeira, where the Laurel was in port. Signals were made to the latter and she came out; the two steamers, being under the British flag, went to the Portuguese island of Porto Santo. Here the cargo of guns, ammunition, &c., on board the Laurel were transferred to the Sea King. The latter was then taken possession of by a rebel officer named Waddell, and a crew mainly of Englishmen and Irishmen, a few of the officers being Americans hailing from the Southern States. The English flag was now hauled down and the rebel ensign hoisted, and the *Sea King*, under the name of the *Shenandoah*, set out upon a mission of destruction. The Laurel returned to England, and although these transactions were shortly afterwards made public, she was not disturbed by the English government.

October 31.—Plymouth, North Carolina, was captured by Commander W. D. Macomb, U.S. Navy, with a fleet of gunboats and small vessels; after some fighting with the shore batteries, the latter were abandoned. 22 guns, a large quantity of ammunition, with small arms, &c., were taken, and also the ram Albemarle, sunk at the wharf. The latter was afterwards raised and put in service.

November 2.—Secretary Seward apprised the mayors of New York and Buffalo, that information had been received from the British Provinces that there was a conspiracy on foot to set fire to the principal cities in the Northern States on election day. Mayor Gunther, of New York, replied: "I have no fears of such threats being carried out, or even attempted."

——— English blockade running steamer Lucy captured off Wilmington, North Carolina.

November 4.—The gunboat Undine, captured from the United States by the rebels, was set on fire by the rebels near Reynoldsburg Island, near Johnsonville, Tennessee. Two Union gunboats which opened upon them were driven back by batteries on shore.

——— The Anglo-rebel privateer Shenandoah, Captain Waddell, formerly the Sea King, captured the United States brig Susan, in latitude 4.30 north, longitude 26.20 west.

November 5.—English blockade runner Ella chased on shore near Wilmington, North Carolina, by the United States gunboat Emma, and destroyed.

——— Forrest's rebel troops under Chalmers and Buford attacked Johnsonville, Tennessee, by cannon planted on the opposite side of the river, and sunk 4 gunboats of 8 guns each, 14 steamers, 20 barges, and destroyed a large quantity of commissary stores on the landing and in storehouses, estimated at 75,000 tons.

November 8.—Election for President and Vice-President of the United States. Electors favorable to Abraham Lincoln and Andrew Johnson were chosen in 25 states, having 233 electoral votes. Three states, New Jersey, Delaware, and Kentucky, having 21 electoral votes, chose electors pledged to the election of George B. McClellan and George H. Pendleton. The popular vote, excluding that of Louisiana and Tennessee, not counted, was for Lincoln and Johnson, 2,203,831; for McClellan and Pendleton, 1,797,019. Lincoln's majority, 406,812.

November 8.—The rebel privateer Chickamauga, *alias* the Edith, Captain Wilkinson, arrived at Bermuda, having run through the blockading fleet at Wilmington, North Carolina. On her passage she made seven captures, including one ship and four barks.

November 9.—John Rantz, Samuel Kline, and William Appleman, of Columbia county, Pennsylvania, accused of conspiring, counselling against, and resisting the draft, which some of them did by the use of arms, were convicted by a court-martial, and ordered to be fined and imprisoned.

——— An attack was made upon Atlanta, Georgia, by rebel infantry and cavalry under General Young. They supposed that the town had been abandoned, but being soon convinced of their mistake, withdrew, having lost 900 prisoners.

——— Major-General Sherman at Kingston, Georgia, issued orders for a grand march, the army to be divided into two wings: the right under Major-General O. O. Howard, composed of the 15th and 17th corps; the left, under Major-General H. W. Slocum, consisting of the 14th and 20th corps. The cavalry an independent command, under General Kilpatrick.

November 10.—Pine Barren Ridge, Florida, captured by Federal troops under Colonel Spilling. They destroyed stores and barracks, and brought back stores and provisions.

——— A party of rebel pirates on "detached service," namely, Captain O. E. Hogg, E. A. Swain, J. L. Black, R. B. Lyon, John Hiddle, and Joseph Higgins, who had arranged a plot to take passage on board the United States packet steamer Salvador, from Panama to San Francisco, and to rise and take possession of the steamer when at sea, as was done in the case of the Chesapeake, were captured on board the Salvador; the vessel being taken possession of by armed crews from the United States frigate Lancaster, near Panama.

——— The resignation of Major-General George B. McClellan, dated November 8th, was received at the War Department and accepted. General Sheridan was appointed to the vacancy in the regular army.

November 11.—A cavalry skirmish near Kearnstown, Virginia, between Union cavalry under Custer and Merritt and the rebel cavalry. The latter advanced in some force, but coming upon the Federal reserves were forced to retreat.

——— General Gillem, at Bull's Gap, Kentucky, was attacked by rebel forces under the rebel General John C. Breckinridge, which attempted to carry the lines by assault, but failed. Union loss, 8 killed and 19 wounded.

——— United States gunboat Tulip, Master William H. Smith, blown up on the Potomac River, by explosion of her boilers. 59 officers and men were killed; but 10 escaped, all of them being scalded and wounded.

November 12.—The army of Major-General Sherman, being ready for a great movement through Georgia, left Atlanta, Rome, and other places of rendezvous, prepared for a campaign of 50 days. The expedition commenced its march upon the evening of the 12th inst., with a division of Kilpatrick's cavalry, under General McCook, and the 20th corps, General Slocum, in advance. This advance was to proceed slowly in the direction of Macon, and to be followed by the 14th corps, General Jeff. C. Davis. The Army of the Tennessee, General Howard, composed of the 15th corps, General Logan: 16th, General Smith; and 17th, General Frank Blair, left Kingston three days before for Atlanta, tearing up the railroad as it went along. On the 11th the Etowah Bridge was destroyed, and from thence to the Chattahoochee River the work of destruction was complete. As these troops proceeded, marching on parallel roads, they tore up railroads, burned bridges, and foraged on the country. General Sherman left Kingston, declaring his purpose, and bidding the North adieu in the following remarkable telegram: "Hood has crossed the Tennessee. Thomas will take care of him and Nashville, while

Schofield will not let him into Chattanooga or Knoxville. Georgia and South Carolina are at my mercy, and I shall strike. Do not be anxious about me, I am all right."

November 12.—Rebel cavalry under Lomax advanced against General Sheridan's lines in the Shenandoah Valley, Virginia. After considerable fighting, they were repulsed. A charge was then made by Colonel Powell, who pursued the enemy several miles, and beyond Front Royal. Rebel loss, 2 guns, 150 prisoners, several wagons and horses. Union loss, considerable.

November 13.—Battle of Panthers' Gap, Kentucky. General Gillem retreating towards Knoxville, having only 2400 men, was attacked by Breckinridge in force, about midnight, on both flanks and in his centre. The command was surrounded, fought bravely, but at length gave way and took to flight. The rebels pursued them twenty-four miles. Union loss, killed, wounded, and missing, 220. It would have been very heavy had it not been for the darkness. Six Parrott guns were lost by Gillem, and half the small arms of his men, which were thrown away, with all his trains, baggage, cattle, &c.

November 14.—Incendiary fires, kindled by rebel emissaries upon detached service, occurred at New York in several large hotels, viz., the St. Nicholas, Lafarge, St. James, Belmont, Metropolitan, Tammany, Lovejoy's, United States, Howard, Fifth Avenue, Astor, New England, and also at the Winter Garden, Barnum's Museum, and Niblo's Garden theatres. The fires occurred about the same time and under similar circumstances, camphene, turpentine, and phosphorus being used in the rooms where the flames originated, and an arrangement being made to assist in the rapid spread of the fire. The excitement was very great; but, luckily, the damage done was very small.

——— Kilpatrick's cavalry, of Sherman's army, made a dash into Jonesboro', Georgia, driving out the rebel Wheeler, who burnt his stores before the retreat.

——— Wheeler, with his cavalry and militia, 4000 strong, was defeated at Lovejoy by Kilpatrick's cavalry, who carried the earthworks by a charge. 2 guns were taken, and 40 rebels killed.

——— The following was published in the Northern papers:—

"In the Richmond *Whig*, of July 24th, appeared the following proposition:—

"'The Devoted Band.—It is believed that there are five or ten thousand men in the South ready and willing to share the fate of Curtius, and devote themselves to the salvation of their country. It is proposed that all who are willing to make this sacrifice shall arm themselves with a sword, two five-shooters, and a carbine each, and meet on horseback at some place to be designated, convenient for the great work in hand. Fire and sword must be carried into the houses of those who are visiting those blessings upon their neighbors. Philadelphia, and even New York, is not beyond the reach of a long and brave arm. The moral people of these cities cannot be better taught the virtues of invasion than by the blazing light of their own dwellings.

"'None need apply for admission to the 'Devoted Band' but those who are prepared to take their lives in their hands, and would indulge not the least expectation of ever returning. They dedicate their lives to the destruction of their enemies.

"'A. S. B. D. B., Richmond.

"'All Southern papers are requested to give this notice a few insertions.'"

November 16.—Preparations for the evacuation of Atlanta, Georgia, being made. The public buildings were fired, and the town abandoned. The two wings of the army began the movement simultaneously, the right moving directly south, and the left due east from Atlanta. General Howard's wing, with a large cavalry force in advance, moved through Eastpoint, and at Rough and Ready encountered a cavalry force under General Iverson, and a brisk but brief engagement followed, in which the rebels were driven. Slocum encamped that night near Jonesboro'. The left wing, under General Slocum, moved out to Decatur, where the two corps divided, one going direct by the Covington road, parallel with the Georgia Railroad, while the other moved north of the railroad by way of Rockbridge, each destined for Covington.

November 17.—Wheeler's rebel cavalry were driven out of Jonesboro' and McDonough, Georgia, by Howard's troops. The court-house and public buildings at McDonough were burned.

——— Same day, Slocum entered Social Circle and burned the buildings there.

——— Rebels in front of General Butler's picket-lines, on the James River, Virginia, surprised the guards and captured the positions, taking about 60 prisoners, losing, themselves, 15.

November 18.—General Butler recaptured his picket-lines, taken by the rebels on the previous night.

——— A company of scouts under Captain Brasher, intending to surprise Moseby's rebel guerrillas, fell into an ambush, and the whole party was defeated, losing, killed, 22; wounded, 8; prisoners, 32.

November 19.—The rebel General Beauregard issues a proclamation, from Corinth, to the people of Georgia, advising them to "obstruct and destroy all roads in Sherman's front, flank, and rear, and his army will soon starve in your midst."

——— Hood's advance, under General Frank Cheatham, entered Waynesboro', Tennessee.

——— Governor Joseph E. Brown, of Georgia, issues a proclamation, from Milledgeville, ordering a levy *en masse* of the whole white population of the state between 16 and 65 years of age, to resist the advance of General Sherman.

November 20.—Kilpatrick's cavalry carried several lines of rebel works, in advance of Macon, Georgia. They halted two miles from the town, where they took 8 guns, which they were unable to bring away. Meanwhile, the main force was operating upon the railroad, and destroying it.

November 22.—Battle at Griswoldville, Georgia. The rebels made an attack upon Howard's division of Sherman's army, and were repulsed, leaving 300 dead on the field.

——— Brigadier-General A. L. Lee, U.S. Army, arrived at Baton Rouge after an expedition to Liberty and Brookville, Louisiana, in which were captured 200 prisoners, 25 officers, 3 guns, and 700 horses and mules.

——— Battle of Rood's Hill, Virginia, between two divisions of United States cavalry, under Generals Powell, Custer, and Tibbetts, and Early's rebel force, 15,000 strong. There was considerable fighting, and charges were made on both sides. The object of the Federal cavalry being a reconnoissance of the rebel position, after acquiring the desired information they withdrew. Federal loss, 60 killed and wounded.

November 23.—Sherman's troops entered Milledgeville, Georgia. The legislature, previously in session, had abandoned the town. The penitentiary, arsenal, and magazine were destroyed.

November 24.—Mrs. Sarah Hutchings, of Baltimore, Md., found guilty by a military commission of attempting to send a sword to the rebel Colonel Harry Gilmore, was sentenced to pay $5000 fine and to be imprisoned 5 years. She was sent to the Fitchburg Penitentiary, Massachusetts.

——— Skirmishing at Columbia, Tennessee, between Hood's army and General Thomas's rear guard. Thomas had evacuated Pulaski, Huntsville, and Decatur, and was retiring before the advance of Hood. Federal loss, on the 24th, 44 men killed and wounded. Rebel loss, 264, including one colonel.

——— 2000 cavalry set out from Vicksburg, under Colonel E. D. Ostrand. They carried the Big Black Bridge, on the Mississippi Central Railroad, on the 27th, and cut off Hood's supplies at Jackson. Railroad tracks, depots, buildings, bridges, cars, locomotives, and provisions were destroyed.

November 25.—Hon. Edward Bates, Attorney-General of the United States, resigned, to take effect December 1.

November 27.—The United States steamer Greyhound, used by Major-General Butler as a dispatch-boat, took fire in the James River. Major-General Butler, Major-General Schenck, and Rear-Admiral Porter were on board, with many other officers. All persons on board were taken off by another steamer, but the horses, stores, and other articles were destroyed.

November 27.—Kilpatrick's cavalry, of Sherman's army, on an excursion towards Millen, Georgia, were attacked by the rebels under Wheeler, near Waynesboro', who followed on their flanks and made constant attacks.

November 28.—Fighting between Kilpatrick's and Wheeler's rebel cavalry. The latter did not succeed in preventing the Federal advance. Kilpatrick made 30 miles march that day.

—— The prize steamer Florida, captured at Bahia, was sunk near Fortress Monroe, being in a leaky condition, in consequence of a collision with a transport.

—— New Creek, Virginia, was taken by Payne, with 2000 rebel cavalry. It was defended by a small infantry force. The buildings were blown up and stores destroyed. The rebels went up to Piedmont, and destroyed the railroad buildings there.

—— The Anglo-rebel blockade runner steamer Beatrice run ashore below Charleston, South Carolina, and was destroyed by the guns of the United States fleet.

November 29.—Battle of Spring Hill, Tennessee, between Thomas's army, in retreat, and Hood's army pushing on towards Nashville. The Federal cavalry was hardly pressed and driven back on the infantry lines.

November 30.—A raiding party of United States cavalry, 5000 strong, left Baton Rouge, Louisiana, under General Davidson, with 12 pieces of artillery, for operations in Eastern Louisiana.

—— Battle of Honey Hill, 3 miles east of Grahamsville, South Carolina. The rebels, under General Gustavus W. Smith, behind field-works, repulsed United States troops under General Foster. Rebel loss, 15 killed and 80 wounded. Union loss, 600 killed and wounded.

—— Battle of Franklin, Tennessee. The rebel army with two corps made an attack upon the Federal army of Thomas, the rear guard being then under command of General J. M. Schofield. The enemy was repulsed at all points, having made four desperate charges, and losing between 5000 and 6000 killed and wounded, 1000 prisoners, including General Gordon, and 30 stand of colors. In consequence of the Federal troops fighting behind breastworks, they were much protected. The rebels lost by making desperate charges under a terrible musketry and artillery fire. On the night of the battle the Federal army withdrew and crossed the Harpeth River, and resumed the retreat to Nashville. Wounded on the Federal side, Major-General Stanley, General Bradley, Lieutenant-Colonel Stockton, 72d Illinois, Major James, 72d Illinois, Colonel Walters, Colonel Conrad, Major Starling, Major Goodspeed. Killed on Federal side, Colonel Oblehr, 85th Illinois; Lieutenant Burdick, 23d Ohio; Lieutenant Kimball, 104th Ohio; Captain Lowrey, 107th Ohio. Killed on the rebel side, Major-General Pat. Cleborne, Brigadier-Generals John Williams, Adams, Gist, Strahl, and Granberry. Wounded, Major-General John Brown, Brigadier-Generals S. Carter, Manigault, Quarlls, Cockerell, and Scott.

December 1.—Davidson's raiders captured Tangipaho, Mississippi, and burned the rebel camp there and the railroad.

—— The Great Sanitary Fair held in New York closed its accounts, the net proceeds being $1,180,091.27.

December 2.—A reconnoissance was made to Stony Creek, Virginia, by General Gregg's division of cavalry. They took a fort, 3 cannon, 1200 rifles, corn, potatoes, &c., and destroyed them, together with a railroad bridge. They returned with 181 officers. Federal loss, 27 killed and wounded.

—— Sherman's troops entered Millen, Georgia.

—— The rebel General John C. Breckinridge, at Wytheville, Virginia, issued an order stating "that it has become of vital importance to husband small arms, ammunition, and lead. All lead which can be gleaned from battle-fields, or otherwise obtained, will be collected by the brigade ordnance officers, and be sent to the nearest arsenal. All arms to be relieved of their loads for cleaning; the balls should be withdrawn, if possible; otherwise the loads should be discharged into boxes of sand or dirt, so that the lead may be recovered and turned into the ordnance department." By another order, special commands are given to insure economy in the use of forage.

December 3.—The English blockade-running steamer Vixen, attempting to enter Wilmington, North Carolina, was captured by the United States steamer Massachusetts.

—— An English blockade-running steamer was chased on Marshall's Shoals, off Cape Fear River, by Union gunboats. A shot penetrated her boiler, and the boat was blown up.

December 4.—Battle of Overall's Creek, Tennessee, a block-house 4 miles north of Fort Rosecrans, near Murfreesboro', Tennessee. The rebels in strength attacked the block-house, which was well defended. Colonel G. M. L. Johnson was sent to the assistance of the little garrison. They were reinforced after some fighting. Federal loss, about 100.

—— Same day (?), battle of the Cedars, which resulted from following up the rebels. They came to a stand at intrenchments to which they had fallen back. An attack was made on these works, which were carried by assault, putting the rebels to flight. Federal loss, 23 killed, 185 wounded; Major Reid was killed. The rebel loss believed to be as heavy as our own.

—— Waynesboro', Georgia, was taken by Kilpatrick's cavalry after a lively fight with Wheeler. The latter retreated. Kilpatrick's losses were 60 killed and wounded.

—— The English blockade-running steamer Susannah captured by the United States steamer Metacomet, Captain Jouett.

—— The English blockade-running steamer Armstrong, loaded with cotton, was captured by United States gunboats Cuyler and Gettysburg.

—— An expedition sent out from Vicksburg by General Dana returned to that place, having destroyed the Mississippi Central Railroad for 30 miles above Big Black Crossing, including the long bridge at the latter place. 2500 bales of cotton, and property worth $300,000 were destroyed.

December 5.—The rebels, being reinforced by Forrest, made demonstrations against Murfreesboro', and also on the 6th and 7th, with no success.

December 6.—English blockade-running steamer Emma Henry captured by United States steamer Cherokee.

—— Salmon P. Chase was appointed Chief Justice of the United States by the President, and immediately confirmed by the Senate.

—— Battle of Gregory's Landing, South Carolina, between United States troops under General Potter, landing on Broad River, and rebels intrenched there. The fight continued during the greater part of the day, and in the meanwhile intrenchments were thrown up, to secure which was the main object of the movement. The position commanded the Charleston & Savannah Railroad for several miles. Federal loss, 40 killed and wounded.

—— Annual Message of President Lincoln sent to Congress. He took the grounds that any offer of terms to the insurgent leaders would do no good; and that, although the people of the South might accept terms, until the power of the so-called rebel government was broken, a cessation of the war could not be hoped for. He said that the people of the South could at any moment have peace by laying down their arms and submitting to the national government. The report of the Secretary of the Navy contained some interesting statements. The general exhibit of the navy, including vessels under construction, on the 1st of December, 1864, showed a total of 671 vessels, carrying 4610 guns, and of 510,396 tons, being an actual increase during the year over and above all losses by shipwreck and battle, of 83 vessels, 167 guns, and 42,427 tons. The total number of men in the naval service, including officers, was about 51,000. There were captured by the navy during the year 324 vessels, and the whole number of naval captures since hostilities commenced was 1379, of which 267 were steamers. The gross proceeds arising from the sale of condemned prize property thus reported amount to $14,396,250.51. The total expenditure of the Navy Department, of every description, including the cost of the immense squadrons that have been called into existence, from the 4th of March, 1861, to the 1st of November, 1864, was $238,647,262.35.

December 7.—Major-General Warren, with 4 divisions of infantry and 1 of cavalry, left General Grant's lines before Petersburg, and moved in the direction of Weldon, North Carolina. He was accompanied by Generals Griffin, Ayres, Crawford, Mott, and Gregg, and crossed the Nottoway River by pontoons, near the former site of Freeman's Bridge.

——— Battle at Wilkinson's Pike, Tennessee, between Federal troops and Forrest's command. The latter were intrenched, but were utterly routed. Federal loss, 30 killed and 170 wounded. The rebel loss was greater, and also 207 prisoners and 2 guns.

December 8.—William Smith, rebel governor of Virginia, sent a long message to the legislature, in which, among other things, he recommended the employment of negro troops to aid the rebel cause.

——— General Warren's expedition, after some skirmishing, reached Nottoway Bridge, on the Weldon Railroad, which was destroyed, together with a considerable portion of the railroad.

——— An expedition under General Miles left General Grant's lines, composed of cavalry and infantry. The latter marched on the morning of the 9th, and moved south. They crossed Hatcher's Run, meeting with some opposition, but carrying the rebel works by assault. The troops remained at Hatcher's Run, weatherbound, for a day, during which they destroyed a dam and bridge.

December 9.—The United States gunboat Narcissus was blown up in Mobile Bay by a torpedo.

——— United States gunboat Otsego was sunk in Roanoke River by a torpedo, which was attached to a floating log.

——— Same day United States transport Bazely blown up in same way. The boats were proceeding up the river upon an expedition which failed in consequence of non-co-operation of land forces. The expedition returned December 23d, having accomplished nothing, and having met with severe losses.

——— General Warren's expedition was at Jarrett's Station on the Weldon Railroad, and from thence moved south, destroying the road as it advanced; at night the troops were at Bellfield Station, on Meherrin River, having destroyed the railroad for 20 miles. The enemy were found strongly posted at Hick's Ford, and General Warren having accomplished his purpose, which was the destruction of the railroad, returned, devastating the country. He arrived safely within General Grant's lines on the 11th.

December 10.—The rebel General John C. Breckinridge issues a proclamation guaranteeing protection to citizens of Tennessee who, having entered the Federal service, shall return home and enter upon their pursuits as peaceable citizens; also to all persons who went beyond the Federal lines to escape from rebel service.

——— The rebel General Lyon, with 2500 cavalry, crossed the Cumberland River at Yellow Creek, and advanced on Hopkinsville, Kentucky.

——— General Miles's expedition, sent to Hatcher's Run as a diversion in favor of General Warren, returned, its purpose being accomplished.

December 12.—Skirmish near Kinston, North Carolina, on the Neuse road.

——— 4000 mounted men, under Major-General Stoneman, General Burbridge, and General Gillem, left Bean's Station, Kentucky.

——— The first communication from General Sherman since he left Atlanta was received by General Foster by scouts, which left the command of General Howard on the 9th, the army then being 10 miles from Savannah.

December 13.—Stoneman met and defeated Duke's rebel brigade at Kingsport, taking 85 prisoners and killing and wounding 15.

——— The rebel General Lyon entered Hopkinsville, Kentucky, conscripted Union men, robbed stores, and burnt property.

——— The case of the St. Albans raiders was decided at Montreal by Justice Coursol, who gave judgment that the arrests had been made upon illegal warrants, that there was no law which justified him in holding the accused parties, and that they should be discharged. The prisoners left the court, and immediately afterwards the whole amount of the money which they had stolen from the St. Albans banks was restored to them.

——— Fort McAllister, upon the Ogeechee River, below Savannah, was taken by assault by General Hazen's division of the 15th army corps, with 21 guns, 200 prisoners, munitions of war, &c. This victory opened Ossabaw Sound to General Sherman, and he was enabled to communicate with the United States fleet. Before opening communication he had completely destroyed all the railroads leading into Savannah, and invested the city. General Sherman reported to the War Department that he had not lost a wagon on the march, but had gathered a large supply of mules, negroes, horses, &c., and his teams were in better condition than when he started. His army also destroyed 200 miles of railroad and consumed stores and provisions that were essential to Lee's and Hood's armies.

——— A large naval expedition left Fortress Monroe under command of Admiral Porter, the troops being under command of Major-General B. F. Butler and Major-General Godfrey Weitzel, destined for an attack upon Fort Fisher, at the mouth of Cape Fear River, North Carolina. The fleet consisted of 150 vessels of all descriptions. The war vessels were 65, of 570 guns.

——— The correspondence between M. Barboza, Brazilian chargé des affaires, and Mr. Seward, in regard to the seizure of the Florida in the port of Bahia, resulted in the United States declaring that Captain Collins, of the Wachusetts, should be suspended and directed to appear before a court-martial; that the consul at Bahia should be dismissed, the flag of Brazil saluted, and the crew of the Florida released and sent abroad. Whilst consenting to that much, Mr. Seward says: "It is not to be understood, however, that this government admits or gives credit to the charges of falsehood, treachery, and deception which are brought against the captain and the consul. These charges are denied on the authority of the officers accused, and the secretary also takes occasion to say that his government disallows the assumption that the insurgents of this country are a lawful naval belligerent, and, on the contrary, it maintains that the ascription of that character by the government of Brazil to insurgent citizens of the United States who have hitherto been and who are still destitute of naval forces, ports, and courts, is an act of intervention, in derogation of the laws of nations, and unfriendly and wrongful, as it is manifestly injurious to the United States." The action resolved upon was declared to have been determined by the fact that Captain Collins acted without authority.

——— Skirmishing between Rousseau's Federal and Bates's rebel troops, near Murfreesboro.

December 14.—Davidson's raiders reached West Pascagoula, Louisiana, after a long march through the state, and considerable results in the destruction of railroads and other property. The loss during the trip was 2 killed, 8 wounded, and 35 prisoners. The object of the expedition was supposed to have been to menace Mobile. Governor Watts issued a proclamation December 11, calling out all the old men and boys in Alabama to resist the expected invasion.

——— Bristol, Virginia, captured by General Stoneman, who took 250 prisoners, 5 locomotives, two trains of cars, and immense quantities of stores.

December 14.—Abingdon, Virginia, captured by General Burbridge, of Stoneman's expedition. 1 gun, a large amount of stores and rolling stock were taken.

—— Same day General Gillem defeated Vaughan at Marion, Virginia, taking 50 prisoners.

—— Same day the rebels defeated at Mount Airy, Virginia. They lost 7 guns, some prisoners, and a large wagon train.

—— Same day Brown's brigade of Burbridge's expedition captured Wytheville, Virginia, defeating the Home Guard, and capturing 5 pieces of cannon and 8 caissons.

—— Major-General Dix, upon information of the discharge of the St. Albans robbers at Montreal, issued his General Orders No. 97, commanding all military commanders on the frontier, upon the occasion of future depredations, "whether by marauders or persons acting under commissions from the rebel authorities at Richmond, to shoot down the perpetrators if possible while in the commission of their crimes; or, *if it be necessary, with a view to their capture, to cross the boundary between the United States and Canada, said commanders are hereby directed to pursue them wherever they may take refuge*, and, if captured, they are under no circumstances to be surrendered, but are to be sent to these headquarters for trial and punishment by martial law."

December 15.—An expedition from New Orleans, under General Granger, landed at Pascagoula, Louisiana, and pushed towards Mobile. A skirmish occurred on the same day at Franklin, Louisiana.

—— Glade's Spring captured by Major Harrison, 12th Kentucky Volunteers; the Virginia Central Railroad was destroyed for some distance. He continued along the road, destroying it all the way to Wytheville, with bridges, depots, rolling-stock, ironworks, &c.

—— The Anglo-rebel blockade runner Petrel was driven ashore near New Inlet, Cape Fear River, North Carolina, by United States gunboats, and destroyed.

—— Battle of Nashville, Tennessee, 1st day. Major-General Thomas attacked Hood's army, intrenched before Nashville. On the right the Federal lines were advanced 5 miles; the rebel centre was pushed back from 1 to 3 miles, with a loss to them of 18 guns and 1000 prisoners. Hood's whole army, except his cavalry under Forrest, and a small force of infantry near Murfreesboro', were engaged. Rebel loss estimated at 600 killed and wounded and 1200 prisoners.

December 16.—Battle of Nashville, 2d day. The rebels at daylight were found to be retiring. They were pressed heavily along the whole line, and lost prisoners, guns, and killed and wounded. At night the rebels were in full retreat, being utterly routed. Captured from the rebels, 30 cannon, 7000 small-arms, 5000 prisoners. Taken prisoners, rebel generals Edward Johnson, Smith, and Rucker, 3 colonels, and 209 officers.

—— General Burbridge's raiding expedition in West Virginia entered Wytheville. The rebels retiring.

—— Pollard, Alabama, was occupied by United States troops under Colonel D. G. Robinson, who burned the government and railroad buildings of the Mobile, Great Northern, Alabama, and Florida railroads.

December 17.—The rebel General Lyon was defeated at Ashbyville, Kentucky, by General E. D. McCook. Lyon lost 1 gun and a considerable number of his men.

—— The President of the United States, by official order, disapproves of that part of the order of Major-General Dix, No. 97, which instructs military commanders on the frontier, in certain cases therein specified, to cross the boundary-line between the United States and Canada, and directs pursuit on neutral territory. The said instruction is revoked.

—— The Secretary of State promulgated an official order, directing that no person should be allowed to enter the United States from a foreign country without a passport, except immigrants entering directly an American port by sea. This regulation was intended to apply especially to persons proposing to come directly to the United States from the neighboring British Provinces.

—— A fight at Escumbia, Alabama, between Colonel Robinson's expeditionary force, on its return, and rebels under Colonel Olmstead. A charge was made on the latter, who were driven away. Colonel Robinson was wounded, and Colonel Olmstead killed.

December 18.—Battle of Staley's Creek. The rebel General Breckinridge, who was following Colonel Brown, of Burbridge and Stoneman's expedition, was overtaken by General Burbridge near Marion. An engagement ensued which lasted 36 hours. At the conclusion, Breckinridge attempted to retreat to Saltville, but, by other United States troops, was forced from that line, and compelled to retreat to North Carolina.

—— A cavalry force, under Major-General Torbert, Brigadier-Generals Devin, Powell, Gibbs, Tibbetts, and Colonel Capehart, left Winchester, Virginia, on an expedition up the Shenandoah Valley.

—— General Thomas's army in pursuit of Hood, arrived at Pulaski, beyond which the infantry did not go.

December 19.—General Custer's cavalry division started on a reconnoissance up the Valley of the Shenandoah.

—— Andrew G. Magrath was inaugurated Governor of South Carolina, at Columbia.

December 20.—The lead-mines near Saltville were destroyed by Colonel Buckley.

—— Saltville, Virginia, captured by Burbridge and Stoneman. 8 pieces of cannon were taken, and the extensive salt-works destroyed. 708 kettles were broken, and 92,000 bushels salt damaged.

—— Call for 300,000 more troops by the President of the United States, to make up for deficiencies under former calls.

December 21.—An attack was made on Custer's cavalry, below Newmarket, Virginia, by Payne's rebel cavalry. The latter, after sharp fighting, were driven back. The rebel infantry being known to be in advance, the Federal cavalry returned. 15 rebels were killed, as many wounded, and 33 prisoners were taken. Federal loss, 2 killed, 22 wounded, and 35 prisoners. Custer's cavalry returned without molestation, reaching their camp on the 23d.

—— The bill passed by Congress creating the grade of Vice-Admiral in the navy, who is to be the ranking officer in the service, was signed by the President. Rear-Admiral David G. Farragut was immediately nominated for the position, and confirmed at once by the United States Senate.

—— A cavalry force was sent out from Memphis, Tennessee, by General Dana. It struck the Mobile & Ohio Railroad below Corinth, and destroyed the track below Okalona, with bridges, railroad cars, wagons, carbines, &c.

—— The city of Savannah was occupied by General Sherman's United States troops. General Hardee, anticipating the contemplated assault, escaped with the main body of his infantry and light artillery, on the afternoon and night of the 20th, by crossing the river to the Union causeway, opposite the city. The rebel iron-clads Georgia and Savannah were blown up, and the navy yard burned. All the rest of the city was intact, and contained 20,000 citizens, who were quiet and well disposed. The captures included 800 prisoners, 150 guns, 13 locomotives in good order, 190 cars, a large supply of ammunition and materials of war, 3 steamers, and 33,000 bales of cotton, safely stored in warehouses. All these valuable fruits of an almost bloodless victory were fairly won.

December 22.—A fight at Liberty Mills, Virginia, between Torbert's cavalry expedition and rebel cavalry and infantry under Lomax. The rebels, retreating across the Rapidan, burned the bridge; but the position being flanked by means of fords above and below, the enemy, after a sharp skirmish, again retreated, being pursued vigorously for many miles. Torbert took 2 guns, ammunition chests, and many small-arms.

December 23.—Torbert's expedition went within 2 miles of Gordonsville, Virginia, which being found well defended by a force too strong to be attacked, the United States cavalry withdrew, having attained the object of the reconnoissance.

December 23.—United States transport steamer North Carolina foundered at sea. 259 soldiers were on board, of whom 194 were lost. The rest were saved by a passing vessel.

December 24.—A bombardment was made on Fort Fisher, at the mouth of the Wilmington River, North Carolina, by Admiral Porter's fleet, who fired upon it heavily until dark, and kept up an occasional firing during the night to keep the garrison awake.

——— Lyon's rebel cavalry struck the Louisville & Mississippi Railroad at Elizabethtown, Kentucky, and destroyed a bridge there. They were followed closely by McCook's Union cavalry.

——— Bombardment of Fort Fisher, at the entrance of Cape Fear, North Carolina, an outward defence of Wilmington, by the United States fleet under Admiral D. D. Porter. The firing was very heavy. The operations by the fleet commenced by the explosion of a grand caisson "powder-boat" or torpedo-boat, which contained 582,400 pounds of gunpowder. The effects of the explosion, it was supposed by Major-General Butler, who projected the floating mine, would be to dismantle the rebel works and so demoralize them that they could not resist a vigorous attack. The idea proved to be a great mistake. The caisson or boat, which was made out of the old transport Louisiana disguised as a blockade-runner, was sent in within 350 yards of Fort Fisher, and the train ignited. The crew then pushed off, and got away safely. The vessel burned for some time and then exploded, but with so little effect that the rebel works were not injured, and they supposed that one of the United States vessels had taken fire and blown up. In their official report they scarcely noticed the explosion. The caisson was blown up about 3 A. M. Immediately afterward the fleet steamed in and commenced a vigorous bombardment of the fort, which was continued until night.

December 25.—Second day of the bombardment of Fort Fisher, North Carolina. An attack made specially on Flag Point Battery on shore resulted in its capture with 69 men. In the afternoon 3000 troops were landed in boats on the beach above the fort. 200 boys belonging to the Junior North Carolina Reserves, few of them being over 17 years old, were captured. Near the fort a reconnoissance made by General Curtis succeeded in reaching the parapets; a few men clambered up, and one soldier tore the rebel flag from its staff and brought it away. A rebel bearer of despatches was captured, and his horse was taken from him. General Butler, with whom General Weitzel agreed, was of opinion that the fort was too strong to be taken by assault. The debarkation of the troops was therefore resolved upon. A portion of the men were taken away the same night, but the sea becoming very rough, about 1000 men were left on shore. They were got off the next day. The fleet in this enterprise lost about 45 men, from the bursting of 6 Parrott guns on board of various vessels. The rebels reported a loss of 3 killed and 55 wounded; also that 20,000 shots had been fired from the Federal fleet and 1202 by themselves. General Butler reported a loss of 1 man drowned, 2 killed, 1 taken prisoner, and 2 wounded. 300 prisoners were taken from the rebels, and 4 guns were captured.

——— The advance of Thomas's army in pursuit of Hood reached a point 21 miles south of Columbia, Alabama.

December 26.—Jeff Davis issued a proclamation stating that Bennett G. Burley, arrested in Canada for the piratical attempt on Lake Erie, was a regular officer in the Confederate service, authorized to capture the United States gunboat Michigan, and release the rebel prisoners of war on Johnson's Island.

——— Skirmish at Pine Hook between General Wilson, U. S. Army, and Forrest's rebel cavalry. Federal loss 20. The rebels fell back during night.

——— The pursuit of Hood's routed army by General Thomas substantially ceased. He had reached Pulaski, Tennessee. The rebel army had divided and taken different roads. General Thomas reported that the rebels admitted a loss of 18 generals, killed, wounded, and captured, since they started north, and 68 pieces of artillery lost.

The following estimate has been made of the losses of the whole of Thomas's and Hood's campaign.

FEDERAL LOSS.

Killed and wounded before the battle of Franklin (about)	100
Killed and wounded at the battle of Franklin (official)	2100
Killed and wounded at the battle of Nashville, December 15 and 16 (official)	2900
Killed and wounded since the 16th (about)	1000
Rousseau, at Murfreesboro,' killed and wounded	100
Total, killed and wounded	6200
Missing before the battle of Franklin (about)	300
Missing at the battle of Franklin (official)	300
Missing in the battle of Nashville	200
Missing since—none	
Total missing	800
Total killed and wounded	6100
Total missing	800
Total	6900

REBEL LOSS.

Killed and wounded before the battle of Franklin (about)	100
Killed and wounded at the battle of Franklin	7000
Killed and wounded at Murfreesboro'	100
Killed and wounded in battles of Nashville	2500
Killed and wounded since battle of Nashville	1000
Total killed and wounded	10,700
Prisoners taken before the battle of Franklin (official)	100
Prisoners taken at battle of Franklin (officia·)	842
Prisoners taken at Nashville, first day's fight (official)	2002
Prisoners taken, second day's fight (official)	4440
Prisoners taken afterwards	2000
Total prisoners	9384

Total rebel loss, killed, wounded, and prisoners 20,034

Cannon taken 68, and small-arms in great number. Hood also lost 6 general officers killed, 7 wounded, and 4 taken prisoners,—total, 18.

December 27.—United States gunboats under Admiral Lee destroy a fort, 2 guns, and 2 caissons at Chickasaw, and all visible means by which Hood's army might be transported across the Tennessee River.

December 28.—Forrest's rebel cavalry were so closely pursued by General Wilson's horsemen that the rebels abandoned 150 wagons, and crossed the Tennessee. This practically closed the pursuit of Hood's routed army.

December 29.—Francis P. Blair and his son Montgomery Blair left Washington to go to Virginia: it was supposed upon some business or informal transaction connected with negotiations for peace with the rebels. F. P. Blair returned January 2d, General Grant refusing to give him authority to pass through the lines.

——— Major-General Stoneman arrived at Nashville, Tennessee, from his great raid in East Tennessee and West Virginia. Stoneman left Knoxville December 18, Burbridge having previously left Bean's Station, Kentucky. Their operations were subsequently, after a junction, under command of General Stoneman. The loss to the rebels was very severe. All the railroad bridges from New River, Virginia, to the Tennessee line, were destroyed. Thirteen railroad trains, with locomotives, several trains and extra cars, without engines, were captured and destroyed. All the depots of supplies in South-western Virginia, railroad depots, all the foundries, mills, factories, storehouses, wagons, and ambulance trains, and turnpike bridges, were destroyed. In addition, was captured 2500 rounds of artillery ammunition, 2000 pack saddles and a large amount of harness, a great quantity of small-arms, 2000 horses, and 1000 mules. The severest losses to the rebels were the destruction of the salt-works at Saltville and the lead-works at Leadville. Both were rendered valueless. Federal losses very small, not exceeding 200 killed, wounded, and missing. Among the killed was Colonel Boyle, of the 11th Kentucky cavalry. The captured rebel prisoners amounted to 24 officers and 845 men.

December 30.—The *Lynchburg Virginian* reports that "the gallant and high-souled Breckinridge is chafing like a lion deeply wounded, at the enemy's audacious raid into his department."

1865. *January 1.*—The *Richmond Sentinel*, Jeff Davis's organ, contained a long and remarkable article upon the prospects of the Confederacy, in which the exhausted condition of the country is acknowledged. It is suggested that sooner than yield to the United States it would be better to surrender to Great Britain, France, or Spain. The *Richmond Sentinel*, commenting on the above article, endorses its arguments and views, and declares in favor of a treaty with France or England, abolishing slavery, if those nations will guarantee Confederate independence.

—— The United States sloop of war San Jacinto was lost off No Name Key, Bahama Islands, having struck upon a reef. The crew and most of the cargo were saved.

—— Citizens of New York made a New Year's gift of $50,000 to Vice-Admiral D. G. Farragut, as a testimonial of public gratitude.

—— Citizens of Philadelphia presented to Lieutenant-General Grant a handsome house, completely furnished.

—— The Dutch Gap Canal, at Farrar's Island, in the James River, was finished by having the bulkhead blown out. The earth, however, fell back into the canal, and although the water flowed through it there was not a depth sufficient for navigation. The head of the canal was also commanded by powerful rebel batteries.

January 6.—Francis P. Blair left Washington upon a visit to Richmond, Virginia, having at this time the necessary passes.

January 7.—United States transport steamer Melville, from New York to Hilton Head, foundered at sea. There were 50 passengers, very few of whom were saved.

January 8.—Major-General B. F. Butler, of the Army of the James, was relieved from his command by order of the President of the United States.

January 11.—The State Convention of Missouri passed an ordinance, which decreed the immediate freedom of all slaves in the state. The vote for the proposition was 60 against 14.

—— Same day the Union State Convention for reorganizing civil government in Tennessee, met at Nashville.

—— Beverly, Virginia, was attacked by a force under the rebel General Rosser, and the Federal troops there were taken prisoners.

—— Francis P. Blair arrived at Richmond.

January 12.—The United States gunboat Iroquois arrived at Capetown, having on board the crew of the whaler *Edward*, of Boston, and schooner *Lizzie M. Stacey*, which had been captured by the Anglo-rebel privateer *Shenandoah* and burned. The crews were sent ashore at the island of Tristan D'Acunha, whence they were taken by the Iroquois.

January 13.—A party of guerrillas made a dash into Bardstown, Kentucky. They burned the depot, but were ultimately driven out of the town by United States troops.

—— The United States fleet, under Admiral Porter, opened fire on Fort Fisher, North Carolina, a heavy bombardment. Same day, the army under command of Brigadier-General Alfred H. Terry was landed on the beach.

January 14.—Second day of the attack upon Fort Fisher. The firing from the fleet was heavy all day, and the military were active on shore.

—— Pocotaligo Bridge, South Carolina, captured by 17th United States army corps with 12 guns. Federal loss, 40 killed and wounded.

—— General Sherman resumed his operations for his march northward. The 15th and 17th corps left Savannah in transports for Beaufort.

January 15.—Fort Fisher, North Carolina, was carried by assault by General Ames's division, and the 2d brigade of the 1st division of the 24th army corps, then under command of Brigadier-General Alfred H. Terry, aided by a battalion of marines and seamen from the navy. The assault was preceded by a heavy bombardment from the Federal fleet, and was made at 3.30 P. M., when the 1st brigade (General Curtis) of Ames's division effected a lodgment upon the parapet, but full possession of the work was not obtained until 10 P. M. All the works south of Fort Fisher fell at the same time; 72 guns were taken, and the rebel commanders Major-General Whiting and Colonel Lamb were taken prisoners. The rebel loss was estimated at 500 killed and wounded and 1800 prisoners. The assault was led by Colonels Curtis, Pennypacker, and Bell. Colonel Bell and Colonel J. W. More and Lieutenant-Colonel Lyman, 203d Pennsylvania Volunteers, were killed, and Colonels Curtis and Pennypacker severely wounded; also Lieutenant-Colonel Coan, 88th New York. In the navy Lieutenant S. W. Preston and Benjamin H. Porter were killed. Federal loss of soldiers and seamen about 850 killed and wounded. Federal loss in army, 119 killed, 545 wounded.

January 16.—Forts Caswell and Campbell, Smith's Island, Smithville, and Reeves's Point, North Carolina, were abandoned by the rebels, who blew up the works: 89 guns were taken by the United States troops.

—— Francis P. Blair arrived in Washington from Richmond, and was "in good spirits."

—— An explosion occurred at the magazine of Fort Fisher, caused by the carelessness of Federal soldiers who were wandering through the captured works; 240 officers and men lost their lives by this calamity.

January 17.—An expedition in three divisions left Savannah under General Fuller, and took the road towards the Altamaha River. They destroyed the railroad track, bridges, &c., for many miles.

—— The United States monitor Patapsco was blown up by a torpedo in Charleston harbor; 40 or 50 of the crew were drowned.

January 20.—Captain Corbett, of the British steamer "Sea King," which was taken to Madeira, and transformed into a rebel privateer under the name of the "Shenandoah," was arrested in London and committed for trial for a violation of the foreign enlistment act.

—— Major-General Thomas, in his official report of the operations of his army, from the 7th of September, 1864, to January 20, 1865, says: "There were captured from the enemy during the various actions, 13,189 prisoners of war, including seven general officers and nearly 1000 other officers of small grades; 72 pieces of serviceable artillery, and a number of battle flags. During the same period over 2000 deserters from the enemy were received, and to whom the oath was administered. Our losses will not exceed 10,000 in killed, wounded, and missing. The larger number of ammunition chests captured were filled with ammunition in good condition, and 6 wagons loaded with similar ammunition were captured before Nashville." Other important captures are mentioned.

—— The left wing of General Sherman's army left Savannah to undertake the great campaign against South Carolina and North Carolina. Two divisions (Jackson's and Ward's) of the 20th corps, crossed the Savannah River at the city of Savannah on the 20th, and plunged into the swamps of South Carolina. General Geary's division was ordered to go to Sister's Ferry, 60 miles above Savannah, by the Georgia road. Williams travelled up the South Carolina shore, the others up the Georgia bank, without incident but laboriously, till

Saturday, January 28, when Jeff C. Davis reached the ferry. Steamboats with supplies were sent up the river to that point, so that, after concentration, the left wing might cut loose from civilization again with plenty of provisions. There was plenty of water in the river, and vast piles of stores were soon accumulated at Sister's Ferry.

January 21.—Anglo-rebel blockade-runner steamers Stag and Charlotte were captured while attempting to run up the Cape Fear River, North Carolina, their commanders being ignorant of the fall of Fort Fisher.

January 22.—Francis P. Blair left Washington on the United States steamer Don, on a second visit to Richmond.

January 23.—Lieutenant-General J. B. Hood was officially relieved of the command of the rebel Army of Tennessee.

January 24.—British blockade-running steamer Blenheim captured off Wilmington by United States fleet.

—— Salkahatchie, South Carolina, occupied by United States troops, the rebels abandoning it upon our advance.

—— The Governor-General of Canada sent a message to the Parliament, recommending that $90,000 in gold be appropriated to pay the losses of the banks of St. Albans, Vermont, in consequence of the perfidious conduct of Justice Coursol, who gave up the money to the thieves.

January 25.—The Richmond squadron of five vessels came down the James River and attempted to get past the obstructions in the river placed there by the Federals. Their design was to make a grand attack on City Point. The United States forts fired on them, and they were driven back, one vessel being blown up and another seriously damaged.

—— The Anglo-rebel pirate Shenandoah, alias Sea King, Captain Waddell, arrived at Melbourne, Australia, having, since leaving Madeira in October, captured 11 Federal merchant vessels, 9 of which were destroyed and 2 bonded.

January 26.—Francis P. Blair arrived at Annapolis, on his return from Richmond.

January 29.—Alexander H. Stephens, Vice-President of the Confederacy; R. M. T. Hunter, Senator from Virginia; and J. A. Campbell, formerly Assistant Secretary of War, left Richmond, Virginia, having been appointed by Jefferson Davis to negotiate informally for peace. The appointment of these persons was made in consequence of the visits of F. P. Blair to Richmond, and of his interviews with Jefferson Davis. On the second visit, Mr. Blair had brought the consent of Mr. Lincoln to receive and confer with any agents sent informally, with a view to the restoration of peace. Stephens and the others were therefore sent forward as informal agents and without formal credentials.

January 31.—The House of Representatives of the Congress of the United States passed the amendment to the Constitution of the United States abolishing slavery, by a vote of 119 yeas to 58 nays; members absent or not voting, 8. By the Constitution, in order to make this amendment binding, it must be ratified by three-fourths of the States. This amendment was introduced into the Senate by Mr. Henderson, of Missouri, January 1st, 1864. This amendment was adopted by the following States at the dates mentioned: Illinois, Feb. 1; Rhode Island, Feb. 2; Michigan, Feb. 2; New York, Feb. 2; Massachusetts, Feb. 3; West Virginia, Feb. 3; Maryland, Feb. 3; Pennsylvania, Feb. 3; Maine, Feb. 7; Missouri, Feb. 7; Indiana, Feb. 13; Wisconsin, Feb. 21. Rejected by Kentucky, Feb. 23; by New Jersey, March 1.

—— Messrs. Stephens, Hunter, and Campbell were allowed to pass through the Federal lines, and were sent to Hampton Roads for the purposes of their conference.

February 1.—Federal troops landed at Young's Island, South Carolina, and made a demonstration toward the line of the Charleston & Savannah Railroad.

—— Robert E. Lee was nominated by Jefferson Davis to the rebel Senate, as commander-in-chief of the Confederate armies, and confirmed on the same day.

February 2.—President Lincoln left Washington to meet the rebel peace commissioners.

—— A conference was held on board the steamer River Queen, in Hampton Roads, Virginia, between President Lincoln and Secretary Seward, on behalf of the United States, and Messrs. Stephens, Hunter, and Campbell, the rebel peace commissioners.

—— General Sherman's troops advanced across Whippy Swamp, South Carolina, driving off the rebel cavalry.

February 3.—The 17th army corps crossed the Salkahatchie River, South Carolina, in force, and carried the rebel works, which were very strong, after a brief skirmish.

—— Kilpatrick's cavalry, in the advance of Sherman's army, crossed the Savannah River into South Carolina, at Sister's Ferry.

—— The Canadian government delivered over to the United States, at the Suspension Bridge, Niagara Falls, Bennett M. Burley, one of the leaders in the piratical enterprises upon Lake Erie.

February 4.—The rebel iron-clad ram Stonewall, formerly the Olinde, put into Ferrol, Spain. This ship was built in France, and was taken to Copenhagen under the pretence that it had been sold to the Danes. It left Copenhagen with a crew of rebel officers and men on board, and hoisted the rebel flag at sea.

—— All Saints Parish, Little River, North Carolina, captured by Lieutenant William F. Cushing, U.S. Navy, who destroyed some cotton and other stores.

—— The rebel Senate adopted a device for a new flag, being the third change made in the ensign during 4 years. It was described as follows: "The width two-thirds of its length, with the union now used as a battle-flag, to be in width three-fifths of the width of the flag, and so proportioned as to leave the length of the field on the side of the union twice the width below it, to have a ground of red and broad blue saltier thereon, bordered with white and emblazoned with mullots or five-pointed stars, corresponding in number to that of the Confederate States; the field to be white, except the outer half from the union, which shall be a red bar extending the width of the flag."

—— President Lincoln and Secretary Seward returned to Washington, the Peace Conference in Hampton Roads having proved to be a failure.

February 5.—The 5th corps, 2d corps, and Gregg's cavalry, of the Army of the Potomac, moved out from their camps in a south-west direction. They crossed Hatcher's Run, and passed on the other side. In the afternoon the rebels massed their forces and made a desperate charge in three lines of battle. They were received with such a deadly fire that they could not withstand it, and they fell back in confusion. Two other attempts were made by the rebels to break the Federal lines, but with no better success. At the end of the day the Union troops held their positions, the rebels having met with heavy losses. The Federal loss was about 100, the rebel loss about 500. Gregg's cavalry moved via Ream's Station to Malone Bridge, over the Rowanty River, and so on to Dinwiddie Court House. They had some slight skirmishing, but no severe action during the day. This movement was undertaken in the hope that the Federal lines could be extended towards the Boydtown Plankroad and Southside Railroad.

—— Major Harry Gilmore, notorious in the invasion of Maryland in 1864, and in the burning of Chambersburg, was captured near Moorfield, Virginia.

—— The United States frigate Niagara, in pursuit of the rebel ram Stonewall, entered the port of Corunna, Spain.

—— Wheeler's cavalry, disputing the advance of Sherman's army, was routed by Logan's corps at Orange Court House, on the Little Salkahatchie, South Carolina. They were driven out by a charge of General John A. Smith's division, made through a swamp, the men being up to their hips in mud and water.

ney's Mills. The move-
otomac beyond Hatcher's
onable success, during the
ear night a sudden attack
resulted in that body of
 was broken for a time,
and the old position was
the day, about 600. Ge-
re wounded. The rebel
General Sorrell mortally
fman severely wounded.
 a consequence of this
s were extended across
Dabney's Mill.
ge assumed the position
bel government, in place

as held in the African
 invitation to the recent peace
lation to the recent peace
made a speech, in which
ake peace upon any other
f the Confederacy. "He
at home, who are able to
e already in the army in
at thereby we would com-
twelve months to *petition*
ms."
ond at 4600. Gold sold

ing of Sherman's army
vannah Railroad at Ban-
ip the track for some dis-

ing of Sherman's army
at Halmar's Bridge.
was held in the African
 to the late peace confer-
y Hunter, Benjamin, Gil-
le object of the meeting
ns to fight against the
s were very bitter.
e, of Kentucky, recom-
at state to ratify the Con-
hing slavery, upon condi-
s would pay Kentucky
ue of her slaves in 1864.
ncoln sent to the Senate
on to the recent conference
of the rebels. The follow-
 Mr. Seward as the only
States could consent to

the national authority

Executive of the United
from the position assumed
sage to Congress and in

ties short of an end of the
the forces hostile to the
 them that all proposi-
t with the above will be
a spirit of sincere liber-
y may choose to say and
assume to definitely con-

result of the conference:
nce of the instructions to
before recited, was stated
ng was said inconsistent
party it was not said that
on they ever would con-
qually omitted to declare
They seemed to desire a
and the adoption of some
ome of them seemed to
ad to reunion, but which
nt to an indefinite post-
ded without result."

Mr. Seward in his report of the conference to Minister Adams said: "What the insurgent party seemed chiefly to favor was a postponement of the question of separation upon which the war was waged, and a mutual direction of the efforts of the Government as well as those of the insurgents to some extraneous policy or scheme for a season, during which passions might be expected to subside, and the armies be reduced, and trade and intercourse between the people of both sections be resumed.

"It was suggested by them that through such postponement we might now have immediate peace, with some, not very certain, prospects of an ultimate satisfactory adjustment of political relations between the Government and the states. section or people, now engaged in conflict with it. The suggestion, though deliberately considered, was nevertheless regarded by the President as one of armistice or truce, and he announced that we can agree to no cessation or suspension of hostilities except on the basis of the disbandment of the insurgent forces, and the restoration of the national authority throughout all the states in the Union collaterally, and in subordination to the proposition which was thus announced."

———— Kilpatrick's cavalry fight. Federal loss, 100 killed and wounded. Rebel, 600 killed and wounded.

February 11.— General Blair of Sherman's army (right wing) crossed the North Edisto opposite Orangeburg, after some resistance by the rebels.

———— Cavalry skirmish at Aiken, South Carolina, between rebels under Wheeler, and Atkins's brigade of Kilpatrick's cavalry. The latter were repulsed, and withdrew for reinforcements to Johnson's Station. It was found that the whole of Wheeler's cavalry were in front of them. Federal loss, 31 killed, wounded, and prisoners.

———— Fight at Honey Hill, North Carolina. A reconnoissance was made by General Terry's troops towards Wilmington, and Hoke's rebel soldiers were driven forward.

February 14.—Major-General E. O. C. Ord was assigned to the command of the department of Virginia, including the Army of the James.

February 15.—From 2000 to 3000 Federals landed at Grimball's on James's Island, below Charleston. Some skirmishing took place, but no general engagement. Grimball's is on the Stono River, about 2 miles southwest of Charleston, the Ashley River, 2000 yards wide, intervening.

———— Lexington Court-House, South Carolina, was occupied by Geary's division of Sherman's army (left wing).

———— All the corps of Sherman were united at the Congaree, being concentrated for the purpose of making an attack upon Columbia, South Carolina.

February 17.—The rebel flag-of-truce boat Schultz was blown up on the James River by a torpedo.

February 18.—The rebel cavalry officer Forrest issued an address to his troops, recounting their exploits during the previous year. He said: "that they had fought 50 battles, killed and captured 16,000 of the enemy, captured 2000 horses and mules, 67 pieces of artillery, 14 transports, 20 barges, 300 wagons, 50 ambulances, 105 stand of arms, and forty block-houses; destroyed 36 railroad bridges, 2000 miles of railroad, 6 locomotives, 100 cars, and $15,000,000 worth of property."

In accomplishing this, he admits that they were occasionally sustained by other troops, but says their regular number never exceeded 5000. 2000 had been killed or wounded, and 2000 had been taken prisoners. He tells them to prepare for renewed action, and warns them against being allured by the syren song of peace, "for there can be no peace save upon their separate independent nationality."

———— Charleston, South Carolina, was evacuated by the rebels. In consequence of the operations of General Sherman in the interior of the state, it was no longer possible to hold the city. The rebel troops were therefore withdrawn at 9 o'clock in the morning. Mayor Macbeth surrendered the city, which was occupied by our troops. Before the evacuation, the rebels burned arsenals, cotton, warehouses, bridges, railroad tracks, quartermasters' stores, three iron-clad vessels, and vessels in the ship-yard. The United States troops captured Forts Sumter, Moultrie, Castle Pinckney, and all the rebel works; 450 pieces of artillery and a large quantity of ammunition, 8 locomotives, and many cars. During the evacuation an explosion took place in the railroad depot, by which several hundred citizens lost their lives. By the burning the flames were spread to houses in the city, and an extensive destruction was the result. None but the poorer classes of people remained in the city. They were found in extreme destitution, and without anything to eat. Their situation was described as much worse than that of the inhabitants of Savannah after the capture of that city. The lower part of the city within reach of our guns was in effect a ruin, and was almost uninhabited. Comparatively few persons dared to remain there. Some of the houses were knocked down; bricks and timbers were lying everywhere, and the streets in particular were strewn with the fragments, in many places entirely obstructing travel. Shells were lying among the ruins. The appearance of the city, the lower part uninhabitable, and the upper part in flames, was described as dreary and desolate in the extreme.

February 18.—Columbia, the capital of South Carolina, was entered by General Sherman, the rebels having abandoned it. Before the occupation, the rebel storehouses were broken open and the people helped themselves. General Sherman captured 43 cannon and immense arsenals, &c. On leaving the town, he destroyed the public property in the arsenals, depots, and public warehouses. Some cotton standing in the streets, which had been placed there by Beauregard to be burned, but was abandoned in his retreat, took fire from sparks, and occasioned a general conflagration, which destroyed all the houses on the main street for a mile and a half. The destruction was very great.

—— John Yates Beale, a rebel spy, pirate, and incendiary, was hanged at Governor's Island, New York harbor. He was tried before a court-martial, and convicted upon a charge of acting as a spy at Kelly's Island, Ohio, and the Niagara Suspension Bridge; of being concerned in the piratical seizure of the steamboats Philo Parsons and Island Belle on Lake Erie; and of attempting to throw a railroad train loaded with passengers from the track by placing obstructions upon it, between Dunkirk and Buffalo, with design also to rob the safe of an express car.

February 19.—Fort Anderson, below Wilmington, North Carolina, was taken by the United States army under General J. M. Schofield, and the navy under Admiral Porter. The attack commenced on the 17th by the troops, the fleet also enfilading the works. The attack was continued on the 18th, upon which day General Cox worked round to the rear of the fort upon the right. The rebels, discovering this, left the fort in the night, carrying off 5 or 6 pieces of light artillery, but leaving 10 heavy guns in the fort, ammunition, &c. Loss in the fleet, 3 killed and 5 wounded.

February 20.—The Army of the Tennessee broke camp around Columbia, and resumed its march. The 17th corps had destroyed 30 miles of railroad towards Winnsboro'.

—— Battle of Tom Creek, North Carolina. General Cox, U. S. A., operating towards Wilmington, flanked the rebels, took them in the rear, and routed them, taking 2 guns and 300 prisoners.

February 21.—General Cox pushed to the Brunswick River, opposite Wilmington, North Carolina, and found the bridge on fire. The rebels began to burn cotton and rosin in the city.

—— A detachment of rebel cavalry penetrated the Union lines, and dashed into Cumberland, Maryland, before daylight, and captured Major-Generals Kelly and Crook in their hotels, and carried them off prisoners.

—— The United States gunboat Sacramento, in pursuit of the rebel ram Stonewall, entered the port of Corunna, Spain, and joined the Niagara.

February 22.—The United States frigate Niagara and gunboat Sacramento left Corunna, Spain, and entered the port of Ferrol, observing the Stonewall.

—— Wilmington, North Carolina, was entered by the United States troops under Schofield, Terry, and Cox.

February 23.—Georgetown, South Carolina, was taken by the fleet under Admiral Dahlgren, aided by a land force. The rebels abandoned Battery White, mounting 15 guns. The town was surrendered shortly afterwards.

February 24.—Camden, South Carolina, was occupied by Sherman's army, and 4000 bales of cotton, with provisions, rations, depots, and public property, were destroyed.

February 26.—General Joseph E. Johnston assumed command of the rebel Army of the Tennessee and of all the troops in the department of South Carolina, Georgia, and Florida.

February 27.—General Sheridan left Winchester, Virginia, in command of an expedition of cavalry intended to operate in the Shenandoah Valley. There were with him Generals Custer, Merritt, Devins, and Colonel Capehart, in command of a brigade.

—— The United States steamer Arizona, the flagship of Admiral Thatcher, was destroyed by fire below New Orleans. 5 of the crew perished.

—— The Richmond, Virginia, papers published two remarkable editorial articles. The *Enquirer* represented that a large number of members of the rebel Congress had left their seats and returned to their homes, thus abandoning the country in the hour of peril. The *Examiner* devoted a serious article to a review of the assertion of Jefferson Davis in a late message to Congress, in which he made the following boasts: "If the campaign against Richmond had resulted in success instead of failure; if we had been compelled to evacuate Richmond as well as Atlanta, *the Confederacy would have remained as erect and defiant as ever.* Nothing could have been changed in the purpose of its government, *in the indomitable valor of its troops, or in the unquenchable spirit of its people.* The baffled and disappointed foe would in vain have scanned the reports of your proceedings at some new legislative seat for any indication that progress had been made in his gigantic task of conquering a free people. There are no vital points on the preservation of which the continued existence of the Confederacy depends. There is no military success of the enemy which can accomplish its destruction. Not the fall of Richmond, nor Wilmington, nor Charleston, nor Savannah, nor Mobile, nor of all combined, can affect the issue of the present contest." In reply to these assertions, the *Examiner* says, prophetically: "Let not this fatal error be harbored till it takes root in the imagination. The evacuation of Richmond would be the loss of all respect and authority towards the Confederate government, the *disintegration of the army, and the abandonment of the scheme of an independent Southern Confederation.* The war would, after that, speedily degenerate into an irregular contest, in which passion would have more to do than purpose; which would have no other object than the mere defence or present safety of those immediately persisting in it. The hope of establishing a confederacy and securing its recognition among nations, would be gone for ever. The common sense of the country, the instinct of every man and woman in the land, contradicts the idea that any possibility of an independent South would remain after its capital was abandoned, its government sent adrift, and its army withdrawn into the solitudes of the interior."

March 1.—Admiral Dahlgren's flag-ship Harvest Moon was blown up by a torpedo while going down the Santee River, after the capture of Georgetown, South Carolina.

March 3.—Chesterfield Court House, South Carolina, was entered by Sherman's army (left wing).

—— Cheraw, South Carolina, was captured by General Sherman, with 25 pieces of artillery, 18 tons of powder, railroad trains, locomotives, several thousand bales of cotton, and a large supply of stores.

March 3.—Battle of Waynesboro', Virginia. General Sheridan attacked the rebel troops under Early. The latter by superior strategy were surrounded. They fired one volley and attempted to run. They were intercepted by Custer and nearly the whole force captured, consisting of 87 officers, 1165 enlisted men, 13 flags, 11 cannon, 100 wagons, small-arms, and ammunition. Federal loss, 12 killed and wounded. Early himself escaped.

March 4.—General Sheridan's expedition entered Charlotteville, Virginia, and captured 3 guns. The next day the cavalry destroyed iron bridges over the Ravenna River and Morse's Creek, and the railroad for 8 miles in the direction of Lynchburg.

—— Abraham Lincoln and Andrew Johnson were inaugurated at Washington, D. C., as President and Vice-President of the United States. The oath of office was administered by Chief Justice Chase.

March 6.—95 tons manufactured tobacco, worth $380,000, were captured at Fredericksburg, Virginia, by a naval expedition with troops sent from Fortress Monroe.

March 7.—Hugh McCulloch was nominated Secretary of the Treasury by President Lincoln, in the place of Fessenden, resigned. He was confirmed by the United States Senate the same day.

—— The *Richmond Enquirer* contained a remarkable article, of which the following is an extract:—

"What mean these rumors of Senatorial Committees approaching the President to submit terms of submission? Is that report true? Are any senators or representatives whipped? Have they approached the President, to press upon him any such base propositions? Who were the senators? What were the propositions? Is there any plan on foot to force the President to compromise with subjugation or resign? Is there any one else ready to volunteer resignation in case he is forced to vacate his place, and if he does, who is proposed to fill that place? *Is any attempt made by rumors to create the impression that General Lee is ready to consider terms for laying down arms under the pretext of preventing the sufferings and sacrifices of a forced surrender?* Who are busy in these plans of surrendering to subjugation? Speak out; the crisis demands boldness and decision, and determined resistance to internal as well as external enemies."

The *Enquirer* replies:—

"R. E. Lee, by and with the consent of the army and the people's wish, grasps the sceptre they may wrench from the hands of Mr. Davis, and wield for the safety and security of his country, liberty, and independence. No cabal of whipped seceders shall capitulate this country into slavery, and crouch it at the footstool of Mr. Lincoln. The Congress has utterly failed. It is incompetent and doing much injury. It has neither capacity nor courage. It is wanting in firmness and resolution. It is unfit for revolution. *The very men who were the foremost to secede are the first to surrender.* A single head and a single man is now needed, and if Congress would consult its patriots it would intrust all power with the President and General Lee, adjourn and go home, and leave the country and its cause in the hands of those two men."

March 8.—Battle of Jackson's Mills, North Carolina. General J. D. Cox, leading the Federal advance from Newbern to Kinston, North Carolina, was attacked by Hill's corps, who got between two divisions of the Federal troops, and took 450 prisoners and 3 guns. The ground lost was recovered by Cox, who re-formed his line and advanced 7 miles. Cox took 200 prisoners.

March 9.—By agreement of exchange, 10,000 Union prisoners held by the rebels were to be delivered at North East, North Carolina. 8684 were brought forward. When the rebel official in charge of the unfortunate prisoners was asked why he did not deliver the complement of 10,000, as promised, he assigned three reasons. First, that a number died at the prisons after their names had been placed on the rolls for exchange, and their persons delivered over to the officer in charge of the train. Second, that a number of the most vigorous jumped from the trains, and took to the woods and swamps, disbelieving the statements of the rebels that they were on their way to be exchanged, thinking the statement but a pretext for conveying them from one rebel prison to another. Third, that a number died on the trains on their way here. Of these 8684, 2000 were unable to move, being what are technically termed "stretcher patients," or patients that are unable to move hand or foot, and must be borne about on stretchers. The condition of these prisoners beggars all description. Many of them were *literally naked;* and not only were they naked, but covered with sores, and their flesh being eaten by vermin. Many of them wore but a pair of filthy and ragged drawers, while some of the more fortunate had a shirt. Some of them had their gaunt and wasted frames shrouded in fragments of blankets and tents. A number of them were demented, stark naked, their bodies bedaubed with mud. Gangrenous, ulcerous, their eyes running out, their toes and fingers dropping off, they were enduring the extreme of human suffering. And to this stage they were systematically and deliberately reduced by fiendish monsters, claiming the names of men, and boasting that they were the exponents of modern "chivalry."

—— Jeff Davis, being informed that the two houses of the rebel Congress were about to adjourn, sent them a message, requesting them to suspend action and prolong their session for a few days.

—— Battle of Wise's Ford, North Carolina. Hoke made three assaults near Kinston upon Cox's troops on the Federal advance, but was repulsed, losing 1 gun, 200 prisoners, and all his dead and wounded left on the field, 300 in number. Up to this time the Federal loss on the advance against Kinston was estimated at 1000 killed, wounded, and prisoners. The rebels lost 12,000 prisoners.

March 10.—Wade Hampton attempted to surprise Kilpatrick's cavalry camps, and actually penetrated into it, taking all his guns, horses, and many prisoners. Kilpatrick re-formed the men and drove the enemy with great loss, recapturing about all that he had lost. Hampton left 86 dead on the field, and his whole loss was estimated at 600 killed, wounded, and prisoners. Loss of Kilpatrick, 100 killed and wounded. Among the rebels who were killed, were General Humes, Colonel Aiken, 5 colonels and 15 lieutenant-colonels wounded.

—— 9 steamers arrived at Annapolis, bringing about 3000 Union prisoners, most of them in a sad state of emaciation, and nearly destitute of clothing. Several died on the passage, and 5 dead were taken from one boat. Some 1500 of the poor fellows had to go to the hospital. A large number of rebel prisoners passed through Baltimore same day, to be exchanged, all in good health and well clothed. Many of them had carpet-bags full of clothing.

—— The rebel General Whiting, who surrendered at Fort Fisher, North Carolina, died at Governor's Island, New York.

—— General Sheridan's expedition arrived at Columbia, Virginia. Since the battle of Waynesboro', the cavalry had destroyed merchandise, mills, factories, bridges on the Ravenna River, all the locks on the James River, canal from Scottsville to within 15 miles of Lynchburg, and had broken down the banks between the canal and the river, the dam over the James at New Capton, all the bridges on the railroad from Swoop's depot, west of Charlottesville, to Charlottesville, all the bridges for 10 miles on the Gordonsville Railroad, and captured twelve canal-boats laden with medicine supplies, &c.

—— James Harlan was nominated Secretary of the Interior by President Lincoln, to take effect May 1st. He was confirmed immediately by the Senate.

March 11.—The President of the United States issued a proclamation warning deserters to return to their respective commands within 60 days, with promise of pardon, if they served out their original terms of enlistment.

—— "Sue Mundy" (Jerome Clark), a noted guerrilla, was taken prisoner with two others, in Webster, Kentucky.

March 11.—Fayetteville, North Carolina, was occupied by General Sherman, who opened communication with General Schofield. 17 guns were taken at this place, making altogether 85 captured since Sherman left Savannah. During the march Sherman captured about 25,000 animals, and gave food and transportation to about 15,000 colored refugees, thus depriving the confederacy of colored soldiers and slaves. He also had about 4000 white refugees with him. He operated over the following districts or counties :—In South Carolina—Beaufort, Barnwell, Orangeburg, Lexington, Richland, Kershaw, Fairfield, Chester, Lancaster, Sumter, Darlington, Chesterfield, Malbourg. In North Carolina—Mecklenburg, Anson, Richland, Union, Robeson, Cumberland, and Moore. The army marched on an average 450 miles; the wings extending some 35 or 40 miles. This would give an area of over 15,000 square miles which was operated over, all the time supporting men and animals on the country. 1000 killed, wounded, and missing will cover the casualties. Several of these were owing to accidental explosions at Columbia and Cheraw. The rebel loss in killed, wounded, and missing, was about 1200, and Sherman captured and brought into Fayetteville over 3000 prisoners.

—— General Couch, marching up from Wilmington, North Carolina, joined Schofield's troops in front of Kinston, North Carolina.

March 12.—The English blockade running steamers Syren, Duc de Chartres, Deer, and Fox, having run into Charleston harbor without knowledge of the surrender, were captured by the United States fleet.

—— The rebels burned the iron-clad ram Neuse, in front of Kinston, and evacuated a part of their lines.

—— General Sherman arrived at Fayetteville, North Carolina, where he captured 20 pieces of artillery and much material of war.

March 14.—The expedition under Major-General Stoneman, which left Knoxville, Tennessee, March 10, struck the East Tennessee Railroad at Wytheville, Christiansburg, and Salem. Between these points 33 bridges were burned, and 25 miles of track totally destroyed, and besides many prisoners were taken, and considerable quantities of corn and other stores destroyed.

March 15.—Jerome Clark, *alias* "Sue Mundy," was hung at Louisville, Kentucky.

—— Major-General Sherman reported from the bridge of the Richmond and Fredericksburg Railroad, across the South Anna River, that, having destroyed the James River Canal as far to the east as Goochland, he marched up to the Virginia Central Railroad at Tollsville, and destroyed it down to Beaver Dam Station, totally destroying 20 miles of the road. General Custer was then sent to Ashland, and General Devin to the South Anna bridges, all of which were destroyed. The amount of property destroyed in his march was enormous. The rebels attempted to prevent the burning of the Central Railroad Bridge over the South Anna, but the 5th United States Cavalry charged up to the bridge, and about 30 men dashed across on foot, driving off the enemy and capturing 3 pieces of artillery, 20-pounder Parrotts. In the course of the expedition mills, tobacco-houses, barns and buildings, produce, and everything that could feed Lee's army was destroyed.

—— Battle of Averysboro', or Moore's Cross Roads, or Taylor's Creek, North Carolina. General Sherman marching really towards Goldsboro', sent out on the left Slocum's 20th corps and Kilpatrick's Cavalry still further in advance, with orders to demonstrate towards Raleigh; 4 miles beyond Averysboro' the foragers met the rebel infantry advancing under Hardee. Kilpatrick dismounted his cavalry, and with 8 pieces of artillery prepared for battle, sending back to the 20th corps for reinforcements. The rebels advanced on Kilpatrick, who fell back, abandoning two pontoons, under the heavy fire of the enemy. Night coming on put an end to the battle.

March 16.—Kinston, North Carolina, was occupied by General Cox, of Schofield's corps, co-operating with General Sherman.

—— Battle of Averysboro', or Moor's Cross Roads, second day. Kilpatrick, being reinforced, advanced with his whole force. The rebels were steadily driven back, until they took refuge in their works at Moore's Cross Roads. Preparations were made for an assault, during which the rebels made strong attempts to turn the Federal flanks, but were repulsed after severe fighting. Later in the day, Major-Generals Williams, Slocum, and Sherman came upon the ground; they ordered assaults to be made on the rebel works, and succeeded in repelling all attacks upon their flanks. The rebels fell back, stubbornly contesting the ground, but during the night they retreated to Raleigh, leaving their killed and wounded on the field. The rebel loss was estimated at 1200 killed, wounded, and missing. Federal loss, 720. Federal loss, 14th corps, killed 21, wounded 100; 20th corps, killed 56, wounded 382. The Federals lost no prisoners. Number of rebel dead buried on the field 101, prisoners taken 197.

March 17.—The 13th and 16th army corps left Dauphine Island for Mobile Point, intending to advance by that route towards Mobile. The expedition was under command of General Canby as commander-in-chief, assisted by General Steele. The navy was under command of Admiral Thatcher.

March 18.—Benton's division, 13th army corps, landed at Mobile Point, and commenced a march against Mobile in that direction.

March 19.—2000 men of Canby's army landed at Cedar Point, and commenced an advance over land against Mobile; two abandoned forts were found.

—— Battle of Bentonsville or Morris Farm, North Carolina, sometimes called the battle of Smithfield. General Johnston, failing at Averysboro', and discovering that the objective point of Sherman was not Raleigh but Goldsboro', withdrew Hardee's troops in haste and ordered them to Bentonsville, where he intrenched himself and awaited Sherman's coming. Generals Duell and Robinson, of Morgan's division, being in the advance, were suddenly turned upon by the rebels, who were retiring. The Federal troops fell back to the railroad, where hasty intrenchments were thrown up, and they held their own in spite of desperate charges by the rebels in columns massed. These charges were made in quick succession and as quickly repulsed. Three of them are noted to have taken place in 35 minutes. Their loss was fearful. Johnston had 40,000 men, and Slocum but a single corps. At night the Federal lines remained intact, the rebel killed and wounded in front of them being very great.

March 20.—General Sherman arrived on the field at Bentonsville, and directed the disposition of the United States troops. The whole day was spent in bringing forward the body of the army, and massing it. Preparations were made for an advance and general battle in the morning. But during the night Johnston withdrew his troops in the direction of Smithville, and there being no obstacle in the way of Sherman's progress to Goldsboro', he took up the line of march. 3 guns were lost by the United States troops on the first day of the battle, which were retaken, with 7 others, and 7000 rebel prisoners were captured. Killed, 14th corps, 152, wounded 623, missing 127. 85 of the rebel dead were buried by this corps, and 232 prisoners were captured.

March 21.—Major-General Schofield, from Newbern, entered and occupied Goldsboro', and Major-General Terry, from Wilmington, secured Cox's Bridge crossing, and laid a pontoon bridge across Neuse River. The advance of General Sherman's army also reached Goldsboro', so that the movement resulted in a glorious success. After a march of the most extraordinary character, nearly 500 miles, over swamps and rivers deemed impassable to others, at the most inclement season of the year, and drawing their chief supplies from a poor and wasted country, they reached their destination in good health and condition, accomplishing the concentration. So skilful had been the plans, almost at the same moment of time, the divergent columns from Savannah, Newbern, and Wilmington, met at the point of rendezvous on the same day.

March 22.—Four divisions of cavalry, under command of Brevet Major-General Wilson, and General Edward McCook, General Lorey, General Upton, and General Hatch, left Chickasaw Bluffs, Alabama, for a grand expedition and march through Alabama and Georgia.

——— General Wilson's cavalry left Chickasaw, Alabama, and started southward, marching on three parallel roads.

March 23.—Major-General Sheridan, having concluded his raiding expedition west and south of Richmond, after a detour to the east, crossed the James River, and came within the lines of Grant and Meade.

——— The corps of General A. J. Smith, intended to operate against Mobile, landed at Danby's Mills, on the left bank of Fish River, 10 miles from Mobile Bay, and 20 miles from Fort Gaines. There was no opposition, an advance by that route not being expected by the enemy.

March 25.—Battle at Fort Fisher, Virginia, in front of the lines of the 6th corps, Army of the Potomac. After the rebel repulse at Fort Steadman, General Wright, who with the 6th corps held the centre, was ordered to push forward. This was done, and the rebel intrenched line in front of Fort Fisher was taken and held by Wright. Federal loss, 47 killed, 401 wounded, and 30 missing. Rebel killed and wounded estimated by General Wright at about 400. Rebel prisoners, 469.

——— Assault upon Fort Steadman, in front of 9th corps, General Meade's lines, and Fort Haskell, by rebels under General Gordon, called by Lee the battle of Hare's Hill. Before daylight, by a sudden rush, the rebels overpowered the Federal pickets, flanked the fort, and drove out the garrison, taking possession of the guns, and turning them against the Federal lines. Soon after, a determined attack was made on Fort Haskell, which was repulsed by McLaughlin's brigade; General McLaughlin and some of his men being taken prisoners. After the rebels had held Fort Steadman for some time, and had repulsed one or two attempts to take it, they were finally driven out by a charge made by reserves under direction of Generals J. G. Parke and Hartranft. The rebels lost 883 prisoners, and 1800 killed and wounded, and 8 battle flags. The rebel General Terry and several officers of rank were wounded. Federal loss, 68 killed, 338 wounded, and 506 prisoners. Immediately upon the repulse of the assaulting party, the Federal lines in front of the 2d and 6th corps were pushed forward by General Grant. They captured the rebels' strongly intrenched picket line and turned it against them. Lee endeavored to retake it, and the battle was continued until 8 o'clock at night, the rebels losing heavily after the battle.

——— General Lee sent in a request for a flag of truce to bury his dead in front of the Union lines. The bold movement at Fort Steadman was well planned, and had it been successful might have deranged the entire campaign of Grant. It would have cut off the main body of the Army of the Potomac from its base of supplies at City Point, and compelled it to evacuate the lines so long held before Petersburg.

——— Battle at Hatcher's Run, Virginia. The 2d corps, on the extreme left of the Federal lines at Hatcher's Run, after the affair at Fort Steadman on the extreme right, advanced in three columns against the enemy's line. They were under Generals Miles, Hayes, and Mott, the movement being superintended by Major-General A. A. Humphreys, the corps commander. The advance was made for about a mile, and the rebel works were then assaulted and carried by the command of Brigadier-General T. A. Smyth. Later in the day the whole line made a charge, and succeeded in capturing a portion of the rebel works defending the Southside Railroad. The losses in the 2d corps were 51 killed, 462 wounded, and 177 missing. Rebel loss estimated by General Humphreys at 2900.

——— Robert C. Kennedy, a rebel spy on "detached service," having been convicted by court-martial of being one of the incendiaries who attempted to set fire to the city of New York, was executed at Fort Lafayette, New York Harbor. He confessed that "it was originally intended to set fire to the city on the night of the Presidential election, but as the phosphorus was not prepared, it was postponed until the night of the 25th of November. Of the eight men who formed the original party, two fled to Canada, leaving but six. I was at first stopping at the Belmont House, in Fulton street, but afterwards moved into Prince street. I set fire to four hotels, or rather to Barnum's Museum, Lovejoy's Hotel, Tammany Hotel, and the New England House. The others only set fire to the house in which each was stopping, and then cut off. Had the entire eight done as I did, we would have set fire to 32 houses, and played a big joke on the Fire Department."

——— Major-General Steele, with the 13th army corps, advancing on Mobile, at Pollard, Alabama, met and defeated rebels under General Clanton, who was mortally wounded. 250 prisoners were taken by Steele, and he tore up the railroad track for several miles.

March 26.—Battle at Mitchell's Fork, Alabama, between 800 rebels and the advance of General Steele's command from Pensacola, marching towards Mobile. The rebels were driven off.

March 27.—The advance of Stoneman's cavalry, which had left Tennessee some time before, entered Boone, North Carolina, and routed a rebel force there, with a loss to them of 10 killed and 65 prisoners.

——— Major-General Granger, with the 13th corps, moved towards Spanish Fort, one of the defences of Mobile, captured the rifle-pits, and established batteries within 400 yards of the fort.

March 28.—The rebel ram Stonewall left Lisbon, Portugal, being warned off by the authorities. The United States frigate Niagara and gunboat Sacramento had arrived the same day, and were prohibited from leaving for 24 hours after the Stonewall had left. In afterwards changing anchorage the Niagara was fired upon by the Belem Fort, the commander of which supposed that the ship was about to disregard the prohibition. For this offence Portugal afterwards made an apology, and dismissed the commander of the fort.

——— A conference was held on board the steamer River Queen, near City Point, on the James River, between President Lincoln, Lieutenant-General Grant, Major-General William T. Sherman, Major-General George G. Meade, Major-General P. H. Sheridan, and Major-General E. O. C. Ord, and the plan of important movements settled and agreed upon.

——— The United States monitor Milwaukie was blown up by a torpedo in Mobile Bay.

March 29.—The United States gunboat Osage was blown up by a torpedo in Mobile Bay.

——— The St. Albans raiders at Montreal, Canada, were released from custody by Justice Smith, of a provincial court. They were afterwards arrested by order of the Canadian government.

——— Wilson's cavalry crossed the Mulberry Fork of the Black Warrior River; between the river and Montevalle they destroyed a large number of furnaces, foundries, machine-shops, rolling-mills, cotton warehouses, &c. They had a skirmish with 500 rebels under Roddy, whom they drove out of their intrenchments.

——— The Army of the Tennessee, consisting of the 15th and 17th corps, under command of Major-Generals O. O. Howard, Frank P. Blair, Jr., and John A. Logan, took up the line of march out of North Carolina, bound homeward, via Richmond.

——— Same day the Army of Georgia followed. It was composed of the 14th and 20th army corps, under the command of General Slocum. The 10th and 23d corps remained in North Carolina, with Kilpatrick's cavalry.

——— A forward movement of the whole Army of the Potomac commenced. The 2d corps, on the extreme left, advanced to Dabney's Mills, and took possession, without fighting, of the lines formerly held by the rebels. The lines formerly filled by the 2d corps were filled by the Army of the James, under General Ord, which had been brought to the south side for the purpose. General Meade established his headquarters at the Perkins House, near Gravelly Run, about 10 o'clock in the morning, and Lieutenant-General Grant established his headquarters at Rowanty Creek, about a mile from General Meade, in the afternoon.

March 29.—There was a heavy cannonading in the night, in front of Fort Steadman, occasioned by a supposition that the rebels were endeavoring to make another assault upon that work.

—————— Battle of Quaker Road. The 5th corps, under General Warren, took up the line of march at 3½ A. M., crossed Hatcher's Run, and reached the Vaughan Road at a point distant 3 or 4 miles from Dinwiddie Court-House. Finally, they crossed Gravelly Run in direction toward the Boydtown Plankroad, and took up a position in front of the rebel pickets. Skirmishing commenced at once, and there was more or less fighting on the right and left of the Quaker Road. Federal loss estimated at 300; rebel loss, about equal, with 100 prisoners. The rebels, who were under Bushrod Johnson, finally retired. Killed, Major Charles I. MacEuen, 198th Union League, Pennsylvania regiment; wounded, Brevet Brigadier-General Horatio G. Sickel.

—————— Major-General Sheridan, with 9000 cavalry under Major-Generals Merritt and Crook, moved by way of Reams's Station on the Weldon Railroad, and Maler's Crossing, on Rowanty Creek. He was bound for Dinwiddie Court-House, from which point he was to make a grand cavalry raid against the Southside Railroad and thence join General Sherman or return to Petersburg, as circumstances might permit. But, during the night of the 29th, General Grant sent Sheridan instructions to abandon the contemplated raid, and act in concert with the infantry under his immediate command, and turn the right flank of Lee's army, if possible.

March 30.—Second day of the grand operations of the Army of the Potomac before Petersburg, Virginia. Major-General Humphreys, with the 2d corps, again advanced, driving the enemy into his main line of works, and by night occupying a line from the Crow House, on Hatcher's Run, to the intersection of the Dabney's Mill and Boydton Plankroad. Major-General Warren, during the day, advanced on the Quaker Road to its intersection with the Boydton Plank, and pushed Ayres's division in a northwesterly direction over to the White Oak Road. No fighting of any consequence occurred this day, except picket skirmishing and exchange of artillery shots from the respective lines, now close to each other. The principal advance was upon the left wing, which had, in the operations of the previous days, extended itself and swung round on a right wheel.

.—————— General Merritt, of Sheridan's cavalry, by reconnoissance found the rebels posted in strong force on the White Oak Road, near Five Forks. There was some heavy skirmishing throughout the day.

—————— The rebels made an attack upon Granger's line, in front of Spanish Fort, below Mobile.

March 31.—Battle of Chamberlain's Creek; or, Five Forks. First day. The advance of the first division of Sheridan's cavalry got possession of the Five Forks. But in the meantime the 5th army corps, which had advanced toward the White Oak Road from the Vaughan Road, were attacked and driven back. The rebels then made an attack upon the United States cavalry at Five Forks, who, after a gallant resistance, were forced back, and cut off from the rest of the army. In order to rescue them, Sheridan ordered an attack upon another part of the line by Generals Gibbs, Gregg, and Custer, in which the rebel wounded fell into our hands. But the rebels fought with tenacity, and pressed on. The result was that at night Sheridan's forces were back at Dinwiddie Court-House — the operations of the day having been unsuccessful in consequence, General Sheridan alleged, of the failure of Warren, with the 5th corps, in the morning, to support the movement of the cavalry. Sheridan's loss was estimated at 800.

—————— About 10 A. M., Ayres, under General Warren's orders, advanced to dislodge the enemy in position on the White Oak Road. Ayres's attack was unsuccessful, and was followed by such a vigorous attack of the enemy that Ayres was compelled to fall back upon Crawford, who, in turn, was so strongly pressed by the enemy as to force both divisions back, in considerable disorder, to the position occupied by Griffin, when the pursuit of the enemy ceased. Immediately on ascertaining the condition of affairs, Major-General Humphreys was ordered to move to Warren's support, and that officer promptly sent Miles's division to attack in flank the force operating against Warren. This movement was handsomely executed by Miles, who, attacking the enemy vigorously, drove him back to his former position on the White Oak Road, capturing several colors and many prisoners. In the meantime Warren advanced with Griffin's division, supported by such portions of Ayres's and Crawford's divisions as could be rallied, and, regaining the position held by Ayres in the morning, Griffin attacked with Chamberlain's brigade, driving the enemy and securing a lodgment on the White Oak Road. The 5th corps lost 100 prisoners. 400 rebel prisoners and 2 battle-flags were taken. The loss of the 5th corps during the day was estimated at 1200.

March 31.—From 9 o'clock A. M. until dark, the 2d division 24th army corps was engaged with Heath's division of Hill's rebel corps. The operations were distinguished by brisk skirmishing and occasional heavy fighting. The losses of the corps during the day were estimated at 200 killed and wounded. 200 prisoners were taken from the rebels.

—————— The 2d corps advanced and fought Bushrod Johnson's division of A. P. Hill's corps. The fighting was severe, but the result was an advance, along the front of the 2d corps, of a mile and a half. General W. Dennison was wounded. Colonel Wm. Sergeant, 210th Pennsylvania, afterwards died.

—————— United States transport steamer General Lyon was burned off Cape Hatteras. There were on board from 550 to 600 persons, of whom but 29 were saved.

April 1.—Battle of Five Forks, Virginia. The Federal troops, cavalry and infantry, being under command of Major-General P. H. Sheridan. General Warren, with Griffin's and Crawford's divisions, moved between 7 and 8 o'clock in the morning. Meantime Sheridan moved his cavalry force at daylight against the enemy's lines in front, which gave way rapidly, moving off by the right flank and crossing Chamberlain's Creek. This hasty movement was accelerated by the discovery that two divisions of the 5th corps were in their rear and that one division was moving toward their left and rear. Sheridan then determined that he would drive the enemy with the cavalry to the Five Forks, press them inside of their works, and make a feint to turn their right flank, and meanwhile quietly move up the 5th corps with a view to attacking their left flank, crush the whole force, if possible, and drive westward those who might escape, thus isolating them from their army at Petersburg. Happily, this conception was successfully executed. The rebels were pressed and driven by repeated charges of the cavalry. At 2 o'clock the enemy was driven within his works on the White Oak Road, and his skirmish line was driven in. General Merritt was then ordered to demonstrate on the right flank, while Sheridan expected to strike a heavy blow on the left flank with the 5th corps. In the execution of these movements, General Warren was charged by General Sheridan with unwillingness in bringing up his men, and of making his dispositions slowly, and not endeavoring to exert himself to insure a victory. He therefore removed General Warren from command before the operations of the day were concluded, and appointed General Griffin to the command of the 5th corps. After this was done, the corps was brought up to efficient work, and secured the success of the day. The 5th corps, on reaching the White Oak Road, made a left wheel, and burst on the enemy's left flank and rear like a tornado, and pushed rapidly on, orders having been given that if the enemy was routed there should be no halt to reform broken lines. The firing of the 5th corps was the signal to General Merritt to assault, which was promptly responded to, and the works of the enemy were soon carried at several points. The enemy were driven from their strong line of works and completely routed, the 5th corps doubling up their left flank in confusion, and the cavalry of General Merritt, dashing on to the White Oak Road, capturing their artillery and turning it upon them, and riding into their broken ranks, so demoralized them, that they made no serious stand after their line was carried, but took to flight in disorder. Between 5000 and 6000 prisoners fell into our hands, and the fugitives were driven westward, and were pursued until long after dark, by Merritt's and McKenzie's cavalry, for a distance of six miles. Killed, on the Federal side, General Winthrop, Major Glenn, 198th Pennsylvania. Wounded, General Dennison, Brevet Brigadier-General Gwyn, Colonel Trenlay, Colonel Doolittle, 188th New York; Colonel Boweman, commanding a brigade; Colonel Berwick, 7th Indiana. 4 cannon, the ambulance and baggage teams, and 28 battle-flags, were captured by Sheridan.

April 1.—About 4 o'clock in the afternoon, the rebels of Davis's, Cook's, and Teall's brigades, of Hill's corps, under General Heth, made an attack upon the line of General Foster, of Ord's 24th corps. They made a sudden dash and got possession of the Federal intrenchments, but were driven out after a hand-to-hand fight, losing nearly 100 killed and wounded and 200 prisoners.

———— The 2d corps was engaged in active fighting with the rebels in its front all day, and gradually fixed its line firmly in spite of their sharp firing. The left of the corps extended beyond the Boydtown Road and rested on the White Oak Road, there connecting with the 5th corps. In front of the 2d corps the enemy had a part of their 3d corps (Hill's), the other part being opposed to the 24th corps, which lay on the right of the 2d. The ground in which the 2d corps was fighting was in most part thick pine woods, and though they afforded very good cover, they were very unfavorable for the action of lines in close order. The ground was, therefore, much in favor of the enemy.

———— The 6th and 9th corps were quiet all day, scarcely a shot being fired in front of the lines which they held.

———— Battle of Ebenezer Church, Alabama, between Wilson's cavalry and 5000 rebels under Forrest, Chalmers, Armstrong, and Adams. The rebels were beaten, losing 4 guns and many small-arms. Federal loss, 30 killed and wounded. Rebel loss equally heavy, and 300 prisoners.

April 2.—Fourth day of the operations against Petersburg, Virginia. Generals Grant and Meade believing from the operations on the rebel line on the right that the left of the line was thinly held, ordered Major-Generals Parke, of the 9th corps, and Wright, of the 6th corps, to attack at 4 A. M. Major-General Wright carried everything before him, taking possession of the enemy's strong line of works, and capturing many guns and prisoners. After carrying the enemy's lines in his front, and reaching the Boydtown Plank-Road, Major-General Wright turned to his left and swept down the enemy's line of intrenchments till near Hatcher's Run, where, meeting the head of the 24th corps, General Wright retraced his steps and advanced on the Boydtown Plank-Road towards Petersburg, encountering the enemy in an inner line of works immediately around the city. Major-General Wright deployed his corps confronting their works, in conjunction with the 24th and part of the 2d corps. Major-General Parke's attack at 4 A. M. was also successful, carrying the enemy's lines, capturing guns and prisoners; but the position of the 9th corps, confronting that position of the enemy's line the longest held and most strongly fortified, it was found he held a second and inner line, which Major-General Parke was unable to carry. Receiving a despatch during the morning from Major-General Parke, reporting his being pressed by the enemy, the troops left in City Point defences, under Brigadier-General Benham and Brevet Brigadier-General Collis, were ordered up to General Parke's support; their prompt arrival enabling them to render material assistance to General Parke in holding his lines. So soon as Major-General Wright's success was reported, Major-General Humphreys was ordered to advance with the remaining divisions of his corps; Hays, on the right, advanced and captured a redoubt in front of the Crow House, taking a gun and over 100 prisoners. Mott, on the left, on advancing on the Boydtown Plank-Road, found the enemy's line evacuated. Hays and Mott pushed forward and joined the 6th corps, confronting the enemy. Early in the morning, Miles, reporting his return to his position on the White Oak Road, was ordered to advance on the Claiborne Road simultaneously with Mott and Hays. Miles, perceiving the enemy were moving to his right, pursued and overtook him at Sutherland's Station, where a sharp engagement took place, Miles handling his single division with great skill and gallantry, capturing several guns and many prisoners. On receiving intelligence of Miles being engaged, Hays was sent to his support, but did not reach the field till the action was over. At 3 A. M. of the 3d of April, Major-Generals Parke and Wright reported no enemy in their front, when, on advancing, it was ascertained Petersburg was evacuated. Before the evacuation of Petersburg, the rebels fired eight cotton and tobacco warehouses, destroying $11,000 worth of cotton and 1500 hogsheads of tobacco. The Norfolk Depot was also burned. The colored people welcomed the Union troops with demonstrations of joy, and hundreds of people thronged the streets, listening to the music of the bands as the troops passed by. The rebel Lieutenant-General A. P. Hill was killed in the fight before Petersburg. Killed, Colonel John N. Crosby, 61st Pennsylvania Volunteers.

April 2.—Battle of Selma, Alabama, between Wilson's cavalry and 7000 rebels, with 30 pieces of artillery. The works were taken by assault and the rebels driven out. Wilson captured 2400 prisoners, 32 pieces of artillery, mounted, and 70 in the arsenals, beside small arms, &c. Federal loss, 324 killed, wounded, and missing. Rebel loss about 300 killed and wounded. On the Federal side was killed, Colonel George W. Dobb, 4th Ohio; wounded, General Eli Long, Colonel Miller, 17th Indiana, Colonel McCormick, 7th Pennsylvania, Colonel Boggs, and other officers. All the arsenals and rebel government property at Selma were burned.

April 3.—Richmond, Virginia, was entered by Major-General Weitzell, of the 25th army corps. Lee telegraphed Davis, at 3 P. M. on Sunday, that he was driven back, and must evacuate. This was announced in church. All the leading men got away that evening. Four rebel iron-clads were exploded, and five wooden vessels. The Virginia was sunk in the James River above the obstructions. Ewell set the city on fire, and all the business portion of the main street to the river was destroyed. The bridges across the river were also destroyed. General Weitzel captured in Richmond 1000 well prisoners, and 5000 rebel wounded were found in the hospitals; 500 pieces of artillery and 5000 small-arms were captured. Admiral Porter took possession of two small vessels.

———— Immediately after the capture of Petersburg, which was garrisoned, the remaining troops of the 2d, 6th, and 9th corps moved up the river, and at night were at Sutherland Station. The pursuit was made along the river road and the magazine road by the cavalry and the 2d, 5th, and 6th corps. The 9th corps was detached to guard the Southside Railroad.

———— Fight at Deep Creek, Virginia, between rebel infantry and Sheridan's cavalry in pursuit; many prisoners were taken during the day, with 5 pieces of abandoned artillery and several wagons.

April 4.—Major-General Sheridan reached Jetersville, Virginia, where he learned that Lee and his whole army were at Amelia Court-house. Sheridan intrenched and prepared to hold Lee until the main army could come up.

———— The steamer Harriet Deford, plying between Baltimore and ports on the Patuxent River, was seized near Fairhaven by 27 rebels, who came on board disguised as passengers. The crew and passengers were put on shore.

April 4.—General Grant telegraphed that the losses of his army would not exceed 7000 killed, wounded, and missing, of whom from 1500 to 2000 were captured, and many but slightly wounded. The rebels lost 13,000 prisoners and over 100 guns. Among the prisoners were officers from generals down to sergeants. Wounded before Petersburg, General Potter, Colonels Getchell, 31st Maine, Gregg, 179th New York, Lieutenant-Colonel Winslow, 179th New York, Majors Betton, 31st Maine, and Morrow, 205th Pennsylvania.

April 5.—Battle at Paine's Cross Roads, Virginia, or Howe Cross Roads. General Davies, sent out by Sheridan to make a reconnoissance, struck a train of 180 wagons which he captured, beside 5 pieces of artillery, and routing the rebel cavalry's artillery. The wagons were destroyed, and a large number of prisoners were brought in. The rebels attempted to cut off Davies's brigade, but it being supported by Gregg and Smith's brigades, the movement was unsuccessful.

——— The 2d and 6th corps reached Jetersville, where they found the 5th corps intrenched and Sheridan's cavalry.

——— The St. Albans raiders were discharged from custody at Montreal, but were immediately rearrested and sent to Upper Canada. A strong force of cavalry and artillery guarded them to the train.

——— William H. Seward, Secretary of State, was thrown from his carriage, and his arm broken and his face much bruised.

April 6.—Battle of Sailor's Creek, Virginia. The 2d corps came up with the enemy, and commenced a rearguard fight, which continued all day till evening, when the enemy was so crowded in attempting to cross Sailor's Creek that he had to abandon a large train. Guns, colors, and prisoners were taken in these successful operations of the 2d corps. The 6th corps, on the left of the 2d, came up with the enemy posted on Sailor's Creek. Major-General Wright attacked with two divisions, and completely routed the enemy. In this attack the cavalry under Major-General Sheridan was operating on the left of the 6th corps, while Humphreys was pressing on the right. The result of the combined operations was the capture of Lieutenant-General Ewell and four other general officers, with most of Ewell's corps. The cavalry under Sheridan attacked the rebel trains near Deatonsville, attempting to escape under escort of infantry and cavalry, just south of Sailor's Creek. Custer, Crook, and Devin took 16 pieces of artillery, 400 wagons, and many prisoners; three divisions of the rebels were cut off from the line of retreat.

——— General Sherman, being about to commence his northern march, estimated the strength of Joe Johnston's army at Smithfield to be about 45,000 men.

April 7.—The pursuit of Lee's army was continued. There was a skirmish at High Bridge, over the Appomattox. 3 spans of the railroad bridge were burned by the rebels, who also attempted to burn the common bridge, but did not succeed. Humphreys crossed, and continued the pursuit, taking 18 abandoned guns at this point. At the junction of the High Bridge and Farmville Roads, the rebels were found to be intrenched, with the intention of making a stand, to cover the withdrawal of their troops. Barlow detached, and sent towards Farmville, successfully attacked a portion of the rebels, and hastened the evacuation. Miles's division, in the front of Humphreys, made an attack which was unsuccessful. The 6th corps, under Wright, reached Farmville in the afternoon, and found the bridge destroyed; a pontoon was laid down, and the corps crossed about nightfall. General Thomas A. Smith was killed, Major-General Mott wounded, and General Gregg was taken prisoner.

——— Lieutenant-General Grant, commanding the United States armies, sent a note to General Lee, suggesting to the latter, that a surrender of his armies would prevent a further effusion of blood, and offering honorable terms.

April 7.—General Lee, while declining to admit that further resistance would be hopeless, asked what terms would be offered.

April 8.—Sheridan continued the pursuit of Lee. 4 trains of cars were captured by General Custer at Appomattox depot. The cavalry pushed on in the direction of Appomattox Court House, capturing many prisoners, 25 pieces of artillery, a hospital train, and a large park of wagons. The fighting continued until after dark, and the rebels were driven to Appomattox Court House. By this time, in addition to the cavalry of Sheridan, the 2d, 5th, and 6th army corps—the army of the James consisting of the 24th corps—had come up under General Ord, and one division of the 25th corps.

——— General Grant replied to General Lee, in reference to the proposition to the latter, that he should surrender, that all he would require would be, "that the men surrendered shall be disqualified for taking up arms again against the government of the United States until properly exchanged."

——— The left lunette of the Spanish fort below Mobile, having been previously taken by General Smith, the rebels evacuated the other parts of the fort at daylight on the 9th, and Colonel Bertam's brigade immediately occupied the fort, and found 5 mortars and 25 guns, a large quantity of ammunition, a number of mules and horses, but few rations. All the guns were spiked with nails. The prisoners taken were 25 officers and 5381 men. The capture of Spanish Fort caused the fall of Forts Alexis, Eugene, and Bleakely.

April 9.—At 12 M., the head of the 2d corps was within 3 miles of Appomattox Court House, where it came up with the enemy.

——— General Lee replied again that the emergency had not yet arisen for a surrender of his army, but proposed to meet General Grant, to consider questions connected with a general restoration of peace. General Grant replied that he had not power to negotiate a general peace, and that an interview would, therefore, be fruitless. Same day General Lee wrote to General Grant requesting an interview with reference to Grant's first proposition.

——— General Grant replied same day, as follows:— "I propose to receive the surrender of the Army of Northern Virginia on the following terms, to wit:—Rolls of all the officers and men to be made in duplicate. One copy to be given to an officer designated by me, the other to be retained by such officer or officers as you may designate. The officers to give their individual paroles not to take arms against the government of the United States until properly exchanged, and each company or regimental commander sign a like parole for the men of their commands. The arms, artillery, and public property to be parked and stacked, and turned over to the officers appointed by me to receive them. This will not embrace the side-arms of the officers, nor their private horses or baggage. This done, each officer and man will be allowed to return to their homes, not to be disturbed by United States authority, so long as they observe their parole and the laws in force where they may reside." Same day General Lee notified General Grant that these terms were accepted; a truce was established, and measures taken to perfect the formalities necessary on the surrender of the rebel Army of Northern Virginia.

——— General Sherman's army took up the line of march from Goldsboro', North Carolina. There was some skirmishing at the bridge over Little River.

April 10.—Blakely River, below Mobile, being cleared of torpedoes, the United States monitor Octorara, and the iron-clads were enabled to move up and bombard Forts Huger and Tracy with great effect.

——— The President issued a proclamation releasing certain southern ports, formerly declared to be blockaded, from the blockade, and declaring them henceforth closed as ports of entry, and also designating which southern ports should be considered open.

——— The President issued a proclamation notifying foreign nations that the United States demanded for their war-vessels in foreign ports the same privileges as were conceded to other maritime nations, and that they would no longer submit to the restrictive rules which had been imposed upon United States vessels during the war, stating that retaliation would ensue by the United States denying to war-vessels of the nations which should refuse to withdraw those restrictions, the privileges heretofore accorded to them in our ports, and adding, "*The United States, whatever claim or pretence may have existed heretofore, are now at least entitled to claim and concede an entire and friendly equality of rights and hospitalities with all maritime nations.*"

April 11.—Forts Huger and Tracy, below Mobile, were evacuated by the rebels, and possession of them taken by the United States forces.

—— A rebel ram, coming down the Roanoke River, was blown up by a torpedo.

—— Lynchburg, Virgina, surrendered to a lieutenant and a scouting party.

April 12.—Battle of Salisbury, North Carolina. General Stoneman arrived at Grant's Creek, 5 miles from Salisbury, the rebel line for the defence of the town, at 6 A. M. This line, defended by artillery and infantry, was now forced, and our forces entered Salisbury at 10 A. M., capturing 8 stand of colors, 10 guns, 1164 prisoners, shells, with powder, clothing, and an immense quantity of supplies. 13 pieces of artillery were brought away, and all other stores not needed for our immediate command were destroyed. The greater part of these supplies had just been received from Raleigh. One large arsenal, machinery complete, with depots, 2 engines and trains, several bridges between Greensboro' and Danville, with several miles of railroad track, were destroyed. Our loss was very few in killed and wounded. Among the latter, Captain R. Morrow, Assistant Adjutant-General of Stoneman's staff.

—— Montgomery, Alabama, was surrendered to Wilson's cavalry, the rebels having evacuated it after burning 209,000 bales of cotton. All the government property in the town was destroyed by the United States cavalry.

—— Admiral H. K. Thatcher took 8000 men to the west side of Mobile Bay for the purpose of attacking Mobile. On their arrival, it was ascertained that the rebels had evacuated their defences and retreated, with their gunboats, up the Alabama River. Fort Pinto, the Spanish river battery, Cheseteau Point battery, and 3 heavy forts below within Garnero's Bend, were now in possession of the United States.

—— Edwin M. Stanton, Secretary of War, announced that his Department, after mature consideration and consultation with the Lieutenant-General upon the results of the recent campaigns, had come to the following determinations, which were to be carried into effect by appropriate orders to be immediately issued: First, To stop all drafting and recruiting in the loyal states. Second, To curtail purchases for arms, ammunition, quartermasters' and commissary supplies, and reduce the expenses of the military establishment in its several branches. Third, To reduce the number of general and staff officers to the actual necessities of the service. Fourth, To remove all military restrictions upon trade and commerce, so far as may be consistent with the public safety.

—— R. M. T. Hunter, John Letcher, William C. Rives, and other Virginians, issued an address calling on the late rebel legislature to assemble at Richmond, with the late governor and other state officers, to consult upon the situation of affairs. General Weitzel approved of this movement, and promised passes and safe conduct to the parties who might assemble.

April 13.—General E. O. C. Ord, who had succeeded General Weitzel in command at Richmond, issued an order revoking the privilege granted to the ex-rebel politicians and members of the legislature to assemble at Richmond for consultation. At the same time, he issued an order notifying the signers of that paper that if they remained in the city for twelve hours longer they would be arrested.

—— Kilpatrick's cavalry entered Raleigh, North Carolina, which was formally surrendered to the United States.

April 14.—The old flag of Fort Sumter, Charleston Harbor, South Carolina, which was hauled down upon the formal ceremony of surrender by Major Anderson, April 14th, 1861, was raised again at 12 o'clock, by the hands of Major-General (late Major) Anderson, assisted by as many of his old garrison as had survived the war. Reverend Henry Ward Beecher, by appointment of the President, delivered an address.

—— Mobile was surrendered to General Granger, of the 13th army corps, and Admiral Thatcher. The city, having been evacuated by the rebel soldiers, there were captured 215 heavy guns, 2000 stand of arms, and 30,000 bales of cotton, besides immense quantities of corn and other grain, and it was also estimated that 100,000 bales of cotton and 75,000 barrels of rosin were hidden in the swamps along the Alabama, most of which was within reach of our forces.

—— The United States despatch-boat Rose was blown up by a torpedo near Mobile.

—— Abraham Lincoln, President of the United States, was assassinated at Ford's Theatre, Washington, by John Wilkes Booth, about 9.30 P. M. The murderer approached the President while sitting in a private box with Mrs. Lincoln, Miss Harris, and Major Rathburn. During the third act, and while there was a temporary pause for one of the actors to enter, the sharp report of a pistol was heard, which merely attracted attention, but suggested nothing serious, until a man rushed to the front of the President's box, waving a long dagger in his right hand, and exclaiming "*Sic semper tyrannis!*" and immediately leaped from the box, which was of the second tier, to the stage beneath, and ran across to the opposite side, thus making his escape, amid the bewilderment of the audience, from the rear of the theatre, and, mounting a horse, fled.

—— About the same hour a man rang the bell at the house of William H. Seward, Secretary of State. The call having been answered, a person at the door, afterwards ascertained to be William H. Payne, or Powell, said he had come from Dr. Verdi, Secretary Seward's family physician, with a particular direction concerning the medicine. He insisted on going up, although repeatedly informed that no one could enter the chamber. He pushed the servant aside and walked quickly to the Secretary's room, and was there met by Mr. Frederick W. Seward, of whom he demanded to see the Secretary, making the same representation which he did to the servant. Mr. Seward refused him admission, when Payne struck him on the head with a billy, severely injuring the skull, and felling him almost senseless. Payne then rushed into the chamber and attacked Major Seward, Paymaster in the United States Army, and Mr. Hansell, a messenger of the State Department, and two male nurses, disabling them all. He then rushed upon the Secretary, who was lying in bed in the same room, and inflicted three stabs in the neck. He then rushed down stairs, mounted his horse at the door, and rode off before an alarm could be sounded, and in the same manner of the assassin of the President.

April 15.—Abraham Lincoln died at Washington at 7.22 A. M., from the effect of the pistol-ball by which he was shot. He was unconscious from the time of the assault until his death, and never spoke. After his death it was ascertained by the surgeons that the ball entered the skull midway between the left ear and the centre of the back of the head, and passed nearly to the right eye. The ball and two loose fragments of lead were found in the brain. Both orbital roofs were fractured inwardly, probably from contre-coup.

—— Andrew Johnson, late Vice-President of the United States, took the oath of office as President, before Hon. Salmon P. Chase, Vice-President of the United States, about 10 o'clock, A. M.

April 16.—West Point, Georgia, captured by La Grange's brigade of McCook's division of Wilson's cavalry. The arsenal, locomotives, cars, and other public property were destroyed.

April 16.—Columbus, Georgia, was taken by General Upton, of Wilson's cavalry. The works were carried by assault, with a Federal loss of only 5 killed and 12 wounded. 2000 rebel prisoners were taken, and 70 pieces of artillery. The arsenal, factories, locomotives, cars, cotton-mills, &c., were burned.

April 18.—A memorandum, or basis of agreement, was determined upon, at or near Durham's Station, North Carolina, between Major-General William T. Sherman, commanding army of United States, and General Joseph E. Johnston, commanding rebel army, upon the following terms:—

First. The contending armies now in the field to maintain the *status quo* until notice is given by the commanding general of any one to his opponent, and reasonable time, say forty-eight hours, allowed.

Second. The Confederate armies now in existence to be disbanded and conducted to their several state capitals, there to deposit their arms and public property in the state arsenal; and each officer and man to execute and file an agreement to cease from acts of war, and to abide the action of both State and Federal authorities. The number of arms and munitions of war to be reported to the Chief of Ordnance at Washington City, subject to the future action of the Congress of the United States, and in the mean time to be used solely to maintain peace and order within the borders of the states respectively.

Third. The recognition by the Executive of the United States of the several State Governments, on their officers and legislatures taking the oath prescribed by the Constitution of the United States; and where conflicting State Governments have resulted from the war, the legitimacy of all shall be submitted to the Supreme Court of the United States.

Fourth. The re-establishment of all Federal Courts in the several states, with powers as defined by the Constitution and laws of Congress.

Fifth. The people and inhabitants of all states to be guaranteed, so far as the Executive can, their political rights and franchises, as well as their right of person and property, as defined by the Constitution of the United States and of the states respectively.

Sixth. The Executive authority or Government of the United States not to disturb any of the people by reason of the late war, so long as they live in peace and quiet, and abstain from acts of armed hostility, and obey the laws in existence at the place of their residence.

Seventh. In general terms it is announced that the war is to cease; a general amnesty, so far as the Executive of the United States can command, on condition of the disbandment of the Confederate armies, the distribution of arms, and the resumption of peaceful pursuits by officers and men hitherto composing said armies.

This arrangement was disapproved of by the President and Cabinet, for the following, among other reasons:—

First. It was an exercise of authority not vested in General Sherman, and on its face shows that both he and Johnston knew that Sherman had no authority to enter into any such arrangements.

Second. It was a practical acknowledgment of the rebel government.

Third. It undertook to re-establish rebel State Governments that had been overthrown at the sacrifice of many thousand loyal lives and immense treasure, and placed arms and munitions of war in hands of rebels at their respective capitals, which might be used as soon as the armies of the United States were disbanded, and used to conquer and subdue loyal states.

Fourth. By the restoration of rebel authority in their respective states, they would be enabled to re-establish slavery.

Fifth. It might furnish a ground of responsibility on the part of the Federal Government to pay the rebel debt, and certainly subjects loyal citizens of rebel states to debt contracted by rebels in the name of the states.

Sixth. It puts in dispute the existence of loyal state governments, and the new state of West Virginia, which had been recognised by every department of the United States government.

Seventh. It practically abolished confiscation laws, and relieved rebels of every degree, who had slaughtered our people, from all pains and penalties for their crimes.

Eighth. It gave terms that had been deliberated repeatedly and solemnly rejected by President Lincoln, and better terms than rebels had ever asked, in their most prosperous condition.

Ninth. It formed no basis of true and lasting peace, but relieved rebels from the presence of our victories, and left them in a condition to renew their efforts to overthrow the United States government, and subdue the loyal states, whenever their strength was recruited and any opportunity should offer.

General Sherman was ordered to resume hostilities immediately; and he was directed that the instructions given by the late President in the telegram which was penned by Mr. Lincoln himself at the capitol, on the night of the 3d of March, were approved by President Andrew Johnson, and were reiterated to govern the action of military commanders. It was as follows:—

"Washington, March 3, 1865, 12 P. M. Lieutenant-General Grant: The President directs me to say to you that he wishes you to have no conference with General Lee, unless it be for the capitulation of General Lee's army, or on some minor and purely military matter.

"He instructs me to say that you are not to decide, discuss, or confer upon any political questions. Such questions the President holds in his own hands, and will not submit them to military conference or conventions. In the mean time you are to press to the utmost your military advantages.

"EDWIN M. STANTON,
"Secretary of War."

General Grant immediately repaired to North Carolina to take the command of the army, if necessary, or to superintend subsequent negotiations for the surrender of Johnston's army.

April 19.—In accordance with the recommendation of William Hunter, Acting Secretary of State, this day was observed throughout the United States as a day of general mourning, the funeral services having been held in Washington, and the body of the President having been taken from that city on its mournful journey to its last resting place.

April 20.—Secretary Stanton issued a proclamation offering the reward of $50,000 for "the murderer of the late President, in addition to all other rewards offered by municipal authorities or state executives, $25,000 for the arrest of G. A. Atzerott, sometimes called 'Port Tobacco,' $25,000 for the arrest of David C. Harold, accomplice of Booth."

—— Andrew Atzerott charged with complicity with the murder of President Lincoln, was arrested at Washington, D. C.

April 21.—Macon, Georgia, was captured by Wilson's cavalry, who were asked to suspend proceedings in consequence of the first truce between Sherman and Johnston. The results of Wilson's raid, up to this time, were summed up as follows:—The capture and occupation of four of the most important cities in the Confederacy, 6000 prisoners, over 200 guns, a large supply of small arms, devastation of the country, and destruction of at least five hundred millions of dollars worth of property, either directly or indirectly belonging to the rebel government.

April 22.—Major-General Henry Wager Halleck assumed command "of the military division which embraces the Department of Virginia, the Army of the Potomac, and such part of North Carolina as may not be occupied by the command of Major-General Sherman."

April 23.—The rebel ram Webb, commanded by Captain C. W. Read, ran out of the Red River, passed the United States blockading fleet, at the mouth of that stream, and proceeded down the Mississippi River at a high rate of speed.

April 24.—President Johnson issued a proclamation, appointing Thursday, May 25, to be observed throughout the United States as a day of public mourning, on account of the assassination of Abraham Lincoln.

April 24.—Secretary Stanton telegraphed to General John A. Dix, New York:—"A despatch from General Sherman states that 'Wilson held Macon on the 30th, with Howell Cobb, G. W. Smith, and others as prisoners, but they claimed the benefit of my armistice, and he has telegraphed me through the rebel lines for orders. I have answered him that he may draw out of Macon, and hold his command for further orders, unless he has reason to believe the rebels are changing the status to our prejudice.'"

—— Secretary Stanton telegraphed to General John A. Dix, New York:—"This department has information that the President's murder was organized in Canada and approved in Richmond. One of the assassins, now in prison, who attempted to kill Mr. Seward, is believed to be one of the St. Albans raiders."

—— Attorney-General Speed published an opinion to the effect, 1st, that the surrender of Lee's army did not give to the rebel soldiers who were paroled a right to return to the loyal states; 2d, that civilians, formerly residing in the loyal states, were not granted such privileges; 3d, that paroled rebel officers had no right to continue to wear their old uniforms.

—— Fifty-one rebel flags, captured by General Sheridan's cavalry, in the campaign from Petersburg to Appomattox Court-house, Virginia, were presented to the War Department.

—— General Grant reached Raleigh, North Carolina, and immediately delivered to General Sherman the reply to his negotiations with Johnston. Notice was at once given the latter terminating the truce, and informing him "that civil matters could not be entertained in any convention between army commanders."

April 25.—The steamer Hamilton, with United States troops on board, struck a torpedo below Mobile; 13 persons were killed and wounded.

—— The United States steamer Massachusetts came into collision with the packet-boat Black Diamond, near Fortress Monroe, and was sunk. The Massachusetts had on board paroled and exchanged Union prisoners, 50 of whom were drowned.

April 26.—12 flags, captured by the 5th corps in the late campaign at Petersburg, &c., were presented to the War Department.

—— J. Wilkes Booth and David C. Harold were chased from a swamp in St. Mary's county, Maryland, to Garrett's farm, near Port Royal, on the Rappahannock, by Colonel Baker's force. The rear of the barn in which they took refuge was fired. Booth, while in the barn, was shot through the head by Sergeant Boston Corbett and killed, lingering about three hours, and Harold surrendered. Booth's body and Harold were brought to Washington the next day.

—— The rebel General Joseph E. Johnston surrendered the forces in his command, embracing all from Raleigh to the Chattahoochie, to General Sherman, on the basis agreed upon between Lee and Grant for the Army of Northern Virginia.

April 27.—The grand jury of Toronto found a true bill against Jacob Thompson, C. C. Clay, W. H. Cleary, William Lawrence, and Messrs. Donald and Bennet Young, for a breach of the neutrality laws.

—— The steamer Sultana, laden with 2176 United States soldiers and the crew, blew up about 7 miles above Memphis. 700 were rescued, and 1400 were scalded to death and drowned.

—— Secretary Stanton telegraphed to General Dix, New York:—

"This department has received the following despatch from Major-General Halleck, commanding the Military Division of the James. Generals Canby and Thomas were instructed some days ago that Sherman's arrangement with Johnston was disapproved by the President, and they were ordered to disregard it and push the enemy in every direction.

"EDWIN M. STANTON, Secretary of War.

"'RICHMOND, 2.30 P. M., April 26.—Hon. E. M. Stanton, Secretary of War: Generals Meade, Sheridan, and Wright are acting under orders to pay no regard to any truce or orders of General Sherman respecting hostilities, on the ground that Sherman's agreement could bind his own command only, and no other. They are directed to push onward, regardless of orders from any one except General Grant, and cut off Johnston's retreat.

"'Beauregard has telegraphed to Danville that a new arrangement had been made with Sherman, and that the advance of the 6th corps was to be suspended until further orders. I have telegraphed back to obey no orders of Sherman's, but to push on as rapidly as possible.

"'The bankers have information to-day that Jefferson Davis's specie is moving south from Greensboro' in wagons as fast as possible.

"'I suggest that orders be telegraphed through General Thomas that General Wilson obey no orders from Sherman, and notifying him and Canby and all commanders on the Mississippi to take measures to intercept the rebel chiefs and their plunder. The specie taken by them is estimated here at from six to thirteen millions.
"'H. W. HALLECK,
"'Major-General Commanding.'"

April 27.—The following summary of what General Stoneman's command had done since previous advices, was received at Knoxville: One portion of the command, under Colonel Palmer, moved down the Catawba River, dispersing parties going southwest from Johnston's army. He captured upwards of 2000 prisoners, and 2 pieces of artillery, and, amongst other things destroyed, was the immense railroad bridge over the Catawba River, 1125 feet long and 60 feet high. Then, learning that a general armistice had been entered into between Sherman and Johnston, Colonel Palmer ceased operations. The other portion of the command, under General Gillem, attacked and routed a rebel force under Major-General McCowan, at Morgantown, taking 1 piece of artillery, and afterwards forcing the pass through the Blue Ridge held by the rebel forces under General Martin, taking 6 guns, and could have captured or destroyed the whole force, had General Gillem not been met by General Martin, with a flag of truce, and bearing a letter from General Sherman, countersigned by General Johnston, and directed to General Stoneman, ordering a general suspension of hostilities, and a withdrawal of the forces under General Stoneman.

April 28.—The 6th corps, General Wright, occupied Danville, Virginia, being sent there after news was received of Sherman's first arrangement with Johnston. 13 locomotives, 117 box-cars, ironwork, machinery, &c., were captured. The march to Danville, 100 miles, was made by the 6th corps in 4 days.

—— Orders were issued by the War Department for the reduction of the expenses of the army, by the discharge of ocean transports not needed for service, stoppage of purchases of horses, mules, and wagons for transportation, stoppage of purchases of supplies, railroad construction and transportation, arms, ammunition, and material of war, stoppage of work on field fortifications, the discharge of soldiers in hospitals and prisoners of war, reduction of the number of clerks and employees, the discharge of prisoners of war willing to take the oath of allegiance, &c.

April 29.—Major-General J. M. Schofield assumes command of the Department of North Carolina, and publishes a proclamation, at Raleigh, announcing the cessation of hostilities and the return of peace, and requesting the citizens of the state to assist in the work of restoration. Another proclamation declared that all persons heretofore held as slaves were free, and recommended that contracts for labor be entered into between them and their late masters.

—— President Johnston postponed the day of general mourning upon account of the death of Abraham Lincoln until June 1st.

—— The President of the United States, by proclamation, withdrew all restrictions upon internal, domestic, and coastwise commercial intercourse in such parts of the states of Tennessee, Virginia, North Carolina, South Carolina, Georgia, Florida, Alabama, Mississippi, and so much of Louisiana as lies east of the

Mississippi River as was embraced within the lines of national military occupation, excepting only such restrictions as are imposed by acts of Congress and regulations in pursuance thereof, prescribed by the Secretary of the Treasury and approved by the President; and also excepting goods contraband of war.

May 1.—The President of the United States issued a proclamation, declaring that "The Attorney-General of the United States hath given his opinion that the persons implicated in the murder of the late President, Abraham Lincoln, and the attempted assassination of the Honorable William H. Seward, Secretary of State, and in an alleged conspiracy to assassinate other officers of the Federal Government at Washington City, and their aiders and abettors, are subject to the jurisdiction of and legally triable before a Military Commission." It was, therefore, ordered, that military officers be selected to hold the court by the Adjutant-General, that Advocate-General Holt prepare charges, and that Brevet Major-General Hartranft be provost-marshal of the court. The court was composed of the following officers:—Major-General David Hunter, President; Major-General Lewis Wallace, Major-General J. G. Foster, Major-General Kautz, Brigadier-General Ekin, Brigadier-General Howe, Brigadier-General Harris, Colonel Clendonin, 8th Illinois cavalry, Colonel C. H. Tompkins, U. S. Army. General Joseph Holt, Judge Advocate; Colonels Bingham of Ohio, and Burnett, of Indiana, Assistant Judge Advocates.

—— The rebel ram Webb passed New Orleans. When midway she lowered the Stars and Stripes and hoisted the rebel flag. She was fired upon, and one 125-pound ball passed through her bow. Our gunboats started in pursuit, and when twenty-four miles below the city the ram was fired by her crew, and at 4.30 P. M., blew up. Her crew, consisting of 64 men, including 8 officers, took to the woods on the left side of the river. Her deck and boilers were protected by cotton-bales, and the bales were destroyed by the burning of the ram. Captain Reed, in coming down the Mississippi, had the telegraph attached to his vessel, in this way tearing down many miles. Reed and most of the crew were subsequently captured.

May 2.—The President of the United States issued a proclamation reciting that, "It appears from evidence in the Bureau of Military Justice, that the atrocious murder of the late president, Abraham Lincoln, and the attempted assassination of the Honorable William H. Seward, Secretary of State, were incited, concerted, and procured by and between Jefferson Davis, late of Richmond, Virginia, and Jacob Thompson, Clement C. Clay, Beverly Tucker, George N. Sanders, William C. Cleary, and other rebels and traitors against the government of the United States harbored in Canada." For the arrest of the accused, the following rewards were offered:—$100,000 for Jefferson Davis; $25,000 for Clement C. Clay; $25,000 for Jacob Thompson, late of Mississippi; $25,000 for George N. Sanders; $25,000 for Beverly Tucker; $10,000 for William C. Cleary, late clerk of Clement C. Clay.

May 3.—Benjamin G. Harris, of Maryland, member of the United States Congress, was arraigned before a court martial at Washington, charged with inciting paroled rebel prisoners to return to the rebel army, and fight against the United States, the offence having been committed about the 26th of April.

May 4.—The remains of President Lincoln, after a solemn journey from Washington to Springfield, Illinois, mainly over the route which he had travelled in 1861, upon going to Washington to assume the presidency, were interred at Oak Ridge Cemetery, near Springfield, Illinois, with appropriate ceremonies.

May 5.—General Meredith, commanding in West Kentucky, issued a proclamation requesting all bands of armed men acting against the United States Government to surrender before May 20th, or be treated as outlaws.

—— Commodore Ebenezer Farrand, of the rebel navy, surrendered to Admiral Thatcher, U. S., at Cottonville, Alabama, all the naval property, officers, and men under his command in the Tombigbee River, Georgia.

May 6.—The 5th and 2d army corps, Army of the Potomac, marched through Richmond, Virginia, on their way to Washington, and were reviewed by General. Halleck.

—— The trial of Dr. Samuel A. Mudd, David E. Harold, Lewis Payne, Edward Spangler, George A. Atzerott, Michael McLaughlin, Samuel Arnold, and Mrs. Mary Surratt, commenced at Washington, before the military commission. The accused were charged with conspiring with John H. Surratt, John Wilkes Booth, Jefferson Davis, George N. Sanders, Beverly Tucker, Jacob Thompson, William C. Cleary, Clement C. Clay, George Harper, George Young, and others unknown, to kill and murder Abraham Lincoln, Andrew Johnson, William H. Seward, and Ulysses S. Grant, with intention to deprive the army and navy of the United States of a constitutional Commander-in-Chief, and to deprive the armies of the United States of their lawful commander, and to prevent a lawful election of President and Vice-President of the United States, and to aid and comfort the insurgents engaged in armed rebellion against the United States, and thereby to aid in the subversion and overthrow of the United States. Edward Spangler was charged with aiding and assisting John Wilkes Booth to obtain entrance to the box in the theatre, in which Abraham Lincoln was sitting at the time he was assaulted and shot, and with aiding and abetting Booth in making his escape after the murder; Harold, with assisting Booth in the murder and in his escape; Payne, with having made the murderous assault upon Secretary Seward, Frederick W. Seward, Augustus W. Seward, Emrick W. Hansel, and George N. Robinson; Atzerott, with lying in wait for Andrew Johnson, with intent to murder him; Michael O'Laughlin, with lying in wait to murder General Grant; Samuel Arnold, with combining with Booth and the others to commit the murders; and Mrs. Surratt, with conspiring with them, harboring, concealing, and assisting them, and helping them to escape from justice.

May 8.—The rebel ram Stonewall, *alias* the Olinde, arrived at Nassau, and came to anchor outside of that port.

May 9.—President issued a proclamation declaring that "armed resistance to the authority of this government in certain states heretofore declared to be in insurrection may be regarded as virtually at an end, and the persons by whom that resistance, as well as the operations of insurgent cruisers, were directed, are fugitives or captives." The proclamation enjoins the army and navy to endeavor to arrest said cruisers, and bring the persons engaged in them to justice. It was also declared that if, after reasonable notice, neutral nations should afford hospitality to such cruisers, "the government will deem itself justified in refusing hospitality to the public vessels of such nations in the ports of the United States, and in adopting such measures as may be deemed advisable towards vindicating the national sovereignty."

May 10.—At daylight, Colonel D. B. Pritchard, commanding 4th Michigan cavalry, captured Jeff Davis and family, together with his wife, sisters and brother, his Postmaster-General Reagan, his private secretary, Colonel Harris, Colonel Johnston, A. D. C. on Davis's staff, Colonel Morris, Colonel Lubbick, and Lieutenant Hathaway; also a train of 5 wagons and 3 ambulances. Shortly afterwards a most painful mistake occurred, by which the 4th Michigan and 1st Wisconsin collided, which cost 2 killed and Lieutenant Boutelle wounded through the arm in the 4th Michigan, and 4 men wounded in the 1st Wisconsin. This occurred just at daylight, after Pritchard had captured the camp, and was occasioned by the advance of the 1st Wisconsin. They were mistaken for the enemy.

May 11.—The rebel ram Stonewall arrived at Havana.

May 13.—A force of United States troops, white and colored, sent up from Brazos Santiago, on the Rio Grande, towards Brownsville, Texas, was ambushed and outnumbered, defeated, and driven back, losing 220 men out of 300.

May 19.—The steamer W. P. Clyde arrived at Fortress Monroe, having on board Jeff Davis and family, Alex. H. Stephens, Vice-President of the rebel states, Clement C. Clay, late on "detached service" in Canada, General Wheeler and staff, and others.

May 22.—The President of the United States issued a proclamation, removing the blockade from all the southern ports, except Galveston, La Salle, Brazos de Santiago, Point Isabel, and Brownsville, in Texas, after July 1st. Notice was given that foreign vessels attempting to enter any Texan port would not be allowed any pretence of belligerent rights, and would be treated as pirates.

May 23.—The 2d and 5th corps of the Army of the Potomac, and Sheridan's cavalry, marched through Washington, D. C., and were reviewed by the President, General Grant, and other officers.

—— Generals Price, Buckner, Brent, and staff officers arrived at Memphis, Tennessee, as commissioners from Kirby Smith's army. Together with Dick Taylor, they had an interview with Generals Canby and Hearn, upon the subject of the surrender of the rebel armies in the Trans-Mississippi Department, on the same terms as were accorded to Johnston and Lee.

May 24.—General Sherman's army marched through Washington, D. C., over the route passed over the previous day by the Army of the Potomac, and were received with enthusiasm.

—— The Anglo-rebel blockade runner steamer Denbigh was destroyed off Galveston, Texas, by United States steamer Fort Jackson.

May 25.—The ordnance depot and magazine exploded at Mobile, Alabama, destroying many buildings, and killing and wounding 500 persons. The total loss of property was estimated at $3,000,000.

—— Sabine Pass, and Forts Mannahasset and Griffin, were captured by Captain B. F. Sands, U.S. Navy.

May 26.—The grand jury of Washington county, D. C., found bills of indictment against Jeff Davis and John C. Breckinridge for high treason.

—— It was agreed at New Orleans that Kirby Smith's army should be surrendered, on the terms of Lee's army, by agreement between General Canby and the rebel Generals Price, Buckner, and others.

May 27.—The War Department issued an order, directing that in all cases of sentences by military tribunals during the war, the sentences should be remitted and the prisoners discharged.

May 29.—President Johnson issued a proclamation, granting amnesty and pardon to all persons who have directly or indirectly participated in the existing rebellion, with restoration of all rights of property, except as to slaves, and except in cases where legal proceedings under the laws of the United States providing for the confiscation of property of persons engaged in rebellion have been instituted; but upon the condition that each person should take the oath of allegiance and keep it. The following classes of persons were excepted from the benefits of this proclamation:—

First. Civil or diplomatic officers, or otherwise domestic or foreign agents of the pretended Confederate government.

Second. All who left judicial stations under the United States, to aid the rebellion.

Third. Military or naval officers of the rebel government, above the rank of colonel in the army or lieutenant in the navy.

Fourth. All who have left seats in the Congress of the United States, to aid the rebellion.

Fifth. All who resigned or tendered resignations of their commissions in the army or navy of the United States, to evade duty in resisting the rebellion.

Sixth. All who engaged in any way in treating otherwise than lawfully, as prisoners of war, persons found in the United States service, as officers, soldiers, seamen, or in other capacities.

Seventh. All absentees from the United States, for the purpose of aiding the rebellion.

Eighth. All military and naval officers in the rebel service who were educated by the government in the Military Academy at West Point or the United States Naval Academy.

Ninth. All persons who held the pretended offices of governors of states in insurrection against the United States.

Tenth. All persons who left their homes within the jurisdiction and protection of the United States, and passed beyond the Federal military lines into the so-called Confederate States, for the purpose of aiding the rebellion.

Eleventh. Persons who have been engaged in the destruction of the commerce of the United States upon the high seas; all persons who have made raids into the United States from Canada, or been engaged in destroying the commerce of the United States upon the lakes and rivers that separate the British provinces from the United States.

Twelfth. All persons who, when they apply to take the oath, were in military, naval, or civil confinement or custody, or under bonds of the civil, military, or naval authorities or agents of the United States as prisoners of war or persons detained for offences of any kind, either before or after conviction.

Thirteenth. All persons who have voluntarily participated in the rebellion, and the estimated value of whose taxable property is over $20,000.

Fourteenth. All persons who have taken the oath of amnesty, as prescribed in the President's proclamation of December 6th, A. D. 1863, or an oath of allegiance to the Government of the United States since the date of said proclamation, and who have not kept and maintained the same inviolate: Provided, that special application may be made to the President for pardon by any person belonging to the excepted classes, and such clemency will be liberally extended as may be consistent with the facts of the case and the peace and dignity of the United States.

May 29.—The President issued a proclamation, appointing Wm. W. Holden Provisional Governor of North Carolina, with instructions to prescribe the rules and regulations necessary for calling a convention of citizens of the State loyal to the United States, so as to amend the Constitution, and present it in a form that will entitle the United States to guarantee to North Carolina a republican form of government. Also declaring that the authority of the United States shall be re-established in the State by the appointment of United States officers, opening of courts, establishment of the custom-house, post-office, revenue agencies, &c.

May 31.—Brazil withdrew the rights of belligerents hitherto accorded to the rebels.

June 1.—Brownsville, Texas, was taken possession of by General Brown, United States Army, the rebels under Slaughter having evacuated—many of them going to Mexico.

—— This day was observed throughout the United States as a day of humiliation and prayer, upon account of the murder of President Lincoln.

June 2.—Earl Russel addressed the British Admiralty Board, stating that permission to enter British ports must henceforth be withdrawn from rebel vessels; also, that all rebel vessels already in such ports shall be forced to withdraw therefrom. But when such rebel vessel should depart, it was declared that "national good faith" required that the former rule prohibiting pursuit within twenty-four hours should be put in force against the United States. Furthermore, it was declared that the commander of any Confederate vessel of war lying within a British port at the time of the reception of the order, or entering within one month, might be allowed "to divest his vessel of her warlike character, and after disarming her, to remain without the Confederate flag within British waters"—at his own risk.

—— Alexandria, La., was occupied by General Herron, United States Army. 22 pieces of artillery were captured.

—— The rebel Generals Kirby Smith and Magruder met in the harbor of Galveston, General A. J.

Smith representing General Canby, and there signed the terms of surrender previously agreed upon at New Orleans, including all the troops and naval forces of the rebels in Texas.

June 3.—The rebel Red River fleet was surrendered by Lieutenant-Commander J. H. Carter, commanding the rebel forces, to Commander W. E. Fitzhugh, U. S. Navy, in accordance with the terms of surrender agreed upon with Buckner and Price. The iron-clad Missouri, a formidable ram, was yielded up to the United States.

June 5.—Galveston, Texas, was taken possession of by the United States forces, and the national flag was raised.

June 7.—James Speed, Attorney-General of the United States, issued an order, by direction of the President, requiring that all persons who made application for pardon under the amnesty proclamation, should take the oath of allegiance, as a precedent condition to the consideration of their petitions.

June 8.—The last vessel of the transport fleet, which was to transfer the United States troops under General Weitzel to Texas, left Fortress Monroe.

—— The 6th corps of the Army of the Potomac, which did not reach Washington until after the previous reviews of Meade's and Sherman's armies, marched through Washington, and were reviewed by the President and General Meade.

June 9.—United States quartermasters' buildings, at Chattanooga, took fire, and stores worth $250,000 were destroyed.

—— United States quartermaster and commissary storehouses, at Nashville, Tennessee, were destroyed by fire. Loss computed to be between $8,000,000 and $10,000,000.

June 13.—William L. Sharkey was appointed Provisional Governor of Mississippi, by the President of the United States, on the same terms as were prescribed in the case of North Carolina.

—— By proclamation, the President of the United States removed the restrictions hitherto remaining in force against trading with ports on the Mississippi, with the exception of goods contraband of war, &c.

June 14.—John Mitchell, formerly editor of the Richmond Examiner, who had come to New York and undertook to edit the New York Daily News, was arrested at the office of the latter paper, and sent to Fortress Monroe, in Virginia.

June 16.—James Johnson, of Georgia, was appointed Provisional Governor of that state, by President Andrew Johnson.

—— Andrew J. Hamilton, formerly military governor of Texas, was appointed Provisional Governor of the same state.

June 17.—Secretary Seward announces to Secretary Welles, that France has withdrawn belligerent rights from the rebels, and all restrictions heretofore imposed upon United States naval vessels in French ports.

—— Alexander H. Stephens, ex Vice-President of the Confederacy, and Robert E. Lee, ex-General and commander-in-chief of the rebel army, apply to the President of the United States for pardon.

—— A monument erected to the memory of Luther C. Ladd and Addison Whitney, two soldiers of the 6th Massachusetts regiment, who were killed in the streets of Baltimore, on the 19th of April, 1861, was dedicated at Lowell, Massachusetts.

June 18.—P. P. Pytchlin, governor and principal chief of the Choctaw Nation, issued a proclamation, calling a grand council of all the Indians of the Indian Confederation, and of the prairies, September 1st, at Armstrong Academy, Choctaw Nation, to consult with commissioners of the United States, with reference to a permanent and lasting peace—all hostilities to cease meanwhile.

June 19.—Secretary Seward wrote to Secretary Welles, in relation to the British orders of June 2d, partially withdrawing belligerent rights from rebel cruisers, and stated the results to be as follows:—

1st. Great Britain withdraws her concessions heretofore made of a belligerent character from the insurgents.

2d. That the withdrawal of the twenty-four hours' rule has not been made absolute by Great Britain, and that, therefore, the customary courtesies are not to be paid by our vessels to those of the British Navy.

3d. The right of search of British vessels is terminated. Of course this has no bearing upon the operation of the existing slave-trade treaty.

4th. Any insurgent or piratical vessel found on the high seas may be lawfully captured by vessels of the United States.

June 21.—By proclamation, the President of the United States appointed Lewis E. Parsons Provisional Governor of Alabama.

—— The legislature of Virginia convened at Richmond, by Governor Pierpoint, pass an Act of Assembly abolishing the "Alexandria oath," as a test of citizenship, and substitute instead "the United States amnesty oath."

June 23.—The President of the United States, by proclamation, declared that the blockade was rescinded, as to all ports in the United States, inclusive of Texas, and that from July 1st they would be open to foreign commerce.

June 22.— The Anglo-rebel privateer Shenandoah captured and burned the American bark Jireh Swift off Cape Thaddeus, in the North Pacific Ocean. About the same time, the Shenandoah captured and burned the whalers Edward Casey, Hector, Abigail, Euphrates, William Thompson, Sophia Thornton, and the Susan and Abigail. The Milo was captured and bonded for the purpose of taking off the crews. Waddell, the commander of the Shenandoah, was informed of Lee's surrender and the collapse of the rebellion, but did not believe. He believed in Lincoln's assassination, *for he expected it.* The Shenandoah called last at Melbourne. She was manned by English and Irish sailors. Some of the captured whalemen joined her.

June 23.—Rear-Admiral Samuel F. Dupont died in Philadelphia, in the 65th year of his age.

—— A treaty was entered into near Doaksville, Choctaw Nation, between United States Commissioners Lieutenant-Colonel A. C. Matthews and Adjutant W. C. Vance, and Stand Watie, governor and principal chief of that part of the Choctaw Nation hitherto allied with the rebels in acts of hostility against the United States, by which it was agreed that the Cherokees should retire to their homes and remain at peace. The agreement to remain in force until the general council at Armstrong Academy, September 1st, 1865.

June 24.—A delegation of citizens of South Carolina waited on the President of the United States in relation to the means necessary to be taken to restore the state to the Union. The President said, among other things, "The government cannot go on unless it is right. The people of South Carolina must have a convention and amend their constitution by abolishing slavery, and this must be done in good faith; and the convention or legislature must adopt the proposed amendment to the constitution of the Union, which prohibits and excludes slavery everywhere."

June 27.—A proclamation was issued by the President removing restrictions upon internal trade and coastwise commercial intercourse between the states west of the Mississippi River.

—— By order of the President the United States are divided into 5 military divisions and 18 departments, to be commanded by the following officers :—

1. Division of the Atlantic, Major-General George G. Meade, headquarters at Philadelphia.
2. Division of the Mississippi, Major-General T. W. Sherman, St. Louis.
3. Division of the Gulf, Major-General P. H. Sheridan, New Orleans.
4. Division of the Tennessee, Major-General G. H. Thomas, Nashville.
5. Division of the Pacific, Major-General H. W. Halleck, San Francisco.

, Major-General Joseph
oral W. S. Hancock, Bal-
ton, Major-General C. C.
jor-General E. O. C. Ord,
e, Major-General George
, Major-General John M.
Major-General John Pope,
Major-General Alfred H.
Carolina, Major-General
Carolina, Major-General
iad.
Major-General James B.
Major-General John G.
pi, Major-General H. W.
a, Major-General C. B.
na and Texas, Major-
Orleans.
is, Major-General J. J.
la, Brigadier-General G.
ia, Major-General Irwin
eorge G. Meade issued a
ers of the Army of the
hat that army had ceased
' the President, Benjamin
ional Governor of South
a Army of the Potomac,
I into a provisional corps
brigades, commanded by
formerly of the 6th corps.
entences of the Military
, 1865, for the trial of the
sassination of President
verture the Government
re approved by Andrew
ited States, and returned
or execution. Mary E.
s Payne, and David E.
ung on Friday, July 7th.
Arnold, and Dr. Samuel
ife, and Edward Spangler
lade to Judge Wylie, of
istrict of Columbia, for a
Mary Surratt, declaring
by Major-General Han-
et of Washington. The
, with a special endorse-
ading the writ of habeas
nence of which the Court
ieneral Hancock to bring
t. Same day, about 1.30
ias Powell, Harold, and
rsenal Yard, Washington,
of the Military Commis-

rmance was announced to
e, Washington, in which
killed. Before the hour
taken possession of by
rder of the War Depart-
ere prevented.
Tassara, Spanish Minister

to the United States, officially informs Secretary Seward that the Government of Spain has determined to deliver to the United States the rebel ram Stonewall, surrendered at Havana to the Captain-General of Cuba. Sixteen thousand dollars, disbursed on account of said vessel, were claimed to be due, but not demanded as a condition of delivery. Secretary Seward (July 17) acknowledged the communication, accepted the vessel, and gave notice that orders had been issued to repay the Spanish Government the sixteen thousand dollars.

July 20.—The Anglo-rebel privateer Shenandoah, alias Sea King, destroyed the American vessel Susan Abigail near the Gulf of Anadir. San Francisco papers of July 10th were furnished Waddell, the captain of the Shenandoah, showing the utter collapse of the rebellion; but he refused to pay any attention to them. He sailed towards Behring's Straits and the Arctic Ocean, where he destroyed 7 vessels. One of these was bonded, and arrived at San Francisco, with the officers and crews of the vessels which had been destroyed, on the 3d day of August.

July 24.—Ford's Theatre, Washington, was rented by the United States Government for $1500 per month, with privilege of purchase for $100,000, the intention being to appropriate it to the purpose of a depository of rebel archives and records.

July 25.—An election was held in Richmond, Virginia, for city officers, and certain candidates were elected who had recently been prominent in the rebellion, whilst candidates of known Union sentiments were defeated by considerable majorities.

——— Battle at Platte's Bridge Station, in the Indian Territory. 1000 Cheyennes, Sioux, Arrapahoes, Blackfeet, and Camanche Indians, made an attack on the station, but were repulsed by the garrison of 250, after two days' fighting. Federal loss. Lieutenant Collins and 1 man killed and 34 wounded. Indian loss, heavy.

July 28.—By special order of General Terry, No. 72, the election held in the city of Richmond, July 25, is set aside because voters were excluded by reason of absence as soldiers of the United States Army during the rebellion, when no such ground was taken against soldiers absent in the rebel army. Also because the officers elected, with but few exceptions, had been conspicuous in inaugurating and sustaining the rebellion, and because the issue was distinctly made and openly avowed at the election as between those men who had aided and abetted the war against the United States authority, and those who had with their lives defended the flag of their country.

July 30.—General George Wright, assigned to the command of the Department of Columbia, was drowned while on his way to the department to assume his duties, by the wreck of the steamer Brother Jonathan, which struck upon a rock off Crescent City, Oregon. At the same time a large number of passengers also lost their lives.

August 1.—Secretary McCulloch issued an official statement of the public debt, which amounted to $2,757,253,275.86, showing an increase of $122,000,000, between that time and May 1, which was mainly occasioned by the payment of large sums due to the troops upon mustering them out of service.

——— By direction of the President the Secretary of War ordered the following army corps to be discontinued as organizations:—The 2d, from June 28; the 4th, from August 1; the 5th, from June 28; the 6th, from June 22; the 7th, from August 1; the 8th, from August 1; the 9th, from July 28; the 10th, from August 1; the 14th, from August 1; the 15th, from August 1; the 17th, from August 1; the 20th, from June 1; the 23d, from August 1; and the 24th, from August 1.

August 14.—The Mississippi State Convention met at Jackson, and organized by the election of officers, &c.

August 16.—The whalers James Maury, Joseph Maxwell, and Richmond arrived at Honolulu, Sandwich Islands, from the Arctic Ocean, the former under bond, with 150 sailors, comprising the crews of vessels burned by the Shenandoah. She reports the total captures by the

Shenandoah, up to her departure from the Arctic Sea, at 30 vessels, of which 26 were burned and 4 bonded. The Maxwell reports that 10 whalers escaped. The Emily Jordan and John P. West had previously sailed for the Ochotsk Sea.

August 18.—A military commission was appointed for the trial of Captain Henry Wirz, charged with barbarities to the Federal prisoners held by the rebels at Andersonville, Georgia. The prisoner was charged with conspiring with Robert E. Lee, James A. Seddon, John H. Winder, Lucius D. Northrop, Richard B. Winder, R. R. Stephenson Moore, and others unknown, to impair the health and destroy the lives of soldiers in the military service of the United States, then held and being prisoners of war within the lines of the so-called Confederate States, and in the military prisons thereof, to the end that the armies of the United States might be weakened and impaired, in violation of the laws and customs of war. Also with murdering prisoners under his charge as keeper of the prison. The specifications were numerous, and charged most wicked and revolting acts upon the accused.

August 19.—Provisional-Governor Sharkey, of Mississippi, issued a proclamation calling on the people of the state to organize, under the militia laws of the state, in each county a force to detect and apprehend criminals, and to prevent crime. Immediately after the issue of this proclamation, Major-General Slocum, commanding in Georgia, issued a proclamation forbidding the organization of the militia.

August 21.—The state convention of Mississippi adopted an ordinance abolishing slavery in the state, and also declaring that the secession ordinance passed in 1861 was null and void.

August 23.—The Commission to try Captain Henry Wirz was reorganized and composed of the following officers: Major-General Lew. Wallace, U.S. Volunteers; Brevet Major-General G. Mott, U.S. Volunteers; Brevet Major-General J. W. Geary, U.S. Volunteers; Brevet Major-General L. Thomas, Adjutant-General U.S. Army; Brigadier-General Francis Fessenden, U.S. Volunteers; Brevet Brigadier-General J. F. Ballier, Colonel 98th Pennsylvania Volunteers; Brevet Colonel T. Allcock, Lieutenant-Colonel 4th New York Artillery; Lieutenant-Colonel J. H. Stibbs, 12th Iowa Volunteers; Colonel N. P. Chipman, Additional Aide-de-camp, Judge-Advocate of the Commission. The charges and specifications were amended by striking out the names of Robert E. Lee, James A. Seddon, Lucien D. Northrop, and Moore in the charge of conspiracy.

August 29.—Carl Shurz, government agent in Georgia, sent a despatch to the President, calling his attention to the proclamation organizing the militia of the state, and expressing fears of the consequences.

August 30.—The President replied to the despatch of Carl Shurz in reference to Governor Sharkey's plan of organizing the militia of Georgia, approving of the effort. He said: " It is believed there can be organized in each county a force of citizens or militia to suppress crime, restore order, and enforce the civil authority of the state and of the United States, which would enable the Federal government to reduce the army and withdraw to a great extent the forces from the state, thereby reducing the enormous expenses of the government. If there was any danger from an orginization of the citizens for the purpose indicated, the military are there to suppress, on the first appearance, any move insurrectionary in its character. One great object is to induce the people to come forward in the defence of the state and Federal government. General Washington declared that the people or the militia was the Army of the Constitution or the Army of the United States, and as soon as it is practicable the original design of the government should be resumed under the principles of the great charter of freedom handed down to the people by the founders of the Republic. The people must be trusted with their government, and, if trusted, my opinion is that they will act in good faith, and restore their former constitutional relations with all the states composing the Union."

September 1.—Major-Ge[n] in Georgia, issued a procla[mation] tion had been received th[at] rate and United States f[orces] the state in the hands of appearing that the peace citizens, and the security o[f] endangered, it was ordered hereafter, all such arms c[…] with all ammunition and now in the hands of priv[ate] turned over to the neare[st] was given that in case o[f] order, the arms would be s[…]

—— Battle of Powder[…] troops under General Can[by] Cherokees, and Arrapahoe[s] were repulsed, losing heav[ily] the attack and were aga[in] battle was renewed and th[e] slaughter, losing from 200[…] They attempted to renew t[he] again repulsed.

September 2.—Major-Ge[neral] the President to counterm[and] to the organization of th[e] vernor Sharkey.

September 4.—An electi[on] Convention was held in […] mation of Governor Perry.

September 6.—A letter Henry A. Wise to Lieute[nant] lished in the Richmond, seeks a restoration of his [rights] States, and uses the follow[ing] my being opposed to the n[…] the condition of slaves fre[e] *lation I have in the result o[f] ever abolished; that not on[ly] freed from bondage, but* Long before the war end[ed] my mind actively to advo[cate] the South. I had deter[mined] descendants should never I have been subject to by [the] edness of slavery; and lawful and humane the v[iews] which it has been abolishe[d] heartily as an accomplish[ed] not only to abide by it and by all the means in my p[ower] both races and a blessing unfeignedly rejoice at the many of the worst calamit[ies] now convinced that the wa[r] God, unavoidable by the [….] tear loose from us a bla[ck] never have been separate[d] those of fire and blood, sw[…]

September 11.—Captain [….] ington about $200,000 in g[old] at Augusta, Georgia, and [….] carried off from Richmond

September 14.—The ch[iefs of] Creek, Chickasaw, Cowski[n] and Quapaw Indians sig[ned a] promising to be bencefor[th] and renouncing their treat[…]

September 15.—The Sta[te of] lina passed an ordinance Secession without debate, [….] negative.

September 16.—The Pre[sident] suspended the writ of ha[beas corpus] Samuel, Charles, and O[…] stealing government horse[s]

September 19.—The Sout[h] an ordinance *repealing* the

September 21.—A trea[ty] United States Commissio[n]

ico and friendship between tribes, promising that they in compelling the Indians aceful relations with each he territory, and with the hall be abolished for ever; ily provided for; that land of Kansas and elsewhere; e granted to railroads, and Indian tribes, with a territ shall be recommended by ouncils. The Commission

ntion of Alabama passed iry for ever by a vote of 89

ention of the Protestant i, in response to a pastoral imending reunion with the urch for the United States, it to postpone compliance Church Council of Virginia. ' Alabama adopted a resonce of secession of 1861

, of Mississippi, by proway with the necessity of s in that state, "and beutional amendment which ll laws which constituted a and in declaring that the his person and property, of themselves entitle the id, as a necessary incident le competent as a witness, ence of the state," declares civil or criminal, in which volved, either for injuries erty, or in matters of cones may be received, subject evidence as regards comi prevail in regard to white

ention of South Carolina ew constitution abolishing

inance of secession of 1860

ntion of Alabama declared purposes during the secesid void.

as held in Connecticut to idment to the constitution hes a right to vote, should y a majority of about 6000. umphreys, formerly comide, was elected Governor

n of North Carolina passed the secession ordinance of

n of North Carolina passed avery in the state by an irs voting.

e President, Alexander H. Vice-President, John H. master-General, George A. na, late Secretary of the y, together with John A. Justice of the United States Clark, late rebel Governor l from close confinement, ion to the authority of the for pardon. They are to be to appear and answer when

tion of the President, the 64, suspending the habeas al law in Kentucky is modiball be no longer in force.

October 14.—A delegation of citizens of South Carolina called on President Johnson, seeking the pardon of Jefferson Davis and Ex-Governor Magrath of South Carolina. In relation to the former, the President said: "that if treason has been committed, there ought to be some test to determine the power of the Government to punish the crime. He was free to say that it was not a mere contest between political parties, or a question as to *de facto* governments. Looking at the Government as we do, the laws violated, and an attempt made at the life of the nation, there should be a vindication of the Government and the Constitution, even if the pardoning power were exercised thereafter. If treason has been committed, it ought to be determined by the highest tribunal, and the fact declared, even if clemency should come afterward. There was no malice or prejudice in wishing to carry out that duty."

October 18.—President Johnson sent a telegraphic dispatch to Wm. W. Holden, Provisional Governor of North Carolina, declaring that before the state could hope to be admitted to the Union, every dollar of the rebel war debt must be repudiated finally and for ever.

October 19.—The convention of North Carolina passed an ordinance preventing any future legislature from assuming or paying any debt created directly or indirectly for the prosecution of the rebellion.

October 20.—Champ Ferguson, a rebel guerrilla, convicted by court-martial of numerous murders, was hanged at Nashville, Tennessee.

——— Henry C. Magruder, a rebel guerrilla, convicted of the murder of 17 men, was hanged at Louisville, Kentucky.

October 23.—The British steamship Hibernian, from Liverpool, brings copies of the correspondence between Charles F. Adams, American Minister at London, and Earl Russell, in reference to the claims of the United States on Great Britain, for compensation for damages done to American commerce by the Alabama and other rebel privateers, fitted in England and permitted to escape from British ports. Earl Russell refused to admit any claim for compensation, refused to submit the question to arbitration, but suggests a commission for the settlement of such claims as it shall be agreed upon to refer to them.

October 27.—The convention of Georgia repealed the Ordinance of Secession.

——— Georgia State Convention adopted an article abolishing slavery, with a proviso, that this acquiescence in the emancipation of slaves, is no estoppel to future claims for compensation.

October 28.—Governor James Johnson, of Georgia, was officially informed by Secretary Seward, that the President cannot recognize the people of any state as having resumed their relations of loyalty to the Union, that adheres to as legal, the obligations contracted or debts created in their name to promote the war of the rebellion.

——— President Johnson issued a proclamation assigning the first Thursday of December a day of national thanksgiving to Almighty God, that it has pleased Him to relieve our beloved country from the fearful scourge of civil war, and to permit us to secure the blessings of peace, unity, and harmony, *with a great enlargement of civil liberty*.

——— Secretary Seward addressed a despatch to Governor Marvin, of Florida, informing him that the President had directed him to say, "that he regards the ratification by the legislature of the Congressional Amendment to the Constitution of the United States as indispensable to a successful restoration of the true loyal relations between Florida and the other States, and equally indispensable to the return of peace and harmony throughout the republic."

October 31.—The Secretary of the Treasury made return of the national debt at $2,748,854,758.96. Reduction since September 30, $4,000,000. Reduction since July, nearly seventeen millions. Legal tenders in circulation, $638,700,611. Amount of debt bearing interest, $138,938,078.59. Interest payable in coin, $67,670,340.59.

INDEX.

Abbeville, Miss., taken, 47. Fight, 81.
Aberdeen, Miss., Grierson's raid at, 68.
Abingdon, Va., captured, 91.
Abolition, (see "Emancipation," "Slaves.")
Accomac, Va., rebels dispersed, 15.
Ackworth Station, Ga., taken, 76.
Acquia Creek, Va., skirmish at, 8. Skirmish, 22.
Adairsville, Ga., battle, 75.
Adams, General, rebel, killed, 89.
Adirondack, frigate, wrecked, 38.
Admirals appointed, 35.
Aiken, S. C., skirmish, 95.
Aiken, Col., rebel, killed, 97.
Alabama secedes, 5. Lewis E. Parsons, Provisional Governor, 108. Nullifies secession and abolishes slavery, 111. Declares war debt void, 111.
Alabama (rebel cruiser) sunk, 77. Correspondence about, 111. See "Privateers."
Albemarle, rebel iron clad, attacks U. S. Fleet, 71. Blown up, 86.
Albemarle Sound, N. C., naval fight, 72.
Aldie, Va., cavalry fight, 57.
Alert, gunboat, blown up, 56.
Alexandria, Va, occupied, Ellsworth killed, 8.
Alexandria, La., taken, 54. Franklin and Smith, at, 70. Occupied, 107.
Alimosa, (New Mexico,) skirmish, 12.
Allatoona, Ga., battle, 85.
Allatoona Creek, Ga., advance to, 76.
Allatoona Mountains, Ga., rebel General Johnson at—flanked by Sherman, 75.
Allatoona Pass, Ga., captured 76.
Alleghany camp, Va., fight, 17.
Allegiance, oath of, violators shot, 43.
Allen, Col., rebel, killed, 59.
Allen, Henry W., rebel, Governor La., advocates use of negro soldiers, 84.
Alligator Harbor, Fla., salt works destroyed, 57.
All Saints, S. C., taken, 94.
Altoona, Pa., conference of Governors at, 43.
Amnesty. See "Proclamations."
Anderson's Cross Roads, Tenn., fight, 63.
Anderson, Robert, Major, U. S. A.,—ordered to Fort Moultrie—evacuates it and takes possession of Fort Sumter, 5. Surrenders the Fort, 6.
Anderson, Gen., rebel, killed, 42.
Andersonville. rebel prison barbarities at, 110.
Andrews, Lieut., killed, 32.
Annandale, Va., skirmish, 16.
Annapolis occupied by U. S. troops, 7.
Anti-draft riots, New York, 60. Boston, Staten Island and Brooklyn, 60.
Antietam, Md., battle, 41.
Antray, Col., rebel, killed, 49.
Apache canon, New Mexico, fight, 23.
Apalachicola, Fla., taken, 23.
Appomattox court-house, battle.—Lee's surrender, 102. Rebel flags captured at, 105.
Appointments to command—Banks, 22, McDowell, 23.
Arkansas secedes, 7. Provisional government, 57.
Arkansas river, battle near, declined, 61.
Arkansas post, taken by storm 49.

Armistead, General, rebel, killed, 59.
Armstrong's Mill, Va., reconnoisance, 86.
Army, U. S., memorial to increase, 33. Reduction of force, supplies, etc., 103. Expenses to be reduced, soldiers discharged, etc., 105.
Army (Sherman's) marched through Washington, 107.
Army corps discontinued, 109.
Army of the Cumberland—Grant takes command, 64. Maj.-Gen. Thomas commands, 73. March commenced, 57.
Army of Georgia moves on Raleigh, 99.
Army of Northern Virginia, Sheridan succeeds Hunter in command, 81.
Army of Ohio, Maj.-Gen. Schofield commands, 73..
Army of Potomac, address to, 22, 31. Address to,. at Harrison's Landing, 33. Corps numbered,. 35. McClellan's address, 35. McClellan removed from command—Burnside appointed,. 46. Reorganization, 46. Attempt to move frustrated by the mud, 49. Burnside resigns command, Hooker appointed, 49. Reorganized by Gen. Hooker, 50. Crosses Rappahannock, 53. Meade appointed to command, 58. Reorganization by Grant, 70. Gen. Sheridan commands cavalry, Hooker 1st corps, Howard 4th corps, 70. Crosses Rapidan, 72. Burnside relieved from command of 5th corps, 81. Conference on the plan of final battles, 99. Final movements against Petersburg and Richmond, 99. Battles, 100, 101, 102. March through Richmond, Va., 106. March through Washington, 107. 6th Corps march through Washington, 108. Meade's farewell address,, 109. Provisional corps to be formed, 109.
Army of Tennessee, Maj.-Gen. McPherson commands, 73. Maj-Gen. Howard commands, 80.. Moves on Raleigh, 99.
Army of Virginia formed, 31. Pope's address to, 34. Pope's order to subsist on the enemy,. etc., 34. Order of Pope to arrest persons who do not take the oath of allegiance, 34.
Arnold, Sam., tried for the assassination of the President, 106. Condemned to imprisonment,. 109.
Arsenals, U. S., seized. Fayetteville, S. C.,. Mobile, Baton Rouge, Little Rock, Augusta, 5 Liberty, Fayetteville, 7. St. Louis, 7.
Ashby's Gap, Va., skirmish. 42. Cavalry fight,. 57.
Ashby, Turner, Col., rebel, killed, 30.
Ashbyville, Ky., fight at, 91.
Ashland station, Va., taken, 74.
Assessments, St. Louis, secessionists, 38—39.
Atlanta, Ga., rebels retreat to, 79. Operations against, 79. Battle near, 80. Battle. Partly taken. Battle, 80. Bombarded, 81. Assaulted, 81. Attack on Logan's lines, 81. Flanked, 82. Taken, 83. Losses in campaign before its capture, 83. Inhabitants ordered to remove, 83. Attacked, 87. Evacuated and burned, 88.
Atalanta, rebel ram, taken, 57.
Atlantic, steam ship, sent with supplies to Fort Sumter. South Carolina notifies the United States that it will be fired into, 6.

(113)

Atlantic Division, Gen. Meade, 108.
Athens, Ala., fight, 84.
Athens, Mo., fight, 10.
Athens, Tenn., fight, 67.
Atzerott, G. A., reward offered for—arrested, 104. Tried for assassination, 106. Condemned, 109. Hung, 109.
Augur, Gen. C. C., to command Department of Washington, 109.
Augusta, Ky., skirmish, 43.
Austin, Miss., burned, 55.
Averill's raid, W. Va., 66.
Avery, Col., rebel, killed, 22.
Avery, Col., rebel, killed, 59.
Avery, Col., rebel killed, 74.
Averysboro' N. C., battle, 98.
Avoyelles Prairie, La., battle, 74.
Aylett's Station, Va., destroyed, 56.
Bachelor's creek, N. C., skirmish, 67.
Back river, Va., vessels burned, 10.
Bacon, A. G., Capt., killed, 17.
Bailey, Godard, defalcation discovered, 5.
Bailey, Col., killed, 29.
Bailey, Lieut.-Col., releases Red river fleet, 74.
Bainbridge, brig, foundered, 61.
Baker's Creek, Miss., battle, 55.
Baker, E. D., Col., killed, 13.
Baker, Col., killed, 44.
Baker, Lieut., killed, 23.
Ballinger's mill, Mo., skirmish, 46.
Ball's Bluff, battle, 13.
Baltimore, attack on Massachusetts and Pennsylvania troops—destruction of property by rebels, 7. U. S. Volunteers march through—occupied by Gen. Butler, 7. Marshal Kane and Police Board arrested for treason, 9. Martial law, 58. Merchants arrested for holding intercourse with rebels, 86.
Baltimore cross roads, skirmish, 58.
Banbury, S. C., Sherman at, 95.
Banks suspend specie payments, 5. Take national loan, 10.
Banks, N. P., Maj.-Gen., appointed commander of the Shenandoah department, 23. Expedition, 47. Supersedes Butler at New Orleans, 47. Expedition, Louisiana, defeated, 71.
Barboursville, Va., skirmish, 9.
Barbus, Va., skirmish, 46.
Bardstown, Ky., captured, 77. Attacked, 93.
Barksdale, Gen., rebel, killed, 59.
Barney, Major, killed, 39.
Barrol, J. L., Editor, sent south, 53.
Bartleston, Col., killed, 83.
Barton, F. G., General, rebel, killed, 10.
Bates, Edward., Attorney-General, resigned, 88.
Bath, Va., fight, 18.
Baton Rouge, La., battle, 36. Taken, 47.
Battery Rock, Ohio river, attacks, 41.
Bayard, James A., U. S. Senator, resigns, 67.
Bayard, Gen., killed, 47.
Bayou Coteau, La., battle, 64.
Bayou Metoe, Ark., battle, 62.
Bayou Sara, La., taken, 36.
Beale, John Yates, rebel spy, hung, 96.
Bealeton Station, Va., skirmish, 64.
Bear Creek, Miss., batttle, 60.
Bean's Station, Tenn., battle, 66.
Beaufort, S. C., taken, 14.
Beauregard, P. G. T., late Major U. S. army, takes command of the rebel troops at Charleston, 5. Attacks Fort Sumter—surrender of the same, 6. Proclaims raising of the blockade of Charleston, 49. Takes command of the rebel army of the west, 86.
Beaver Dam, Va. battle, 31. Railroad destroyed, 34. Taken, 73.
Beckwith, Mo., skirmish, 13.
Bee, Bernard E., General, rebel, killed, 10.
Beech Grove, Tenn., flanked, 58.
Bell, John, nominated for President—his vote, 5. Addresses the people of Tennessee, 6.
Bell, Col., killed, 93.
Bellers' Mill, Va., skirmish, 11.
Belligerent rights withdrawn from rebels by Brazil—Great Britain, 107. Secretary Seward's complaints that British withdrawal is only partial, 108. France, 108.
Belmont, Mo., battle, 14.
Benedict, Col., killed, 71.
Bentonsville, N. C., battle, 98.
Berlin, Va., bridge burned, 8.
Berlin, Md., skirmish, 17.
Bermuda Hundred, Va., occupied, 72. Rebel works taken, 74. Night attack on, 74. Lines attacked—Attacked by Beauregard, 75 Attack on lines, 76. Butler's pickets surprised, 88.
Berry, Gen., killed, 54.
Berryville., Va, occupied, 21. Occupied, 80. Train captured, 81. Sheridan at, 82. Battle, 83.
Bertrand, Mo., skirmish, 16.
Bethesda Church, Va., battle, 75.
Beverly Ford, Va., cavalry fight, 56.
Beverly, Va., fight, 86. Attacked, 93.
Bible Ridge, Tenn., fight, 63.
Bidwell, Gen., killed, 86.
Big (or Great) Bethel, battle, 8. Reconnoisance, 23. Occupied, 23.
Big Black River battle, 55.
Big Black Bridge, Miss., battle, 55. Loss at, 59.
Big Blue, Mo., battle, 86.
Big Creek, Ark., fight, 80.
Big Creek Gap, Tenn., fight, 20.
Big Hill, Ky., skirmish, 45.
Big Hurricane Creek, Mo., fight, 13.
Big Mound, Dakotah, battle, 61.
Big River bridge, Mo., skirmish, 13.
Big Shanty, Ga., battle, 78. Taken, 85. Battle, 85.
Biloxi, Miss., taken, 17.
Black, Samuel W., Col., killed, 31.
Black, Col., rebel, killed, 49.
Blackwater river, N. C., battle on, (naval,) 43. Fight, 43. Fight, 51. Battle, 49.
Black Walnut creek, Mo., skirmish, 16.
Blair, Francis P., goes on a peace mission to Richmond, 92. Second visit to Richmond, 93. Returns, 93.
Blair, Montgomery's, house burned, 79. Postmaster General, resigns, 84.
Bland, Col., rebel, killed, 63.
Blitz, Major, killed, 31.
Blockade proclaimed, 7. Charleston, 7.
Blockade runners captured, chased, injured or destroyed:—Adelaide, 15. Admiral, 17. Prince Albert, 81. Albion, 16. Alliance, 46. Alliance, 71. Anglia, 45. Ann, 32. Armstrong, 89. Banshee, 65. Bat, 85. Beatrice, 89. Bermuda, 26. Blenheim, 94. Boston, 79. Mary Bowers, 83. Calhoun, 18. Caroline, 45. Ceres, 65. Charlotte, 94. Chatham taken, 65. Cheshire, 17. Constance, 83. Columbia, 37. Condor, 85. Cuba, 55. Cumberland, 68.

Duc de Chartres, 98. Dee, 67. Dee, 98. Denbigh, 107. Dolson, Clara, 30. Don, 70. Donegal, 76. Douro, 50, 63. Ella, 87. Ella Warley, 18, 26. Eolus, 86. Emily, 33. Emily, 68. Emma, 18. Fannie and Jennie, 68. Flamingo, 86. Florinne, 86. Florida, 26. Fox, 98. Habana, 83. Havelock, 56. Emma Henry, 89. Hope, 86. Ivanhoe, 80. Stonewall Jackson, 52. Ladona, 34. Laura, 67. Little Ada, 79. Lucy, 87. Lynx, 84. Mabel, 15. Mary, 69. Matagorda, 83. May Flower, 66. Memphis, 35. Minho, 45. Minna, 66. In Mississippi Sound, 16. Nando, *alias* Let-her-rip, 86. Nassau, 29. Nicholas I, 51. Night Hawk, 84. Nostro Signora de Regla, 26. Nutfield, 67. Patras, 29. Pet, 68. Peterhoff, 53. Petrel, 91. Presto, 67. Princess Royal, 49. Ranger, 66. Reliance, 34. Rose, 76. Rosita, 67. Rouen, 78. Emily St. Pierre, 22; Rescued, 25. Scotia, 45. Scotia, 68. Isaac Smith sunk, 56. Spunkie, 68. Stag, 94. Stettin, 28. Susan, 46.. Susannah, 89. Syren, 98. Transports, 19. Tropic, 49. Tubal Cain, 34. Union, 46. A. D. Vance, 67. Venus, 64. Vesta, 66. Vixen, 89. Wachuta, 45. Wm. Curry, 46. West, Florida, 55. Wild Dayrelle, 67. Young Republic, 73.
Bloomfield, Mo., fight, 38. Attacked, 40.
Blooming Gap, Va., taken, 19.
Blue's Gap, Va., skirmish, 18.
Blue Mills, Mo., fight, 12.
Blue River, Mo., fight, 86.
Blue Springs, Ky., battle, 63.
Bluffton, S. C., destroyed, 56.
Bluntsville, skirmish, 52.
Blythe, Col., rebel, killed, 24.
Board, Col., rebel, killed, 80.
Bohlen, Henry, Gen. killed, 37.
Bolivar, Tenn., skirmish, 39. Fight, 72.
Bolivar, Va., skirmish, 13.
Bollanger, Col, killed, 73.
Bollinger's Mills, Mo., skirmish, 35.
Bombshell, steamer, sunk, 72. Retaken, 72.
Bone Mills, Va., skirmish, 17.
Bonsecours Bay, Ala., salt works destroyed, 83.
Boone, N. C., occupied, 99.
Boone Court House, Va., skirmish, 11.
Booneville, Mo., battle, 8. Skirmish, 11. Fight, 33. Price's speech at, 85.
Booneville, Miss., raid upon, 29.
Boonsboro' Gap, Md., battle, 41.
Booth, John Wilkes, murders President Lincoln, 103. Killed, 105.
Boston Mountain, march across, 48.
Bottom's Bridge, Va., taken, 72.
Bottom Narrows, Ky., fight at, 55.
Bouliusburg, Miss., battle, 53.
Bowling Green, Ky., skirmish, 18. Evacuated, 19. Skirmish, 37.
Boydtown Plank Road, Va., reconnoisance to, 86. Skirmish, 100. Battle, 101.
Boyle, Col., killed, 93.
Bradford, Gov. of Maryland, house burned, 79.
Bragg, Proclamation by, to Kentucky, 37.
Bramlette, Thos. E., elected Gov. of Kentucky, 61.
Branch, Gen., rebel, killed, 42.
Brandy Station, Va., skirmish, 37. Skirmish, 61.
Brandywine, sloop of war, burned, 83.
Brasher, defeated by Mosehy's guerrillas, 88.
Brashear City, La., taken, 58.
Brazil withdraws belligerent rights from rebels, 107.

Brazos Santiago, Texas, taken, 64.
Bread riot at Richmond, Va., 51. Mobile, 62.
Breckinridge, John C., rebel, nominated—his vote, 5. Public dinner to, at Baltimore, 10. General, issues an order about saving arms and lead, 89. "Chafes like a lion," 93. Appointed Secretary of War, 95. Indicted at Washington, 107.
Brentwood, Tenn., taken—skirmish afterward, 51.
Brewster, gun boat, blown up, 73.
Bridgeport, Ala., taken, 26.
Bridgeport, Ga., occupied, 26.
Bridges destroyed—Hannibal and St. Joseph Rail Road, 17. Mobile and Ohio Railroad burned, 21. Kentucky Central Railroad burned, 34. Kentucky and Edgefield Railroad—Red River, burned, 37. See "Raids."
Bristol Station, Va., taken, 38. Battle, 63.
Bristol, Va., captured, 90.
Bristol, Ky., skirmish, 63.
Britton's Lane, Tenn., fight, 40.
Brodhead, Thornton, Col. killed, 39.
Brooks, Major-General, commands in Pennsylvania, 56.
Brooks, Colonel, killed, 80.
Brown, Joseph E., rebel, Governor of Georgia, orders out the reserve militia, 79. Calls out the whole population of the State, 88.
Brown, J. M., Colonel, killed, 29.
Brown, Colonel, killed, 39.
Brown, General, rebel, killed, 44.
Brown, Colonel, rebel, killed, 11.
Brown, Captain, rebel, killed, 11.
Brown's Ferry, Tenn., taken, 64. Battle at, 64.
Brownsville, Arkansas, skirmish, 62.
Brownsville, Kentucky, skirmish, 16.
Brownsville, Missouri, skirmish, 35.
Brownsville, Tenn, skirmish, 45.
Brownsville, Texas, taken, 64. Opened to commerce, 68. Skirmish—near the last fight of the war, 106–7. Taken, 107.
Brunswick river, N. C., reached, 96.
Buchanan, James, defence, and reply to General Scott, 46.
Buchanan, Thomas McKean, Commander, U. S Navy, killed, 49.
Buckhannon, Va., taken, 39.
Buckner, S. B., farm confiscated, 15.
Budd, Thomas A., Lieutenant, killed, 22.
Buell, Don Carlos, Major-General, removed, 45.
Buffington, Ohio, skirmish, 60.
Bullock, Colonel, rebel, killed, 65.
Bull Run, Va., battle, 9. Second battle, 39.
Bull's Bay, S. C., naval expedition, 19.
Bull's Gap, Va., evacuated, 70.
Bull's Gap, Tenn., evacuated, 86.
Bull's Gap, Ky., fight, 87.
Bull's Island, S. C., battery captured, 24.
Burch, Lieutenant-Colonel, killed, 65.
Burdick, Lieutenant, killed, 89.
Burk's Station, Va., skirmish, 21.
Burksville, Va., raid to, 78.
Burley, Bennet M., rebel pirate, surrendered by Canada, 94.
Burnham, General, killed, 84.
Burnside's corps goes to Acquia Creek, 35.
Burnside, A. E., General, appointed to command the Army of the Potomac, 46. Offers to resign, on account of the battle of Fredericksburg, 47. Resigns command of the Army of Potomac, 49. Issues "Order 38," at Cincinnati, denouncing

penalty of death against persons aiding the rebels, 52. Relieved from command at Knoxville, Tenn., 66. Relieved from command of Fifth Corps, 81.
Bute la Rose, La., captured, 53.
Butler, Mo., burned, 16.
Butler, B. F., Major-General, appointed to Gulf Department, 22. Seizes specie at New Orleans, 28. Preparing for operations on James River, 72. Relieved from command, 93.
Cabin Creek, Kansas, train taken, 84.
Cainesville, Tenn., skirmish, 50.
Calf River, Tenn., skirmish, 36.
Calhoun, Ky., skirmish, 17.
Calhoun, Tenn., skirmish, 66.
California, Mo., captured, 85.
Camden, S. C., taken, 96.
Camden, Ark., taken—evacuated, 72.
Cameron, Simon, Secretary of War, resigns, 18.
Cameron, Colonel, killed, 9.
Camp Finegan, Fla., taken, 68.
Camp Wildcat, Ky., fight, 14.
Campbell's Station, Tenn., battle, 64.
Campbell, Colonel, killed, 40.
Campbell, Major, killed, 14.
Campbell, Captain, killed, 38.
Campbell, John A., rebel, released, 111.
Canby, E. K. S., General, to command Department of Louisiana, 109.
Cane Hill, Ark., battle, 47.
Cane River, La., battle, 70.
Canton, Miss., taken, 60. Captured, 63. Skirmish, 78.
Cantwell, Colonel, killed, 39
Cape Girardeau, Mo., battle, 38. Fight, 53.
Carlisle, Pa., bombarded, 58. Occupied by the rebels, 58. Rebels evacuate, 58.
Carmel Church, Va., fight, 34.
Carcifex Ferry, Va., battle, 11.
Carpenter, Colonel, killed, 48.
Carpenter, Major, killed, 48.
Carrick's Ford, Va., battle, 9.
Carrington, Colonel, rebel, killed, 59.
Carrion Crow Bayou, La., battle, 64.
Carrol Station, Tenn., fight, 85.
Carrol, Colonel, killed, 73.
Carson, Captain, killed, 24.
Carter's Creek, Ky., fight, 53.
Carter's Raid, East Tenn., 47.
Carter, Captain, killed, 24.
Carter, Colonel, rebel, killed, 59.
Carter, Colonel, rebel, killed, 74.
Carthage, Mo., battle, 9.
Caseyville, Ohio, River Guerillas, 41.
Cass, Lewis, resigns from the Cabinet, 5.
Cassville, Ga., fight, 75.
Castleman's Ferry, disasters at, 25.
Castle Rock, Mo., fight, 85.
Catawba River, bridge destroyed, 105.
Catlett's Station, Va, raid, 37.
Cedar Bluff, Ga., skirmish, 52.
Cedar Creek, Va., battle, 86.
Cedar Mountain, Va., battle, 36.
Cedar Point, Ala., occupied, 98.
Cedars, Tenn., battle, 89.
Celina, Tenn., skirmish, 53.
Centralia, Mo., massacre at, 84.
Centreville, Va., occupied, 21.
Chaffin's farm, Va., battle, 84. Battle, 85.
Chamberlain's Creek, Virginia, battle, 100.
Chambers, Lieut., killed, 23.

Chambersburg, Pa., captured, 44. Taken, 57. Abandoned, 57. Reoccupied, 57. Taken and burned, 80.
Chambliss, General, rebel, killed, 81.
Champ, Colonel, rebel, killed, 29.
Champion Hill, Mississippi, battle, 55.
Chancellorsville, Virginia, battle, 53, 54.
Chandeleur Island, Louisiana, occupied, 12.
Chandler, J. R., Major, killed, 54.
Chantilly, Virginia, battle, 39.
Chapin, Lieutenant-Colonel, killed, 54.
Chaplin Hills, Kentucky, battle, 44.
Chapman, Co onel, killed, 36.
Chapman, Colonel, killed, 73.
Chapman, Major, killed, 54.
Chapmanville, Virginia, fight, 12.
Charles City Court House, Virginia, taken, 66.
Charles City Cross Roads, Virginia, batt e, 32.
Charleston blockaded 7. Great fire at,16. Stone fleet, 17, 18. Attack on United States fleet by rebel rams, 49. Iron clad fleet abandons, 52. Morris Island batteries taken—assault on Fort Wagner, 60. Sumter and Morris Island bombarded—surrender demanded—swamp angel—Char!eston bombarded—complaints of foreign consul—Greek fire—condition of Sumter, 61. Fort Moultrie bombarded, 62. Rebel steamer sunk in harbor, 62. Second demand to surrender Fort Sumter—assault on, 62. Forts Wagner, Gregg and Morris Island taken, 62. Attempt to blow up the Ironsides frigate, 63. Bombarded, 64. Torpedo boat sunk, 72. John's Island occupied, 78. Assault on Fort Johnson, 78. Battery Simkins taken, 78. Federals driven from John's Island, 79. Patapsco, monitor, blown up, 93. Evacuated—taken possession of by United States troops, 95, 96. United States flag finally raised at Fort Sumter, 103.
Charlestown, Virginia, skirmish, 45. Abandoned, 45. Occupied, 46. Fight, 47. Captured, 64.
Charleston, Illinois, Riot, 70.
Charleston, Tennessee, fight, 66.
Charlestown, West Virginia, Hunter at, 78.
Charlestown, Missouri, skirmish, 20.
Charlottesville, Va., fight at, 69. Taken, 97
Chase, S. P., Secretary of the Treasury, offers his resignation, 47; declined, 47. Re-igned, 78. Appointed Chief Justice of the United States, 89.
Chattahoochie, rebel ram, blown up, 57.
Chattahoochie river, Georgia, Sherman at, 78. Crossed by Sherman. 79. Losses, 83.
Chattanooga, Ga., cannonade, 30. Bragg retreats to, 59. Rosecrans before, 61. Taken, 62. Bombarded, 63. Battle, 65. Fire, 108.
Cheatham, General, rebel, killed, 49.
Cheek's Cross-roads, skirmish, 70.
Cheraw, S. C., taken, 96.
Cherokee Indians adhere to the Confederacy, 10.
Chesapeake, steamer, seized by pirates, 65. Retaken, 66. Rebel crew of, rescued in Nova Scotia, 66. Capture adjudge l piracy, 68. Pirates ordered to be surrendered to the United States, 69. Warrant of extradition refused, 69. Vessel surrendered to United States, 70.
Chesterfield Court House, S. C., taken, 96.
Chickasaw Bluffs, battle, 48.
Chickasaw, Miss., taken, 19.
Chickahominy, Va., crossed, 79.

Chickamauga, Ga., battle, 62, 63.
Chicomacomico, N. C., skirmish,—fight with gunboats, 12.
Childs, Colonel, killed, 41.
Chowan River, skirmish, 69.
Christianburg, Va., taken, 98.
Chuckatuck, Va., fight, 67.
Chuckatuck Creek, Va., skirmish, 70.
Cincinnati, Ohio, threatened, 40. Martial law suspended, 41.
Cincinnati, gun-boat sunk, 56.
Citico Creek, Tenn., battle, 65.
City Point, Va., Butler lands at, 72. Ordnance boat explodes, 81. Designed attack on by rebel fleet, 94.
Clark (Fort), N. C., captured, 11.
Clark, Charles, released, 111.
Clark, Jerome ("Sue Mundy"), taken prisoner, 97. Hung, 98.
Clark, Colonel, killed, 56.
Clarkson, Mo., skirmish, 45.
Clarksville, Tenn., taken, 20. Surrendered, 37. Skirmish near, 52.
Clarksville, Ky., re-occupied, 40.
Clay, C. C., rebel peace negotiations, 79. Indicted in Canada, 105. Reward for his arrest, 106. Taken prisoner at Fortress Monroe, 107.
Claybrook, Major, rebel, killed, 58.
Cleary, W. C., indicted in Canada, 105. Reward for his arrest, 106.
Cleborne, Patrick, General, rebel, killed, 80
Clinton, Ga., fight near, 81.
Clinton Road, Tenn., skirmish, 64.
Cloyd Mountain, Va., battle, 73.
Cobb, Howell, resigns from the Cabinet, 5.
Cobb, T. R., General, rebel, killed, 47.
Cobb's Point, N. C., naval battle, 19.
Cochran's Cross-roads, Mo., skirmish, 40.
Cochrane, John, nominated for Vice-President, 75-6. Withdraws, 84.
Cockpit Point, Va., taken, 21.
Coggswell, Colonel, killed, 36.
Coin captured from rebels after flight from Richmond, 110.
Cold Harbor, Va., battle, 31. Skirmish—battle, 75. Battle—fight—losses, 76. Battle near,— another battle, 76. Flanked, 77.
Coldwater Bridge, Mo., burned, 40.
Coldwater River, operations on, 49. Expedition to, 50.
Cole (Camp), Mo., fight, 8.
Coleman, Colonel, killed, 41.
Coles, Robert, Captain, rebel, killed, 19.
Collet, Lieutenant-Colonel, killed, 38.
Collet, Colonel, killed, 54.
Colliersville, Tenn., battle, 64.
Collins, Lieutenant, killed, 109.
Colored troops—permission to recruit in Massachusetts, 49. At Port Hudson, 56.
Columbia, Ark., fight, 10.
Columbia, S. C., taken, 96.
Columbia, Va., taken, 97.
Columbia, Tenn., skirmish, 88.
Columbia Furnace, Va., skirmish, 25.
Columbus, Ga., taken, 104.
Columbus, Ky., evacuated, 20.
Colquitt, General, rebel, killed, 42.
Combahee River, S. C., expedition, 56.
Commodore Jones, gun-boat, blown up, 78.
Concordia, Ark., burned, 47.
Conestoga, gunboat, sunk, 68.

Confederacy organized at Montgomery, Ala.— sends commissioners to United States Government, who are not received, 6.
Congaree, S. C., Sherman at, 95.
Congress (United States), meets, 9.
Congress of seceding States meets at Montgomery, Ala., 5.
Congress, frigate, sunk, 21.
Conklin, Major, killed, 39.
Connecticut, defeat of State Constitution to grant negro suffrage, 111.
Connell, Colonel, killed, 39.
Conscription Bill, 50.
Conventions, 1860—Democratic, Seceders, Republican, Constitutional Union, Peace, Secession, 5. Peace, 6. National Union, to be held at Baltimore, 69. Of the Radical Democracy, 75. Peace, at Syracuse, N. Y., 82. Democratic, at Chicago, Ill.—Peace resolutions, 83. Nominations, 83.
Coons, J. C., Colonel, killed, 74.
Cook, Major, killed, 36.
Cooke, General, rebel, killed, 63.
Coosawatchie, River, S. C., operations on, 45.
Corbett, Boston, Sergeant, shoots Booth, 105.
Corbett, Captain of the Sea King, arrested, 93.
Corbin, W. F., Captain, rebel spy, hung, 59.
Corinth, Miss., skirmishes, 28. Reconnoisance— Taken, 29. Battle, 44. Skirmish, 47. Evacuated by Federals, 67.
Corpus Christi, Texas, bombarded, 42.
Corse, General, rebel, killed, 74.
Corsons, Ky., skirmish, 17.
Cotton, export prohibited by rebel congress, 8.
Cotton, Lieutenant-Colonel, killed, 48.
Cotton Plant, Ark., battle, 33.
Couch, D. N., Major-Gen., commands a corps, 50. Commands in Pennsylvania, 58.
Courtland, Ala., taken, 35.
Cove Creek, N. C., fight, 46.
Cove Mountain Gap, Va. battle, 73.
Covode, George, Colonel, killed, 78.
Covington, Ky., in danger, 40.
Cowles, Daniel S., Colonel, killed, 56.
Cowleyville, Ohio, fight at, 60.
Cox's Creek, Ky., skirmish, 45.
Cox's Mills, Va., skirmish, 36.
Crane, Colonel, killed, 36.
Crane, Lieutenant-Colonel, 65.
Creelsboro', Tenn., skirmish, 53.
Creighton, Colonel, killed, 65.
Croasdale, Samuel, Colonel, killed, 42.
Crook, General, taken prisoner, 93.
Crosby, John N., Colonel, killed, 101.
Cross, Colonel, killed, 59.
Cross-Keys, Va., battle, 30.
Cross-Lanes, Va., skirmish, 11.
Crystal Springs, Miss., destroyed, 55.
Culpepper, Va., occupied, 33. Fight, 64.
Culpepper Court House, Va., fight, 54. Cavalry fight, 56.
Culp's Farm, Ga., battle, 78.
Cumberland, Md., entered, 96.
Cumberland, frigate, sunk, 21.
Cumberland Gap, Va., reconnoisance, 22.
Cumberland Gap, Tenn., taken, 30. Evacuated, 43. Retaken, 62. Fight near, 69.
Curlew, Ohio River, guerillas attack, 41.
Curtin, Governor of Pennsylvania, Proclamation for defence of the State, 57. Second Proclamation, 58. Proclamation for 60,000 militia, 58

Calls for 12,000 volunteers, 78. Proclamation for 30,000 volunteers, 81.
Cutters, Revenue, etc. (U. S.), seized by rebels—Aiken, Dana, McClellan, Cass, 5—Dodge, 6.
Cynthiana, Ky., taken, 34. Skirmish and battle, 77.
Cypress Bridge, Ky., skirmish, 15.
Dabney's Mills, Virginia, battle, 95.
Dahlgren, Uric, Colonel, killed, 69.
Dallas, Georgia, battle, 75.
Dallas, Alabama, losses, 83.
Dalton, Georgia, skirmishes near, 69. Evacuated, 74. Train captured near, 77. Fight, 82. Surrendered, 85.
Dam No. 4, Virginia, skirmish, 16.
Dam No. 5, Va., skirmish, 16.
Damonville, Arkansas, fight, 62.
Danby's Mills, Alabama, occupied, 99.
Danbridge, Tenn., skirmish, 66. Battle, 66, 67.
Danville, Virginia, occupied, 105.
Darbytown Road, Virginia, battle, 85.
Dardanelles, Arkansas, taken, 75.
Dardanelles, Missouri, Price at, 83.
Darien, Georgia, burned, 56.
Dauphine Island, Alabama, expedition from, 98.
Davis, Colonel, killed, 24.
Davis's, (Garret,) farm, Kentucky, skirmish, 34.
Davis, Colonel, killed, 24.
Davis, B. F., Colonel, killed, 56.
Lavis, Lieutenant-Colonel, killed, 74.
Davis, Col., rebel, killed, 29.
Davis, Jefferson C., Major-General, kills General Nelson, 43.
Davis, Jeff., inaugurated permanent President of Confederacy, 20. Cabinet, 22. Recommends violation of parole, 22. Retaliatory order against Pope and Steinwehr, 35. Issues proclamation threatening to hang Gen. McNeill, 46. Issues a proclamation threatening to hang Gen. Butler, 48. Message of retaliation for emancipation proclamation, 49. Proclaims fast day, 50. Orders a conscription, 61. Announces to his soldiers the beginning of the Tennessee campaign, 84. Speech in the African church, Richmond, 95. Asks rebel Congress not to adjourn, 97. Rumor of plots against, 97. Reward for his arrest, 106. Captured, 106. Taken to Fortress Monroe, 107. Indicted at Washington, 107.
Davis's Mill, Tenn., fight, 47.
Dayton's Gap, skirmish, 52.
Dead Buffalo Lake, Dakota, fight, 61.
Debts due northern creditors confiscated, 7.
Debt, National, August 1, 1865, 109. October 31, 1865, 111.
Decatur, Ga., occupied by Sherman, 79. Battle, 80.
Decatur, Alabama, operations at, 25. Rosseau at, 79. Fight, 86.
Decatur, Tenn., skirmish near, 35.
Decker, Lieut., killed, 25.
Deep Bottom, Va., battle, 81.
Deep Creek, Va., battle, 101.
Deep Run, Va., battle, 81.
De Kalb, gunboat, blown up, 60.
Delaware refuses to receive secession commissioners, 5.
Democratic national convention, 1860, 5.
De Montieuil, Colonel, killed, 19.
Dennison, Postmaster General, appointed, 84.
Dentonsville, Va., fight, 102.
De Rosset, Colonel, rebel, killed, 42.

De Saussure, Colonel, rebel, killed, 59.
Deshler, General, rebel, killed, 63.
Deserters shot, 61.
Dickerson's Farm, Va., skirmish, 15.
Dillon, Captain, killed, 24.
Dinwiddie Court House, Va., skirmish, 94.
Dix, General, appointed to Middle Department, 23. His orders about raiders from Canada, 91. Disapproved, 91.
Dobb, George W., Colonel, killed, 101.
Doken, Major, rebel, killed, 24.
Donahue, Edw. Jr., convicted of preparing fraudulent soldiers' votes, 86.
Donald, ——, indicted in Canada, 105.
Donaldsonville, La., battle, 58.
Doughty, Colonel, killed, 57.
Douglass, S. A., nominated for President—his vote, 5. Death of, 8.
Downe, James, Editor, sent south, 53.
Draft, ordered, 35. Citizens liable to, not to go abroad, 36. Law, 50. Riots, New York, 60—Staten Island, 60—Boston, 61—Brooklyn, 61. For 500,000 men, 67. Proclamation, 70. Persons convicted of obstructing and resisting, 87. Drafting stopped, 103. See "Proclamation."
Dranesville, Va., reconnoisance to, 15. Expedition to, 16. Battle, 17. Fight, 69.
Drake, Colonel, killed, 76.
Droop Mountain, battle, 64.
Drury's Bluff, James River, naval fight at, 28.
Dry Fork, Va., skirmish, 18.
Dudley, W. W., Colonel, killed, 59.
Dufie, General, captured, 86.
Dug Spring, Mo., battle, 10.
Dumfries, Va., skirmish, 23. Skirmish, 48.
Dunlop, Lieutenant, rebel, executed as a spy, 56.
Dupont, Samuel F., Admiral, death, 108.
Dutch Gap, Va., rebel prisoners put to work, 85. Canal, finished., 93.
Duval's Bluff, Ark., taken, 49.
East Bay, Fla., Salt-works destroyed, 68.
East Point, Tenn., fight, 85.
Eastport, Miss., operations at, 25.
East Tennessee, Carter's raid, 47.
Ebenezer Church, Ala., battle, 101.
Edenburg, Va., skirmish, 23. Occupied, 23.
Edenton, N. C., taken, 19.
Edgefield Junction, Tenn., skirmish, 37.
Edgefield Station, Va., fight, 37.
Edisto Island, S. C., skirmish, 25.
Edisto River, S. C., expedition, 78.
Edmonds, Colonel, rebel, killed, 59.
Edwards' Ferry, Va., skirmish, 8. United States troops withdrawn from, 14.
Edwards' Station, Miss., battle, 55.
Egypt Station, Miss., raid at, 68.
Elison's Mills, Va., skirmish, 28.
Elizabethtown, Ky., taken, 48. Gen. Lyon, rebel, at, 92.
Elk Creek, Kansas, fight, 60.
Elkford, Ky., skirmish, 48.
Elkhorn, Ark., battle, 20. Beauregard's address at, 26.
Elkwater, Va., skirmish, 11.
Ellet, Charles Jr., Colonel, killed, 30.
Elliott, Lieutenant-Colonel, killed, 65.
Ellis, Colonel, killed, 24.
Ellsworth, E. E., killed at Alexandria, Va., 8.
Enlistments suspended, 23.
Erie (Lake), raid, 84. Burley surrendered, 94. John Y. Beall, hung, 96.

nt-Colonel, killed, 20.
l batteries, 52.

taken, 75.
-works burned, 75.
, rebel, killed, 44.
ed for Vice-President—

)els, held in Liverpool,
Sanitary, proceeds, 89.
2.
charge through by ca-
alls back to, 13. Skir-
).
), 67.

red, 53.
mish, 9. Lee's army
60.
sh, 15.
sh, 27. Battle, 27.
, battle, 63.
l.
perations against Mo-
)e-Admiral, 91.
l, surrenders navy, 106.
sted, 10.

0. Skirmish, 34. Skir-

by Gen. Sherman, 98.
80.
l, hung, 111.
0.
preparing fraudulent

inted Secretary of the

led, 74.
34.
ed, 10.
, 49.

0, 101.
ted, 94.
.ransfer, 43.
4. Taken, 56. Skir-
)es at, 85.
ates property seized, 5.
itutional amendments

captured by, 79. Cap-
il, 85. Sunk, 89. Cor-
—satisfaction to, 90.
idicted for Indian bond

ander, killed, 71.
l as hostage, 59. Ex-

)ointed Flag-officer of
iral, death of, 58.

dismissed the service

ton—taken possession

78.
l, 74.
8.

Forrest, William, Colonel, rebel, killed, 69.
Forts (United States), seized by rebels—Moultrie, Castle Pinckney, Macon, Wilmington, in Mississippi, Pulaski, Caswell, Johnson, Jackson, Morgan, St. Phillip, Pickens, Barrancas, McRae, 5. Brown, 6. Smith, 7.
Forts taken, bombarded and besieged during the war:—Alexis, Ala., taken, 102. Anderson, N. C., taken, 96. Arkansas Post, 49. Bartow, N. C., taken, 19. Beauregard, S. C., captured by United States, 14. Blanchard, N. C., taken, 19. Bleakley, Ala., taken, 102. Campbell, N. C., taken, 93. Caswell, N. C., taken, 93. Chereteau Point, Ala., taken, 103. Chickasaw, Tenn , destroyed, 92. Clark, taken, 11. Corpus Christi, Texas, taken, 33. De Russy, La., taken, 54, 70. Donelson, Tenn., taken, 19—Repulse at, 38—Attacked, 49. Esperanza, taken, 65. Eugene, Ala., taken, 102. Fisher, N. C., attack on, 90—Bombarded, 92—Attack on abandoned, 92—Second bombardment, 93—Captured, 93—Magazine explosion, 93. Fisher, Va., battle, 99. Gaines, surrendered, 81. Garnero's Bend, Ala., taken, 103. Gibson, attacked, 66. Gray, N. C., assaulted, 71. Gregg, S. C., taken, 62. Griffin, Texas, taken, 107. Grumball. S. C., taken, 26. Hatteras, taken, 11. Henry, Tenn., taken, 18. Hudson, Fla., taken, 84. Huger, Ala., bombarded, 102—Taken, 103. Jackson, La , attacked, 25—Taken, 26. Johnston, Va., taken, 20. Johnson, S. C., assaulted, 78. Livingston, La., taken, 26. Lunette, Warwick River, Va., taken, 26. McAllister, Ga., bombarded, 49, 50—Taken, 90. Mannahasset, Texas, taken, 107. Macon, N. C., invested, 23—Sortie, 25—Taken, 26. Morgan, Ala., surrendered, 82. Moultrie, S. C., bombarded, 62—Retaken, 96. Pemberton, bombarded, 50—Siege abandoned, 52. Pinckney (Castle), retaken, 96. Pinto, Ala., taken, 103. Pillow, Ky., invested, 25—Taken, 70—Massacre, 71. Port Hudson, Miss., attempt to pass, 50—Bombarded, 55—Surrendered, 59. Port Royal, S. C., taken, 17. Powell, Ala., bombarded, 69, 70—Taken, 81. Powhatan, Va., taken, 60—Skirmish near, 67—Battle, 75. Pulaski, Ga., taken, 24. Randolph, Miss. River, taken, 29. St. Mark's River, taken, 30. St. Phillip, La., attacked, 25—Taken, 26. Sanders, Tenn., assaulted, 65. Scott, Kan., skirmish, 10. Sinkins, S. C., taken, 78. Smith, Ark., taken, 62—Attacked, 81. Spanish, Ala., fight, 99—Attacked, 100—Taken, 102. Spanish River, Ala , taken, 103. Steadman, Va., battle, 90—Fight at, 100. Stevens, D. C., attack on, 79. Sumter, S. C., bombarded, 51—Grand attack on, 61—Retaken, 96—United States flag formally raised, 103. Tracy, Ala., bombarded, 102—Assaulted, 103. Wagner, assaulted, 60—Rifle pits taken, 62—Taken, 62. Walker, S. C., captured by United States, 14. Warrenton, Miss., destroyed, 55. West Branch, Va., stormed, 53. Wright, Miss. River, invested, 25—Taken, 29. Yazoo River, 38.
Foster, J. G., Major-General, takes command at Knoxville, Tenn., 66. To command Department of Florida, 109.
Fowler, Colonel, rebel, killed, 46.
Four Mile Creek, Va., battle, 80.
Fourteen Mile Creek, loss at, 59.
France withdraws belligerant rights from rebels, 108.

Francisville, La., burned, 37.
Frankfort, Ky., threatened, 33. Secession convention at, 50. Threatened, 76.
Franklin, Va., skirmish, 47.
Franklin, Tenn., skirmish, 50. Battle, 52. Fight, 59. Battle, 89. Losses at, 92. Report of losses, 93.
Franklin, Major-General, commands centre army of the Potomac, 46. Relieved from command, 49. Taken prisoner—escape, 79, 80.
Frederick, Md., occupied by rebels, 40. Federals at, 41. Skirmish—taken, 79.
Fredericksburg, Va., skirmish, 25. Evacuated, 39. Burnside at, 46. Sumner demands surrender, 46. Fight at, 46. Battle of, 47. Sedgwick at, 53. Tobacco captured, 97.
Fredericktown, Mo., battle, 14. Occupied, 84.
Freestone Point, Va., shelled, 16.
Fremont, John C., Major-General, orders slave property of rebels in Missouri confiscated—President partially revokes the order, 11. Retires from the command of the Army of Missouri, 14. Nominated for President, 75–6. Withdraws, 84.
Fribley, Colonel, killed, 68.
Pricke's Lick, Mo., skirmish, 41.
Front Royal, Va, skirmish—battle, 28. Retaken —reconnoisance from, 29. Occupied by rebels, 57. Fight, 82. Skirmish near, 88.
Fulton, Mo., skirmish, 9. Rebels captured, 14.
Funkstown, Md., fight, 59.
Fry, James B, Colonel, appointed Provost-Marshal General, 51.
Gadberry, Colonel, rebel, killed, 39.
Gadsden, Ga., skirmish, 52.
Gaines' Mills, Va., battle, 31.
Gainesville, Va., fight, 64. Flanked, 77.
Gainesville, Fla., taken, 68.
Gallatin, Tenn., taken, 36, 37.
Galveston, Texas, taken by the rebels, 48. Bombarded, 49. Taken, 108.
Garesche, Lieutenant-Colonel, killed, 48.
Garland, General, rebel, killed, 41.
Garlick Landing, Va., Stuart's raid, 30.
Garnett's Farm, Va., battle, 31.
Garnett, Gen., rebel, retreats—is killed, 9.
Garnett, General, rebel, killed, 59.
Garnett, T. S., Colonel, rebel, killed, 54.
Garretsburg, Ky., skirmish, 46.
Gates County, N. C., expedition to, 27.
Gauley, Va., bridge burned, 10. Skirmishing, 14. Floyd retreats from, 14. Evacuated, 41.
Gavan, Colonel, rebel, killed, 58.
Gavitt, Major, killed, 14.
Geiger's Creek, Ohio, capture at, 60.
Germantown, Va., skirmish, 19.
Georgetown, S. C., taken, 96.
Georgia appropriation by, for war—United States property seized—secedes, 5. Jas. Johnson, Provisional Governor, 103. Carl Schurz upon militia, 110. Organization of militia approved of by President, 110. Proclamation of General Steadman against distributing arms among Georgians, 110. Repeals secession ordinance—abolishes slavery conditionally, 111. Instructed that she must repudiate the rebel debt, 111.
Georgia, rebel cruiser, captured by the frigate Niagara, 82.
Gettysburg, Pa., occupied by rebels, 58. Battle, 59.
Geyer Lake, Ky., fight at, 40.

Gherardie, General, rebel, killed, 81.
Gilmore, Q. A., Major-General, commands department of the South, 57. To command department of South Carolina.
Gilmore, James R., peace negotiations, 80.
Gilmore, Harry, Major, rebel, captured, 94.
Gist, General, rebel, killed, 89.
Glade Spring, Va., captured, 91.
Glasgow, Mo., fight, 16.
Glasgow, Miss., battle, 86.
Glass, Lieutenant-Colonel, killed, 65.
Glendale, Va., battle, 32.
Glenn, Major, killed, 101.
Gloucester, Va., bombardment, 26. Evacuated, 27. Kilpatrick at, 55.
Godard, Major, killed, 24.
Godwin, General, rebel, killed, 84.
Gold, prices, 70. Bill to punish frauds in price of, 71. Bill signed, 77. Prices of, 77. Price in Richmond and Philadelphia, 95.
Goldsboro' N. C., taken, 47. Occupied, 98.
Golgotha, Ga., battle, 77.
Goodrich, Colonel, killed, 42.
Goose Creek, Florida, salt works destroyed, 69.
Gordonsville, Va., fight at, 77. Menaced, 91.
Gove, Colonel, killed, 31.
Governors, rebel, consultation held at Augusta, Ga., 86.
Grafton, Va., occupied by United States troops, 8. Skirmish, 10.
Granberry, General, rebel, killed, 89.
Grand Gulf, La., bombardment, 30. Bombarded, 53. Taken, 54. Battle, 79.
Grant, U. S., Major-General, takes command of the army of the Cumberland, 64. Nominated Lieutenant-General, 69. Assigned to command armies of the United States, 70. "Will fight it out on this line," 74. House presented to him by citizenz of Philadelphia, 93. Goes to South Carolina to assist Sherman, 104.
Grant's Creek, N. C., battle, 103.
Graves, Major, rebel, killed, 63.
Great Bethel, battle, 8.
Great Britain issues a proclamation of neutrality, 7. Proclamation against the exportation of articles used in making gunpowder and firearms, 16. Forbids the exportation of saltpetre, 16. Surrender to, by the Confederates advocated, 93. Withdraws belligerent rights from rebels, 107. Withdrawal—complaints that it is partial, 108.
Greble, J. T., Lieutenant, killed, 8.
Greeley, Horace, peace negotiations, 79.
Green, Lieutenant-Colonel, killed, 60.
Green, General, rebel, killed, 71.
Green, Major, rebel, killed, 30.
Greenbrier, Va., skirmish, 12.
Greencastle, Md., taken, 59.
Green Hill, Ky., skirmish, 51.
Greenland Gap, W. Va., defended, 53.
Green River, Ky., skirmish, 16.
Greenupsburg, Ky., retreat to, 43.
Greenville, Tenn., skirmish, 83.
Greenwalt, Lieutenant-Colonel, killed, 74.
Greenwich, Va., fighting at, 38.
Greenwood, Miss., fight, 50.
Gregg, Maxcy, General, rebel, killed, 47.
Gregg, General, rebel, killed, 85.
Gregory's Landing, S. C., battle, 89.
Grenada, Miss., taken, 47, 61.
Grice, Colonel, rebel, killed, 74.

Grierson, Colonel, raid through Georgia and Alabama, 52.
Griffith, General, rebel, killed, 32.
Grimballs, S. C., occupied, 95.
Griswoldsville, Ga., battle, 88.
Groner, Colonel, rebel, killed, 59.
Grover, A. J., Major, killed, 59.
Groveton, Va., battle, 39.
Guiney Station, Va., occupied, 75.
Gulf Division, General Sheridan, 108.
Gum Swamp, N. C., taken, 55.
Gunboat Fleet, transfer, 43.
Gunpowder River Bridge, Md., burned, 79.
Guntown, Tenn., battle, 76.
Guyandotte, W. Va., massacre of Union troops at, 14—Burned, 14.
Guy's Gap, Tenn., skirmish, 57.
Gwyn, Captain, U. S. Navy, killed, 48.
Habeas Corpus, suspended by the President, 110. Suspended, 62.
Hackleman, Brig'r-General, killed, 44.
Hagerstown, Md., taken, 41. Taken by Lee's advance, 57. Retaken, 78. Evacuated, 78. Occupied by rebels, 81.
Haggerty, Lieutenant-Colonel, killed, 9.
Haines Bluffs, Miss. River, shelled, 48. Evacuated, 55.
Half Mountain, Ky., fight, 71.
Hall, Colonel, killed, 24.
Halleck, H. W., Major-General, appointed commander of all the armies, 33. Chief of Staff, 70. Commands Department of Virginia, etc., 104. Advises that no regard be paid to Sherman's treaty with Johnston, 105. Commands Pacific Division, 108.
Hallsboro', Va., skirmish, 45.
Hamilton, N. C., taken, 33. Taken, 46.
Hamilton, A. J., Provisional Gov'r of Texas, 108.
Hamilton, Captain, rebel, killed, 29.
Hamlin, Hannibal, nominated Vice-President—his vote, 5. Election—inauguration, 6.
Hampton, Va., occupied, 7. Burned by Magruder, 9. Abandoned by U. States troops, 10.
Hampton, Colonel, rebel, killed, 57.
Hancock, W. S., Major-General, commands Second Corps, 70. To command Middle Depart't, 109.
Hanover Court House, Va., battle, 29.
Hanover Gap, Tenn., skirmish, 57.
Hanover Junction, Pa., cavalry fight, 58.
Hanson, Gen., rebel, killed, 49.
Hard, Col., rebel, killed, 63.
Harker, G. C., General, killed, 78.
Harlan, James, nominated Sec'y of Interior, 97.
Harney, General, arrested, and released. 7.
Harper, Col., rebel, killed, 63.
Harper's Ferry, Va., evacuated and burned by U. States troops, 6. Also by rebels, 8. Skirmish, 16. Shelled, 19. Taken by Banks, 29. Taken by "Stonewall" Jackson, 41. Evacuated, 43. Skirmish near, 66. Retreat to, 80.
Harris, Benj. G., M. C. from Maryland, motion to expel from Congress—censured, 71. Court-martialled, 106.
Harrisonburg, Va., occupied, 25. Skirmish, 26, 27. Fight, 30.
Harrison's Landing, Va., address to troops at, 33. Skirmish, 33, 35. Evacuated, 37.
Harrisonville, Mo., skirmish, 9.
Harrold, David E.—a reward offered for his arrest, 104. Taken prisoner, 105. Tried for assassination, 106. Condemned, 109. Hung, 109.

Hart, John, Lieut., U. S. Navy, killed, 48.
Hartsfield, Colonel, rebel, killed, 74.
Hartsville, Tenn., captured, 47.
Hartville, Mo., fight, 49.
Haskel, Col., killed, 76.
Hatch, Lieut. Col., killed, 31.
Hatchie, Miss., battle, 44.
Hatcher's Creek (or Run), Va., reconnoisance, 86.
Hatcher's Run, Va., battle, 94, 99.
Hatteras and Clark (forts), N. C., bombarded and captured, 11.
Hatteras, steamer, attacked by the privateer Alabama, and sunk, 49.
Hatton, General, rebel, killed, 29.
Hawes' Shop, Va., battle, 75.
Hawk's Nest, Va., skirmish, 10.
Haxall's Farm, Va., battle, 80.
Haycock, Major, killed, 54.
Hayes, Alex'r, General, killed, 73.
Hays, Colonel, killed, 73.
Hayward, General, rebel, killed, 82.
Heath, Colonel, killed, 65.
Helena, Ark., Gen. Curtis at, 33. Skirmish, 35, 50. Battle, 59, 60. Fight near, 80.
Helm, B. H., Gen., rebel, killed, 63.
Henderson, Ky., skirmish, 32. Taken, 34. Skirmish, 38.
Henderson's Hill, La., fight, 70.
Hendricks, Colonel, killed, 20.
Hesser, Theodore, Lieutenant-Colonel, killed, 65.
Heth, Lieutenant-Colonel, killed, 31.
Hewlings, Colonel, killed, 74.
Hickman, Ky., occupied, 11.
Hidden, Lieutenant, killed, 21.
Higham, Captain, killed, 14.
High Bridge, Va., skirmish, 102.
Hill, A. P., General, rebel, killed. 101.
Hillsboro', Ky., skirmish, 13.
Hillsboro', Ga., fight near, 81.
Hinks, Colonel, killed, 32.
Hinks, Colonel, killed, 42.
Hodges, Colonel, rebel, killed, 74.
Hogg, Lieut. Col., killed, 39.
Hoke, Major, rebel, killed, 22.
Hoke's Run, Va., skirmish, 9.
Holcombe, J. B., Peace negotiations, 79.
Holden, Wm. W., appointed Provisional Governor of North Carolina, 107.
Holly Springs, Miss., occupied, 30. Captured, 47.
Holston River, Tenn., crossed by Gen. Sturges, 67.
Holt, Colonel, rebel, killed, 74.
Honey Hill, S. C., battle, 89. Reconnoisance, 95.
Hood, J. B., Gen., rebel, takes command of Army of the Tennessee, 79. Campaign to Tennessee announced by Jeff. Davis, 84. Commenced, 84. Retires before Gen. Sherman, 86. Pursuit of his army ceases, 92. His losses, 92, 93. Report of losses, 93. Deprived of command, 94.
Hooker, Joseph, Major-Gen., commands left wing Army of Potomac, 46. Appointed Commander Army of Potomac, 49. Commands First Corps, 70. Resigns from command of Twentieth Corps, 80. Commands Department of the East, 109.
Hopkinsville, Ky., fight, 85. Taken, 90.
Horses burned, Washington, D. C., 17.
Horse-Shoe, Ky., fight at, 55.
Hospitals (U. States), seized by rebels at New Orleans, 5.
Hostages—Flynn and Sawyer held as, 59. Rebel Gen. W. Fitzhugh Lee and Col. Winder held as, for Capts. Sawyer and Flynn, 60. Capts. Saw-

yer and Flynn exchanged for Gen. Lee and Capt. Winder, 70. Gen. John H. Morgan, rebel, held as, for Col. Straight. 61.
Housatonic, gunboat, sunk by a torpedo, 68.
Houston, Mo.. captured, 14.
Howard, Major-Gen., commands Fourth Corps, 70. Commands Army of Tennessee, 80. Commands right wing of Gen. Sherman's army, 87.
Howard, Charles, Ensign, U. S. Navy, killed, 63.
Howe's Cross-roads, Va., battle, 102.
Hubbs, Major, killed, 31.
Hudson, Mo., skirmish, 17, 40.
Hudson, Colonel, killed, 73.
Huey, Colonel, killed, 78.
Hughes, General, rebel, killed, 36.
Humansville, Mo., skirmish, 23.
Humboldt, Tenn., skirmish, 36.
Humes, General, rebel, killed, 97.
Humphreys, B. G., elected Governor of Mississippi, 111.
Humphreys, West H., United States Judge, Tennessee, impeached and removed, 31.
Hunnewell, Mo., skirmish, 11. Skirmish, 18.
Huntoon's Mills, Tenn., skirmish, 49.
Hunter, David, Major-General, appointed to the department of the south, 22. Commands in West Virginia and Shenandoah, 75. Virginia expedition ended, 78. Removed from command, 81.
Hunter, William, acting Secretary of State. 104.
Hunter, R. M. T., calls on Virginia Legislature to assemble, 102. Meeting forbidden, 103.
Hunter, Major, killed, 24.
Hunter, General, steamer, blown up, 71.
Hunter's Chapel, Va., skirmish, 16.
Huntersville, Va., taken, 18.
Hunts Cross Roads, Tenn., skirmish, 48.
Huntsville, Ala., taken, 24. Surrender demanded, 85.
Huron, Ind., railroad accident, 12.
Hurricane Creek, Miss., fight, 81.
Hutchings, Mrs. Sarah, of Baltimore, found guilty of attempting to send a sword to Gilmore, a rebel, 88.
Hutter, midshipman, rebel, killed, 21.
Independence, Mo., skirmish, 20. Skirmish, 22. fight, 36.
Indian country, fight, 33.
Indians hung at Mankato, 48. Defeated near Salt Lake, 52.
Indians, rebel, surrender of Pytchlin and Stand Watie, 108. Allied to rebels sign treaties with U. S., 110. Treaty with Kansas Indians, 111.
Indian Creek, Mo., skirmish, 22.
Inge, Lieut.-Colonel, rebel, killed, 63.
Iron Age blown up, 66.
Ironsides, New, attempt to blow up, 63.
Ironton, Mo., battle, 84.
Island Ford, Va., battle, 80.
Island No. 10, Mississippi river, battery taken, 23. Bombardment, 23. Passed by Carondelet, 23. Passed by Pittsburg, 24. Evacuated, 24.
Irish Bend, La., fight, 52.
Irvon, Lieutenant-Colonel, killed, 56.
Irwin, Lieutenant-Colonel, killed, 65.
Iuka, Mississippi, battle, 54.
Jackson, Camp, taken by Captain Lyon, 7.
Jackson, Miss., battle, 55. Loss at, 59. Taken, 60. Taken, 67. Entered by Sherman's army, 68. Taken, 78.
Jackson, Tenn., fight, 60.
Jackson's Mills, N. C., battle, 97.
Jacksonville, Fla., occupied, 21. Resolutions against secession, 22. Anti-secession meeting, 23. Taken, 50.
Jackson, Conrad F., General, killed, 47.
Jackson, General, killd, 4e4.
Jackson, Lieutenant-Colonel, killed, 31.
Jackson, T. J., "Stonewall," rebel, killed, 54.
Jacques, James F., Col., peace negotiations, 80.
James Island, S. C., fights, 29.
James River, Virginia, naval battle, 76. Crossed by Grant and Meade, 77. Rebel fleet driven from their moorings, 86. Naval attempt foiled, 94. Canal destroyed, 77.
James, Colonel, rebel, killed, 41.
Jarratt's Station, Va., fight, 72.
Jefferson City, Mo., menaced, 85. Attacked, 85.
"Jeffersonian," newspaper, destroyed at West Chester, Pa., 10. Seizure by U. S. Marshal, 11.
Jenkins, General, rebel, killed, 74.
Jerusalem plank road, Va., battle, 77. Skirmish, 81. Rifle-pits near, taken, 83.
Jetersville, Virginia, Sheridan at, 101, 102.
Jewett, Lientenant-Colonel, killed, 44.
Jewett, J. M., Colonel, rebel, killed, 63.
Jones, J. Richter, Colonel, killed, 55.
Jones, Colonel, killed, 48.
Jones, Lieutenant-Colonel, killed, 48.
Jones, S. M., General, rebel, killed, 74.
Jones, W. E, General, rebel, killed, 76.
Jones, Colonel, rebel, killed, 59.
Jonesboro', Ga., destroyed, 82. Battle, 83. Skirmish, 88. Skirmish, 88.
Jones' Ford, Va., fight, 72.
Jonesville, Va., fight 66.
John's Island, S. C., occupied, 78. Federals driven from, 79.
Johns, Major, killed, 31.
Johnson, Andrew, nominated for Vice-President at Baltimore, 76. Elected Vice-President—his vote, 87. Inaugurated, 97. Inaugurated as President, 103. Receives delegation from South Carolina—terms of reconstruction, 108. Speech to South Carolina delegation, 111. Issues proclamation for a day of thanksgiving, 111.
Johnson, Herschel V., nominated Vice-President —his vote, 5.
Johnson, James, Provisional Governor, Georgia, 108.
Johnson, Waldo P., senator, expelled, 18.
Johnson, Wm. H., deserter, shot, 17.
Johnson, Colonel, killed, 12.
Johnson, Captain, killed, 48.
Johnson, Geo. W., rebel, Governor of Kentucky, killed, 24.
Johnson, Colonel, rebel, killed, 44.
Johnson, B. F., Lieut.-Colonel, rebel, killed, 10.
Johnsonville, Tenn., attacked, 87.
Johnston, Albert S'dney, General, rebel, killed, 24.
Johnston, Jos. E. General, rebel, takes command of South Carolina, etc., 96. Removed from command, 70. His surrender—original terms disapproved, 104. Grant reaches Raleigh, North Carolina, 105. Benefits of, claimed by Howell Cobb, 105.
Joy's Farm, Miss., skirmish, 69.
Kanawha Valley, Va., abandoned, 45.
Kane, George P., arrested for treason, 9.
Kansas City, fight, 15.
Kautz, General, raid in Virginia, 72.

Kearney, Philip, Major-General, killed, 39.
Kearneysville, Va., railroad train robbed, 68.
Kearnstown, Va., skirmish, 87.
Kearsage sinks Alabama, privateer, 77.
Keenan, Major, killed, 54.
Knittsville, Mo., skirmish, 29.
Kell, Colonel, killed, 48.
Kelly, B. F., Gen., taken prisoner, 96.
Kelly's Ford, Va., fight, 51. Battle, 64.
Kenesaw Mountain, Ga., rebels at, 76. Skirmish and battle, 77.
Kenesaw, Ga., fight, 77. Taken, 78. Assaulted— flanked, 78. Evacuated by rebels, 78. Losses, 83.
Kennedy, Robert C., rebel spy and incendiary at New York, hung, 99.
Keokuk, monitor, sunk, 51.
Kentucky, refuses to furnish three months volunteers, 6. To be neutral, 7. Election for members of Congress, 9. Confederate army ordered by Legislature to leave the State, 11. United States flag hoisted by Legislature, 11. Bragg's Proclamation to Kentuckians, 37. Entered by Bragg's rebel army, 40. Recommended to abolish slavery, 95. Released from martial law, 111.
Kettle Run, Va., battle, 38.
Key, Colonel, killed, 63.
Kinderhook, Ky., skirmish, 36.
Kilpatrick's Camp, S. C., fight at, 97.
Kilpatrick, Major-Gen., commands cavalry of Gen. Sherman's army, 87.
Kimball, Lieutenant-Colonel, killed by Gen. Corcoran, 52.
Kimball, Lieut., killed, 89.
King, Colonel, killed, 63.
King George's Court House, Va., skirmish, 47.
Kingsport, Tenn., fight, 90.
Kingston Road, Tenn., battle, 65.
Kingston, Ga., occupied by Gen. Sherman, 74. Train captured near, 77.
Kingston, Tenn., taken, 62.
Kinston, N. C., fight, 47. Taken, 77. Skirmish, 90. Occupied, 98. Junction of troops at, 98.
"Kirke, Edmund"—Peace negotiations, 80.
Kirkville, Mo., fight, 36.
Koltes, John A., Colonel, killed, 39.
Knoxville Road, Tenn., battle, 64. Burnside falls back, 64.
Knoxville, Tenn., battles and skirmishes near, 64, 65. Siege abandoned, 65. Foster in command, 66. Longstreet's return—Sturges's operations, 66, 67. Siege abandoned, 70.
Kyle, Lieutenant-Colonel, killed, 24.
Lacy, Ark, skirmish, 28.
Ladd, Luther C., monument, 108.
Lafayette, Mo., fight, 21.
Lafayette, Tenn., fight, 78.
Lafourche, La., confiscation, 46.
Lafourche Crossing, La., fight, 57.
La Grange, Tenn., skirmish, 46. Fight at, 83.
Lake Erie, rebels from Canada seize steamers on, 84. See 94, 96.
Lake Providence Canal, 51
Lamar, Mo., skirmish, 38.
Lamar, Col., rebel, killed, 74.
Lancaster, Ky., skirmish, 61.
Lancaster, Mo., skirmish, 15.
Lancaster, Colonel, killed, 54.
Lander, F. W., General, died, 20.
Lane, Joseph, nominated for Vice-President—his vote, 5.

Lane, J. H., General, rebel, killed, 65.
Lane, Colonel, rebel, killed, 44.
Lavender, gunboat, lost, 77.
Lavergne, Tenn., skirmish, 44.
Lawrence, Kansas, sacked and burned, 61.
Lawrence, Wm., indicted in Canada, 105.
Lawton, Lieut., killed, 22.
Lea, Edward, Lieutenant, United States Navy, killed, 48.
Lebanon, Ky., burned, 33. Morgan defeated, 48. Surrendered, 59.
Lebanon, Mo., skirmish, 13.
Lebanon, Tenn., skirmish, 27. Occupied, 50.
Lee, W. Fitzhugh, rebel, raid in Virginia, 50. Held as hostage, 60. Exchanged, 70.
Lee, Robert E., appointed commander of Virginia troops, 7. Retreats, 64. Nominated rebel commander-in-chief, 94. Plan to make him Dictator, 97. Advised by Gen. Grant to surrender—negotiations—final surrender, 102. Applies for pardon, 108.
Lee, Lieutenant-Colonel, rebel, killed, 44.
Leesburg, Va., taken, 47. Occupied, 80.
Leetown, Va., fight, 82.
Legareville, S. C., fight, 66.
Letcher, John, calls Virginia Legislature to assemble, 103. Meeting forbidden, 103.
Lewinsville, Va., skirmish, 11. Skirmish, 12. Occupied, 13. Fight, 28.
Lewisburg, Va., battle, 28.
Lexington, Mo., attacked by rebels, 11. Taken, 12. Recaptured, 13. Skirmish, 17. Price retreats from, 19. Battle at, 86.
Lexington, Ky., threatened, 33. Occupied, 40. Occupied, 45. Reoccupied, 45.
Lexington, Va., captured, 77.
Lexington Court House, S. C., occupied, 95.
Liberty Gap, Tenn., skirmish, 57. Taken, 58.
Liberty Mills, Va., fight, 91.
Lincoln, Abraham, nominated President—his vote, 5. Declared elected—plot to assassinate —journey to Washington—inaugurated, 6. Goes to West Point to consult Gen. Scott, 30. Visits Harper's Ferry, 43. Nominated for President at Baltimore, 76. Re-elected President—his vote, 87. Message to Congress, 1864, 89. Inaugurated, 97. Assassinated, 103. Funeral ceremonies, 104. Reward offered for murderers, 104. Assassination organized in Canada and approved at Richmond, 105. Remains interred, 106. Trial of assassins, 106. Assassins of, conviction and execution, 109.
Lindsey, Lieutenant-Colonel, killed, 71.
Linn Creek, Mo., fight, 18.
Linn Creek, Ky., skirmish, 19.
Linn, Colonel, killed, 39.
Little, General, rebel, killed, 42.
Little Platte, Mo., disaster at, 11.
Little River, N. C., skirmish, 102.
Little Rock, Ark., taken, 62.
Little Santa Fe, fight at, 14.
Liverpool Point, Va., skirmish, 20.
Loans, national interest to be anticipated, 70. Part of $75,000,000 awarded, 77.
Lomax, T., Colonel, rebel, killed, 29.
Long, Alexander, M. C. from Ohio, motion to expel from Congress—censured, 71.
Lookout Mountain, Tenn, fight, 64. Battle, 64. Battle, 65.
Lost Mountain, Ga., rebels at, 76. Losses, 83.

London, Tenn., skirmishes, 64.
Loudon Road, Tenn., skirmish, 64.
Louisiana secedes—United States property seized 5. Reinforced, 6. Plan of reorganization, 66. Michael Hahn elected Governor, 69. Constitutional convention called, 70.
Louisville, Ky., threatened, 33. Buell's advance at, 43.
Louisville, Tenn., fight, 65.
Lovejoy's, Ga., fight at, 82. Fight, 88.
Lovettsville, Va., skirmish, 45.
Lowe, Colonel, killed, 10.
Lowe, Colonel, rebel, killed, 14.
Lowere, S., Major, killed, 59.
Lowrey, Captain, killed, 89.
Luray, Va., occupied, 25. Skirmish, 32.
Luray Court House, Va., fight, 84.
Lyman, Lieutenant-Colonel, killed, 93.
Lynchburg, Va., skirmish, 77. Surrendered, 103
Lyon, Nathaniel, Captain at St. Louis—takes Camp Jackson, 7. General, killed, 10.
Lytle, General, killed, 44.
Lytle, General, killed, 63.
MacEuen, Charles I., Major, killed, 100.
McAllister, Colonel, killed, 77.
McClellan, George B., Major-General, commands United States armies, 14. Review at Washington, D. C., 15. Address to United States army, 22. Supersedes Pope, 40. Relieved from command of the Army of the Potomac, 46. Nominated for the Presidency, 83. Accepts the nomination, 83. Resigns from the army, 87. His vote, 87.
McClernand, General, takes command at Vicksburg, 49.
McCullough, Captain, killed, 29.
McConnell, Colonel, killed, 39.
McConnel, Colonel, rebel, killed, 65
McConnellsburg, Pa., taken, 57.
McConnellsville, Pa., skirmish, 58.
McConnough, Lieutenant-Colonel, killed, 76.
McCook, R. L., murdered, 30.
McCulloch, Hugh, nominated Secretary of the Treasury, 97. Statement public debt August 1, 1865, 109. U. S. debt, October 31, 1865, 111.
McCulloch, Ben., General, rebel, killed, 20.
McDonough, Ga., skirmish, 88.
McDowell, Irwin, Major-General, advances from Arlington, Va., 9. To command department California, 109.
McDowell, Va., fight, 27.
McElroy, Colonel, killed, 65.
McFarland, Col., rebel, killed, 44.
McGrath, Lieutenant, killed, 23.
McGraw, T. J., rebel spy, hung, 59.
McIntosh, General, rebel, killed, 20.
McKee, Lieutenant-Colonel, killed, 48.
McKnight, Colonel, killed, 54.
McLane, John W., Colonel, killed, 31.
McLane, Colonel, rebel, killed, 44.
McLean, Colonel, killed, 39.
McLaughlin, Michael, tried for assassination, 106. Hung, 109.
McMinnville, Tenn., occupied, 35. Occupied, 53. Captured, 63.
McNair, Colonel, rebel, killed, 49.
McNeil, Colonel, killed, 42.
McPherson, James B., Major-General, commands army of the Tennessee, 70, 73. Killed, 80.
McRae, General, rebel, killed, 59.
Macon, Ga., fight near, 88. Captured, 104.

Madison Court House, Va., cavalry fight, 63. Burned, 72.
Madisonville, Ky., skirmish, 46.
Magnolia Station, Md., trains captured, 79.
Magoffin, B., rebel Gov. of Kentucky resigned, 37.
Magrath, A. G., rebel Gov. of South Carolina, 91.
Magruder, H. C., guerilla, hung, 111.
Major-Generals, date of rank, 58.
Mallon, Colonel, killed, 63.
Mallory, Colonel, rebel, killed, 54.
Malvern Hill, Va., battle, 32. Fight, 36.
Manassas, Va., battle, 9. Occupied, 21. Second battle at, 38.
Manassas Gap, fight, 61.
Manassas Junction taken, 38.
Manassas Station, Va., burned, 38.
Manchester, Tenn., taken, 58.
Mankato, Minn., Indians hung, 48.
Mansfield, Va., skirmish, 46.
Mansfield, La., battle, 71.
Mansfield, Brigadier-General, killed, 42.
Maple Leaf, blown up, 70.
Marianna, Fla., taken, 84.
Marietta, Ga., advance to, 76. Taken, 78. Rousseau at, 80. Losses, 83.
Marion, Va., fight, 91.
Marrattstown, Mo., fight, 12.
Marshall, Colonel, rebel, killed, 39.
Marshfield, Mo., skirmish, 45.
Martial Law in Baltimore, 58. Withdrawn from Kentucky, 111.
Martinsburg, Va., attacked, 40. Taken by rebels, 57. Skirmish, 80. Reoccupied, 80. Reoccupied by rebels, 82.
Martin, Thos., S., Lieutenant-Colonel, killed, 39.
Martin, General, rebel, killed, 44.
Marye's Hill, Va., battle, 54.
Maryland refuses to receive secession commissioners, 5. Defeats secession ordinance, 7. Elections in 1861, 8. Mayor Brown of Baltimore and members of Legislature arrested for treason, 11. Entered by rebel army, 40. Lee, rebel General's proclamation to citizens of, 40. State Convention authorized, 70. Convention passes resolution to abolish slavery, 78. New Constitution adopted, 85. Constitution proclaimed, 86.
Mason, James M., taken in British steamer Trent, 14, 16. Surrendered, 17. Notifies Earl Russell that his commission is at an end, 63.
Mason, Colonel, rebel, killed, 10.
Massey's Creek, Ky., fight, 57.
Mather, Master, killed, 22.
Matthias Point, Va., skirmish, 9.
Maury, Richard, Colonel, rebel, killed, 74.
May, Major, rebel, killed, 39.
Maysville, Ark., battle, 45.
Meade, George G., Major-General, commands a corps, 50. Commands army of Potomac, 58, 72. Commands Atlantic Division, 108. Farewell address to his army, 109.
Meadow Bridge, Va., fight, 74.
Means, Colonel, rebel, killed, 39.
Mechanicsville, Va., skirmishes, 28. Battle, 31.
Mechanicsville Gap, Va., fight, 12.
Medon, Tenn., fight, 40.
Memminger, G. C., rebel Secretary of Treasury, resigns, 77.
Memphis, naval battle—ram fleet—surrender of city, 29. Taken by guerillas, 33. Forrest in, 82.
Mercedita, gun-boat, surrenders, 49.

Merrimac and Monitor, naval, 21.
Merriam, Lieutenant-Colonel, killed, 74.
Merrill's Crossing, Mo., fight, 63.
Merritt, Henry, Lieutenant-Colonel, killed, 22.
Merriwether, Captain, rebel, killed, 17.
Middle Creek, Ky., battle, 18.
Middleton, Va., skirmish, 41.
Midway, S. C., Sherman at, 93.
Millen, Ga., taken, 89.
Miles, Colonel, killed, 44.
Miles, Lieutenant-Colonel, killed, 74.
Miles, Lieutenant-Colonel, killed, 59.
Milford, Mo., fight, 17.
Milford Station, Va., skirmish, 75.
Mill Spring, Ky., battle, 18.
Milledgeville, Ga., occupied, 88.
Miller, James Colonel, killed, 29.
Miller, Colonel, killed, 42.
Miller, Colonel, rebel, killed, 59.
Milligan, Colonel, killed, 80.
Milliken, Colonel, killed, 48.
Milliken's Bend, La., battle, 56.
Military Departments, commanders appointed, 15.
Military Divisions and Departments established, 108.
Milton, Tenn., fight, 51.
Milwaukee, monitor, blown up, 99.
Mine exploded at Petersburg, Va., 80. Rebel, at Petersburg, exploded, 81.
Mine Run, Va., battle, 65.
Minnesota, frigate, attempt to blow up, 71.
Mint, United States, seized by rebels at New Orleans, 5. Charlotte, N. C., 7.
Minty's fight in Georgia, 86.
Missionary Ridge, Tenn., battle, 65.
Missouri refuses troops to United States, 6. 50,000 troops called out to resist United States, 8. Secession of, proclaimed by Gov. Jackson, 10. A state convention declares offices vacant, and appoints a provisional government, 10. Martial law declared, 11. Rebel slave property confiscated—order modified by President, 11. State election postponed, 13. Proclamation against spies and rebel sympathizers, 16. General Price issues a proclamation for 50,000 volunteers for the Confederacy, 16, 17. Convention passes ordinance emancipating slaves, 93.
Missouri Railroad, raid on, 17.
Mississippi secedes, United States property seized, 5. W. L. Sharkey, Provisional Governor, 108. Division, General Sherman, 108. Convention, 109. Attempt to organize State militia—forbidden by General Slocum, 110. Adopts ordinance to abolish slavery, 110. Nullifies secession ordinance, 110. B. G. Humphreys elected Governor. 111. Governor Sharkey seeks to abolish the black laws, 111.
Mississippi River—U. States assume the whole control of, 16. Naval fight near Fort Wright, 27.
Mitchell, O. M., Major-General, death, 46.
Mitchell's Fork, Ala., battle, 99.
Mitchell, John, rebel editor, arrested, 108.
Mix, Colonel, killed, 71.
Mobile, Ala., threatened, 70. Naval battle—Fort Powel taken—U. States ships sunk, 81. Fort Gaines surrendered, 81. Operations against, 98. Point occupied, 98. Fight at Spanish Fort, 100. Blakely river cleared—Forts Huger and Tracy bombarded, 102. Taken, 103. Spanish Fort—

Forts Alexis, Eugene and Blakeley taken, 102. Forts Pinto, Spanish River, Garnero's Bend, and Chereteau Point, taken, 103. Surrendered, 103. Magazine explosion, 107.
Monitor and Merrimac, naval fight, 21.
Monitor foundered, 48.
Monocacy, Md., Gen. Wallace falls back to, 79. Battle, 79.
Monroe (Fortress), Burnside at, 33. McClellan's army arrives at, 37.
Monroe, Mo., battle, 9.
Montgomery, Ala., surrendered, 103.
Monticello, Ky., taken, 53.
Moore, J. W., Col., killed, 93.
Moore, Thomas, Master, killed, 21
Moore, General, rebel, killed, 44.
Moore's Cross-roads, N. C., battle, 98.
Moore's Mills, Mo., fight, 35.
Moorfield, W. Va, fight at, 49, 67. Battle, 81.
Morehead City, N. C., taken, 22.
Morgan's, John H., rebel Gen., raid in Kentucky, 48. Through Indiana and Ohio, 59. Col. Dick Morgan captured, 61. Repulse at Cowleyville—Capture at Geiger's Creek, 60. Gen. Morgan and Col. Cluke captured, 61. Morgan held as hostage for Col. Straight, 61. He escapes from Ohio Penitentiary, 65. Killed, 83.
Morgan, General, killed, 48.
Morgan, Samuel, Major, rebel, killed, 45.
Morganfield, Ky., skirmish, 39.
Morgantown, Ky., skirmish, 45.
Morgantown, Va., captured, 53.
Morgantown, N. C., fight, 105.
Morganza, La., fight at, 63.
Morris' Farm, N. C., battle, 98.
Morris Island, S. C., fortifications taken, 59. Assault on Fort Wagner, 59. Surrender demanded, 61. Taken, 62.
Morris, Colonel, killed, 76.
Morton, Governor of Indiana, issues a Proclamation, 56.
Morton, Colonel, killed, 44.
Moseby, rebel, defeats Capt. Brasher, 88.
Mosquito Inlet, Fla., skirmish, 22.
Mossy Creek, Tenn., battle, 69.
Mossy Creek, Va., bridge burned, 86.
Mott, Colonel, rebel, killed, 27.
Moultrie, Fort—Major Anderson at—Buchanan refuses to reinforce—Abandoned by Major Anderson—Seized by rebels, 5.
Mounger, Colonel, rebel, killed, 59.
Mount Airy, Va., fight, 91.
Mount Crawford, Va., battle, 76.
Mount Elba, Ark., fight, 70.
Mount Jackson, Va., occupied, 25. Skirmish, 65. Pursuit to, 86.
Mount Sterling, Ky., fight, 35, 51. Taken, 51. Battle, 76. Morgan defeated, 76.
Mount Zion, Mo., fight, 17.
Mouton, Gen., rebel, killed, 71.
Mudd, Sam'l A., Dr., tried for assassination, 106. Condemnation—Imprisonment, 109.
Mulberry Fork, Ala., Wilson at, 99.
Muller, Major, rebel, killed, 71.
Mumford, Wm. B., hung at New Orleans, for tearing down American flag, 30.
Munfordsville, Ky., battle, 41. Surrendered, 42. Recaptured, 42.
"Mundy, Sue," taken prisoner and hung, 97, 98.
Munson's Hill, Va., occupied, 12. Federal army falls back to, 40.

Murfreesboro', Ala., skirmish, 29.
Murfreesboro', Tenn, taken by rebels, 33. Battle, 48. Skirmish, 89, 90. Losses at, 92.
Murray, W. G., Colonel, killed, 22
Muscle Fork, Mo., skirmish, 37.
Nance, Colonel, rebel, killed, 74.
Nansemond River, Va., naval fight on, 52. Reconnoissance, 54. Intrenchments taken, 54.
Nashville, Tenn., fire at, 17. Skirmish, 20. Taken, 20. Surrender demanded, 43. Operations near, 45. Skirmish, 46. Battle, 91. Losses at, 92. Report of Losses, 93. Fire at, 108.
Natchez, Miss., taken, 59.
Natchitoches, La., captured, 70.
National Union Convention, to be held at Baltimore, 69.
Naval gunboat action, 26. See "Privateers," "Vessels."
Navy Yards (United States), seized by rebels—Pensacola, 5—Gosport, 7.
Navy—size of, and losses in 1864, 89. For naval operations, see "Blockade," "Privateers," "Vessels."
Neff, Colonel, rebel, killed, 39.
Nelson, William, Major-Gen., killed, 43.
Nelson, Col., rebel, killed, 10.
Neosho, Mo., skirmish, 26.
Newark, Mo., fight, 35.
Newbern, N. C., battle, 22. Skirmish, 52.
New Bridge, Va., skirmish, 28.
Newburg, Ind., taken, 34.
Newcastle, Ky., skirmish, 42.
New Creek, Va., fight, 81. Taken, 89.
New Hope, Ky, skirmish, 33.
New Hope, Ga., advance to, 76.
New Hope Church, Ga., battle, 75. Losses at, 83.
New Iberia, La., taken, 52.
New Kent Court House, Va., occupied, 72.
New Laurence, Tenn., fight, 64.
New Lisbon, Ohio, Morgan captured at, 61.
New Madrid, Mo., evacuated, 22. Batteries taken, 24.
Newman, Lieutenant-Colonel, killed, 71.
Newmarket, Va., occupied, 23. Battle, 74. Fight at, 91.
Newmarket Cross-roads, Va., battle, 32.
Newnan, Ga., fight, 81.
New Orleans, operations against, 25. U. States army landed below, 26. Taken, 26. Specie seized at, 28. Rebel Fund for defence given to the poor, 36.
Newport, Ky., in danger, 40.
Newport News, Va., rebel camp destroyed, 15.
New River, N. C., gunboat Ellis blown up, 47.
New River bridge, W. Va., battle, 73.
Newton, Henry, Lieut. U. S. Navy, killed, 48.
Newtonia, Mo., skirmish, 43. Battle, 86.
New York City—Draft riots, 60. Plot to set fire to, 87. Proposal to burn, by "devoted band," 88. Hotels and buildings at, fired by rebels, 88. Kennedy, incendiary, hung at, 99.
Niagara (frigate), fired into at Lisbon, 99.
Nickajack Trace, Ga., skirmish, 72.
Nickajack Creek, Ga., Gen. Thomas at, 78.
Noncona, Tenn., skirmish, 53.
Nolensville, Tenn., skirmish, 48.
Norfolk, Va., captured, 28.
Norristown, Tenn., fight, 86.
North, Sam'l, Col., charged with preparing fraudulent soldiers' votes, 86.

North Anna River, Va., fight, 34. Army of Potomac at—skirmish, 75. Battle, 75.
Northampton, Va., rebels disperse, 15.
North Branch, Va., fight, 67.
North Carolina—U. States forts seized, 5. Secedes, 7. Proclamation of M. N. Taylor, Provisional Governor, 15. Convention to repudiate secession, 15. W. W. Holden Provisional Governor, 108. Notified that she must repudiate the rebel debt, 111. Nullifies secession ordinance—abolishes slavery, 111.
North Edisto, S. C., crossed, 95.
North Madrid, Mo., skirmish, 20.
Nose's Creek, Ga., battle, 78.
Nottoway Bridge, Va., burned, 72.
Oakford, R. A., Colonel, killed, 42.
Oak Woods, Va., skirmish, 65.
Oath of Allegiance, violators of, shot, 43.
Oblehr, Colonel, killed, 89.
O'Brien, Colonel, killed in New York riots, 60.
Ocean Pond, Fla., battle, 68.
Occoquan, Va., skirmish, 18. Evacuated, 20. Skirmish, 48.
O'Connor, Colonel, killed, 39.
O'Kane, Dennis, Colonel, killed, 59.
Old Church Tavern, Va., skirmish, 75.
Old Town, Va., block-house surrendered, 81.
Olmsted, Colonel, rebel, killed, 91.
Olustee, Fla., battle, 68.
O'Mara, Col., killed, 65.
Onslow, N. C., taken, 47.
Opelousas, La., taken, 64.
Opequan, Va., battle, 84.
Orange and Alexandria Railroad, Va., fight, 60.
Orange Court House, Va., taken, 34. Fight, 72.
Orange Court House, S. C., fight, 94.
Orangeburg, S. C., skirmish, 95.
Orangetown, Va., reconnoisance, 35.
Ord, E. O. C., General, commands department of Virginia, 95. Commands at Richmond, Va., 103. To command Department of Ohio, 109.
Ordnance boat explodes at City Point, Va., 81.
Orleans, Ind., fight, 57.
Orton, Lawrence William, Colonel, rebel, executed as a spy, 56.
Osage River, Mo., fight, 37.
Ould, Colonel, rebel, killed, 63.
Ould, Robert, Colonel, rebel Commissioner of Exchange at Fortress Monroe, 70.
Overall's Creek, Tenn., battle, 89.
Owensboro', Ky., skirmishes, 42.
Owensville, Ky., fight at, 34.
Oyster Point, Pa., skirmish, 58.
Ozark, Mo., skirmish, 35.
Pacific Division, General Halleck, 108.
Paducah, Ky., taken, 70.
Paine's Cross Roads, Va., battle, 102.
Painesville, Ky., fight, 71.
Paintsville, Ky., fight, 71.
Palmer, Gen., John M., to command Department Kentucky, 109.
Palmetto Station, Ga., destroyed, 80.
Palmyra, Tenn., burned, 51.
Panther's Gap, Ky., battle, 83.
Paris, Ky., taken, 76.
Parker, Colonel, rebel, killed, 42.
Parrisin, Lieutenant-Colonel, killed, 42.
Parsons, Lewis E., Provisional Governor of Alabama, 108.
Parsons, General, rebel, killed, 59.

Paducah, Ky., occupied, 11. Fight near, 15.
Page, Major, killed, 24.
Paine, Colonel, killed, 56.
Paint Lick, Ky., skirmish, 45.
Paintsville, Ky., skirmish, 18.
Palmer, Major, rebel, killed, 27.
Palmyra, Mo., skirmish, 15. Taken, 41.
Pamunkey, Va., naval expedition, 28.
Paoli, Ind., fight, 57.
Papinsville, Mo., burned, 16.
Paris, Ky., fight, 61.
Paris, Tenn., raid to, 19. Skirmish, 21.
Parsons, General, rebel, killed, 59.
Pass Christian, naval fight, 23.
Pascagoula, La., taken, 52. Davidson at, 90. Granger at, 91.
Passports required from Canadians, 91.
Patapsco, monitor blown up, 93.
Patten, Mo., skirmish, 35.
Patterson, Robert, Maj.-General, marches towards Virginia, 8. Advances to Bunker's Hill, Va.,—at Charlestown, 9. Skirmish at Falling Waters, 9.
Patterson, Colonel, killed, 73.
Patterson, Colonel, rebel, killed, 44.
Patterson's Creek, Va., fight, 67.
Pattersonville, La., fight, at, 49.
Payne, Lewis, attacks Mr. Seward, 103. Tried for assassination, 106. Condemned—hung, 109.
Paxon, Colonel, killed, 41.
Paxton, Colonel, rebel, killed, 54.
Pea Ridge, Ark., battle, 20. Thanks to General Curtis, 21.
Pea Ridge, Tenn., reconnoisance, 26.
Peace negotiations in Canada, 79. Lincoln's reply to rebel negotiators, 79-80. Jacques and Gilmore's negotiations, 80. Convention at Syracuse, New York, 82. F. P. Blair's mission to Virginia, 92-93. Blair's second visit to Richmond—return, 94. Interview by President Lincoln and Secretary Seward with rebel commissioners on James River—a failure, 94. The terms of the conference, 95. Conference assembles at Washington, D. C., 5. Plan of, 6.
Peach Orchard, Va., battle, 32.
Peach Tree Creek, losses, 83.
Peeble's Farm, Va., battle, 84.
Pegram, Colonel, killed, 24.
Pegram, General, rebel, killed, 95.
Pelot, Lieutenant, rebel, killed, 70.
Pender, General, rebel, killed, 59.
Pendleton, George H., nominated for the Vice-Presidency, 83. His vote, 87.
Pendleton, Va., saltpetre works destroyed, 62.
Pensacola, Fla., bombardment between forts and U. S. fleet, 15. Skirmish, 17. Evacuated, 27.
Pennsylvania el.ction on Constitutional amendment to give soldiers a right to vote, 81. Troops called out to repel invasion, 41. Divided into military districts, 56.
Perry, Benj. F., appointed Provisional Governor of South Carolina, 109.
Perryville, Ky., battle 44.
Perryville, Ark., retreat of rebels to, 61.
Peterhoff, British steamer, mail bag given up 53.
Petersburg, Va., skirmish near, 73. Cavalry charge at, 76. Attacked by W. F., (Baldy) Smith, 77. Two redoubts taken, 77. Bombarded, 77. Attack on rebel lines, 77. Fight at, 78. Mine exploded, 80. Rebel mine exploded, 81. Attack on Birney's lines, north of James river, 82. Attack on lines, 83. Final battles at, 99, 100, 101. Captured, 101. Losses in battle, 102.
Petrel, gunboat, burned, 72.
Pettigrew, General, rebel, killed, 60.
Pettus, Lieutenant-Colonel, rebel, killed, 53.
Phelps, Colonel, killed, 65.
Phelps, John S., Governor of Arkansas, 34.
Phillimont, Va., skirmish, 46.
Philadelphia, proposal to burn by "the devoted band," 88.
Philadelphia, Tenn., fight, 64.
Phillippi, Va., skirmish, 8.
Pickens, Fort, garrisoned by Slemmer, 5. Opens fire on a steamer, 15.
Piedmont, Va., battle, 76. Fight, 85. Taken, 89.
Piketon, Tenn., skirmish, 53.
Piketon, Ky., skirmishes, 15. Fight, 46.
Pilatka, Flo., taken, 69.
Pilot Knob, Mo., fight at, 13. Battle, 84.
Pine Barren Ridge, Fla., taken, 87.
Pine Bluff, Ark., skirmish, 72. Battle, 64.
Piney Factory, Tenn., fight, 64.
Pineville, Mo., skirmish, 61.
Pine Hook, skirmish, 92.
Pine Mountain, Ga., battle, 77.
Pittsburgh, Tenn., fight, 20.
Pittsburgh Landing, Tenn., skirmish, 22. Battle, 24.
Pittman's Ferry, Mo., skirmish, 40.
Pittman's Landing, Ark., taken, 23.
Platte's Bridge Station, Indian Terr'y, battle, 109.
Platte City, Mo., burned, 17.
Pleasant Hill, La., fight—battle, 71.
Pleasant Hill, Mo., skirmish, 33. Recaptured, 15.
Plymouth, N. C., burned, 47. Occupied by rebels, 71. Taken by rebels, 72. Captured, 87. Attacked, 90.
Plum, J. H., killed, 38.
Pocahontas, Ark., fight at, 62.
Pocotaligo, S. C., fight, 29.
Pocotaligo Bridge, S. C., taken, 93. Battle, 45.
Poindexter, taken, 40.
Point Pleasant, Mo., taken, 21.
Point Pleasant, W. Va., taken and retaken, 51.
Point of Rocks, Md., bridge burned, 8. Skirmishes, 12, 15, 17. Maryland Railroad track taken, 57.
Polk, Trusten, senator, expelled, 18.
Polk, General, rebel, killed, 77.
Po'lard, Ala., occupied, 91. Battle, 99.
Pollock, James, Lieut. U. S. Navy, killed, 48.
Pontotoc, Miss., occupied, 79.
Poolesville, Md., raid on—taken, 86. Fight at, 40. Taken by rebels, 56.
Pope, John, Gen., address to Army of Virginia, 34. Order to subsist on enemy, etc., 34. Oath of Allegiance, 34. Denounced by Jeff. Davis—not to be entitled to privileges of prisoner of war, 35. To command Department of Missouri, 109. Retreat, 37. Superseded by McClellan, 40.
Poplar Spring's Church, Va., battle, 85.
Po River, Va., crossed, 73.
Porcher, Colonel, rebel, killed, 65.
Port Gibson, Miss., battle, 53. Loss at, 59.
Port Hudson, La., passed by Farragut—naval fight at, 50. Bombarded, 55. Assaulted, 56. Second assault, 57. Surrendered. 59.
Portland, Maine, rebel privateer enters, 58.
Port Walthall, Va., battle, 74.
Port Republic, Va., battle, 30.

Porter, Fitz John, Major-General, dismissed from service, 49.
Porter, Colonel, killed, 76.
Porter, Benjamin H., Lt. U. S. N. killed, 93.
Porter's House, Va., skirmish, 18.
Pound Gap, Tenn., taken by Garfield, 22.
Potomac River, crossed by Bradley T. Johnson and Early, 78. Army, order for general movement, 21. Divided in 4 corps, 21. River crossed by whole rebel army, 40. Crossed by Burnside, 45. Crossed by Lee's army in retreat, 60.
Powder River, Indian Territory, battle, 110.
Pratt, Colonel, killed, 31.
Prairie D' Ana, Arkansas, battle, 71.
Prairie Grove, Arkansas, battle, 47.
Preble, Sloop-of-War, blown up, 53.
Preble, Geo. H., Commander U. S. N., dismissed, 42.
Prentice, —— killed, 43.
Prentiss, Miss., burned, 42.
Presidential Election, 1860, 5.
Preston, S. W., Lt. U. S. N., killed, 93.
Preston, Colonel, killed, 76.
Prestonburg, Ky., occupied, 14, 18.
Price, Major (Rebel) killed, 54.
Prichard's Mills, Va. skirmish, 12.
Princeton, Va., skirmish, 28.
Prisoners, exchange of, 34. Exchanged 43. Exchange at Aiken's Landing, 46. Political, discharged, 46-7. Exchange prohibited by Jeff. Davis, 48. Maltreatment of, to be punished, 66. Escaped from Libby, Col. Straight and others, 69. Exchanged, 69. In Richmond, attempt to rescue by Dahlgren, 69. Ould and Butler's negotiations, 70. U. S., at Charleston, put under fire of Federal guns, 77. Rebel officers similarly treated, 77. Exchanged in North Carolina, condition of Union prisoners, 97. Exchanged in Virginia, 97. U. S., held by rebels at Richmond. Va.—released, 13. Federal officers held as hostages for the lives of rebel privateersmen, 15. U. S. officers to be treated as criminals, 49. On Johnson's Island, plot to rescue, 64.
Privateers, rebel cruisers and war vessels, operations by and against:—Alabama or "290," captures by, 43. Alabama, vessels burned by, 43, 44. Sinks the Hatteras, 49. Petition of Liverpool, England, Emancipation Society against, 51. Sunk, 77. Correspondence between Mr. Adams and Earl Russell about the Alabama, 111. Albemarle, attacks of, 71. On Albemarle Sound, 72. Blown up, 86. Alexandra, decision of the House of Lords, 70, 71. Ariel taken, 47. Alice, 56. Arkansas ram passes Federal fleet, 34. Attempt to destroy, 34. Blanche run ashore on the Island of Cuba, 44. Hattie Brock, 70. Cairo blown up, 47. Chapman, 51. Chesapeake steamer seized, 65. Retaken, 66. Case, 68. Warrant for extradition of Chesapeake pirates refused, 69. Crew ordered to be surrendered to the U. S., 69. Proceedings, 70. Chicora attacks the blockading fleet off Charleston, S. C., 49. Chickamauga ran out of Wilmington, N. C., 86, 87. Clifton, 70. Cotton blown up, 49. Cotton Plant sunk, 72. Davis torpedo boat, 68. Harriet Deford steamer seized, 101. "Ovieto" or Florida, escapes from Mobile, 42, 49. Jacob Bell burned by Florida, 50. Captures by, 79. Captured, 85. Sunk, 89. Correspondence with Brazil, 90. Florida No. 2, 56, 58. Japan, alias Georgia, sails, 51. Georgia captured, 52. Indiannola blown up, 50. Jackson sunk, 26. Harriet Lane escapes, 72. R. E. Lee, 65. Little Leila, 66. Lovell destroyed, 52. Manassas sunk, 26. Morgan sunk, 26. Morning Light captured at Sabine Pass, Texas, 49. Nashville at Southampton, England, 18, 50. Blown up, 82. Neuse, iron clad, burned, 98. North Carolina, Rebel ram attacks, 73. Olustee run out of Wilmington, N. C., 86. Palmetto sunk, 26. Palmetto State attacks the blockading fleet off Charleston, 49. Petrel sunk, 10. Phœnix sunk, 26. Queen of the West taken, 50. Ram blown up in Roanoke River, 103. Rebel fleet driven away on James River, 86. Rebel Red River fleet surrendered, 108. Rebel steamers burned at New Iberia, 52. Attempt by Rebel vessels on City Point repulsed, 94. Rebel navy in Georgia surrendered, 106. Retribution, 50. Attempt to capture steamer Salvador, 87. Saxonia destroyed, 52. Selma, gunboat, captured, 81. Sumter, 70. Schultz blown up, James River, 95. Sea King sails from Liverpool, Laurel takes out arms for her—Sea King transferred to Rebels—takes the name of the Shenandoah, 87. Shenandoah's operations, 95. Capt. Corbett of the Sea King, or Shenandoah arrested, 93. At Melbourne, 94. Captures to close of the war, 108. Depredations after the close of the war, 109. Whaling vessels destroyed, 109. Captured, 110. "Olinde" or "Stonewall," at Ferrol, 94. At Corruna, 96. Leave Lisbon, Portugal, 99. At Nassan, 106. At Havana, 106. To be delivered to U. S., 109. Tacony, 58. Comes into Portland, Me., 58. Tallahassee captures, 81. Arrives at Halifax, 82. Ordered off, 82. Tallahassee gets into Wilmington, N. C., 82. Captures by Tallahassee, 82. Ran out of Wilmington, 86. Teaser, 33. Tennessee rebel ram captured, 81. Torpedo boat, rebel, sunk, 68. Torpedo boat sunk, 72. Tuscaloosa seized, 66. Virginia sunk, 101. Webb runs out of Red River, 104. Run ashore and blown up, 106. Yazoo River expedition, 31. Archer, attempt to capture Revenue Cutter Caleb Cushing 58. Alabama, operations of, 46. At Cape of Good Hope, 61. Alice, 29. Allegheny, 46. Arkansas destroyed, 39. Atalanta taken, 57. Baronda Castine, 46. Chattahoochie blown up, 57. Beauregard captured, 15. Calhoun captured, 7. Jeff. Davis wrecked, 10. Wm. Smith of the "Jeff. Davis" convicted of piracy, 14. Federal hostages held for privateersmen prisoners, 15. Eastport taken, 19. Emma burned, 39. Fair Play, 37. Florida, 37. Florida No. 2, Tacony taken by, 56. Fulton destroyed, 63. Georgia at Cape of Good Hope, 61. Joseph L. Gerity captured 65. Gun-boat Rebel sunk, 22. Clarence H. Haldeman taken —fitted out as a privateer, 56. Judith destroyed, 12. General Lee, 36. Rebel ironclad Manassas attacks United States fleet at the south-west pass of the Mississippi River, 13. Merrimac and Monitor, naval, 21. Merrimac comes out, 24, 27. Blown up, 28. Memorial of Liverpool Emancipation Society against, 62. Governor A. Mouton, 28. Nashville takes the Harvey Birch, 15. Nashville, 20. Naval fight, Mississippi river, 27. Naval fight, James river, 28. Tatnall's attack on United States

fleet, Cockspur Roads, Ga., 15. Peterhoff condemned, 61. Planter, steamer, taken, 28. Rebel rams seized at Liverpool by British Government, 63. General Rusk, 44. Bark Saxon captured, 64. Savannah taken, 8. Sumter burned, 37. General Taylor destroyed, 63. Terrible taken, 26. N. B. Terry captured, 10. Tuscaloosa, formerly bark Conrad, at Cape of Good Hope, 61. Vessel destroyed at Quantico, Va., 13. Capture in Urbanna creek, 14. Winchester, 23.

Proclamations, President ordering a return to allegiance, 34. Against rebels and their aiders and abettors, discouragers of volunteer enlistments, resisting the draft, etc., 43. That slaves would be free after January 1, 1863, 43. Of Beauregard, that port of Charleston was opened, 49. Deserters promised pardon, etc., 50. President U. S., fast day, 51. Admission of West Virginia, 53. The national militia law to be put in force—aliens to depart from the country, 55. Amnesty on return to allegiance, etc., and for reconstruction, 65, 66. General Banks, Louisiana, for an election and reorganization, 66. For a draft for 500,000 men, 67. Brownsville, Texas port opened 68. For 200,000 men, 70. Explaining amnesty proclamation, 70. For 500,000 volunteers, 79. Day of Thanksgiving, 83. Beauregard to people of Georgia, 88. Breckenridge, rebel, guarantees protection to Union citizens of Tennessee, 90. For 300,000 troops, 91. By Jefferson Davis, declaring that B. G. Burley, Lake Erie pirate, was a regular confederate officer, 92. Deserters to return in sixty days, 97. Releasing certain ports from blockade—demanding equal privileges for U. S. war vessels in foreign ports, 102-3. By President Johnson, a day of public mourning, 104. Mourning postponed, 105. Restricting intercourse with Southern States withdrawn, 105. Meredith's in Kentucky, for rebels to surrender, 106. "Insurrection virtually at an end," 106. Notice of retaliation to neutral nations entertaining rebel cruisers, 106. Reward for assassins, 106. Court martial to try assassins, 106. Amnesty to certain classes of rebels, 107. Observance of fast day, 107. Ports relieved from blockade, 107. Texas ports not opened, 107. Order to persons applying for amnesty to take the oath of allegiance, 108. Restrictions on trade of Mississippi removed, 108. Pytchlin to rebel Indians, 108. For 75,000 volunteers, 1860, 6. Blockade, 7. For 42,034 volunteers, 7. That seceding States are in insurrection, 10 For a draft, 35. Bragg, rebel, to Kentucky, 37. Lee, rebel General, to citizens of Maryland, 40. Emancipation, 48. In relation to invasion of Maryland, Pennsylvania and Ohio, 57. Governor Morton of Indiana, against resisting draft, 56. Governor Curtin, for defence of Pennsylvania, 57. For 60,000, militia, 58. President's thanksgiving, 60. President's, declaring that colored troops shall be protected—that a rebel soldier shall be hung for every colored soldier treated otherwise than as prisoner of war, etc., 61. Revoking order for 100,000 militia, 61. Suspension of Habeas Corpus, 62. Thanksgiving day, 63. Raising the blockade at Alexandria, Va., 63. For 300,000 men, 64.

Proclamation, forged, published, 74.

Pryor, Major, rebel, killed, 44.
Purdy, Tenn., bridge burned, 22. Reconnoisance—occupied, 26.
Pulaski, Tenn., skirmish, 27, 84. Hood pursued to, 91.
Pumpkin Vine Creek, general battle, 75.
Putnam's Ferry, Mo., skirmish, 45.
Putnam, Colonel, killed, 60.
Putnam, Colonel, killed, 65.
Pytchlin, proclamation to rebel Indians, 108.
Quaker Road, Va., battle, 100.
Quaker Church, Va., battle, 77.
Quallatown, N. C., fight, 68.
Quantico, Va., rebel vessel destroyed, 13.
Quantrell attacked, 37.
Quitman, Miss., Sherman at, 68.
Raids:—Averill's cavalry, Virginia, 54. West Virginia, 66. Burbridge's, Tennessee and Virginia, 91, 92, 93. Butler's, Virginia, 72. Carter's into East Tennessee, 48. Crooks, Virginia, 72. Custer's, Virginia, 69, 91. Dana's in Mississippi, 89. Tennessee, 91. Davidson, Louisiana, 89. Forrest's, rebel, triumphs and losses, 95. Fuller's, Georgia, 93. Harry Gilmor's, rebel, Maryland, 79. Granger's, Louisiana, 91. Grierson, Mississippi, 68. Wade Hampton's, rebel, on cattle pens, Virginia, 84. Harper, rebel, in Virginia, 53. Hunter's in Virginia, 76. Ended, 78. Imboden's, rebel, in Virginia, 53. Jenkins, rebel, Virginia, 53. Kautz, Virginia, 72. Returns, 74. Kilpatrick's, Virginia, 69. Arrives at Yorktown, 69. In Georgia, 82. Returns, 82. Lee's, in Louisiana, 88. Long, Mississippi, 88. Lyon's, rebel, in Kentucky, 90. McCausland's, rebel, in Pennsylvania, 80. At Chambersburg, Pennsylvania, 80. McCook, at Palmetto Station and Fayetteville, 80. In Georgia, 80. At Newnan, Georgia, 81. In Alabama, 99. Maxwell's to Bertie, N. C., 69. Miles, in Virginia to Hatcher's Run, 90. Morgan, rebel, in Kentucky, 48. Through Indiana and Ohio, 59. Fights and losses, 60, 61. Morgan captured, 61. Morgan, rebel, escapes from Ohio penitentiary, 65. Rebels in Paris, Kentucky, 76. Mosoby, rebel, Virginia, 81. On Baltimore and Ohio Railroad, 85. Mosoby's camp taken, 85. In Poolesville, Maryland, 86. General Dufie taken prisoner, 86. Ostrand's, Mississippi, 88. Palmer's, N. C., 67. Ransom's, Natchez, 59. Rosseau's, Tennessee and Alabama, 77. At Decatur, Alabama, 79. Finished, 80. By rebels on St. Albans, Vt., 86. Raiders discharged by Coursol, 90. Gen. Dix orders troops to cross Canadian lines in pursuit of raiders from Canada, 91. Disapproved, 91. Governor of Canada recommends payment to banks of St. Alban's, 94. Raiders released by Justice Smith, 99. Sheridan's, Virginia, 73. In Shenandoah Valley, 85, 96. On James River Canal and in Virginia, 97. Sheridan on Virginia Railroads, 97. Completed, 99. Sherman's, Mississippi, 67. Slocum's, Mississippi, 78. Battle at Grand Gulf, Louisiana, 79. Smith's at Egypt Station, 68. Aberdeen, Mississippi, 68. Battle at West Point, Mississippi, 68, 69. Return to Memphis, 69. At Ripley, Mississippi, 78. Return, 79. At La Grange, Mississippi, 80. Spear's in Virginia, 72. Steele's in Mississippi, 52. Sturgis, Mississippi, 76. Defeated at Guntown, 76. Stoneman's, 53. In Virginia, 55. Georgia, 80.

Near Macon, Georgia—Clinton, surrender of Stoneman, 81. In Kentucky, 90. In Tennessee and Virginia, 91, 92, 93. Virginia, 98. North Carolina, 105. Straight's cavalry, 51, 52. Stuart, rebel, in Pennsylvania and Maryland, 44. Stuart, Cattlett's Station, 37. Sturges at Ripley, Mississippi, 76. Return, 77. Torbert's, Virginia, 84, 91. Warren's in Virginia, toward Weldon, North Carolina, 90. Wheeler's, rebel, Georgia, 81. In Tennessee, 82, 83. Wilder's, 52. Wilson's, Virginia, Weldon Railroad, 78. Alabama, 99. End of, 104. Wood's, Mississippi, 53. Wright's, Weldon Railroad, 78. Blair's, Mississippi, 56. Clayton's, Arkansas, 55. Cornyn's, Alabama, 56. Davis's, Mississippi, 55. De Bussy's, Mississippi, 60. Forrest's, in Rosecran's lines, 63. Getty's, Virginia, 58. Rebel, into Indiana, 57. Kilpatrick's, Virginia, 56. In Teche country, 56. Pegram's, rebel, Ky., 61. Phillips', Tennessee and Mississippi, 61. Potter's, North Carolina, 60. Quantrell's, rebel, Kansas, 61. Ransom's, Mississippi, 59, 61. Sander's, Kentucky, 58. Scott's, rebel, Kentucky, 61. Selfridges, Red River, La., 60. Spear's, Virginia, 59. Wistar's, Virginia, 63. Wilder's, Tennessee, 58.

Railroads destroyed, 17.—See Raids. Halleck's order against destroyers of bridges, telegraphs and railroads, 17. President to take command of, 16. Louisville and Nashville train captured by Morgan's cavalry, 23.

Rains, J. E., General, rebel, killed, 49.
Raleigh, North Carolina, surrendered, 103.
Randolph, Mississippi, burned, 43.
Randolph, W. W. Colonel, rebel, killed, 74.
Rapidan Station, Virginia, fight, 54.
Rapidan, crossed by Meade—recrossed, 65. Rebels cross, 64.
Rapidan, skirmish, 68.
Rappahanock River crossed by the Army of the Potomac, 53. Naval operations, 25. Reconnoisance, 56.
Rappahannock, cavalry fight near, 64.
Rappahannock Station abandoned, 38. Battle, 64.
Baum, Colonel, killed, 65.
Ravenna, Va., taken and destroyed, 69.
Raymond, Mississippi, battle, 55. Loss at, 59.
Readyville, Tennessee, skirmish, 83.
Reagan, rebel Post Master General captured, 106. Released, 111.
Reams' Station, Va., fight, 78. Battle, 82. Battle, 82. Second battle, 82.
Reconstruction by one-tenth of the loyal citizens, 66. President's plan, appointment provisional governors—Holden and others, 107, 108. Talk with South Carolinians, 108.
Recruiting stopped, 23.
Red Bend, Ky., skirmish, 38.
Red river, bridge burned, 37.
Red River fleet, La., released, 74.
Reed, Lieutenant-Colonel, killed, 68.
Relay House, Md., taken, 7.
Remsem, General, rebel, killed, 86.
Reno, Jesse L., Major General, commands 3d army corps, 40. Killed, 41.
Resaca, Ga., battle—evacuated, 74. Losses, 83. Skirmish, 85.
Reynolds, John F., Major-General, commands a corps, 50. Killed, 59.
Reynolds, General J. J., to command department of Arkansas, 109.

Rhett, General, rebel, killed, 32.
Rhodes, General, rebel, killed, 84.
Rice, General, killed, 73.
Rice, Major, rebel, killed, 63.
Rich Mountain, Va., battle, 9.
Richmond, Colonel, rebel, killed, 63.
Richardson, Major-General, killed, 42.
Richmond, Virginia, bread riot by women, 51. Attempt to surprise—Kilpatrick's, 69. Attempt to surprise—Wistar's, 68. Meeting at African Church, 95. Speculations on evacuation by rebel journals, 96. Evacuated by the rebels— burned—entered by Federal troops, 101. Election at—rebel candidates chosen, 109. Election set aside, 109.
Richmond, Ky., fight, 38. Battle, 39.
Richmond, Miss., taken, 57.
Rienzi, Miss., taken, 76.
Riker, Colonel, killed, 29.
Riley, Colonel, killed, 54.
Ringgold artillery first at Washington, 6.
Ringgold, Georgia, battle, 65.
Ringgold, Colonel, killed, 54.
Riot at New York—negroes attacked, 52. Boston, Staten Island, 52. "Peace," Charleston, Ill., 70. Bread, Mobile, 62. Anti-draft, N. Y., 60. Anti-draft, Boston, 61. On Staten Island, New York, 61. Brooklyn, New York, 60.
Ripley, Missouri, fight, 67.
Ripley, Mississippi, taken, 76. Fight, 78.
Ripley, Va., skirmish, 17.
Rippey, Colonel, killed, 29.
Rives, Wm. C., calls Virginia Legislature to assemble, 103. Meeting forbidden, 103.
Roberts, Colonel, killed, 31.
Roan's Tan Yard, Mo., fight, 18.
Roanoke Island. N. C., captured, 19.
Roanoke River, N. C., fight, 46.
Roanoke steamer, captured by pretended passengers, 84.
Roberts, R. P., Colonel, killed, 59.
Roberts, Colonel, killed, 39.
Roberts, Colonel, killed, 48.
Robinson, James F., rebel Governor of Kentucky, 37.
Rocky Gap, Va., battle, at, 62.
Rocky Face Ridge, Georgia, threatened, 73.
Rocky Mount, N. C., burned, 62.
Rodgers, Geo. W., Fleet Capt. U. S. N., killed, 61.
Rodgerville, Tenn., taken, 64.
Rogers, General, rebel, killed, 44.
Rolla, Mo., train captured, 28. Skirmish, 42.
Rome, Georgia, fight, 85. Occupied by Sherman, 74.
Romney, Va., skirmish, 8. Fight, 14. Occupied, 19.
Rood's Hill, Virginia, battle, 88.
Rosecrans, Wm. S., Major-Gen., appointed to command U. S. army in Kentucky, 45. Marches from Nashville, 48. Commands Army of the Cumberland, 57.
Rosengarten, Major, killed, 48.
Rosewell, Georgia, burned, 79.
Rosso, Colonel, rebel, killed, 54.
Rosseau, Major-General, commands District of Tennessee, 76.
Rossville, Missouri, fight, 70.
Rough and Ready, Ga., fight at, 88.
Round Top Mountain, Virginia, battle, 85.
Rowanty Creek, Sheridan at, 106.
Ruff, Colonel, rebel, killed, 65.

Russell, C lonel, killed, 19.
Russell, David, General, killed, 84.
Russell, Major, killed, 31.
Russelville, Kentucky, skirmish, 43.
Sabine's Cross Roads, Louisiana, battle, 71.
Sabine Pass, Texas, taken, 43. Gunboats Sachem and Clifton taken, 62. U. S. vessels captured, 75. Taken, 107.
Sailor's Creek, Virginia, battle, 102.
St. Albans, Vermont, raid on, 86. Governor of Canada recommends payment to St. Albans banks, 94. Raiders discharged by Coursol, 90. Gen. Dix orders his troops to pass the borders of Canada in pursuit of rebel raiders from Canada, 91. Disapproved, 91. Raiders released by Justice Smith, 99.
St. Augustine, Fla., occupied, 22.
St. Charles, Arkansas, skirmish, 33.
St. John's Bluff, Florida, shelled, 42.
St. Joseph's, Bay, Fla., salt works destroyed, 40.
St. Louis, martial law, 10. Arsenal visited by Illinois volunteers—Capt. Lyon takes command—Camp Jackson taken—Home Guards have a fight, 6. Attack on Kallman's regiment, 8. Secessionists assessed, 39.
St. Marks, Florida, salt works destroyed, 68.
St. Mary's, Florida, shelled, 46.
St. Mary's Church, Virginia, battle, 78.
St. Nicholas, steamer, seized by Capt. Thomas, the French lady, 8. Thomas arrested, 9.
Salatia, Yazoo River, fight, 67.
Salisbury, North Carolina, battle, 103.
Salem, Virginia, taken, 98.
Salem, Mo., skirmish, 16, 22.
Salem, Ind., taken, 59.
Salkhatchie, South Carolina, occupied, 94.
Salkhatchie River, South Carolina, crossed, 94.
Salt Lake, Utah, Indians, near, defeated, 52.
Salt works destroyed, Onslow, N. C., 47. St. Andrew's Sound, 65. Westbay, Florida, 66. St. Marks, Florida—Westbay, Florida, 68. East Bay, Florida, 68. Goose Creek, Florida, 69. Bonsecours Bay, 83. Saltville, Va., 91. St. Joseph's Bay, Fla., 40. Alligator Harbor, Fla., 57.
Saluria, Miss., fight, 56.
Saluria, Texas, U. S. troops captured at, 7.
Saltville, Va., battle, 85. Lead mines destroyed, 91. Salt works destroyed, 91.
Salvador, steamer, attempt to capture by rebel pirates frustrated, 87.
Sanders, George N., peace negotiations, 79. Reward for his arrest, 106.
Sanders, General, killed, 65.
Sanders, General, rebel, killed, 82.
San Jacinto, frigate, lost, 93.
Santa Rosa Island, Fla., attack on Wilson's Zouaves, 12.
Saratoga, Ky., skirmish, 14.
Savage Station, Va., battle, 32.
Savannah captured by Sherman, 91.
Savannah River, naval fight, 18.
Bawtelle, Lieutenant, killed, 49.
Sawyer, H. W., Capt., held by rebels as hostage, 59. Hostage for his safety ordered, 60. Ex changed, 70.
Schofield, General, commands Department of Missouri, 55.
Schofield, Maj.-General, commands 23d corps, 70. Commands Army of the Ohio, 73. Commands in North Carolina, 105. To command Department of North Carolina, 109.

Scott, Winfield, Brevet Lieut.-General, retires from command of the army, 14. Explains his course in the early days of the rebellion, 45. Buchanan's defence and reply to, 46.
Scott, Lieutenant-Colonel, killed, 54.
Scottsville, Ky., captured, 67.
Secession, Democratic National Conventions, 1860, at Charleston, Richmond and Baltimore—Douglas and Johnson nominated—ditto, Breckenridge and Lane—South Carolina senators resign —Georgia appropriation for war—Howell Cobb resigns—Lewis Cass, Secretary, resigns—South Carolina secedes—John B. Floyd, Secretary of War, resigns—Commissioners from South Carolina to President Buchanan—Secretary Jacob Thompson, resigns—Alabama secedes—Florida do, Georgia, do., Louisiana, do., Texas, do.—arsenals and forts, mints, cutters, and vessels of the U. S. seized—Secession Congress meets at Montgomery, Ala., 5.
Secession Convention, Frankfort, Ky., 50.
Secessionville, S. C., battle, 30.
Sedalia, Mo., taken, 86.
Seddon, James A., rebel, resigns Sec. of War, 95.
Sedgwick, John, Maj.-General, commands a corps, 50. At Fredericksburg, 53. Commands sixth corps. Killed, 73.
Sedgwick, Major, killed, 42.
Selma, Ala., battle, 101.
Semmes, General, rebel, killed, 59.
Senatobia, Mo., burned, 40.
Sentences, military, revoked, 107.
Sergeant, William, Colonel, killed, 100.
Seven Days battles, 31, 32, 33.
Sewall's Point, Va., shelled, 27.
Seward, Wm. H., Secretary of State, recommends harbors and seaports of Northern States to be put in a condition of defence, 13. Offers his resignation, 47. Declined, 47. Accident to, 102. Attempt on his life, 103. Trial of assassins, 106, 109.
Seven Pines, Va., battle, 29.
Shady Grove Church, fight, 72.
Shaffer, Colonel, killed, 48.
Sharkey, William L., appointed Provisional Governor of Mississippi, 108. Issues proclamation for organization of a militia, 110. General Slocum forbids it, 110. His order countermanded by President, 110.
Sharpsburg, Md., battle, 41.
Shaw, Colonel, killed, 60.
Shawnee Mound, Mo., skirmish, 17.
Shawneetown, Kansas, burned, 45.
Shawsheen, gun-boat, sunk, 73.
Shenandoah River crossed by Wright, 80.
Shenandoah, rebel privateer, sails—captured, 87. See "Privateers."
Shelbina, Mo., skirmish, 11.
Shelby Farm, Ky., skirmish, 38.
Shelbyville, Tenn., skirmish, 23. Fight, 58.
Shepherdstown, Va., battle, 42, 43.
Sheridan, P. H., Major-General, commands cavalry, Army of Potomac, 70. Raid in Virginia, 73. Commands the Army of northern Virginia, 81. Early's army falls back, 82. Appointed Major-General, regular army, 87. Offers battle at Halltown, Va., 82. Attack on his lines, 82. Destroys crops, etc., in the Shenandoah Valley, 85. Commands Gulf Division, 108.
Sherman, W. T., Major-General, advance in Mississippi, 67, 68. Great raid, Miss., 67. Com-

mands military division of the Mississippi, 70.
Great Southern campaign commences, 73. Losses in campaign from Chattanooga to Atlanta, 83. Rebel losses in same, 83. Issues order for his great march through Georgia, South Carolina and North Carolina, 87. March commences, 87. Adieu to the north, 87. Railroads and bridges destroyed, 87, 88. Operations of his troops, 88. First news of his progress received by General Grant, 90. March, report of, 90. March resumed from Savannah, 93. Left wing leaves Savannah, 93. Campaign in South Carolina, 98. At Goldsboro', N. C., concentration of his army, 98. At conference on James river, 99. Army resumes its march, 99. Estimated strength of Joe Johnson's army, 102. Leaves Goldsboro', N. C., 102. Halleck advises that no regard be paid to Sherman's treaty with Johnson, 105. Commands Mississippi Division, 108.
Shiloh, Miss., battle, 24. Beauregard's address, 26.
Ship's Gap, Ga., taken, 86.
Ship Island, La., taken, 16.
Shipping Point, Va., occupied, 23.
Shully's Ford, Mo., fight, 42.
Sickles, D. E., Major-Gen., commands a corps, 50.
Sigel, Major-General, commands reserve, army of Potomac, 46. Commands a corps, 50.
Sill, General, killed, 48.
Silver Spring, Md., burned, 79.
Simon's Bluff, South Carolina, shelled, 30.
Sinking Creek, Virginia, taken, 47.
Sister's Ferry, South Carolina, crossed, 94.
Skidaway Batteries, Ga., destroyed, 23.
Skillen, Lieutenant-Colonel, killed, 31.
Skinner, Lieutenant-Colonel, killed, 39.
Slaves in Missouri belonging to rebels ordered to be confiscated—order modified by President, 11. President recommends compensation to States that will abolish, 20. Bill for abolition of slavery in D. C., signed by President, 24. Declared free by General Hunter, 27. President revokes Hunter's proclamation, 28. Compensation to any State that will abolish slavery, recommended, 34. To be free after Jan. 1, 1863, 43. Compensation to loyal States for emancipation, 47. Emancipation proclamation, 48. Retaliation by Jeff. Davis for emancipation, 49. West Virginia, Constitution in relation to, 51. Abolition in Maryland, 78. Gov. Allen, rebel, of Louisiana, advocates employment of negroes as soldiers, 84. Employment of negroes as soldiers advocated, 85. Constitution abolishing slavery adopted in Maryland, 85. Constitution proclaimed, 86. Emancipated in Missouri, 93. Constitutional amendment abolishing slavery adopted by Congress and various States, 94. Abolition amendment recommended to Kentucky, 95. Smith, rebel Governor of Virginia, recommends the use of negroes as troops, 90.
Slater's Mills, Va., skirmish, 27.
Slemmer, A. J., Lieutenant, withdraws from Fort McRae to Fort Pickens, Fla., 5.
Slidell, John, taken in British steamer Trent, 14, 16. Surrendered, 17.
Slocum, H. W., Major-General, commands a corps, 50. Commands the 20th corps, 81. Commands left wing of Sherman's army, 87. To command Department of Mississippi, 109.
Slocum, Colonel, killed, 9.

Smith, Charles F. Major-General, died, 26.
Smith, Joseph B., Lieutenant, killed, 21,
Smith, Preston, General, rebel, killed, 63.
Smith, Melancthon, Lieut.-Colonel, killed, 59.
Smith, Thomas H., Lieut.-Colonel, killed, 20.
Smith, Lieutenant-Colonel, killed, 64.
Smith, Kirby, surrender, 107. Surrender completed, 108.
Smith, I. P., gun boat taken, 49.
Smith, William, rebel Governor of Virginia, recommends the employment of negro troops, 90.
Smith, T. A., Major, killed, 42.
Smith, Thomas A., General, killed, 102.
Smith, Colonel, rebel, killed, 59.
Smithfield, North Carolina, battle, 98.
Smithburg, Maryland, captured, 59.
Snake Creek Gap, Georgia, skirmish, 73.
Snicker's Ferry, Virginia, fight, 47.
Snicker's Gap, Virginia, fight, 45, 79.
Snyder's Bluff, Miss., batteries taken, 55. Captured, 55.
Snowhill, Kentucky, skirmish, 51.
Social Circle, Georgia, burned, 88.
Soldier's votes fraudulently prepared, 86.
Somerset, Kentucky, fight, 51.
Sorrell, General, rebel, killed, 95.
South Anna River, Virginia, crossed, 73. Battle and skirmishes—flanked, 75.
South Carolina—senators resign—secedes—revenue cutter seized—palmetto flag raised—forts Moultrie and Castle Pinckney seized—commissioners sent to President Buchanan, 5. Delegation from wait on President Johnson, 108. Convention delegates elected, 110. Repeals secession ordnance, 110. Abolishes slavery, 110. Delegation, speech of President to, 111.
South Edisto, South Carolina, crossed, 95.
Southfield, gunboat sunk, 71.
South Mountain, Maryland, battle, 41.
Southwest Creek, North Carolina, skirmish, 47.
South Mills, N. C., skirmish, 25.
Southwest Mountain, Va., battle, 36.
South West Pass, Mississippi River, naval fight at, 13.
Specie seized at New Orleans by Gen. Butler, 28.
Spring Hill, Tennessee, Morgan defeated at, 28. Battle, 50. Battle, 89.
Stafford, L. A., General, rebel, killed, 74.
Spangler, Edward, tried for assassination, 106.
Condemnation, imprisonment, 109.
Spanish Fort, Mobile, fight, 99. Fight at, 100. Taken, 102.
Spanish River battery Ala., taken, 103.
Spear, Colonel, killed, 54.
Spottsylvania Court House, Va., skirmishes, 73. Battle, attack on rifle pits, 74. Ewell defeated, 75.
Springfield, Missouri, Zagonyi's cavalry charge at, 14. Fight at, 49.
Springfield, Virginia, fight, 67.
Stafford, Lientenant-Colonel, rebel, killed, 54.
Stainrook, Colonel, killed, 54.
Staley's Creek, Virginia, battle, 91.
Stan Watty, rebel Indian, defeated, 33. Makes a treaty, 108.
Stanton, Edwin M., appointed Sec. of War, 18.
Staples, Colonel, killed, 73.
Starke, General, rebel, killed, 42.
Staten Island, N. Y., anti-draft riots, 60.
Staunton, Virginia, taken, 76. Taken, 84.
Steadman, Colonel, killed, 81.

Star of the West, steamer, fired into near Charleston, 5.
"Stark County Democrat" newspaper office destroyed at Canton, Ohio, 10.
Stedman, General James B., to command Department of Georgia, 109. Commands District of Etowah, Georgia, 76.
Steel's raid, Miss., return, 52.
Steinwehr, General, retaliation against, 35.
Stephens, Alex. H., Vice-Pres. Confederate States, 6. Comes down James River as bearer of flag of truce, 59. Avows himself in favor of an armistice and peace, approves of the Chicago Convention, 84. Arrives at Fortress Monroe, 107. Applies for pardon, 108. Released, 111.
Steven's Station, Ala., taken, 24.
Stevens, Isaac L., Brigadier-General, killed, 39.
Stevenson, General, killed, 73.
Stewart's Creek, Tennessee, skirmish, 48.
Stewart's Landing, Tenn., Wheeler at, 82.
Stone, Colonel, killed, 73.
Stone, Lieutenant-Colonel, killed, 36.
Stone, Chas. P., Captain, appointed to command militia of District of Columbia, 5. General, arrested, 19.
Stone Fleet sunk, 17. Second, sunk, 18.
Stone River, battle, 48.
Stoneman, Gen. Geo., raid in Virginia, 52. Surrenders, 81. Raid ended, 92. To command Department of Tennessee, 109. Reconnoisance, Virginia, 20.
Stono River, S. C., I. P. Smith, gunboat taken, 49.
Stoney Creek, Va., crossed, 24. Reconnoissance, 89.
Stony Lake, Dakotah, battle, 62.
Stover, Major, rebel, killed, 54.
Strahl. General, rebel, killed, 89.
Straight, Colonel, cavalry raid, 51.
Strasburg, Va., skirmish, 23, 29. Sigel retreats to, 74.
Strawberry Plains, Tenn., Longstreet retreats from, 68.
Strong, Colonel, rebel, killed, 41.
Strouse, Major, killed, 54.
Stuart, J E. B., General, rebel, raid on Maryland and Pennsylvania, 44. Raid in Virginia, 50. Killed, 74.
Striker, D. C., Colonel, killed, 74.
Suffolk, Va., taken, 28. Skirmishes, 52. Captured, 69.
Sugar Creek, Ark., skirmish, 20.
Sugar Valley, Ga., Sherman at, 74.
Summerville, Va., taken, 41.
Sumner, Major-General, commands right wing army of Potomac, 46. Demands surrender of Fredericksburg, 46. Relieved from command, 49. Appointed to Missouri, 50. Death, 51.
Sumter, Fort, occupied by Major Anderson—bombarded—surrenders, 6. Surrender demanded, 61. Second demand for surrender—attempt to carry by assault, 62.
Surratt, Mrs. Mary E., tried for assassination, 106. Condemned, 109. Hung. 109.
Surrender of Lee, at Appomattox Court House, 102. Johnston's, N. C., original terms of—disapproved of—hostilities to be resumed, 104, 105. Grant at Raleigh, 105. Final surrender, 105. Halleck advises that no attention be paid to Sherman's treaty with Johnston, 105. Benefit claimed by Howell Cobb, 105. Commodore Farrand of rebel navy, Ga., 106. Kirby Smith's army, negotiations, 107. Dick Taylor's army, negotiations, 107. Rebel Red River fleet, 108. Kirby Smith, completed, 108.
Sutherland Station, Va., battle, 110.
Swansboro', N. C., salt works burned, 37.
Sweeden's Cove, Ala., skirmish, 20.
Sweetzer, Lieutenant-Colonel, killed, 31.
Taft, Lieut.-Colonel, killed, 65.
Taggart, Charles F., Major, killed, 64.
Tah-kah-o-kuty Mountain, battle, 81.
Taney, Roger B., Chief Justice, U. S.—died, 85.
Tangipaho, La., taken, 89.
Talladega, Rousseau at, 79.
Tallahassee, rebel privateer, captured, 81.
Tallahatchie River, fight, 50. Crossed by Smith, 69.
Tar River, N. C., fight, 52. Bridge destroyed, 61.
Tavern Hill, Va., advance to, 30.
Taylor, Dick, surrender, 107.
Taylor, Colonel, killed, 59.
Taylor, Captain, killed, 49.
Taylor, Thomas, Colonel, rebel, killed, 17.
Taylor's Creek, N. C., battle, 98.
Taylorsville, Ga., fight, 75.
Tazewell salt works, Va., skirmish, 73.
Tazewell, Tenn., fight—battle, 36.
Tecumseh, monitor, sunk, 81.
Telegraphic dispatches seized all over the U. S., 7. President to take possession of, 18.
Tenallytown, Md., skirmish, 79.
Tennessee Division, General Thomas, 108.
Tennessee River, fight, 67. Crossed by Hood in retreat, 92.
Tennessee votes on secession, 5. Refuses troops to U. S., 6. Attempts to take the State over to the Confederacy, 7. Proclamation of secession, 8. (East) Union Convention, 8. (East) bridges burned by Union men, 15. Union State Convention meets at Nashville, 93.
Tennessee Iron Works destroyed, 19.
Terrill, General, killed, 44.
Terry, Colonel, rebel, killed, 17.
Terry, A. H., General, to command Department of Virginia, 109.
Texas secedes, 5. Weitzel's expedition, 108. A. J. Hamilton, Provisional Governor, 108.
Thoburn, Colonel, killed, 86.
Thomas, Geo. H., commands army of the Cumberland, 73. Commands Tennessee Division, 108.
Thomas, Lieutenant-Colonel, rebel, killed, 65.
Thomas, Captain, disguised as a French lady, captures steamer St. Nicholas—is arrested in Baltimore, 9.
Thomasville, Mo., skirmish, 45.
Thompson, Jacob, resigns from the Cabinet, 5. Indicted in Canada, 105. Reward for his arrest, 106.
Thompson, A. B., General, rebel, killed, 70.
Thompson, Colonel, rebel, killed, 63.
Thornton, John T., Colonel, rebel, killed, 42.
Thoroughfare Gap, Va., 38—skirmish, 46.
Thrush, Colonel, killed, 44.
Tiger Creek, Ga., skirmish, 72.
Tilford, Ga., taken, 62.
Tilghman, General, rebel, killed, 55.
Tillinghart, Captain, killed, 22.
Tishamingo Creek, Ky., battle, 76.
Titus, Major, killed, 38.
Todd, Governor of Ohio, arrested, 51.
Todd's Tavern, Va., skirmish, 73.
Toland, Colonel, killed, 61.

Tolopotomy Creek, Va., battle, 75.
Tom Brook, Va., battle, 85.
Tom Creek, N. C. skirmish, 52. Battle, 96.
Tompkinsville, Ky., skirmish, 29. Fight, 33.
Topping, Lieutenant-Colonel, killed, 39.
Torpedo, rebel gun-boat, flag of truce, 59.
Town, Major, killed, 39.
Town, Colonel, killed, 54.
Townsend, Colonel, killed, 76.
Tracy, General, rebel, killed, 53.
Trenholm, George F., appointed rebel Secretary of Treasury, 77. Released, 111.
Trevillian Station, Va., battle, 76.
Triune, Tenn., fight at, 56.
Trufitt, Major, killed, 74.
Tschudy, Martin, Lieutenant-Colonel, killed, 59.
Tucker, Beverly, reward for his arrest, 106.
Tucker, Colonel, killed, 31.
Tucan, Arizona, taken, 28.
Tullahoma, Tenn., occupied, 58. Evacuated, 59.
Tunica Bend, Miss., fight, 77.
Tunisville, Tenn., skirmish, 66.
Tunnel Hill, Ga., evacuated, 67. Skirmish, 69. Occupied, 73.
Tupelo, Miss., battle, 79.
Turkey Island, Va., Sheridan at, 74.
Tuscumbia, Ala., taken, 50. Recaptured, 53.
Twiggs, David E., General, treacherously surrenders U. S. Army in Texas, 6.
Tyler, John, died, 18.
Tyler, Lieut.-Colonel, rebel, killed, 24
Tybee Island occupied, 15.
Tyrell, Colonel. rebel, killed, 75.
Underwriter, gun-boat, taken, 67.
Uniforms, rebel official order, 29.
Union, Va., skirmish, 46.
Union City, Ky., surrendered, 70.
Union City, Tenn., skirmish, 23.
Unionville, Tenn., fight, 50.
Upperville, Va., occupied, 46. Cavalry fight, 57. Skirmish, 69.
Upton's Hill, Va., occupied, 12.
Vallandingham, C. L., of Ohio—dinner given to, by secessionists at Baltimore, 10. Arrested, 54. Before court-martial, 54, 55. Found guilty, 55. Sentenced to Fort Warren, 55. Sent across the lines, 58. Petition for a certiorari refused, 58. Returns to United States, 77. Nominated Democratic Governor of Ohio, 56. Runs the blockade, 57.
Valverde, New Mexico, battle, 20.
Van Buren, Ark., skirmish, 48.
Van Gilsa, Colonel, killed, 30.
Vanleer, John P., Lieut.-Colonel, killed, 27.
Van Dorn, General, rebel, killed, 55.
Vaugh, Major, rebel, killed, 44.
Venus Point, Ga., fight, 19.
Vermillion Bayou, La., battle, 52. Taken, 64.
Versailles, Ky., skirmish, 45.
Vessels in the service of United States, captured, lost, or destroyed:—Arizona destroyed, 96. Barataria burned, 51. Bazely blown up, 90. Clara Bell, 71. Bombshell sunk, 72. Bombshell retaken, 72. Boston destroyed, 75.— Brandywine, sloop of war, burned, 83. Brewster blown up, 73. Smith Briggs taken, 67. Maria J. Carlton sunk, 26. Caleb Cushing, cutter, seized and burnt, 58. City Belle destroyed, 72. Columbine captured, 75. Conestoga, 68. Covington destroyed, 72. Diana captured, 51. Electric Spark taken, 79. Ellis blown up, 47. Emma destroyed, 72. Granite City captured, 75. Greyhound burnt, 88, 89. Hamilton blown up, 105. Harvest Moon blown up, 96. Hastings taken, 83. Housatonic, 68. General Hunter blown up, 71. Indianola passes Vicksburg, 50. Indianola captured, 50. Iron Age blown up, 66. Island Queen seized on Lake Erie, 84. Commodore Jones blown up, 72. Keokuk sunk, 51. Massachusetts sunk, 105. Melville, 93. Lavender, gunboat, 77. Lebanon taken, 75. General Lyon burned, 100. Maple Leaf, 70. Milwaukee blown up, 99. Minnesota, attempt to blow up, 71. Narcissus, gunboat, blown up, 90. Naumkeag, gunboat, taken, 83. Niagara, frigate, fired into at Lisbon, 99. North Carolina, foundered, 92. Osage blown up, 99. Otsego, gunboat, blown up, 90. Parsons seize i on Lake Erie, 84. Patapsco blown up, 93. Peterhoff sunk, 69. Petrel burned, 72. Preble blown up, 53. Queen City burned, 78. Queen of the West passes. Vicksburg, 49. Queen of the West destroys rebel steamers, 50. Queen of the West is destroyed, 52. Rob Roy, 71. Rose blown up, 108. St. Phillippe sunk at Mobile, 81. San Jacinto, frigate, lost, 93. Shawsheen sunk, 73. Signal destroyed, 72. Sky Lark destroyed, 37. I. P. Smith, gunboat, taken, 49. Southfield sunk, 71. Sultana blown up, 105. Tecumseh, monitor, sunk at Mobile, 81. Titan destroyed, 69. Tulip blown up, 87. Undine destroyed, 87. Varuna sunk, 26. Underwriter, 67. Warner destroyed, 72. Washington, gunboat, destroyed, 52. Water Witch, 16. Wave captured, 75. Henrietta Weed, blown up, 73. Weehauken sunk, 65. West Point sunk, 37. Western gunboat fleet, 43. Two taken on Potomac River, 16. Alert blown up, 56. Bainbridge lost, 61. Callie burned, 37. Cincinnati sunk, 56. Clifton taken, 62. Attempt to blow up Ironsides, 63. De Kalb blown up, 60. . Fanny, propellor, in Hatteras Inlet, 12. Fairfax taken, 13. Platte City captured, 15. Reliance taken and destroyed, 61, 62. Gunboat Sachem taken, 62. Satellite captured, 61. Afterwards destroyed, 62. Skylark taken, 37. Union foundered, 64. Whitehall, gun-boat, burned, 21.
Vice-Admiral, rank created—D. G. Farragut appointed, 91.
Vicksburg, Miss., passed by Farragut, 31. Bombarded, 33. Ceres fired into, 34. Passed by Farragut's fleet, 34. Sherman's expedition against, 48. Advance U. S. troops opposite, 49. Yazoo Pass and Coldwater River operations, 49. Ram Queen of the West passes, 49. Sherman withdraws—McClernand in command, 49. Yazoo Pass expedition, 50. Bombardment, 50. Fort Pemberton attacked, 50. Coldwater River expedition, 50. Fight at Greenwood, Miss., 50. Lake Providence canal, 51. Rams Lancaster and Switzerland attempt to run past, 51. Benton and other gunboats run past the batteries, 52. Yazoo Pass expedition abandoned, 52. Transports run the batteries, 53. Grant lands at Bonlinsburg—battle, 53. Battles at Port Gibson, 53. Raymond, Miss., Jackson, Champion Hills, Big Black Bridge, Walnut Hills, Haines Bluff, Snyders' Bluff, 53. Batteries assaulted, 55. McPherson's, assault, 57. Cincinnati, gunpoat, sunk, 56. Blair's raid, 56. Surrender, 59.

Vienna, Va., skirmish, 8, 16.
Vinegar Hill, S. C., rifle pits taken, 62.
Virginia rejects an ordinance of secession, 6. Refuses to call out militia at proclamation of President—recognizes the Confederacy—secedes, 6. Transferred to the Confederacy, 7. Army of, formed, 31. Retreats, 37. Abolishes the Alexandria oath, 108.
Volunteer enlistments—arrest of persons who discourage, 36.
Wade, Colonel, rebel, killed, 53.
Wadsworth, General, killed, 73.
Wainwright, Captain U. S. Navy, killed, 48.
Wallace, W. H. L., Brig.-General, killed, 24.
Waltham, General, rebel, killed, 63.
Walker's Ford, Tenn., fight, 65.
Walker, L. W., Lieutenant-Col., rebel, killed, 54.
Walnut Hills, battle, 55.
Walthal, Port, Va., battle, 74.
Ward, Colonel, killed, 59.
Ward, Colonel, rebel, killed, 27.
Warfield, Ky., skirmish, 37.
Warrenburg, Mo., skirmishes, 15, 23, 23.
Warren, G. K., Major-Gen., commands 5th corps, 70.
Warrenton, Va., skirmishes, 38, 46.
Warrenton, Miss., forts destroyed, 55.
Warrenton Junction, Va., reconnoisance, 23. Fight, 54.
Washington, D. C., menaced, 79.
Washington, N. C., occupied, 22. Attacked, 40. Invested, 51. Attempt to relieve, 52. General Foster escapes from, 52. Seige raised, 52.
Washington, gunboat, destroyed, 52.
Washington, John A., Colonel, rebel, killed, 17.
Waterford, Va., fight, 38.
Water Witch, gunboat, captured, 76.
Watts, rebel, Gov. of Ala., calls out the boys and old men, 90.
Watt's Creek, Va., skirmish, 23.
Wauhatchie, Tenn., battle, 64.
Waverly, Tenn., fight, 45.
Waynesboro', Tenn., entered by Hood's advance, 88. Fight, 89. Taken, 89.
Waynesburg, Va., Hunter at, 76. Taken, 84. Battle, 97.
Webb, Colonel, killed, 71.
Webster, Fletcher, Colonel, killed, 39.
Webster, Colonel, killed, 44.
Weehawken, monitor, sunk, 65.
Weldon Railroad, Va., battle, 82. Skirmish, 82.
West Bay, Fla., salt works destroyed, 66, 68.
Western gunboat fleet transferred to Navy Department, 43.
Weston, Va., taken, 39.
West Point, Ga., captured, 103.
West Point, Miss., battle at, 68, 69.
West Point, Va., battle, 27.
West Point, steamer, sunk by collision, 37.
West Virginia, meeting at Clarksburg in opposition to Letcher's course, 7. Declares her independence of old Virginia at Wheeling, 8. Resolve to make a new State called "Kanawha," 10. Proposition to form State of "Kanawha" carried, 14. Convention changes the name of the State from "Kanawha" to "West Virginia," 16.
Wet Glaze, Missouri, fight, 13.
Wheaton, Colonel, rebel, killed, 63.
Whippoorwill Bridge, Ky., burned, 16.
Whipple, A. W., General, killed, 54.

Whippy Swamp, S. C., Sherman at, 91.
White's Ford, Md., Wright crosses at, 79.
Whitehall, N. C., fight, 47.
White, Colonel, killed, 12.
White Oak Ridge, Mo., skirmish, 37.
White Oak Road, battle, 106.
White Oak Swamp, Va., battle, 52.
White Stone Hill, N. W. Territory, battle, 62.
White House, Va., evacuated, 31. Burned, 49. Taken, 55. W. F. Smith, (Baldy), at, 75. Fight at, 77.
White Point, S. C., fight, 78.
White River, Ark., naval fight, 30. Fight, 78.
White's Station, Tenn., Sturgis at, 77.
White Tavern, Va., battle, 81.
Whitewater Creek, Ga., crossed, 80.
Whiting, General, rebel, killed, 42.
Whiting, General, rebel, death, 97.
Whitney, Addison, monument, 108.
Wilder's raid, return of, 52.
Wilderness, Va., battle, 72. Flanked, 73.
Wilkes, Charles, Capt. U. S. Navy, takes Mason and Slidell, 13. Commands James River flotilla, 33.
Willet, Colonel, rebel, killed, 74.
Williams, Thomas, General, killed, 36.
Williams, Kit, Colonel, rebel, killed, 24.
Williams, Colonel, rebel, killed, 57.
Williams, Colonel, rebel, killed, 59.
Williamsburg, Va., battle, 27. Taken, 40. Attacked, 52.
Williamsport, W. Va., fight, 67.
Williamsport, Md., Lee's army cross at, 60.— Occupied by Federals, 60.
Williamsport Cross Roads, Va., skirmish, 21.
Williams, John, General, rebel, killed, 59.
Willis, Colonel, rebel, killed, 74.
Willis, Colonel, rebel, killed, 75.
Wilmington, N. C., taken, 95.
Wilmington Island, Ga., skirmish, 26.
Wilson's Creek, Mo., battle, 10.
Wilson's Wharf, Va., battle, 75.
Wilson, Major, rebel, killed, 59.
Winans, Ross, his steam-gun captured—himself captured, 7.
Winchester, Va., occupied, 21. Battle, 22, 23. Evacuated, 40. Surrender, 47. Taken by rebels, 57. Battle, 80. Early retreats from, 81. Reconnoissance, 84.
Winchester, Ky., attack, 61.
Winder, Captain, exchanged, 70.
Winder, Colonel, held as hostage, 60.
Winder, C. S., General, rebel, killed, 36.
Winfield, Va., fight, 86.
Winnsboro, S. C., reached, 96.
Winthrop, General, killed, 101.
Winthrop, Theodore, Major, killed, 8.
Winton, N. C., burned, 20.
Wilkinson's Pike, Tenn., battle, 90.
Williams, Colonel, rebel, killed, 59.
Wirz, Captain Henry, tried for barbarities at Andersonville rebel prison, 110.
Wise, Henry A., writes a letter to General Grant, approving of downfall of slavery, 110.
Wise's Ford, N. C., battle, 97.
Wise, O. Jennings, Captain, rebel, killed, 19.
Wolf, Lieutenant-Colonel, killed, 39.
Wolf River Bridge, Tenn., fight, 65.
Wolford, General, rebel, killed, 63.
Wolfstain, Va., skirmish, 36.
Wood, General, rebel, killed, 44.

Wood, General C. B., to command department of Ala., 109.
Woodbury, Tenn., 38—fight, 51.
Woodside, Colonel, rebel, killed, 22.
Woodstock, Va., occupied, 23.
Woodward, Colonel, killed, 73.
Wright, Major-General, commands 6th corps, 73. Crosses the Potomac, 79.
Wright, George, General, to command department of Columbia, 109. Drowned, 109.
Wrightsville, Pa., skirmish, 58.
Wyman, Colonel, killed, 32.
Wyman, J. B., Colonel, killed, 48.
Wytheville, Va., taken, 61. Cattle near, 73. Taken—retaken, 91. Taken, 98.
Yancey, William L., death, 61.
Yazoo City, Miss., destroyed, 55. Second expedition, 57. Taken, 60. Fight, 67.
Yazoo Pass, operations to open, 49. Expeditions, 50, 52.
Yazoo River expedition, 31.
Yeadon, Richard, offers $10,000 for the head of General Butler, 48.
Yellow Bayou, La., battle, 74.
Yellow Tavern, Va., fight, 74.
York, Pa., rebels at, surrender, 58.
Yorktown, Va., invested, 23. Skirmishes, 25. Bombardment, 26. Evacuated, 27.
Young's Island, S. C., occupied, 94.
Young, Bennett, indicted in Canada, 105.
Zook, General, killed, 59.
Zollicoffer, Tenn., skirmish, 63.
Zollicoffer, F. K., General, rebel, killed, 18.

www.ingramcontent.com/pod-product-compliance
Lightning Source LLC
Chambersburg PA
CBHW022132160426
43197CB00009B/1257